Arthur Scratchley

A Practical Treatise on Savings Banks

Arthur Scratchley

A Practical Treatise on Savings Banks

ISBN/EAN: 9783744724296

Printed in Europe, USA, Canada, Australia, Japan

Cover: Foto ©ninafisch / pixelio.de

More available books at **www.hansebooks.com**

SCRATCHLEY

ON

ASSOCIATIONS FOR PROVIDENT INVESTMENT.

CONTENTS.

DIVISIONS I, II, & III.

Each Division is sold separately.

I.—424 pages.—14*s.*

II.—310 pages.—3rd Edition, 7*s.* 6*d.*

    Continuation of Division II.—192 pages.—4th Edition, 3*s.* 6*d.*

III.—316 pages.—10th Edition, 7*s.* 6*d.*

DIVISION I.

NEW TREATISE ON SAVINGS BANKS.

[*Longmans'*. 424 pages. 14s.]

Contents.

INTRODUCTION.

Nature of the Subject	ix
Of the kind of Persons who are Depositors	x
Of Institutions for Provident purposes	xii
Distinctive advantages conferred by Savings Banks	xiii
Effect of the Establishment of Savings Banks	xv
Of the Social Effects of Economy	xix
Of Security for Savings	xx
Praise of the Legislature, and of Honorary Trustees and Managers	xxii
Such praise not universally merited	xxiv
Effect of the Panic	xxv
Progress of Savings Banks	xxvii

AS TO PRACTICE OF SAVINGS BANKS IN FOREIGN COUNTRIES:—

France	xxxi	Russia	xlv
Belgium	xxxiv	*United States of America:*—	
Switzerland	xxxvi	State of New York	xlvii
Hamburg	xxxvii	Commonwealth of Massachusetts	l
Prussia	xxxviii		
Austria	xl	State of New Jersey	lii
Holland	xlii	*Australia:*—Colony of Victoria	liii
Sweden	xliii		

PART I.
PAST HISTORY AND PRESENT SYSTEM OF SAVINGS BANKS.

CHAPTER I.—*History of Savings Banks.*

	PAGE		PAGE
SEC. 1.—Origin	3	SEC. 5.—Present Condition	20
" 2.—Early Methods of Investment	7	" 6.—Military and Naval Savings Banks	21
" 3.—Course of Legislation	10	" 7.—Penny Banks	22
" 4.—Committee of the House of Commons of 1858	17		

CHAPTER II.—*Present Constitution.*

SEC. 1.—Formation	25	SEC. 6.—Limitation of Deposits	33
" 2.—Rules	26	" 7.—Separate Surplus Fund	34
" 3.—Officers	29	" 8.—Profits of Savings Banks	36
" 4.—Rate of Interest allowed	30	" 9.—Deposits Unclaimed	38
" 5.—Balances in Treasurers' hands	31	" 10.—Expenses.—ERRORS OF THE PRESENT SYSTEM	39

PART II.
FRAUDS IN SAVINGS BANKS; THEIR EVIL CONSEQUENCES, AND THE REMEDIES.

CHAPTER III.—*Defects in the Management of Savings Banks.*

SEC. 1.—Remarks upon the Frauds on Savings Banks	49	II.—The Tralee Fraud	64
		III.—The Rochdale Fraud	65
" 2.—Extent of the Frauds	55	IV.—The Brighton Fraud	68
" 3.—As to the Remarkable Cases of Fraud	59	V.—The Reading Fraud	69
I.—The Cuffe Street Fraud	60	SEC. 4.—Belief of the Public that the Banks had Government Security	70

CHAPTER IV.—THE REMEDY—In the appointment of Government Inspectors and Auditors, with the guarantee of the State for Savings Bank Deposits.

SEC. 1.—As to what is really desirable 76
" 2.—As to the attempts at Legislation, 1850 to 1857 78
SEC. 3.—As to Government Inspection 81
" 4.—As to Government Treasurers 84

CHAPTER V.—*As to Improvements in the Internal Management of Savings Banks.*

SEC. 1.—As to Uniformity of Accounts in Savings Banks 90
" 2.—As to Actuaries.—THEIR FUTURE REMUNERATION & DUTIES 92
SEC. 3.—As to Trustees and Managers 93
" 4.—As to production of Pass Books 97

CHAPTER VI.—AS TO SUNDRY POINTS OF INTERNAL MANAGEMENT.

SEC. 1.—As to Declarations 103
" 2.—As to Withdrawals 105
" 3.—As to Money Payments out of Office Hours... 107
SEC. 4.—As to the Rules and Annual Statements 108
" 5.—As to Books of Account 110

PART III.

FINANCIAL DEFECTS IN THE PRESENT SAVINGS BANK SYSTEM.

CHAPTER VII.—*How the Deficiency in Savings Bank Assets has arisen, and Remarks on the Loss experienced by the Nation.*

SEC. 1.—Preliminary Considerations as to the Correct Principles for valuing Securities 115
" 2.—Statement of the Deficiency in Savings Bank Securities, and of the Errors of the System... 118
" 3.—Statement of the Causes of the Deficiency 122
SEC. 4.—Remarks on the Loss arising from the Rate of Interest allowed to Savings Banks by the Nation 128
" 5.—Remarks on the Losses attending Purchases and Sales of Stock for Depositors' purposes only 131

CHAPTER VIII.—The Operations of the Chancellors of the Exchequer, and their Effect on Savings Banks.

SEC. 1.—As relates to Savings Banks 135 | SEC. 2.—As regards the Nation............ 147

PART IV.

FINANCIAL REORGANIZATION OF SAVINGS BANKS.

CHAPTER IX.—*Fundamental Principles for Financial Reorganization.*

SEC. 1.—Preliminary Considerations 165
" 2.—Of the Field for Savings Banks 168
" 3.—Of Securities for Savings Banks' Investments ... 171
SEC. 4.—Further Preliminary Considerations—How a Deficiency is to be prevented in Future 177

CHAPTER X.—*As to the Alterations that are desirable in the Government Connection with Savings Banks.*

SEC. 1.—General Reorganization suggested 184
SEC. 2.—Of the Commission 186
" 3.—Modes of Investment 187

CHAPTER XI.—*Recommendations.*

SEC 1.—Plan recommended for Payment of Savings Bank Expenses 191
" 2.—Of the Interest recommended to be allowed to Depositors 193
SEC. 3.—Recommendations respecting Notice of Withdrawal 194
" 4.—Changes recommended in the Annual Limit................... 196
" 5.—Of Investment direct with the Savings Bank Commissioners 198

CHAPTER XII.—*Subsidiary Recommendations.*

SEC. 1.—As to the Conversion of Deposits into Stock ... 200
" 2.—Trust Accounts. Changes recommended 203
" 3.—As to Privileges relative to Estates of Deceased Depositors 205
SEC. 4.—Uniformity in the Calculation of Interest recommended.—The "Prospective Plan." 207

PART V.

THE "POST OFFICE SAVINGS BANK" PLAN, AND THE EXTENSION OF LIFE ASSURANCE AND SICK BENEFITS AMONG THE INDUSTRIOUS CLASSES, THROUGH THE AGENCY OF SAVINGS BANKS.

CHAPTER XIII.—*The "Post Office Savings Bank" Plan*, (proposed in 1804.) 215

    SEC. 1.—Mr. Whitbread's Plan and proposed Bill 216
      " 2.—Remarks in favour 223
    SEC. 3.—Objections......................... 224
      " 4.—Recommendations 227

CHAPTER XIV.—*On the Extension of Life Assurance and Sick Benefits among the Industrious Classes, by the aid of Savings Banks, and Mr. Whitbread's Plan of a Poors Assurance Office.* 231

    SEC. 1.—As to Life Assurance ... 231
      " 2.—As to Sick Benefits by Parish Friendly Societies, in connection with Savings Banks 234
    SEC. 3.—Mr. Whitbread's Plan of a "Poors Assurance Office." ... 239
      " 4.—Of Government Life Assurance 247
      " 5.—Of Deferred Annuities & Provisions for Old Age.—Errors of the present System 251

PART VI.

AS TO NON-GOVERNMENT BANKS OF DEPOSIT, AND THE AUDIT OF PUBLIC INSTITUTIONS.

CHAPTER XV.—*As to Non-Government Banks of Deposit; or Independent Savings Banks without State Guarantee.*

    SEC. 1.—As to their Management 263 | SEC. 2.—As to Banks of Deposit 263

CHAPTER XVI.—*As to the Investments of Non-Government Banks, and Section 12 of the Savings Bank Act 9 Geo. IV., c. 92* ... 273

CHAPTER XVII.—*Extracts from Rules of American Deposit Banks* 280

CHAPTER XVIII.—*General Remarks on the Audit and Management of Public Institutions* 283

PART VII.

LEGISLATION ON SAVINGS BANKS SINCE THE YEAR 1859.

CHAPTER XIX.—*Legislation of the year 1860, and Position of the Savings Bank Question at the end of the Session.*

    SEC. 1.—The Nature of Mr. Gladstone's first Bill of 1860, and of the opposition thereto 295
    " 2.—The Act of 1860 (23 and 24 Vict. c. 137), "To make further provision with respect to Monies received from Savings Banks and Friendly Societies." 307
    " 3.—Position of the Savings Bank Question at the end of the Session of 1860.
        I.—As to the 'Trustee' View.
        II.—As to the 'Banker' View.

APPENDICES.

I.—*On the Improvement of Industrial Dwellings, by the aid of Savings Banks.*

    SEC. 1.—Domestic Causes of Vice and Pauperism............ 3
      " 2.—As to Suburban Villages 10
      " 3.—As to Model Lodging Houses 13
      " 4.—Foreign Efforts at Improvement 17
    SEC. 5.—As to Public Playgrounds 20
      " 6.—As to the Unhealthiness of a Town Life 24
      " 7.—As to Manufacturing Trades ... 27
      " 8.—As to the Establishment of Industrial Dwelling Societies... 28

II.—*On the National Debt* 31

    Origin of the National Debt. Life Annuities and Tontines. Commencement of the Funded Debt. Long Annuities. Exchequer Bills. Exchequer Bonds. Present Amount and Cost of the Debt. Real Charge to the Nation. Cause of the Debt. Effect on National Wealth. *How to Liquidate the National Debt.* Effect on National Expenditure.

Division II.

TREATISE
on
BUILDING SOCIETIES, TONTINES, AND COLONIZATION.

3rd Edition, 7s. 6d. (1857.)

Shaw and Sons, Fetter Lane, and Laytons, 150, Fleet Street.

CONTENTS.

PART I.
ON BENEFIT BUILDING SOCIETIES.

	PAGE
Preliminary Remarks	v
Land Credit Associations, &c.	xiii
Chapter 1.—Introduction	1
History of Building Societies	5
2.—New Theorems in Compound Interest, and General Theory	11
Discount and Present Value	16
Annuities or Periodic Payments	18
Doubling of *Money*	22
3.—On Benefit Building Societies as at present constituted:—	
Sec. 1.—The Theoretical Principles of a Terminating Society	26
2.—Societies on Erroneous Principles	33
3.—The Leading Practical Objections to Benefit Building Societies as at present constituted. *Causes of Failure*	41
4.—On Permanent Benefit Building Societies	52
5.—The Practical Management of a Building Society	67
Solicitor ... 68 Arbitrators	72
Surveyor ... 70 Trustees	73
Manager ... 71 Bidding, Rotation, or Ballot	74
Auditors ... 72 Rules	77
6.—The Balance Sheets of Benefit Building Societies	80
7.—Rules for a Permanent Building and Investment Society	94
Copyhold Property	95
Discount on Payments in Advance	96
Transfer Fees, &c.	106
Schedule of Forms	121
8.—On Life or Fidelity Assurance, applied to Building Societies:—	
Sec. 1.—As regards Borrowing Members	125
2.—Life Assurance applied to Investors	135
Building Society Shares as Security for Fidelity in Situations of Trust	137
On the joint combination of Life and Fidelity Assurance in co-operation with the ordinary Principles of Building Societies	139

9.—The Act for the Regulation of Benefit Societies, 6 & 7 Wm. IV., c. 32., 14 July 1836, with Observations and Legal Decisions 140
Limit of Shares ... 143
Borrowing of Money 144
Copyhold Enfranchisement 145
Freedom from Stamp Duty ... 145
Income Tax 145
Minors 145
Enrolment of Rules 147
As to Voting for Members 149
Clauses required in a new Act ... 152

PART II.

ON FREEHOLD LAND SOCIETIES, TONTINE ASSOCIATIONS, AND EMIGRATION SOCIETIES.

PAGE

CHAPTER 1.—Freehold Land Societies 157
    Political Effect and Object, &c. 159
2.—Tontine Associations :—
    Origin 173
    Advantages of the French System— Banques Tontinières 178
    Plan 179
    Defects 180
3.— Sec. 1.—Building Companies and Suburban Villages 187
    Improvement of Industrial Dwellings 190
    2.—Remarks on the Rural Districts 192
    3.—The Necessity for Home Colonization or Systematic Emigration 196
4.—Freehold Life Assurance—Application to the Extension of Emigration and Colonization 199
    Emigration Returns and Colonial Statistics 209, 210
5.—Benefit, Emigration, and Colonization Societies 219
    Draft Rules for the same 225
    Colonial Land Sales 230
    Loan Repayment Guarantee 231

APPENDIX.—On the Mathematical Principles of Compound Interest, Tontines, New Deposit System for Savings Banks, Deposit Life Assurance, &c. :—

SEC. 1.—On the accumulation of a Single Sum at Compound Interest 233
2.—Of Present Value and Discount 246
3.—Of Annuities 252
4.—Practical Considerations relating to Industrial Associations :—
    Profits 267
    Valuations of Liabilities & Assets 271
    Paid-up Shares .. 273
    Withdrawals 274
    Bonuses 275
    Contributions to Management Fund 277
    Deposit System 281
    Annuity Deposits 286
    Purchase of Annuities 287
    Deposit Life Assurance and Tontines 289

PRACTICAL TABLES for Benefit Building Societies, and other Industrial Associations :—

I.—Decimals 298
II, IV, V.—Rates of Interest 299, 302
III, VI.—Accumulations ...301, 303
VII.—Doubling of Money 303
VIII.—Present Values...... 304
IX, X, XI.—Annuities ..:305, 306, 307
XII.—Logarithms 308
XIII, XIV.—Laws of Mortality 308, 309
XV.—Life Annuities 309

Division III.

TREATISE
ON
FRIENDLY SOCIETIES AND LIFE ASSURANCE SOCIETIES.

10th *Edition*, 7s. 6d. (1859.)
SHAW AND SONS, FETTER LANE, AND LAYTONS, FLEET STREET.

CONTENTS.

	PAGE		PAGE
PRELIMINARY REMARKS :—			
Friendly Societies	vii	Errors in Bonus Divisions	xxi
Industrial Life Assurance Societies	xiii	Amalgamations	xxxi
		Tables of Mortality	xxxvi
Failure of Assurance Offices	xvi	Statistics as to Population	xli

PART I.
ON LIFE ASSURANCE.

	PAGE		PAGE
Annuities	54	Half Premium System	29
Assignments	14	Indisputability of Policies	33
Assurance for Leases	49	Industrial Assurance	45
Bonus Principle	8	Marriage Assurances	14
Building Society Assurances	55	Moral Urgency of Life Assurance	65
Capital of an Assurance Company	60	Mortality of Sound Lives	39
Defects of Assurance System, and Modification as regards the Industrious Classes	10	Nature of a Life Assurance Society	1
		Success of Assurance Offices	9
Deposit System	22	Suspension Principle	15
Doctrine of Probabilities	4	Tables of Mortality	7
Fidelity Assurance	43	Tables of Premium	51
Free Reversionary Policies	21	Tontine System, as applied to Capital	62
Guarantee Temporary Annuity Policies	57	Transfer Principle	26

PART II.
ON FRIENDLY SOCIETIES.
SECTION 1.

Failure of Friendly Societies	74	Legislation	83
Fraudulent Claims	77	Necessity of Average	77
Guarantee Shares	81	Public House Meetings	79
Honorary Members	80	Requirements of Industrious Classes	73
Inadequacy of Rates	75	Underwriting of Liabilities	82
Inefficiency of Management	78		

SECTION 2.

Actuarial Investigations	104	Model Tables	93
Burial Clubs	95	Parish Friendly Societies	92
Definition of Sickness	105	Proper Method of obtaining Returns	103
Experience of Friendly Societies	94	Sickness of Females and Children	101
Friendly Societies Institute	90		

SECTION 3.

True Law of Sickness	106	Recoverable and Irrecoverable Sickness	108
Rates of Premium	109		

SECTION 4.

Rules of a Friendly Society		110

MODEL RULES.

Constitution	113	Sickness Assurance	138
Officers and Management	122	Deferred Annuities	142
Members	131	Endowments	142
Life Assurance	136		

		PAGE
New Deposit Tables for Savings Banks & Industrial Associations	145	
Single Deposits	147	
Annuity Deposits		151
Deferred Annuities		155
New Systems of Assurance		158, 159

MATHEMATICAL APPENDICES.

App. 1.—Expectation in Probabilities 1
           Mathematical Expectation 2
           Moral Expectation 5
App. 2.—Valuation of Post Obits and Contingent Reversions .... 1—18
           Tables for Purchase of Post Obits, &c. .... 7—10 & 14—16
App. 3.—Investigations into the Affairs of a Company, for Amalgamation or Bonus Division :—

Sec. 1.—Valuations of Policies and Liabilities	19	Application to Payment of Policies during Life	31
Free Reversionary Policies	24	Sec. 3.—Guaranteed Bonuses	33
		Sec. 4.—Average Ages of Policies	35
Sec. 2.—Divisions of Profits and Allotments of Bonus	26	Limit of Assurance Risk to be kept by a Society	36

App. 4.—True Law of Sickness 38
App.—Act, 18 & 19 Vic., c. 63 41

Continuation of Division II.

TREATISE
ON THE ENFRANCHISEMENT OF
COPYHOLD, LIFE LEASEHOLD, AND CHURCH PROPERTY.

4th Edition, 3s. 6d. (1859.)
Laytons, 150, Fleet Street, and C. Mitchell & Co., Red Lion Court.

CONTENTS.

Transfer of Land ....(Preface)	vi	Sec. 6.—On Church Leases (Stat. Hen., 8 c. 28, 1 Eliz., c. 19, 13 Eliz., c. 10)	69
Agricultural Statistics	ix	Remarks on Principles of Renewal	72
Sec. 1.—Introduction—State of Legislation	1	Parliamentary Evidence	77
Returns of Enfranchisements effected	4	Evidence of Existence of Lives (re Byrne, and C. Anne, c. 18)	93
Practice under Act of 1858	9	Act 16 and 17 Vict., c. 57	95
Origin of the Tenure	13	Sec. 7.—Freehold Land Societies	97
Objections	14	Model Rules under 6 and 7 Wm. 4., c. 32:—	
Diversity of Tenure (Stat. 18 Edwd. i., & 17 Edwd. 2)	15	I.—Constitution	101
Litigation	17	II.—Members	108
Recommendations of Committees	23	III.—Shares and Subscriptions	112
Sec. 2.—Definitions	33	IV.—Meetings	120
Copyhold of Inheritance	34	V.—Management and Officers	122
Copyholds for Lives	35		
Copyholds for Years	36	Appendix.	
Sec. 3.—Practical Considerations	37	Formulæ for Valuation of Life Contingencies	1
Tables of Annuities	39	Of Successive Lives	6
Table of Fines in Perpetuity	41	Tables for Leases, &c	13
Table of Annuity Re-Investments	42	Electoral Franchise (10 Hen. 6, c. 2, 31 Geo. 2, c. 14, 2 Wm. 4, c. 45)	17
Sec. 4.—Mode and Conditions of Enfranchisement (15 & 16 Vic., c. 51)	43	Heriots	18
Schedules	47	Enfranchisement and Extinguishment	21
Sec. 5.—Systematic Enfranchisement by Associations	49	Schedule of Particulars	23
Plan for a Society; under 6 & 7 Wm. IV, c. 32	52	Mortgage Deeds in Freehold Land Societies (Fleming v. Self)	27
Necessity of Association	60	Act 17 and 18 Vict, c. 116	33
Assurance for Renewal Fines in Leases	61	Transfer of Land	41
Objections to Life Leasehold Tenure	63	Numerous useful Tables for Advowsons, Next Presentations, and Life Contingencies	49—55
Tables of Reversion Values	67		

A PRACTICAL TREATISE

ON

SAVINGS BANKS,

CONTAINING A REVIEW OF

THEIR PAST HISTORY AND PRESENT CONDITION,

AND OF LEGISLATION ON THE SUBJECT,

WITH AN

Exposition of the Measures required
for their complete re-Organization, and for placing
them on a sound Financial Basis.

BY

ARTHUR SCRATCHLEY, M.A.,

Of the Inner Temple, Barrister-at-Law;
Formerly Fellow and Sadlerian Lecturer of Queen's College, Cambridge,
Author of a "Treatise on Industrial Investments," &c.

LONDON:
LONGMAN, GREEN, LONGMAN, AND ROBERTS.
MDCCCLX.

NOTICE.

I.—Ten years have elapsed since the publication of our "*Suggestions on the Savings Bank Question,*" in which we proposed measures likely to prevent the recurrence of such frauds as had been discovered during the years 1848 and 1849. Though the Bill, which we drew on that occasion to give effect to those suggestions, came to no result in a legislative form, yet the lapse of time has shewn that the principles upon which it was based were well calculated to attain the desired object. One advantage, moreover, has arisen from the delay: it has afforded opportunity to persons interested in Savings Banks, or engaged in their management, to give full consideration to the views we then advocated, and to the various measures that have been proposed by successive Governments, and, more recently, by the Parliamentary Committee of 1858. The public are also better prepared to appreciate the arguments that may be advanced on *either side with regard to any particular steps towards the reorganization of these institutions.

II.—The Committee of 1858 examined several witnesses of experience with great patience, and at much length; but the chaotic state of the question, and the necessarily limited time devoted to their inquiries, appear to have prevented them from doing more, in their Report, than giving an abstract of the evidence. The Committee, however, concluded with one main

---

* [Some of these arguments will be found in the valuable Report of the Committee, before which we were prevented by temporary ill-health from attending to give evidence. The Committee was excellently constituted. The list of Members comprised the names of Mr. Bonham Carter, and Mr. Adderley, who have taken so active a part in Friendly Society legislation; Mr. Fagan, who exerted himself very nobly on behalf of the unfortunate Cuffe Street Depositors; Mr. Grogan, Mr. Baring, Mr. Henley, Mr. Bouverie, with others (the Right Hon. Sotheron Estcourt, Chairman, Mr. Ayrton, Sir H. Willoughby, &c.), whose names will be found mentioned in subsequent pages.]

recommendation, viz. that a *Savings Bank Commission* should be appointed, to whose future deliberations they seem to have deemed it better to leave all measures actually to be adopted in the future, whether to obviate the recurrence of frauds, or to terminate the errors in political finance that may be said to be at the root of the present Savings Bank system.

III.—In this *treatise we have endeavoured to give to those, who may desire thoroughly to understand the subject of Savings Banks, all the information necessary for their purpose, in a systematic form; and we have stated the principles by which, as we conceive, their internal and financial reorganization should be guided.

This information cannot be said to have been hitherto accessible. It could only be obtained by wading through voluminous Blue Books; by a careful study of the numerous returns made to Parliament during the last twenty-five years from the banks and from the National Debt Commissioners; by an analysis of the mass of Parliamentary evidence dispersed in every variety of form through thousands of answers, abounding in erroneous statements, and embodying conflicting opinions on almost every point; and, lastly, by reference to the rules of the banks themselves (with which we have acquainted ourselves by an examination of every clause in the rules of all the banks but six in the United Kingdom). Such a study, necessarily laborious, would probably be irksome and distasteful to most persons, as well as perplexing to the non-professional inquirer.

IV.—We have, besides, endeavoured to make this volume (*which forms †Division I. of the Treatise on Associations for Provident Investment*) the exponent, not only of the views we have ourselves so long advocated, but of those of a large number

---

* [No systematic Treatise on the question exists either in England or in foreign countries: the numerous publications on the subject have been only in the nature of Essays and Lectures.]

† [Divisions II. and III. can be obtained separately.]

of Savings Bank officials, who have, during the period mentioned, favoured us with letters on the subject—more particularly since the Committee's Report—in reply to a *circular issued, at our suggestion, by the *Friendly Societies Institute*.

These communications display much ability and knowledge of the subject, and, in our selection from the mass of matter thus placed at our disposal, we have given most prominence to those opinions which derive weight from the experience of those who hold them.

V.—Keeping in view the object indicated above we have traced retrospectively the history and law of Savings Banks, although the impending legislation will doubtless introduce great changes. With the same motive, our analysis of past financial errors is accompanied by explana-

* [In order to make the investigation as complete as possible, we issued, also, a circular, containing a variety of questions, to the officials of the principal Savings Banks *abroad*.

In every instance, with striking courtesy, answers were readily returned, and at great length; and a vast number of documents relating to foreign and colonial Savings Banks was sent to the Friendly Societies Institute. The information they afford is, however, too elaborate and extensive to be brought forward in any satisfactory shape in the few pages we are able to devote to it in this Volume, without delaying its publication. We have been compelled, therefore, to confine ourselves to a short sketch, in the Introduction, of the condition and progress of the leading banks. The documents furnished have been of much service to us, however, for we have been enabled to trace the actual practical working in foreign banks of some of the amendments we have recommended for adoption in this country.

In a future Volume, which will be published with the new Savings Bank Act, when passed, we contemplate giving a more full *resumé* of these documents, and of the Laws relating to Non-Government Banks.

The perusal of the Reports, and a comparison of a large number of foreign rules with those of the English banks, has shewn us that a similarity of plan exists in all; which is probably attributable to the fact that they appear to have had for original model the rules and plan of operations in this country. In several instances, however, they have given earlier attention to those defects of principle and practice that have caused such mischief in English banks, and they have sought to introduce remedial modifications of the parental system.]

tions, which some may deem too elementary, as the work would not fulfil its purpose, as a text-book for future Savings Bank Actuaries and others, if these points were not discussed. The present volume is, consequently, divided into several Parts, as follows:—

I.— Past History and Present System of Savings Banks.

II.—The Frauds in Savings Banks, their evil consequences, and the Remedy.

III.—Financial errors in the present Savings Bank system.

IV.—The financial re-organization of Savings Banks on a sound basis.

V.—The "Post Office Savings Bank Plan," and the facilities offered by Savings Banks for the extension of Life Assurance and Sick Benefits among the Industrious Classes.

VI.—Non-Government Banks of Deposits and the Audit of Public Institutions.

In the Appendix, a chapter has been added on the subject of applying a portion of Savings Bank funds to assist Societies for the Improvement of Industrial Dwellings. We have also given a short *résumé* of the history of the National Debt, the security in which, under the present law, all Savings Bank funds are invested.

⁎ In the preparation of this work, we have received the greatest assistance from many eminent and experienced persons interested in the subject: to two of them not mentioned in the text, a recognition of our obligation is specially due: The varied acquirements and rare financial ability of our friend, Mr. W. J. Reynolds (of Chelsea), M.A., have been of the utmost service to us. We have also been fortunate in having had the active co-operation of Mr. E. W. Brabrook, the Corresponding Secretary of the Friendly Societies Institute, whose intimate acquaintance with the Savings Bank question has enabled him to lighten the task of collecting, comparing, and digesting the mass of materials involved.

5 *Essex Court, Temple,*
      January 1860.

INDEX.

	PAGE
Accounts: Uniformity desirable,	90
Acts of Parliament	12
Actuaries	92
America	xlvii
Rules of Deposit Banks	280
Attempts at Legislation	11, 78
Audit of Public Institutions	283
Australia	liii
Austria	xl
Banks of Deposit	268
Belgium	xxxiv
Branches	228
Committee of 1858	17
Declaration on Depositing	103
Defalcations	xxi., 49
Cuffe Street Savings Bank, Dublin	60
Extent of the Frauds	55
Rochdale Savings Bank	65
Deferred Annuities	251
Recommendations	258
Deficiency in Savings Bank Fund:—	
Correct Principle for Valuing Securities	115
Amount of the Deficiency	118
Its Causes	122
How to be prevented in future,	178
Deposits and Depositors:—	
Class of persons who should be Depositors	x
Legal provisions in regard to the amount of deposits	33

	PAGE
Unclaimed deposits	38
Deposits out of bank hours,	52, 107
Future limit	197
Conversion into Stock	200
Exchequer Bills—Appendix	34
Laws relating to Purchase and Funding	147
Debate of March 1859	159
Exchequer Bonds—Appendix	35
Expenses of Management:—	
Savings Banks	39
National Debt Office	44
Future Government allowance,	191
Field for Savings Banks	168
Financial Operations of Chancellors of the Exchequer.	135, 152
Financial Reorganization:—	
Fundamental Principles	165
Alterations desirable	183
Foreign Countries	xxxi
Formation of Savings Banks	25
France	xxxi
Frauds, how to be prevented	287
Government Guarantee: Belief of the Public	70
Government Inspection	81
Hamburg	xxxvii
Holland	xlii
Inspectors	81, 99, 289

INDEX.

	PAGE
Interest: Rate allowed	30
Excess paid to Trustees over the amount received by the Commissioners	128
Uniformity of Calculation	207
Investment:—	
Early Methods	7
Losses attending Sale and Purchase of Stock	131
Difficulty of obtaining Securities	171
Investment through a newly Constituted Commission	186
Improvement of Industrial Dwellings—Appendix	1, 28
Non-Government Banks	273
Life Assurance through Savings Banks	231, 247
Manufacturing Trades—Appendix	27
Massachusetts	1
Military and Naval Savings Banks	21
Model Lodging Houses—Appendix	13
Money Order Offices	223
National Debt—Appendix	31
National Debt Commissioners: their Relation to Savings Banks	142
New Jersey	lii
New York	xlvii

	PAGE
Non-Government Banks	263
Origin of Savings Banks	3
Parish Friendly Societies	234
Pass Books, Inspection of	97
Penny Banks	22
Poors Assurance Office	239
Post Office Savings Bank Plan,	215
Progress of Savings Banks, xxvii, 20
Prospective Interest Plan	209
Provisions for Old Age	251
Prussia	xxxviii
Public Playgrounds—Appendix,	20
Remedy for Defects of Management	76
Rules and Annual Statements, 26, 108
Russia	xlv
Separate Surplus Fund	34
Suburban Villages — Appendix,	10
Sweden	xliii
Switzerland	xxvi
Town Life: its Unhealthiness—	
Appendix	24
Treasurers	29, 31
Government Treasurers	84
Trust Accounts	28, 203
Trustees and Managers, xviii, 50, 93, 112
Whitbread, Mr., his Bill (1807), 11, 216, 239
Withdrawals	105

ERRATA.

Page 20, line 4 from bottom;—*for* " 1,049" *read* "$\overline{1}$,049."
    The 1 is negative—there being a decrease of 951 in the number of Depositors under the column.
  ,, 110, Note: line 2 from bottom; *for* " ou" *read* " on."
  ,, 256, line 3 from bottom; *for* " paie" *read* " place."

*** [The calculations are based on the returns for 1858 where those for 1859 are incomplete or not published.]

A PRACTICAL TREATISE
ON
SAVINGS BANKS.

INTRODUCTION.

I.—Nature of the Subject.   THE subject of Industrial investments in Savings Banks is one of those complicated questions of every-day life, that fall within that branch of political economy of which a writer (whose distinguished abilities have lately elevated him to the financial administration of our Indian empire) has so justly said* that it is difficult to those only who are disposed to give to it but superficial consideration. There are, indeed, in the Savings Bank question, as in that of banking generally, numerous points of the highest importance, which are of a character too abstruse to command, under ordinary circumstances, sufficient consideration from the public at large; so that, as Mr. Wilson remarks, "the only time, when we can hope usefully and entirely to arrest attention to them is when the current events of the day clothe them with more than usual interest."

The present may, perhaps, be deemed such a juncture in the

---

* [Capital, Currency, and Banking, by the Right. Hon. J. Wilson, M.P.]

history of Savings Banks, when a consolidation of the Acts relating to them, with material amendments in their constitution, is anticipated, and recognised as necessary.

The subject of Savings Banks is indeed one well deserving of study by all classes, for these institutions form one of the most remarkable features of the present age. Its importance is admitted by the most eminent *political economists in this country and abroad, many of whom, in their admirable contributions to the discussion of some of the leading financial principles involved, have displayed the genius that characterizes all their writings.

II.—Of the kind of persons who are Depositors. We will here, in a few words, direct the reader's attention to the *politico-social* aspect of the question of Savings Banks. He will at once see that it is one of peculiar delicacy and importance, and that there is a pressing necessity for amending imperfect or erroneous legislation on the subject. For this purpose we may regard the population

---

* [Adam Smith, Ricardo, Malthus, Parnell, Buchanan, and Stuart Mill, with others at home. The most complete essays on the subject are by foreign writers, viz. Baron Charles Dupin and M. Agathon Prévost. Valuable suggestions occur in the works of numerous other authors:— MM. Gustave du Puynode—Coquelin (in his able work "*Du Crédit et des Banques*")—Lemontey (in a popular Tract, "*Les bons effets de la caisse d'Epargne*")—Garnier—Francœur (formerly Professor at the *Ecole Polytechnique*), and Jomard (in Reports to the *Société pour le progrès de l'Instruction élémentaire*)—Navier, the celebrated mathematician, in a paper read before the *Académie des Sciences*—the excellent Cardinal de Chévérus (in his Orations)—MM. Emile de Girardin, E. Salverte, Felix Bodin (in the periodical journals)—le Duc de Larochefoucauld ("*Dialogue entre Alexandre et Benoît*"), in France; and Dr. Otto Hubner, of Berlin, and Dr. Stubenrauch, of Vienna, may be specially mentioned as having made important contributions. Many others have furnished arguments or illustrations to the views advanced in this Treatise, and their names are mentioned in subsequent pages. Indeed, it would not be easy to exhaust the list of distinguished writers whose attention has been arrested, in a greater or less degree, by the subject of Savings Banks.]

of this country as divided into three classes. Of one of these, the members (relatively limited in number) are so rich and prosperous, that in their domestic arrangements they do not even notice whether the prices of bread and meat are rising or falling. Another is composed of a large mass of persons destitute of sufficient resources for their existence. They, of course, have nothing to put in a Savings Bank; they live by public charity, or at least require aid from other sources for what their own exertions are insufficient to supply, and are a charge on the community to the extent of nine millions a-year in poors' rates.

Between these two classes is the great bulk of the population, which lives honourably on the fruit of its labour, whether of the mind or the body; the latter (by custom rather than with correctness of language) being termed the working or industrious classes. The members of this " working" class are the persons for whom Savings Banks were originated, and to whose requirements they are adapted; and their increasing providence may be measured by the fact of their having advanced their *Savings Bank deposits from fourteen millions in 1828 to forty-one millions at the present time. Great, indeed, must have been the industry and self-denial that have enabled them to achieve such results; and commensurate therewith is the keen anxiety they experience for the safety of their money—for they are not without the natural jealousy which gives rise to suspicions on the part of those who are weak, towards those who are strong; suspicions of a class which is open to injury, towards those who, they imagine, may do them disservice. Any inattention, therefore, to evils affecting the places of deposit, into which they have been invited to put trust, is fraught with disadvantage.

---

* [Except where otherwise stated, the deposits of Friendly Societies, direct with the Commissioners, are included under this denomination.]

III.—Of Institutions for Provident purposes.

If it is by the men of business, the extensive manufacturers, the wealthy bankers and merchants, the large capitalists of this country, that commercial enterprises of magnitude and importance are originated and set on foot, so that the effect of its industry and the weight of its power are felt at every extremity of the globe, it is mainly to the efforts of all ranks united—to the landed proprietors, the gentry and clergy as well, that we owe other landmarks of progress, by which mankind has *advanced to civilization: it is to their benevolent spirit that we are indebted for numerous institutions which are specially designed to encourage provident habits among the industrious classes, and have for object to serve as banks for temporary deposits. Whether they be established under the sanction and control of Government, or by private enterprise merely, their purpose is the same: to afford to persons whose time and attention are otherwise occupied, the opportunity of obtaining, with as little expense as possible, a remunerative investment for their savings—under such a system, and with such a security, as shall present little doubt of their money being safely laid out.

That this is both practicable and desirable we have pointed out in Division *II. of the Treatise on Associations for Provident Investment, and shewn that, while it is usually im-

---

* [" A mesure que les sociétés avancent dans les voies de la civilisation, le travail tend à y occuper une place plus élevée. Le principe guerrièr qui est entré si avant dans la constitution sociale de la vieille Europe, semble se retirer devant les progrès du principe industriel qui, chaque jour, se développe et grandit.

On a commencé à comprendre que les conquêtes de l'homme sur la nature sont les plus vraies, les seules durables, les seules qui forment la base de la prospérité des nations comme des individus." (L. Lemaitre: Preface to Condy-Raguet on Banks and Circulation.]

* [Treatise on Benefit Building Societies, Tontines, and Emigration. Third Edition.]

possible for a private individual to obtain an advantageous accumulating interest for the small sums of money he can spare from time to time from his expenses, an aggregation of such amounts, contributed by a number of persons, may be as readily and profitably invested as the larger savings of a richer man. Without such associations, however, each accretion is so small that something of the ridiculous is felt in looking upon it as usefully available towards forming a fund for the future, and it would too often be applied to satisfy some present and seemingly pressing want.

Where the transactions of the association are independent of any question of life or death of the Depositors, the power of withdrawal of the money contributed, with accumulated interest, is almost always conceded; and the large number of millions standing to the credit of the industrious classes in the particular kind at present under our notice, is evidence of the popularity of such institutions.

IV.—Distinctive advantages conferred by Savings Banks. "The secret of their success,"* remarks M. Prévost, "is, that a Savings Bank may be† entered and quitted when and how a man pleases; as long as the money

---

* [Essay on Savings Banks in the "*Cent Traités,*" translated with much ability by Mr. W. Hatton, Actuary to the Brighton Savings Bank.]

† ["At present," wrote Mr. Malthus in the year 1803, "the few labourers, who save a little money, are often greatly at a loss to know what to do with it, and under such circumstances we cannot be much surprised that it should sometimes be ill employed, and last but a short time. It would probably be essential to the success of any plan of this kind, that the labourer should be able to draw out his money whenever he wanted it, and have the most perfect liberty of disposing of it in every respect as he pleased. Though we may regret that money so hardly earned should sometimes be spent to little purpose, yet it seems to be a case in which we have no right to interfere, nor, if we had, would it, in a general view, be advantageous; because the knowledge of possessing this liberty would be of more use in encouraging the practice of saving, than any restriction of it in preventing the misuse of money so saved."]

remains deposited, it is continually increasing for the benefit of the Depositor. Do his wants require the whole or a part? by simply making the demand, he receives what he requires. If in the interval between the demand and the payment his temporary necessity has ceased to exist; if, as it sometimes happens, a salutary thought interposes, and triumphs over a transient whim, the Savings Bank, with a paternal feeling to the Depositor, considers the demand as not having taken place, and retains the deposit without expense or loss of interest, thus encouraging, with all its power, perseverance in the wise paths of economy and saving."

Savings Banks, as they at present exist, differ from the other channels of industrial investment, discussed in the remaining divisions of the Treatise on Associations for Provident Investment, from the fact of their management and supervision being entirely out of the hands of the parties whose money is at stake, and from their presenting no element either of speculative assurance affecting relatively the deposits of members (as in Friendly Societies for sickness or life contingencies), or of commercial trading (as in Benefit Building and other co-operative Investment Societies). Further, the numerous Friendly Societies in the United Kingdom only partially meet the provident requirements of the industrious classes, as it is not to every one that the benefits they afford are an object of necessity or desire; and the peculiar features of their operations, such as an allowance during *sickness*, &c., are only an actual money benefit to those members who happen to fall ill; thus presenting, from the nature of the case, the circumstance of many persons contributing for years, who, by the blessing of continued health, receive but little in return out of the funds of the Society. On the other hand, those self-supporting and self-managing Industrial Associations, of which Benefit Building Societies are a specimen, offer the attractions of possible greater profit than can be obtained by more secure institutions; but every subscriber, in becoming entitled to share in the prospective profits of the Association, would, if he inquired, find that he had also become a participator in the contingencies of loss. These distinctive objections to the respective systems of Friendly Assurance and Benefit Building Societies do not apply to that of Savings Banks.

V.—Effect of the establishment of Savings Banks. In reality, therefore, it is by Savings Banks that the only opportunity is offered to the working man to be provident, in the sense of accumulating with certainty a sum of money for use in the future, as distinguished from the *contingent* advantages offered by Benefit Clubs and Building Societies. Before Savings Banks were established, there were no systematic means of encouragement to thrift, and no provision was made for its gatherings. Through long years of hard saving, and scraping together, and hoarding in his old stocking, some cottager, bent with age, may here and there have attained the end of his desire by the purchase of the freehold of his cottage and garden; but this, in the nature of things, could not be general, and, in our highly artificial civilization, perhaps not desirable, when labour can be so often more profitably employed in service or the work of an artisan. Now, however, those among the labouring population of England, whose industry and frugality enables them to lay aside a portion of their earnings, have (as was remarked by Mr. G. R. Porter, in his "*Progress of the Nation*,") "a readier, and, as regards the community, a far better opportunity for the profitable employment of their money, than can be generally procured by the purchase of a bit of land;" for the Savings Bank is open to receive their deposits, and to yield a moderate, but certain return of interest upon them. A much greater incentive to prudence is thus offered than would generally be found in the desire of acquiring a rood of ground: besides which, the unwise laws and complicated systems that still continue to regulate the *transfer and possession of real property in this kingdom are so intricate in their operation, surrounded by so many difficulties, and attended by so much cost, that it would be quite incompatible with prudence for any poor man to venture upon a speculation dependent on the validity of a title, even if the expensiveness of the deeds rendered such a course possible to him. The success which has attended Freehold Land Societies does not invalidate the argument; for if they have to some extent smoothed legal difficulties by lowering the relative cost of transfer, the movement is altogether partial in its results. They have been confined in their land dealings to the neighbourhood of large towns, where small building sites were in demand by well-off artizans and tradesmen; they have made no dealings in land specially designed to yield the labouring man a livelihood by tillage. Moreover, as Mr. Porter observes:—

"Savings Banks [when honestly conducted] can never involve those, who therein deposit their savings, in any expense, or in the risk proverbial to those who touch bricks and mortar: so long as the money continues in deposit, it produces a small revenue to the owner, unaccompanied by any contingencies of seasons or fluctuations in the money market as far as he is concerned, and, at any moment when the whole amount, or part of it, is required to meet any extraordinary exigency, it is forthcoming, without being subject to any deduction of any kind whatever."

Without habits of forethought and frugality the workingman cannot provide against the ever-recurring contingency of his existence—misfortune; and in forming such habits Savings Banks have done and are doing incalculable good.

---

* [See on this subject the introduction and appendices to our "Treatise on the Enfranchisement of Copyhold and Church Property." Fourth Edition.]

Archbishop *Whately remarks that " if they had become general some ten or twenty years earlier, at the time when wages were at the highest, they would have saved probably much moral degradation resulting from the distress which followed. It happens, as a fortunately countervailing circumstance, that in those very employments which are the most liable to fluctuation, wages are, generally speaking, the highest: so that, in prosperous times, the workman of steady habits, and not, like the savage, a slave to present gratification and thoughtless of the future, may accumulate a little store, which, when employment falls short, may either enable him to subsist till times improve again, or till he shall have acquired a competent skill in some other kindred art; or else to remove with his family to some place where he can earn support."

In times of pressure, the money he has deposited in a Savings Bank allows the working man to look forward to better days: he gains a habit of self-reliance, of depending on his own efforts and foresight for the means of extrication from a difficult but passing crisis; and his very nature is thus elevated by the feeling of his own strength and independence.† For him who looks only to the labour of his hands for his daily bread, it is an absolute necessity to provide against the day when by the failure of work, by sickness, or by the gathering infirmities of age, his earnings may be suspended or terminated.

---

* [Lectures on Political Economy, p. 194.]

† [An excellent prize essay has recently been largely distributed by the Managers of the *Glasgow Savings Bank*, in which is pointed out the general superiority of the workmen who have deposit accounts over those who have none. The former are invited to use every means in their power to lead to the Savings Banks those who have not yet tried them. The sound argument is suggested that the workman, who possesses a little money, is always in a good position to make a stand for fair wages for his labour; whilst the artisan, who is pressed by necessity, is forced to accept whatever is offered, and it is put out of his power to profit by a favourable opportunity when there is a demand for labour.]

"What," says *M. Agathon Prévost*, in the admirable Essay before quoted, "will the labourer then do, if, in his careless thoughtlessness, he has laid up nothing? if he has lived from hand to mouth, without troubling himself for a moment about the difficulties he must sooner or later encounter in his way? Will he beg relief from public charity—a relief which is degrading to any one who ought to be able to do without it, and which he requires entirely through his own fault? Would it not be better for him to provide, long beforehand, for the evil day, and, even at the risk of present privations, prepare himself to meet it?"

This point of view shows well the advantage of *institutions that serve as a stimulus, a constant reminder of the duty of saving: for it is unfortunately frequently that which is useful,

---

* [It is not right to overlook that a few men of eminence doubt the existence of any advantages derived by the working classes from the establishment of Banks for Savings. One learned writer, who has given great attention to the subject—*Dr. Hubner*, of *Berlin*, says:—" If we may credit the testimony of history, the habit of saving was not less prevalent before than after the establishment of such institutions. Formerly the little savings of the poorer classes were deposited with tradespeople and master mechanics. The rate of interest was, perhaps, not higher than that now given by the Savings Banks, but the Depositor had the double advantage of acquiring a *friend*, a connection with his capital. The interest was not the only profit derived from saving and industry; they also generated mutual trust and confidence in case of need or want of money in business and trade, and the artisan was always morally sure to find reciprocity in his transactions with old customers, to whose hands he had entrusted his former savings. There is no compensation for such social benefits in the Savings Banks, where the clerks receive the little savings, hardly looking at the Depositor, or even granting him the least mark of civility. All he gets from the representative of *humanity* is a slip of paper, and his savings and hard earnings go to the strong box, but not to the *heart* of the receiver. Being in need and pressed for money before the time, he receives it back with a reduction of interest (according to the practice of the Prussian banks in reference to withdrawal). A half life-time of saving and industry does not procure him either friend or credit."]

if not indeed necessary, which must be retrenched with an eye to the future. How much, it may be asked, of the immense amount deposited would have been saved, had not these institutions existed?

VI.—Of the Social Effects of Economy. A provision for the inexorable necessities of the future having been once completed, then follows the natural desire on the part of the Depositor still further to improve his worldly condition. Each hopes that he may escape in times of commercial depression the necessity of touching his little hoard, and that he may anticipate the day, when, possessed of sufficient capital, he will be enabled to take a small business of his own, become a master, and have workmen under him.* Thus it is that †Capital, which is nothing but the

---

* ["The young workman," observes M. Droz, (*Principes de la Science des Richesses*, 2nd Edit. p. 46,) "whose only possession is the gains of his labour, can never, if he dissipate all his earnings, improve his position. But the intelligent and well-conducted young man, who qualifies himself to work on his own account, may in time save enough to take the lease of a shop, and to become himself an employer of labour."

Dr. Chalmers had a great idea of giving to every man, if possible, a stake in the country, and thus a sense of the value of social order:

"*Dr. Chalmers*," says Mr. Mill, "inculcated on capitalists the practice of a moral restraint in reference to the pursuit of gain; while Sismondi deprecates machinery, and the various inventions which increase productive power. They both maintain that accumulation of capital may proceed too fast, not merely for the moral, but for the material interests of those who produce and accumulate; and they enjoin the rich to guard against this evil by an ample productive consumption. Yet, remarked M. Rœderer, in his Mémoires sur quelques points d'Economie Publique (p. 67):—

"Une épargne ne peut se faire que par des privations, ou en se ménageant une grande surabondance de consommation par un travail qui passe la mesure des besoins actuels. Or on ne cherche à obtenir un superflu par le travail ou par des privations, qu'afin d'étendre par là ses jouissances à venir.

"Ainsi, sans espérance de profit, point d'épargnes, point de capitaux, point de culture au delà des besoins des propriétaires et de leur serviteurs."]

† ["Le capital," said M. Bastiat (*Harmonies Economiques*, pp. 285,

produce of labour saved, marks the progress of society, and, as Adam Smith pointed out before Savings Banks were set on foot, every man, who wastes his money, is a public enemy who diminishes the profits of intelligent labour, while he who saves it ought to be regarded as a benefactor to society.

VII.—Of security for Savings. It is strange that while the most eminent members of both Houses, as *individuals*, recognise the great extent to which the self-denying economy of the body of the people tends, not only to the increase of the national wealth, but also to great moral improvement, yet they have, in their *collective* capacity as *legislators*, neglected, for eleven years, to provide the necessary security for the deposits they have invited;—not that they can say that none is required, when they have still ringing in their ears the sad complaints of numerous unfortunate Depositors as to the unfairness with which the nation has allowed them—miserably poor as they were—to lose the money of which they have been defrauded. (See Part II.)

One of the first cares of every Legislature should be not only to promote habits of frugality among the labouring population, but to provide a secure depository for the savings of their industry. If there be a public fund of a more sacred

---

286), " a sa racine dans trois attributs de l'homme : la Prevoyance, l'Intelligence et la Frugalité. Pour se déterminer à former un capital, il faut en effet prévoir l'avenir, lui sacrifier le présent, exercer un noble empire sur soi-même et sur ses appétits, résister non seulement à l'appât des jouissances actuelles, mais encore aux aiguillons de la vanité . . . . .
Il faut surtout être animé de l'esprit de famille et ne pas reculer devant des sacrifices dont le fruit sera recueilli par les êtres chéris qu'on laissera après soi.

"Capitaliser c'est préparer le vivre, le couvert, l'abri, le loisir, l'instruction, l'indépendance, la dignité aux générations futures. Rien de tout cela ne se peut faire sans mettre en exercice les vertus les plus sociales, qui plus est, sans les convertir en habitudes."]

character than another, or to which inviolability should attach, it is that which poor men have accumulated with so much toil and almost heroic self-denial.

This inviolability is obviously essential as an incentive to saving. Any one, who has mixed largely with working men still ignorant of provident notions, will readily testify that the first obstacle opposed to lessons of economy is the ever-recurring doubt of security for their savings—that, in fact, the fundamental difficulty with operatives, and all who receive wages, is to induce them to make a beginning in habits of order, foresight, and economy. If a servant or an artisan can once be persuaded to place in a bank, week by week, his smaller economies of a shilling or so, he will keep on accumulating with the hope of having *pounds*, where at first only *shillings* are stored, and we may be certain, that before that result is obtained, he will have acquired a knowledge of the advantage of saving, a taste for it, and a desire to continue it. To use a common French expression, he is no longer " *un proletaire sans avenir*," but has joined the ranks of those who are marked by the excellence of their conduct and by their habits of morality; and he is found a better workman, a better husband, and a better * citizen.

---

* [The director of the Paris Savings Bank stated, in proof of this, that not a single Depositor in that Institution had ever been prosecuted for joining in any political disturbance—a notable circumstance in France. Whatever amelioration there might be in the material condition, or in the inner life of the working classes, he attributed quite as much to the influence of Savings Banks, as to the spread of elementary education.

It cannot be overlooked, however, that these agents of progress have much to effect in the United Kingdom: for direct investigation shews, that, of the population of 30,000,000, no less than 175,000 may be taken to belong to the criminal classes, whose yearly depredations average £14,400,000, or £82 to each individual. If to these be added the paupers, 1,300,000, who cost annually £9,000,000 in poors rates, we obtain £23,000,000 of money as the yearly loss to the nation by the useless portion of its population, exclusive of the expenses of looking after and punishing their malpractices.]

VIII.—Praise of the Legislature, and of Honorary Trustees and Managers.

Until recent events, the Legislature was supposed to have done all it could, by successive enactments, to place these admirable institutions on a sound footing. So much was this opinion general, that when the Chambers of France were discussing a *projet de loi* for the regulation of Savings Banks in that country, one of their most eminent economists pronounced the following high eulogium to the assembled Peers on the bold measures of encouragement adopted by the English Parliament—so different, as he said, from the sentiments of fear which occupied the mind of the French Legislature, lest some great and sudden financial difficulties should arise, from too much liberty of principle being adopted with regard to the Depositors:—

* "Savez vous ce qui fait la force et le salut du gouvernement Anglais ? C'est le même sentiment qui faisait, au plus beau temps du peuple-roi, la force et le salut du sénat Romain : *il croit en lui : il croit à la fortune virile de l'empire britannique*; il vendrait le champ occupé par un nouvel Annibal, celui-ci fût-il aux portes de Londres. Il a confiance dans la nation et la nation l'en recompense en triomphant, sous sa conduite, de difficultés et de dangers que l'univers entier repute insurmontables."

These sentiments were not only largely shared by those for whose benefit these institutions were devised, but multiplied throughout the land among all classes—and eminent writers† accorded a high place and praise to the existing Savings Bank system, proclaiming:—

That "the labouring classes may now feel assured that their savings, and the interest accumulated upon them, would be faithfully preserved to meet their future wants."

---

* [M. Charles Dupin, Chamber of Peers, 17 July 1843.]

† [Mr. McCulloch's Statistical Account of the British Empire, II., p. 668. See also sec. 4, chap. III. of this Treatise.]

Much praise, at home and abroad, was also considered due to the excellent men of all classes, who, carrying out the design of the Legislature, heartily co-operated in the establishment of banks for savings, and subscribed considerable sums to defray necessary expenses of management in the smaller places; besides making it their duty, for many years together, to give their personal services gratuitously in supervising the commonest operations. Many of them, though engaged in affairs of the greatest moment, were known to be regular in their attendance on the days fixed for them by rotation, and to be discharging with untiring patience the minor duties connected with the receiving and registration of the most trifling sums: content if, by their presence in the office of the bank, they gave confidence and encouragement to the industrious classes.*

---

* [" L'artisan qui veut placer la petite somme economisée dans la semaine,"—remarks M. Dupin, with something of a rhetorical expansion of the facts—"s'il vient au bureau de la caisse d'épargne, au lieu d'un employé subalterne, trouve à tour de rôle les citoyens les plus eminents, des magistrats, des fonctionnaires, des savants, des manufacturiers, des commerçants. *Voilà les commis du peuple*, qui dérobent à leur vie laborieuse des moments précieux, pour en faire un admirable usage, en inscrivant de leur main les versements de l'ouvrier. En même temps, nos plus riches capitalistes sont fiers de présider à la compatibilité d'un établissement qui reçoit avec bonheur les moindres économies de l'artisan et du soldat, comme les plus humbles dépôts de l'orphelin et de la veuve. Tel est l'établissement que s'enorgueillissait à juste titre de présider, l'illustre duc de Larochefoucauld-Liancourt, celui qui, non content d'apporter la vaccine aux enfans du peuple français, aspirait à leur assurer l'aisance dans l'âge mûr, et *le confort* dans la viellesse."

" Savings Banks have, above all, an inestimable advantage in forming a bond of fraternity and of Christian charity between rich and poor—between all classes of society. When men, distinguished by their wealth, by their position at the bar, in the magistracy, in learning, or in arts—many of them the bearers of those historical names which form one of the glorious inheritance of France,—when these men are seen voluntarily devoting themselves to the administration of the Savings Banks; giving up to them their time, their attention, and even their money; constituting themselves the servants of the poor man, and occupying them-

IX. — Such praise was not universally merited.
A series of facts, however, subsequently brought to light, shewed, unhappily, that all Trustees and Managers did not, after the first enthusiasm was over, continue the effective discharge of the duties for which they were receiving public esteem and admiration. It was also found that the Legislature—while endeavouring to give practical effect to the wide sympathies between class and class, which honourably distinguish our age from all others in the world's history—had not in its efforts at social law-giving been invariably successful, and had not always sufficiently regarded the simplest principles of political economy.

After thirty years (up to 1848) had been devoted to developing, in what was thought a satisfactory manner, the progress of Savings Banks, the friends of these excellent institutions imagined that no improvement could be necessary, unless, perhaps, to give greater facilities to the public. Within the last twelve years, however, the reputation of Savings Banks has undergone a change; to the praise that used to be awarded to them has succeeded censure of the most bitter kind; to the confidence, which was universal, has succeeded distrust. It has been found, not only that their system of management has become imperfect and given rise to frauds and losses, but also that considerable* financial errors have been committed in the

---

selves with his interest with a zeal as enlightened as it is indefatigable; the labourers—that numerous class which earns its bread by the sweat of its brow, throw aside the feelings of hate which evil suggestions seek in vain to inspire. They see that, if they are not the eldest sons of the great human family, they are not, after all, entirely disinherited: they see that there are sympathetic hearts to love them, and good dispositions to serve them; thus they reconcile themselves to an order of things which none can change: and should Savings Banks have produced no other good, they would even thus deserve the gratitude of mankind."—*Prévost.*]

* [In Part III. Art. 19. it will be shewn that errors in the fundamental principles of finance have produced a Deficiency of over 4½ millions on the 41 millions due (20 November 1859) to Savings Banks and Friendly

principles upon which the Government has dealt with Savings Banks.

X.—Effect of the Panic. The panic that ensued on the discovery of the Savings Bank frauds would, but for the serious character of the delusion, form no unamusing chapter in the history of popular credulity. The one leading fact disclosed was that the public really knew little of the legal position of what was deemed so simple a matter, coming home to the experience of every-day life, as a Savings Bank. *Complete ignorance prevailed of the fundamental nature of these institutions, and of the relation which subsisted between the Depositors on the one hand and the Government on the other. The delusions which existed in the public mind were not confined to the illiterate, but were participated in by persons eminent from the high political positions they had filled. The alarm which followed was re-echoed by the Press, and loud were the clamours of the hour for change, dictated more by pressing fears, than by due regard to the reasons which really existed for a change; but public fear, when the first apprehension of the imminence of greater disasters had passed away, was more tempered with rationality than public faith had been, for it set itself with commendable promptitude and calmness to the task of inquiring into the facts of the case.

Societies, which is equivalent to £10 . 13s. 7d. in every £100 that the nation has taken charge of. The operations of the Chancellor of the Exchequer will be shewn to have produced a Deficiency of £315,801, which is equivalent to £1 . 4s. 1d. per cent.

Up to 20th November 1858, the following causes had assisted in creating this Deficiency:—

1. *Paying more interest than received:*   over 3½ *millions.*   (*Art.* 14. *Part III.*)
2. *Loss on purchases and sales of stocks* : . . ¾ *of a mil.*   (*Art.* 16. *Part III.*)
The discovered Frauds amounted to . . . . ¼ *of a mil.*   (*Art.* 9. *Part II.*)]

* [See illustrations of this in Sect. 4, Chap. 3.]

Thus the great panic, which, about ten years ago, threatened to be such a check, financially and morally, to the future provident habits of the labouring classes, has not been without beneficial results. It has proved, what does not seem to have been thought of before, that large and difficult questions, legal and economical, are mixed up with a matter apparently so simple as the accumulation and safe deposit of odd pence and shillings, saved up by thrifty labouring men.

This is abundantly evidenced by the grave and patient consideration, which Parliament has been compelled to give to the measures introduced, session after session, and by the numerous pamphlets and essays that have been written on the subject of late. The public has thus had placed within reach the means of acquiring a better knowledge of the actual and legal relations between the Savings Banks and the Government, and is able to guard against the false and unsound confidence in which it previously reposed. The working classes have learnt how delusive and how dangerous was their faith in the security of the State for the safe keeping of the fruits of their economy. The disclosures of the criminal tribunals and the discussions in Parliament have demonstrated how completely divided responsibility has set at naught whatever of security, it may have been designed to provide by the original acts of legislation. Yet the public has still very much to learn respecting the constitution and operations of prudential institutions, although the faith of ignorance is giving way to the good faith that comes of knowledge, and although there is reasonable ground to believe that all classes of the nation, whether the governing or the governed, have made no inconsiderable advance, in the decade that is just closing, in appreciation of the principles that ought to regulate the safe custody and increase of the savings of the people. We may therefore hope that the discovery of the accidental defects in institutions in themselves so beneficial and beneficent, will lead to a reorganization that may effectually obviate the recurrence of the calamities of that period, to assist in the consideration of which, we have given, in our Chapter on Savings Bank Frauds, very full details of the various circumstances by which the unsound elements in the constitution and management of these banks were brought to light.

XI.—As to progress of Savings Banks. In spite of all the discouragement to Savings Banks, caused by the neglect of the Legislature to provide for the complete security of their deposits, the degree in which the labouring classes are willing to avail themselves of these institutions is shewn in a remarkable manner by numerous facts; and the rapid increase in the number of small Depositors is a very satisfactory feature of the inquiry. Even in respect to the larger deposits, it is probable that their owners have accumulated them by a long and *patient economy.

It appears from the parliamentary returns that the Investments in England and Wales are in proportion of about £1.12s. to each person of the gross population, and that the average amount to each Depositor is about £26.

That one in sixteen of the population of England and Wales are Depositors in Savings Banks, and that this proportion is on the increase.

---

* [" Combien de vertus cachées, combien d'empire sur soi-même, combien de résistance aux séductions du plaisir, aux entrainements de la débauche, combien d'amour filial, combien d'amour paternel et maternel, combien d'inspirations providentielles et de sentiments religieux sont cachés sous ce trésor de cent millions épargnés, centime à centime, et gagnés a la sueur du front des classes laborieuses !"—*Lecture of Baron Charles Dupin ' sur les Progrès moraux de la Population Parisienne depuis l'établissement des Caisses d'Epargne.'*]

That the number of Depositors (as compared with the *population) is less, and the amount of individual deposit much smaller, in †Scotland than in England.

That in Ireland the banks are fewer than in Great Britain, but the average of deposits is higher.

Various attempts have been made to classify the Depositors according to *occupation;* but from difficulties of definition, no absolutely certain results can be obtained, and the Parliamentary classification is full of confusion. Thus in one class, amounting to nearly one-fourth of the whole Depositors, two distinct elements are unfortunately mixed up: tradesmen and farmers being aggregated with certain artisans.‡ For want of better published information, the following Table is deduced from the Parliamentary Report for 1858, and from returns we have obtained from some of the largest banks. Approximate results show that, speaking generally, *only one-third* of the total number of Depositors may be deemed "workingmen:" more than one-third are *females,* and one-sixth *minors,* making, for females and minors, more than one-half of the total amount of deposits. Not 3 in 100 are gentlemen, professional men, or teachers.

---

* [The following are the proportions of the population, in other countries, who are Depositors :—

France (Report to the Emperor), year 1858 . .	1 in 37
Belgium	1 in 8¼
Germany (Dr. Hubner's Treatise) . . .	1 in 42
America—New York	1 in 14
,, Massachusetts	1 in 6]

† [Although the balance due in the Glasgow Savings Bank to 35,838 Depositors on the 20th November 1858, was £724,280 . 15s. 1d., or an average of £20 to each, yet out of 92,743 receipts from Depositors during the currency of the year, no fewer than 76,435 consisted of sums varying from 1s. to £5.]

‡ [The author of an article in the eighth edition of the Encyclopædia Britannica, published in 1859, based upon the Committee's Report of 1858, seems to have overlooked these circumstances (as well as the general inaccuracy of such descriptions as "minors," &c.), and to have relied on the imperfect Table there given as the basis of certain arguments.]

Class.	Occupations.	Number belonging to each class in every 100 Depositors.	Per-centage of the total Deposits (exclusive of Friendly Societies that their accounts amount to.
I.	Charwomen, Dressmakers, Female Artisans, Laundresses, Milliners, Needlewomen, Nurses, Sempstresses, Servants and their wives, Shopwomen.	25	per cent. 26
II.	Artisans and Mechanics (not described as Journeymen) Small Farmers, Tradesmen and their Assistants, and their wives,	24	26
III.	Minors having accounts in their own names (including apprentices).	15	8
IV.	Carmen, Carriers, Farm Servants, Journeymen Mechanics, Labourers, Porters, and their wives.	12½	14
V.	Females, described as Married Women, Widows, or Spinsters.	12	14
VI.	Miscellaneous, not included in other Classes.	5	4½
VII.	Clerks and Employés in public and other offices, Gentlemen, or persons of independent means, Persons engaged in education, Professional men and their wives.	3	3
VIII.	Boatmen, Fishermen, Letter Carriers, Mariners and Soldiers (exclusive of Military Banks), Pensioners, Policemen, Railway men, Revenue Officers, Steamboat, Cab, and Omnibus men, and their wives,	2	3
IX.	Trust monies and Joint Accounts,	1½	1½
		100	100

We find also that:—

Classes 1 and 7 are proportionately greatest in the *metropolitan* divisions of England.

Class 2 is least, and class 3 greatest, in the *agricultural* counties.

Class 4 preponderates in Scotland and the manufacturing districts.

Class 5 is greatest, and class 6 least, in *Ireland*.

Classes 8 and 9 are least in Scotland.

*AS TO THE PRACTICE OF SAVINGS BANKS IN FOREIGN COUNTRIES.

1.—*France.*

Savings Banks in France require for their establishment the authorization of the Government, which exercises a surveillance over their management and accounts. Their funds are deposited in account current with the " *Caisse des Dépôts et Consignations,*" which is administered under †guarantee of the public treasury, and pays the interest; they are not, properly speaking, " Government Institutions," as the Depositors have no other security than that of the Savings Bank itself, which is conducted on the volun-

---

* [All foreign systems appear to be based upon principles and rules of English origin, which are still followed very closely; but, starting from that point, they have introduced many improvements. In respect to account-keeping, personal examination has satisfied us that the best system is that in use in the Paris Savings Bank, of which M. Prévost is justly proud.

We are indebted to Dr. E. H. Michelsen, of the Board of Trade (an accomplished linguist), for assistance in procuring from abroad official information of the most reliable character; and to Mr. L. Frädersdorff, of Hamburg, for valuable details in reference to the German, Swedish, and several other continental Savings Banks.]

† [During the Revolution of 1848 the Provisional Government found itself in great difficulties, the amount due to Depositors being 356,000,000f., with only 66,000,000 of specie in the Treasury to provide for it. The rate of interest was in consequence raised to 5 per cent.; and all Depositors above 100f. were compelled to take a per-centage of the amount due to them in Treasury Bonds at four and six months' date, and in coupons of *rente* at 5 per cent. Ultimately, under the empire, the loss incurred by the Depositors on sale of these securities was reimbursed to them.]

tary system, as in England, by a Board of *Directeurs*, who supervise the *management, and by a number of *Administrateurs*, who attend at the office of the bank to witness receipts and payments.

The following Acts of Legislation apply to them:—Laws of 28 *Floreal, An* VII., 5th June 1835, 31st March 1837, and 22nd June 1845; Ordonnance of 28th July 1846; Law of 30th June 1851; Decree of 15th April 1852 (which regulates the system of account keeping); Law of 7th May 1853; and Decree of 15th May 1858.

On the 1st January 1859 there were 379 Savings Banks in operation in France: thirty more had been authorized by the Government, but were not yet opened at that date.

The account of a single Depositor is limited to 1000f. †(£40); and no sum beyond 300f. can be paid in at one time.

The *rate of interest* granted to the banks by the Caisse des Dépôts et Consignations is *fixed at* 4 per cent. by Art. 1 of the Law of 1853. Of this sum 177 banks retain $\frac{1}{4}$, and 202 retain $\frac{1}{2}$ per cent., for expenses of management; the statutory limit, by the law of 1851, is $\frac{1}{2}$ per cent. in the provinces, and 1 per cent. for the Paris Bank.

A few cases of malversation have occurred, but of trifling importance: they were, however, sufficient to attract the attention of the Government, and led to the system of Uniform account-keeping

---

* [The Parliamentary Committee of 1858 were given to understand by one of the witnesses that French Saving Bank Depositors have a State guarantee, but this is not the case. The Committee also gathered that there were no Trustees or Managers, but the law is as follows:—
"Les opérations de chaque caisse d'épargne sont dirigées et surveillées par un conseil de directeurs ou d'administrateurs. Les statuts determinent la composition et les fonctions de ce conseil." (*Decree*, 1852, *art.* 1.) In the Paris Banks there are about 1200 *administrateurs*, and in the provincial banks there are altogether about 6800.]

† [When a deposit account exceeds 1000 f., either by interest or by fresh deposits, a portion, sufficient to buy 10 f. of *rente*, is transferred from it, and the Depositor is made a proprietor of stock to that amount. See Part IV.]

and surveillance prescribed in 1852. To this is added periodic inspection by the Government 'Inspecteurs de Finance.'*

With the exception of the Paris Savings Bank (which is a private undertaking, authorized by the Government as an 'establishment of †public utility,' and is administered by a Council of twenty-five Directors, annually elected) they are municipal establishments combibing, however, the voluntary system of unpaid Managers. The bank officials are required to deposit actual money or government stock by way of security. Each year the ‡Minister of Agriculture, Commerce, and Public Works, publishes a report to the Emperor, accompanied by statistical documents on the condition and operations of the Savings Banks.§

---

* [" Les caisses d'épargne sont soumises aux vérifications des Inspecteurs de finances. Les inspecteurs peuvent porter leur examen et leurs investigations sur *toute la gestion* des établissements."—*Art.* 21, *Décret du* 15 *Avril*, 1852.]

† [Established as a *Société anonyme* 22nd May 1818, on the model of the English Savings Banks, under the presidency of the Duc de la Rochefoucauld Liancourt, by M. Benjamin Delessert, and twenty other gentlemen belonging to the *Compagnie Royale des Assurance maritimes*, who, to acquire a legal standing, each subscribed stock representing 50 fr. annual rente. The bank receives a "subvention," partly departmental and partly municipal, amounting in 1858 to £1000. To M. Agathon Prévost, the present Agent-general, from whose writings on the subject we have freely quoted, we are indebted for much valuable information.]

‡ [The most recently published accounts of the investment of Savings Bank money by the "Caisse des Dépôts et Consignations" shew that only 20 per cent is really laid out in the purchase of *Rentes sur l'Etat*, the remainder being carried to an *account current* with the Treasury (by which it is used for State purposes, and not invested at all) with the exception of a small portion lent on the obligations of various railways.]

§ [The number of Depositors in France is 978,802, or 1 in every 37 of the population. The total amount due to Depositors is £11,000,000 sterling—about 6s. per head for every inhabitant. The early progress of Savings Banks in France was not great: up to 1832 (fourteen years after the establishment of the Paris Bank) only twelve had been founded: in the next two years, only thirteen more. Now there are, on the average, over four for each of the eighty-six departments, which is, however, only one for every 100 *Communes*.]

The Paris Caisse is under the direct surveillance of the Minister of Finance, and makes a separate annual *report*, containing extended statistical information of its own affairs. The following is an abstract of its *operations from its commencement in 1818 to the 26th December 1857 :—

	fr.	£
Deposits received	743,663,131	29,746,525
Deposit Accounts opened	848,665	
Invested in Stock on Account of Depositors.†	83,144,121	3,325,765
Expenses	6,655,905	266,236

On the 26th December 1857 the number of Depositors in the Paris Savings Bank was 226,224, holding accounts to the amount of 44,607,255f., or £1,784,290. Of this number 33,227 were opened in the year 1857.

2.—*Belgium.*

There are Savings Banks in Brussels, Liège, Tournai, and in several other towns in Belgium. They are directed, either by the administration of the towns in which they are situated, or by financial establishments.

The principal Savings Banks have been founded as subsidiary departments to :—

1. The ‡Société Générale for the Encouragement of National

---

* [The bank offices are open every day of the week (including Sunday). The transactions average 1000 a-day. Many improvements of detail, which we have mentioned in subsequent pages, are adopted in its management One of the most important is the prospective plan of crediting interest. See Part IV.]

† [Stock purchased, 4,021,484 f. a year, or £160,859 (20¾ years' purchase.)]

‡ [For the information in this chapter we are indebted to the Manager of the abovenamed Institution, through the kindness of M. Hamoir de Reus, Directeur-agent-general to the Compagnie des Propriétaires Réunis, and to M. Charles de Hoffman of Brussels. The distinguished M. A. Quételet has, also, been obliging enough to make inquiries on our behalf.]

Industry at Brussels, which has branches at Antwerp and other chief towns, and several agents in the provinces; and

2. The Banque Liégeoise at Liége.

There is no general law of the state relating to these Institutions. The rules are settled by the founders of the banks. The Companies mentioned above are " Sociétés Anonymes."

In a recent session of the Legislative Chambers, the Minister of Finance deposited a "projet de loi," which has not yet been published, for the organization of a Savings Bank for the whole kingdom.

Savings Banks are therefore, at present, private undertakings. No security is given them by the State, nor does the Government interfere in their management, although it affords them its *sanction.

The Société Générale and the Banque Liégeoise guarantee the deposits of the bank founded by them: the others are under the guarantee of the cities where they are established.

There are two classes of accounts opened by the banks—one for private persons, the other for public establishments.

The maximum amount allowed to be deposited by private individuals is 2000 f. (£80), while the deposits of Public Institutions are not limited, but each is made by special demand.

The rate of interest is now uniformly 3 per cent.: some time ago 4 per cent. was allowed. The conditions of allotment differ: those adopted by the Société Générale are considered the most favourable to Depositors.

Savings Banks in Belgium do not appear to be prospering very

---

* [The law relating to Communal administration expressly recommends the magistrates of towns to encourage the operations of Savings Banks, and charges them with the duty of rendering an annual account of the position of the banks: but it appears that the provisions of this law have been more or less neglected; and it is confessed in official documents that the Savings Banks in Belgium are far from answering to the necessities of the population.]

greatly: the last report of the Société Générale furnishes the following remarkable figures:—

On 31st December.	Number of private Depositors.	Amount Deposited.
		fr.
1847	40,600	46,810,000
1848	19,900	22,510,000
1852	25,400	20,690,000
1857	25,800	19,230,000
1858	28,000	19,100,000

shewing, since 1847, a great decrease in the number of Depositors and in the amounts deposited.

3.—*Switzerland.*

This country is entitled to the credit of having established the oldest Savings Bank of those now existing in Europe: the one at Zurich having been in operation since the year 1805.

The most considerable bank in Switzerland is that founded in Geneva in 1816 by M. Tronchin, a worthy citizen, who bound over his own property for the security of the Depositors to the extent of 60,000 florins (£1100), and contributed during twenty-six years, a sum of 2400 florins (about £44) annually towards the expenses of management. The Managers of the bank are nominated by the Council of State, and render to it an annual account of their management. Deposits are received from 2s. up to £10. The maximum limit of a deposit account is £50. Interest is granted at 3 per cent., and *three months' notice* is required before *withdrawal*. This rule, however, is not rigidly enforced, and payment is usually made on the first Monday of the month following the notice. No withdrawals are allowed till the deposits have been twelve months in the bank. The funds are invested in stock of the Canton, and on bills of exchange, bearing the signatures of two inhabitants of Geneva.

4.—*Hamburg.*

There is one Savings Bank for the State of Hamburg, which has six District Banks in the city, and three in the country, placed in convenient localities.

The Government has nothing to do with the administration of these banks, which is carried on as prescribed by the Ordinance of Law of 1827.*

They are directed by merchants and others gratuitously. One of the Senators is President of the Direction. Five of the Directors officiate each time the banks are open; one receives the money, and enters it in the Depositor's book; the second and third sign their names against the amount; the fourth stamps the book; and the fifth enters in the bank-book the sum received, and, on calling out the number of the book, hands it to the †Depositor.

No more than 60 marks, Hamburg currency (£3. 12s. 6d.) can be deposited at one time (once a-week, Saturday evening, from six to eight o'clock); but the Depositor may place a similar sum weekly in the bank to an unlimited amount. To evade the weekly limitation, two or more books are frequently obtained: indeed there are

---

* [On the 31st December, 1856, the number of Depositors was 36,037, and the amount deposited £685,400, or £19 to each. Taking the population of the State at 200,000, this is equivalent to 1 Depositor in every 5.]

† [An excellent plan is adopted by these banks to prevent errors. Each book is enclosed in a red pasteboard case, on which its number is stamped. The Depositor hands his book to the official, but retains the case, which thus serves the purpose of identifying him as the owner of the book, as well as of keeping it clean.]

instances of one Depositor having eight or ten books for his own deposits.

On application to withdraw, the deposit is returned to the *holder* of the pass-book, and no concern is taken, as a rule, as to his authority or right to receive the money.

By clause 5 of the Law of 1827, however, it is enacted that monies of wards or minors, of Charitable Institutions, and Corporations, shall not be permitted to be withdrawn without the special authority of the party in whose name the account is opened.

The investments are made as follows:—nine-tenths on mortgages (to be approved by five Directors) of houses which, in Hamburg, are held by freehold tenure, and insured by the State.

Only one-third of the value of the property, as estimated for ground-tax, is advanced by the banks, and but a low rate of interest is generally obtained. The remaining one-tenth of the Savings Bank monies is employed in discounting good Bills of Exchange, to be approved of by three Directors of the chief bureau.

The rate of interest allowed Depositors is at present $3\frac{1}{8}$ per cent., but will be *reduced* from 1st January 1860, *to* $2\frac{1}{2}$ *per cent.*

5.—*Prussia.*

On the 31st December 1856 there were *365 Savings Banks in

---

* [In the last " Zeitschrift des Centralvereins in Preussen für das Wohl der arbeitenden Klassen" (Leipsig 1859) is an able article on the Savings Banks of Brandenburg, which have increased in number from five in the years 1835 to sixty-four in 1857.

	Thalers.
Deposits in the 19 years, from 1838 to 1857 .	19,771,015
Withdrawn in the same period . . .	17,483,744
Remaining due to Depositors . . .	2,288,171
Add for Interest	1,857,684
Total due to Depositors . .	4,145,855
Or in English money . . .	£621,877]

Prussia, and on the same date in 1857 their number had increased to 405.

They are in no sense Government Institutions, but are of two kinds:—1st, private commercial undertakings, of which the State takes no cognisance; and 2nd, banks conducted under the supervision of the municipal or county (*Kreis*) authorities, whose rules are required (according to the law of 12th December 1838) to be confirmed (*bestätigt*) by the provincial Government. The local authorities have, however, been urged in several rescripts to encourage Savings Banks, and in some counties the tax-receivers have become agents to the Savings Banks, and collect deposits with the taxes. This plan Dr. Otto Hubner, of Berlin, Director of the Royal Statistical Central Archives (to whom we are indebted for this information) states to have been very useful, and to offer, particularly in country parts, increased facilities to investors.

The rate of interest allowed by the Prussian banks* varies with the expenses of each Institution, the law requiring that it shall be fixed so as to leave a balance between the interest paid by the banks and that received on their investments, to cover expenses of management, and to furnish a small surplus to be accumulated to a guarantee fund.

The maximum amount of †deposit for any one year varies considerably, but Depositors may hold accounts to the extent of 500 thlrs. (£75), although many banks enforce as low a limit as 200 thlrs. (£30).

---

* [In the province of Brandenburg the rate allowed averages 2½ to 3¼ per cent. Many banks which originally granted a higher rate have reduced it to these figures.]

† [In some banks when the deposits have attained a certain amount, they are converted into stock (under the provisions of the law relating to *pupillarische* security) without notice being given to the Depositor. He continues to receive the Savings Bank rate of interest, but is liable to the losses, and entitled to any profit that may arise in the course of exchange.— (Zeitschrift des Centralvereins, pp. 397,409)]

The report for 1857 shews that there were invested at the end of that year for the whole of Prussia:—

	Thalers.	£
On Mortgages in Towns	9,732,683	1,459,902
Ditto in Country Districts	9,762,056	1,464,308
In Public Securities	10,263,084	1,539,463
In Personal ditto	4,697,231	704,585
In Dead Pledge (*Faustpfand*)	3,202,901	480,435
With Public Corporations	4,086,460	612,969
	41,744,415	6,261,662

6.—*Austria.*

Savings Banks in Austria are established either by Joint-Stock Companies or by Civic Corporations; but they are all placed under the supervision of Government, especially as to the employment of their funds and the strict observance of the rules and regulations. The funds may be invested in loans on landed property of double the value (provided the buildings be previously insured), to be repaid by certain fixed instalments; in advances on, or purchase of, Government stocks and bonds bearing interest; also in advances to *Monts de Piété* or Pawn and Credit Institutions; and on private Bills of Exchange, bearing three good signatures.

The largest investments are made in loans and mortgage or landed property, and the total of such investments amounted in 1858 to about £7,300,000 (or about four-fifths of the whole).

The average rate of interest allowed for deposits is about 4 per cent. The withdrawal of deposits of £10 or more requires one month's notice, while lesser sums are repaid on demand.

The Savings Banks were first introduced *at Vienna* in 1819 on a very small scale, but are spreading gradually throughout the empire.

The number of Savings Banks has increased from 14 in 1842, to 66 in 1855. The amount of deposits has increased in the same period from £4,286,805 to £9,036,773, while the amount of withdrawals has increased from £969,808 to £3,013,677. The

Reserve Fund has increased from £236,731 to £652,584. The number of Depositors has increased from 73,630 to 903,677.

The average amount due to each Depositor is about £10.

There are in Austria and Prussia other institutions for savings, under the title of "*Spar-und-Consumo Vereine*," the principle of which will be found described in Professor von Stubenrauch's work (pp. 162—167). Their operations will perhaps be best understood by quoting the following preamble to the Rules adopted by some of them:—

"*The members propose to themselves, as a common object, to make savings from their daily earnings for the purpose of investing them each week in a Savings Bank, and of buying, for the support of existence during the winter, provisions wholesale, especially bread, fuel, and potatoes.*"

They are also referred to by M. Moreau-Christophe, as having produced satisfactory results. He says:—

"*La fourmi met de côté, pendant l'été, de quoi se nourrir quand la bise est venue.* Telle est l'idée mère des sociétés d'épargne qui se sont etablies à Berlin, et de là dans les autres villes de la Prusse et dans les autres États germaniques, depuis plusieurs années. Ces sociétés, partout où elles existent, procurent à leurs associés une économie de cent pour cent sur les denrées de première nécessité. Les distributions qui se font ainsi sont doublement préférables à celles qui se pratiquent en quelques lieux, au moyen de magasins que des personnes bienfaisantes ont établis pour vendre à prix coûtant les denrées d'un usage habituel. Elles ont, sur ce dernier mode, l'avantage de ne pas participer du caractère de l'aumône, et surtout celui de faire, de la prévoyance qu'elles reclament, la condition des ressources qu'elles offrent."

---

* [For further information respecting the Austrian Banks the reader is referred to 'Sonnleithner—Erläuterung der Statuten und des Reglements der, mit der ersten Oesterreichischen Sparcasse vereinigten Versorgungsanstalt,' Vienna 1826, and 'Geschichtliche Darstellung der Entstehung und des Wirkens der ersten Oesterreichischen Sparcasse,' Vienna, 1854. The particulars given above are from the elaborate Statistical Treatise of Professor Moritz von Stubenrauch, who has, with the greatest kindness, answered our inquiries in reference to the Savings Banks of Austria.]

² [Du Problème de la Misère, et de sa Solution chez les Peuples anciens et modernes," tom. 3, pp. 306, 307. See also *Annales de la Charité*, 1847 note by Dr. *Julius*, "sur les Sociétés d'Epargne," p. 634 et seq.]

It was partly with a similar object—viz. to establish Co-operative Stores—that *Mr. Slaney's Industrial and Provident Societies'* Act was passed in 1852.

That it has not been acted upon to any great extent is attributable (as much as to any other cause) to the fact that the members of societies, registered under it, are exposed to unlimited liability, whilst ordinary joint-stock companies are enabled, by a recent Act, to limit the responsibility of their shareholders.

VII.—HOLLAND.

In Holland there were 127 Savings Banks in operation in the year 1857.

There are no Acts of Legislation specially relating to them. They are wholly private undertakings, but are considered benevolent institutions, and the Directors are bound by an article of the Poor-law to make annual *returns of their operations.

The rate of interest usually allowed is 3 per cent., although a few banks allow 4 per cent.

The investments are made in Government stocks, on mortgages, and on loans on the public funds for short terms. *Some years ago, from depreciation of securities, several †banks had to suspend payment.*

---

* [Digest in the Statistical Annual, Amsterdam 1858.]

† [Mr. J. Langerhuizen, Manager of the Dutch Society for Life Assurance at Amsterdam, writes to us that :—

In 1830, the then existing Savings Bank at Amsterdam failed, by the fall of the national funds, in which the money was placed. The disappointment was great, and to win back the confidence of the public, another Savings Bank was set on foot as a private undertaking; a guarantee capital of 400,000 guilders being subscribed by private individuals, to bear interest at 2½ per cent., and to be liable to the losses of the bank; but to receive no further dividend out of its profits, if any.]

"The leading Savings Bank, that at *Rotterdam*," according to an account with which Mr. W. Six, of the Central Statistical Commission at the Hague, has favoured us, "is conducted like those in many other cities, by some members of a philanthropic Society called 'Maatschappy tot Nut van het Algemeen' (Society for public benefit or general utility). In that bank the smallest sum which is accepted on deposit is two-pence: interest is allowed, on sums of one guilder (1s. 8d.) and upwards, at 3 per cent., which is added to the capital three times a year, viz. on the last days of April, August, and December.

"Deposits are received twice a-week, but they can only be withdrawn twice a-month.

"Principal and interest are entered at the same time, in the books of the bank and in the pass-books kept by each Depositor.

"Sums of 25 guilders (£2. 1s. 8d.) and more will not be returned until after giving notice.*

"Disputes between the officers of the bank and the Depositors, if they take place, are settled, *not* by the justices, but always by the Directors of the 'Maatschappy.'"

The Rotterdam Bank began its operations in the year 1818. On the 30th April 1819 there had been invested by 466 Depositors a sum of 18,558 guilders (£1550), and on the 30th April 1858, these figures were respectively increased to 10,064 Depositors, and 1,788,790 guilders (£150,000).

VIII.—SWEDEN (exclusive of Norway).

There were reported to be 130 Savings Banks in Sweden at the

---

* [In the *Amsterdam* bank the maximum deposit allowed is £100, and the interest paid is 4 per cent. in quarterly instalments.
For withdrawals notice is required
From 10 guilders (16s. 8d.) to 50 guilders (£4. 3s. 4d.) 1 week.
„ 50 „ (£4. 3s.) to 200 „ (£16. 13s.) 2 weeks.
„ 200 „ (£16. 13s.) to 600 „ (£50) and above, 4 weeks.
It is prescribed in this bank that not more than ¼th of the capital shall be placed in Government securities.]

end of the year 1858 : 13 of these had been opened during the year.

The amount of deposits at that date was 26,102,360 rixdollars (£1,491,500),* the increase during the year being only £1400.

There is no general Act of Legislation relating to these banks, but each institution obtains a special statute from the Government authorising the carrying out of the particular views of its promoters; and any change, that may afterwards be considered necessary by the Directors in the statutes, is submitted to the Government for revisal.

The Savings Banks, like all other charitable institutions in Sweden, are exempt from any tax or contribution to the Government.

They are wholly *private undertakings*, with subscribed capital for the necessary guarantee funds, and are managed by Directors elected among the founders, or by those who are voted to replace them. The functions of Governors or Directors are gratuitous.

There is no uniform system of book-keeping, but many banks have obtained forms of account from the Stockholm bank as models.

Deposits may be made in that bank, once a week, for as small an amount as 25 öre (about 4d.).

The total amount that may be paid in, in a year, is 300 Rd. (£17).

A Depositor may hold an account to the extent of 2000 Rd. (£115). Deposits may be withdrawn at a week's notice, though

---

* [The Reports of the Savings Banks in the larger towns are published every year in the papers. The *Stockholm* Bank also prints a pamphlet separately. Its return for 1858 shows that to 20,624 Depositors there was due a balance of £184,000
   Deposited during the year 32,000
   Surplus Fund (excess of assets over liabilities) . . . 17,000
   Out of the whole funds of this bank only 2,900
is invested in Government securities. It appears that in the city of Stockholm, which has a population of 90,000, one person in every 4 inhabitants is a Depositor.]

power is reserved to require longer* notice if circumstances render it necessary.

For the accommodation of Depositors who are not able to attend at the banks during the week-days, payment is allowed of money to delegates in their own parish before service on Sundays.

Interest is calculated from the 1st of the month after the deposit is made, and is added to the capital at the end of the year. In the Stockholm Savings Bank the rate of interest allowed was 5 per cent. from 1821, when the Bank was established, until 1830, when it was reduced† to 4 per cent., which rate still continues.

In some banks the interest is higher, but in no case exceeds 6 per cent.

The banks invest their moneys (within fixed limits) on mortgages, and in Government stock, or in bonds issued by corporations sanctioned by Government.

Private bonds with personal security are *not* accepted.

In case of need, they have a privilege to draw‡ on the Bank of Sweden to a fixed amount, and they may also deposit money at 3 per cent interest.§

IX.—RUSSIA.

There are but two Savings Banks in Russia—at St. Petersburg and Moscow. (The ¶Colleges of Public Charity in Russia, and the

---

* [Deposits *unclaimed* after ten years cease to bear interest; but power is reserved to the Direction to waive this regulation. Deposits of deceased persons, leaving no representatives, are forfeited to the Bank. (Stockholm Savings Bank Rules, as revised, 15th July 1859.)]

† [In 1857, the *Christiania* Savings Bank (Norway), adopted the same course: the result, however, was an *excess of withdrawal* during the year of £28,000 sterling.]

‡ [In the year 1857, several of the banks found it necessary, through the large amount of withdrawals demanded, to avail themselves of this privilege.]

§ [For much information relating to Sweden, we are indebted to Dr. F. T. Berg, and to M. Herman Arosenius, who have very obligingly forwarded to us copies of the forms in use in the Stockholm and other Savings Banks.

¶ [For its rules, see Russian Code of Laws, vol. xiii. §§ 1. to 1711.]

Agricultural Bank in the Baltic province of Courland, are authorised to accept deposits, but their operations are of another nature, and with different objects.)

They are entirely Government institutions, under the Imperial regulation of 30th October 1841, inserted in the Russian Code of Laws (vol. xi.), under the Chapter entitled "Rules of Credit Establishments," §§ 1636—1666, and are directed by the Council of the Orphan Asylum (called " Lombard ").

In the course of the reforms now in progress in the Russian legislation on banks generally, modifications are expected to be introduced in the regulations of the Savings Banks.

The system of account-keeping is the same in both banks.

*The amount that may be deposited at a time ranges between 50 copecks silver (1s. 8d.), and 25 rubles silver (£4. 3s. 4d.), but not more than 50 rubles (£8. 6s. 8d.) can be received in the course of a year; and the total amount that a Depositor may have to his credit is 750 rubles silver (£125).

Deposits are under the guarantee of the Lombard.

Interest is allowed at the rate of 3 per cent. per annum (compound): previous to the 1st November 1857, 4 per cent. was given, but the rate was reduced by Imperial Ukase of 20th July 1857.

The following is from the Report of the Minister of Finance on the Russian Establishments of Credit for 1858, laid before the Council at its annual meeting, 15th June 1859:—

"SAVINGS BANKS.

	Silver Rubles.	£
"1858, 1st January—		
"Amount of Capital deposited	3,456,388	576,065
"New sums deposited during the year 1858	1,566,096	261,016
"Paid back	1,458,278	243,046
"1859, 1st January—		
"Balance remaining in Savings Banks, including Interest up to this date	3,634,220	605,703
"Number of Accounts open	46,644	
"Average of each account	£13	

---

* [For information in reference to Russia we are indebted to the kindness of Mr. James Thal, of St. Petersburg.]

AMERICA. xlvii

In the capital of Russian Poland (Warsaw), a Savings Bank is formed, having 10,830 Depositors, and a capital of £78,000, or, on the average, £7 to each Depositor.

United States of America.

We find, by a perusal of the *rules of American Savings Banks, that their plans of operation present great similarity.

The most complete arrangements for securing sound management and prosperity are observable in the rules of the banks of New York, Massachusetts, and New Jersey: we subjoin a short statement of their operations :—

X.—*State of New York.*

The number of Savings Banks in operation in this State was 57 on the †31st December 1858. Each of these institutions is organized under separate ‡Acts of the Legislature, passed during various Sessions. The provisions of these Acts do not materially differ in respect to their powers, and in all cases provide for the appointment of a Board of Managing Trustees; but the ||Govern-

---

* [The reader will find a variety of Clauses from Rules of American Savings Banks dispersed through this Treatise.]

† [Superintendent's Report, 9th February 1859.]

‡ [The laws 1835 (May 9); 1839 (May 6); 1847 (December 15); 1850 (March 25); 1853 (April 15 and June 30); and 1857, cap. 136; apply to all Savings Banks.

It is remarkable how frequently the American Statutes are altered, thereby carrying out the ample precedent furnished by England. Indeed, the Acts are sometimes altered twice or thrice in the same Session.]

|| [The Act of 1857, however, appointed an officer (Mr. James M. Cook) the Superintendent of the Banking Department, whose official residence is in the City of Albany, to supervise and report annually upon the condition of the Savings Banks in the State. It is also part of his duty to suggest, from time to time, any amendments in the law which he may think desirable.]

ment does not interfere with or control the action of such Trustees, and the Savings Banks are wholly private institutions.

Some of the Savings Banks allow 6 per cent. per annum on sums of 500 dollars (£100) and under, and 5 per cent. on larger deposits. Others allow 5 per cent. up to 500 dollars, and 4 per cent. on larger amounts, with an occasional bonus. The law of the State permits an accumulation of a surplus fund up to 10 per cent. on the whole amount of deposits. The Trustees of each bank declare the rates of interest according to its profits. They have, as a rule, been as above stated.

Investments are required to be made, generally, in Government securities, or public stock, created under any of the laws of the United States, or of the several States of the Union, or by the cities of the State of New York (when authorised by the Legislature), and on bond and mortgage on improved unencumbered real estate of double the value of the amount loaned. No investments are allowed to be made on merely personal security.

Some of the Savings Banks limit the original deposit of one person to an amount not exceeding 1000 dollars, others not exceeding 3000 dollars, but allow the accumulation of interest, which is treated as principal if not withdrawn. In most of the banks, however, there is no limit to the amount of a deposit, except that a Depositor can have but one account standing in his own name, though he may have accounts as Trustee for members of his family, or other persons. The Trustees of the banks, however, discourage large deposits, and the lowering the rates of interest operates, also, as a check upon them.

No *frauds* have been officially reported: it is known, however, that there have been some, but they were not remarkable in character, or of sufficient magnitude to affect the deposits, either in principal or interest.*

---

* [For the information given above we are indebted to *Mr. Andrew Warner*, of the Institution for the Savings of Merchants' Clerks, and *Mr. Charles Newcomb*, of the Mercantile Mutual Insurance Company, New York. A large number of rules and statements issued by the various Savings Banks have been forwarded to us in the most obliging manner by those gentlemen.]

A remarkable agitation has been carried on for some years, having for object the transfer to the State of the deposits remaining unclaimed after a period of ten years. It was, in fact, asserted *in the Senate, and for several years reiterated, "that more than 20 millions of dollars were locked up in Savings Banks for which no claimants could be found."

During recent Sessions it was found " that an impression existed in the minds of many of the Members, that large unclaimed deposits were lying in the vaults of these institutions, and the Speaker of the House, with other Members of large legislative experience, expressed similar views."

This attempt, however, has been warmly resisted by the Trustees of the banks, who have urged, very properly, that money in a Savings Bank, being the absolute property of the Depositor, may be, and frequently is, claimed after a long interval of years. By the Trustees of the †Seamen's Bank for Savings, New York (February 7, 1859), it was alleged "that these attempts in the Legislature to appropriate unclaimed balances in the Savings Banks had caused a much more general habit than formerly of presenting books to be written up, by which accounts were renewed; while, from the same cause, many accounts had been withdrawn altogether; and that the amount of unclaimed deposits was too small to be an object to the State, even if they could reconcile their views to a measure which would be abhorrent to the feelings of the community at large, and would greatly diminish the confidence of Depositors."

In the Report for 1859 of the Chamber of Commerce of New York (pp. 266, 267), it was remarked, that the continued efforts made in the Legislature to deprive Savings Banks of the unclaimed deposits could only be characterized as equivalent to

---

* [Protest of Mr. Thomas Jeremiah, President, and Mr. Giles H Coggeshall, Secretary, on behalf of the Bowery Savings Bank, 1859.]

† [Statement of Mr. P. Perit, President, and Mr. W. H. Macy, Vice-President, on behalf of the Seamen's Bank.]

"repudiation," and, indeed, "confiscation;" and the 'Chamber' invoked "public disapprobation against that legislative action which would weaken general confidence in what are vested rights." So strong, indeed, was the opposition to the measure, that, if not finally abandoned, it will have to be very much modified before it can pass into law.

The average of *deposits per account in the State of New York is £41, and the proportion of Depositors (230,074) to population (2,880,000) is 1 in 13.

11.—*Commonwealth of Massachusetts.*

In this State there are 86 Savings Institutions. They are incorporated companies, each created by special Charter. They are partly private and partly public institutions. The members of the corporation elect their own associates and successors, and have the entire management and control of its affairs, although they have no compensation or profits; and the Depositors have the whole profits and earnings, but no voice in the management of the corporation; and in these particulars the institutions may be called *private.* They are created by special Acts of the Legislature, and these Acts may be altered, amended, or repealed by the same power;† they are also regulated by the general laws of the State,

---

* [It is remarkable that the average deposit in the Philadelphia Savings Bank is nearly the same, viz. £40. In Baltimore there are one or two banks, however, with an average of £60.]

† [*Revision of the general Statutes of Massachusetts. Report of Commissioners* (Joel Parker and William A. Richardson), 1858, No. 2, cap. 57, pp. 179 to 211, and cap. 68, pp. 317 to 327. See also Judge Richardson's admirable Compendium of the Banking Laws of Massachusetts (Lowell, 1855). To this gentleman, whose opinion is acknowledged as of the highest authority on these matters, we are indebted (through the kindness of Dr. Josiah Curtis, of Boston, who has forwarded to us voluminous valuable returns, Statutes, and other documents) for the information contained in the text.]

are subject to examination by the Bank *Commissioners appointed by the Governor, and the members of the corporations having no compensation or profits are supposed to labour wholly for the public good. In these particulars the institutions may be called *public*. No great changes in the law are contemplated: individuals often propose some change in detail, but none of very great importance. The "bye-laws" of the several institutions differ as to the payment of *interest*. Some few pay all the earnings every six months in equal proportions among the Depositors, reserving only a small sum for contingencies. Most of the institutions pay a fixed rate of interest, semi-annually, from 2 to 3 per cent. (2 and $2\frac{1}{2}$ being the most common), and at the expiration of three or five years divide the surplus earnings in equitable proportions among the Depositors. The law relating to investment of funds is extremely liberal: it allows, under certain restrictions, loans upon bank and railway stock, and even personal security.†

By Statute, no Savings Institution can "hold at the same time more than 1000 dollars (£200) of one Depositor, other than a religious or charitable corporation;" and by the bye-laws of some institutions the amount is limited to 500 dollars, but there is no annual limit. The Treasurer of one small Savings Bank has recently proved a defaulter to the amount of about 15,000 dollars (£3000), but it is supposed this may be fully secured by his official bond and his private property. No other remarkable frauds have taken place.

The total deposits in the 86 Savings Banks of the State ‡amount to 33,914,972 dollars (nearly 7 millions sterling), be-

---

* [These functionaries were first appointed in 1851. In the year ending 30th September 1858, they report that they have examined into the condition of forty-two Savings Banks, and that "their general management is highly creditable to the officers, and reflects credit on the Commonwealth." (Public Document No. 6, 1858, pp. 100—126, 128.]

† [Revised Statutes, cap. 57. ss. 138. to 141., No. 2, pp. 206, 207.]

‡ [Abstract of Returns to the last Saturday in October 1858, prepared by Oliver Warner, Secretary of the Commonwealth. Public Document, No. 7, p. 121.]

longing to 182,655 Depositors, or an average of 186 dollars (£37) to each. The population of the State (census 1855) is 1,132,369, giving an average Savings Bank deposit of 30 dollars to each individual. The dividends (paid as interest to Depositors) have averaged, for the last five years, 6¾ per cent., and the expenses of management are equivalent to 6s. 3d. in every £100 sterling deposited.

3.—*State of New Jersey.*

The banks in this State are 7 in number, each governed by a Charter, and bearing the same relations to the Government and to Depositors as in the States already detailed. The management of the banks corresponds almost entirely with that of the leading Savings Institutions in the State of New York. Six per cent. interest is granted on all deposits in the *Newark* Savings Bank. Investments are made chiefly on bonds and mortgages. There is no limit to the amount of deposits receivable from individuals. No frauds have occurred.*

The "Provident Institution for Savings," which has a capital of 340,000 dollars, grants interest to its Depositors on the following excellent scale of graduation :—

Sums not exceeding 500 dollars (£100) . 6 per cent.
Not exceeding 1000 dollars, on the excess above 500 dollars, ... 5 ,,
On the excess above 1000 dollars, for any amount . . . . . . 4 ,,

---

* [We are indebted to Charles King, Esq., Treasurer of this bank, for a complete set of the forms and regulations adopted therein, and to B. C. Miller, Esq., of the Mutual Benefit Life Insurance Company, New Jersey, and Charles Newcomb, Esq., of the Mercantile Mutual Insurance Company, New York, for a large amount of information. including the above.]

INTRODUCTION.

AUSTRALIA.

13.—*Colony of Victoria.*

There are 8 Savings Banks in this colony, viz. at Melbourne, Geelong, Portland, Belfast, Castlemaine, Sandhurst, Ballarat, and Maryborough. One is about being opened at Warnambool. They are governed by the provisions of the *"Savings Bank Act, 1853,"* (16 Vict. c. 37.), which appointed a Board of five Commissioners and a †Comptroller, to manage the investments of the Savings Banks and superintend their operations. The Commissioners supply the banks with pass-books, books of account, and forms for returns. They invest partly in Government Debentures of the Colony, partly in bank fixed deposit receipts (12 months), and partly in mortgage of freehold estate. The Commissioners do not, however, propose to lend moneys in future on mortgage securities. The maximum rate of interest permitted by the Act is 4 per cent., which is the rate allowed by all the banks during the last five years; *but when an account is closed during a financial year only 2½ per cent. per annum is added to the balance due on the previous 1st July.* There is no *annual* limit, and a Depositor may have as much as £1000 to his credit, but interest is not allowed on more than £500. No frauds whatever have taken place. The Commissioners annually appoint *Auditors* to examine the accounts of each bank, and the *Depositors' books.*

On the 30th June 1858, the number of Depositors in the Colony was 7732, and the balance due to them £432,250.

---

* [This Act very ably consolidated all the previous enactments. Its provisions correspond very closely with those of the English law, but it provided, seven years ago, the very same central authority which we proposed in 1851, and is now recommended in the Report of the English Committee.]

† [The office of Comptroller is at present held by Mr. Charles Flaxman, who has, in the most obliging manner, answered our inquiries, and (through Mr. W. H. Archer, Registrar-General of the Colony, whose great abilities as an Actuary were well known to his friends in this country) forwarded to us copies of the Annual Reports of the Commissioners, and of the various regulations they have made for the guidance of the banks.]

PART I.

PAST HISTORY AND PRESENT SYSTEM

OF

SAVINGS BANKS.

CONTENTS OF PART I.

Chap. I. *History of Savings Banks.*

§ 1. Origin - - - - - - - 3
§ 2. Early Methods of Investment - - - 7
§ 3. Course of Legislation - - - - - 10
§ 4. Committee of the House of Commons of 1858, 17
§ 5. Present Condition - - - - - 20
§ 6. Military and Naval Savings Banks - - - 21
§ 7. Penny Banks - - - - - - 22

Chap. II. *Present Constitution.*

§ 1. Formation - - - - - 25
§ 2. Rules - - - - - - - 26
§ 3. Officers - - - - - - 29
§ 4. Rate of Interest allowed - - - - 30
§ 5. Balance in Treasurers' hands - - - 31
§ 6. Limitation of Deposits - - - - - 33
§ 7. Separate Surplus Fund - - - - 34
§ 8. Profits of Savings Banks - - - - 36
§ 9. Deposits Unclaimed - - - - - 38
§ 10. Expenses - - - - - - - 39

CHAPTER I.

HISTORY OF SAVINGS BANKS.

Section 1.—Origin.

ART. 1.—In order that our readers may have a right understanding of the present condition of Savings Banks (which will be found investigated hereafter), it is necessary to consider their past history, and the various steps of legislation which have preceded their existing constitution. We propose, therefore, to give a rapid review of the measures that have been devised, both by the Legislature and by benevolent private individuals, to benefit the industrious classes in respect to Savings Bank deposits.

The credit of introducing these excellent institutions into *Great Britain is claimed on behalf of at least three different persons; but we do not doubt that there may be earlier unrecorded instances of arrangements having been made to receive

---

* [The first institution of the kind, it is generally believed, was formed at Berne, in Switzerland, in the year 1787. It is remarked, as worthy of notice, by M. le Baron Dupin (in *"La Caisse d'Epargne et les Ouvriers:"* Leçon donnée au Conservatoire royal des arts et metiers, le 22 Mars 1837) that "it was not an opulent country in which these new establishments originated, but one, which for its rocks, its climate, and, above all, for the spirit of its inhabitants, might very well be called the Scotland of the Continent." M. Gustave du Puynode, however, in his learned work "*De la Monnaie, du Credit, et de l'Impôt,*" (Tome i., p. 413. Paris, 1853.) states that a Savings Bank was founded at Hamburg so early as 1778.]

small savings from the poor and to return them, on demand, with interest.

2.—In the year 1798, a "Friendly Society for the benefit of Women and Children," was established at Tottenham High Cross, under the superintendence of Mrs. Priscilla Wakefield; and before the year 1801 there had been combined with its main design two other objects, viz. a fund for loans and a bank for savings.

The principal rules were as follows:—

"*The honorary members pay five shillings on entrance and twelve shillings annually.

"The benefited members pay two shillings on entrance: they are divided into three classes according to their age. The first class, which consists of those between twenty and thirty, pay sixpence monthly; those of the second class are between thirty and forty, and pay ninepence monthly; those of the third class are between forty and fifty, and pay one shilling monthly.

" No one is to contribute after sixty. From sixty-five to seventy, each member is to receive a pension of one shilling weekly; and from seventy to the end of their lives two shillings weekly, even should they be obliged to retire into a workhouse. In case of sickness, four shillings weekly are allowed for four months in one year and two shillings afterwards; and if a member dies, after having subscribed six years, thirty shillings are allowed for the funeral.

" The honorary members, thinking themselves entitled to risk part of their contributions, have authorized the Stewardesses, at their discretion, to lend small sums from five shillings to thirty to the benefited members, on such occasions as they may approve. These loans are directed particularly to enabling them to purchase necessaries at the wholesale price, or to supply themselves with

---

* [Reports of the Society for Bettering the Condition and Increasing the Comforts of the Poor, vol. 3, p. 186.]

articles for sale, materials for work, a pig, or any other thing likely to produce a profit. These loans are repaid in small monthly payments.

"Children of either sex, or whatever age, whether belonging to a member or not, are permitted to bring any sum above one penny to the monthly meeting of the Stewardesses, to be laid up in the fund of the society, where their small earnings may accumulate in security till wanted for an apprentice fee, clothing on going to service, or some such important purpose; and in case of death, the sum laid up is returned to the parents of the child.

"The business of the society is managed by six Stewardesses and a Treasurer, who meet monthly: four of the Stewardesses are chosen from the honorary members, and two from the benefited members. These offices are filled in alphabetical order at an annual meeting of the whole Society. It should be added, that great attention is paid to the moral character of those who are admitted members; and a notorious irregularity of conduct incurs expulsion."

In 1804 this Bank for Savings was more regularly organized, and Trustees were appointed, viz. Mr. Eardley Wilmot, M.P., and Mr. Spurling.

3.—A prior claim is raised, however, on behalf of the Rev. Joseph Smith, of Wendover, who, in the year 1799, circulated in his parish *proposals to receive any sums in deposit during the summer, and "to return the amount at Christmas, with the addition of one-third to the whole as a bounty upon the Depositors' economy.

"It was expressly and wisely stipulated that the Depositors might receive back the sums respectively due to them at any time before Christmas, on demand; and that the fruit of their economy should not exclude them from parish relief in case

---

* Ibid. No. 59.

of sickness or want of employment; a comfortable addition at home to the family Christmas dinner was to finish the year's account. These curious proposals were ushered in by a text, which, though not applied to its original purpose, was, as a motto, sufficiently appropriate—'Upon the first day of the week, let every one of you lay by him in store, as God hath prospered him.' The peasantry of the parish readily embraced the offer held out to them, and, during the first season, sixty subscribers brought their weekly savings with great regularity."

This institution, however, though highly praiseworthy in its way, must be held to be the precursor of the modern "Penny Banks" (see § 7), rather than of the more important Savings Bank system.

4.—The first publication in this country of the idea of a Savings Bank is also attributed to the celebrated Jeremy Bentham, in whose well-known schemes for the management of paupers (1797)* was included a system of Frugality Banks, as he called them. The suggestions of Mr. Bentham were, however, never acted upon.

5.—The Society next formed, of which we have any account, was opened in 1808, at †Bath (chiefly through the instrumentality of ladies), for receiving deposits from female servants. In 1806 the ‡Provident Institution of London was established by the exertions of Mr. Barber Beaumont, Managing Director of the County Fire Office, for Loans, Life Assur-

---

* [Arthur Young's Annals of Agriculture, 1797; Pauper Management Improved, 8vo., 1812; Report of Commons Committee on Penitentiary Houses, 1811., App.]

† [Porter's Progress of the Nation.]

‡ [Essay on Provident or Parish Banks, by Barber Beaumont, 1816.]

ance, and Deferred Annuities. To this undertaking a Savings Bank was at first attached, but it was shortly afterwards discontinued, and the institution became simply a Life Assurance office.

6.—In 1810, the first Savings Bank in Scotland was formed by the Rev. Henry Duncan, minister of Ruthwell, Dumfriesshire. Various papers were published by him upon the subject of forming banks for savings in the different parishes of the country, and the regular and simple organization of his "Parish Bank" served as a model for other institutions. He communicated the rules to the Edinburgh Society for the Suppression of Mendicity, and the result was the establishment, in 1814, of the Edinburgh Savings Bank, under the auspices of Mr. Forbes. Similar institutions were, about the same time, commenced at Kelso and Hawick. In gratitude to Mr. Duncan, who died in 1846, a Savings Bank house was shortly after erected to his memory in the county town of Dumfries.

In Nov. 1815, the Provident Institution of Southampton was established, to which the zeal and influence of the Right Hon. George Rose in a great degree contributed.

Section 2.—As to early Methods of Investment.

ART 7.—It will be interesting to notice, here, the methods which were employed in the early days of Savings Banks, before their adoption by the Government, to procure for the depositors a safe, intelligible, and remunerative means of investment.

The founders of these institutions considered that—as it was not customary in England for ordinary private banks to allow interest on the deposits made with them, and as in other private investments, where interest might be obtained, the security would not always be good—the only source whence interest could be derived with a due measure of safety was the public funds.

Lord Monteagle, who has filled the high official position of Chancellor of the Exchequer, in his evidence before the Select Committee on Savings Banks in 1858, speaking of the advantages and disadvantages of this medium of investment, said:—

"Fortunately the accumulation of wealth in this country has been so great, that there has been what may be called an appetite for Three per Cents. that seems insatiable, so that you can, as a general principle, assume that, on a series of years, you will seldom find a time when the market is not in that condition gladly to take off Three per Cents.; but all that is a speculation, and it is against speculation in these matters that I take the liberty of very earnestly and very firmly protesting. The more the management of the thirty-eight millions of Savings Banks deposits is freed, as a matter of business, from speculation, the better. And remember, after all, you are trustees for these funds, and 'speculation' is just the word which ought to be excluded from the room in which trustees meet to transact the business of their *cestui que trust.*"

8.—It was first proposed that each Depositor should be paid whatever the funds produced. The inconvenience of this system, however, arising from the fluctuations of price, was speedily found to be too great, and a fixed rate of interest was given; but the difficulty arose, on withdrawals, of the loss attending the rise and fall of the securities on which the Savings Banks money would be invested. Many and various were the schemes devised for this difficulty. The plan upon which Dr. Haygarth proceeded, in the bank which his strenuous exertions were the means of setting on foot in Bath, was to make every Depositor to the value of one or more pounds of stock a proprietor of stock to that amount, entitling him to receive, every six months, the same dividends as those paid at the Bank of England, one-sixth being deducted for the expenses of the institution. In the constitution* of this bank, no part of the management, and no control over it, were given to the Depositors.

Several Trustees and Managers were constituted, with powers of supplying vacancies; and the money of the depositors was vested in the public funds in the names of a certain number of the Trustees.

9.—The Southampton Bank, which was formed on very nearly the same plan as that at Edinburgh, was composed of a large number of noblemen and gentlemen, who formed themselves into an association for banking the money of the poor; excluding entirely the intervention of the Depositors. It differed from the bank established at Bath, which gave the Depositors a proportion of the dividends, and left them to the chance of gain or loss by the fluctuation of the stock which their money had purchased. The Southampton Bank, though it vested the money in Government Securities, undertook to pay a fixed rate of interest of 4 per cent. on each sum of 12s. 6d.; and to repay the deposit when demanded without diminution. The bank, in this way, took upon itself the chance of any rise or fall in the price of the funds. This bank, like the one at Edinburgh, placed a limit to the deposits which it would receive from any one individual, and fixed the amount at £25.

10.—These local and limited attempts were followed by others on a more extensive scale. The " Society for Bettering the Condition of the Poor " took measures for interesting a sufficient number of noblemen and gentlemen to establish a

---

* [Article on Savings Banks in the 1824 edition of the Encyclopædia Britannica.]

large Savings Bank (or Provident Institution, which was deemed a preferable name), for the whole of the western metropolis. Several meetings were held during the month of March 1816. The plan of the bank of Southampton, to pay a certain fixed rate of interest, and return the net deposit on demand, was first proposed. This, with regard to the facility of giving satisfaction to the contributors and of avoiding misconception on their part, injurious to the prosperity of the institution, was highly desirable. But, after a due consideration of the danger to which the bank would, on this plan, be exposed, in the event of any great depression in the price of stock, it was resolved to follow the example of Bath—to render each Depositor a stockholder, and consequently to make him liable to either the profit or the loss, which the fluctuation of stock might occasion. This institution was composed of the noblemen and gentlemen by whom it was promoted, who formed themselves into an association, consisting of a President, Trustees, and Managers; wholly excluding the co-operation of the Depositors, and all intervention and control on their part. It is said by Mr. Willich to have been commenced in a very humble way, in a room over a butcher's shop in Panton Street, Haymarket, on the 15th April following; and it is now the St. Martin's Place Savings Bank, the largest as well as the oldest of the metropolitan banks, with deposits at the present time to the extent of more than a million and a half.

Section 3.—*As to the course of Legislation to the end of the Year* 1859.

ART. 11.—We now arrive at the era of the first legislation on the subject.

The first Act, in relation to Savings Banks, was passed in 1817; and, up to the time of the passing of that Act, there had been formed, by the voluntary association of benevolent persons, no less than seventy banks in England, four in Wales, and four in Ireland. The first Act affecting the Scottish banks was not passed till two years later. Unsuccessful attempts had been made previously, even before Savings Funds were thought of, to obtain a legislative encouragement of provident habits among the industrial classes. In 1773, a Bill passed the House of Commons, on the motion of Mr. Dowdeswell, to enable the *purchase of deferred annuities or provisions for old age* to be secured out of the *poors rates* of the parish to which the purchasers belonged, in case the funds subscribed should prove insufficient to pay the annuities. This Bill was thrown out by the Lords, from its defective character; for, among other things, it made no provision against the very probable case of a too limited number of annuity purchasers being found to protect the poors rates from loss.

Another Bill, prepared in 1789, had for its object, mainly, to enable the labouring poor to provide support for themselves in old age by small weekly savings. This Bill also was rejected by the House of Lords. In 1807, Mr Whitbread introduced into the House of Commons a Bill of a most comprehensive character, for the creation of an office in the metropolis, under Government control and guarantee, to afford advantages to the provident working classes, very similar to those at present held out by the Savings Banks. This *Bill was ultimately withdrawn.

12.—At last, however, " the †Legislature appear to have become sensible of the advantages, that would arise to the public

---

* [*See Part* V., *in which we have given this Bill at length, on account of the remarkable plan contained in it for facilitating the receipt of deposits by the agency of the* POST OFFICE.]

† [Tidd Pratt's History of Savings Banks.]

at large, from judiciously fostering the provident spirit which was gradually developing itself among the industrious classes. Legislative protection and encouragement were felt to be desirable, not only as affording positive advantages to the poor, whom it was professed to have principally in view, but to secure certain collateral benefits, which would be of no mean importance to the whole community. It was seen that every person, who had vested his savings in the public funds, had a stake in the security of the country, measured not merely by the sum total of those savings, but by the value of that amount to himself, and that he would be deterred from abetting in or compassing disturbance in his native land by a personal motive, added to the influence of duty;—that he would also feel the importance of public peace and public credit through that strong conviction which individual interest never fails to inspire;—and that the fair answer to any objection, on the part of those who might be jealous of the support thus accorded to the ruling powers, was, that he who possesses property in a country is not interested in the mere stability of any particular administration, but in the perpetuation of universal order and good government."

13.—Acting under these convictions, the Acts 57 Geo. III. c. 105., "To encourage the establishment of Banks for Savings in Ireland," and c. 130., for the like purpose in "England," were passed by both Houses, and followed, in 1819, by the Statute 59 Geo. III., c. 62., "for the Protection of Banks for Savings in Scotland."*

These Acts defined the associations, for whose benefit they

---

* [The advantages afforded by this last Act, however, related principally to exemptions from stamp duties. The privilege of depositing with the Commissioners was not extended to Scotland till 1835, in consequence. Previous to that date, Savings Banks in that country existed only on a very limited scale. Now they are considerably more flourishing than in Ireland.]

were enacted, as "any society for the purpose of establishing and maintaining any institution, in the nature of a bank to receive deposits of money for the benefit of the persons depositing the same, to accumulate the produce of so much thereof as shall not be required by the Depositors, their executors, or administrators, at compound interest, and to return the whole, or any part of such deposit, and the produce thereof, to the Depositors, their executors, or administrators (deducting out of such produce so much as shall be required for the necessary expenses attending the management of such institution), but deriving no benefit whatever from any such deposit, or the produce thereof"* (s. 1.).

14.—In 1818, an amending Act, the 58 Geo. III. c. 48., relating to England only, was passed, providing for the deposit of funds that had accrued before the passing of the Act (s. 15.);

---

*[Re-enacted by 9 Geo. IV. c. 92.
s. 2.
s. 3.
s. 6.
s. 25.
s. 28, 29.
s. 7.
s. 8.
s. 11.
s. 11.
s. 15.
s. 14.
s. 10.
s. 30.
s. 41.
s. 43.
s. 44.
s. 62.

These Acts provided for the filing of Rules (ss. 2.); that the Trustees and Managers must derive no benefit from the funds (ss. 3.); the Rules to be legally binding (ss. 4.); that the savings of minors might be invested (ss. 5); that Friendly Societies might subscribe to Savings Banks (ss. 6.); for the taking of security from officers (ss. 7.); the effects of the bank to be vested in the Trustees (ss. 8.); funds to be deposited in the Bank of England and Ireland (ss. 9.), to the credit of a "Fund for the Banks for Savings" (ss. 10.), by an order of two of the Trustees (ss. 11.), and to be invested by the National Debt Commissioners in Bank Annuities only (ss. 14.); penalties for depositing under a false declaration (ss. 17.); for the responsibility of the Treasurer as to funds in his hands (c. 105., s. 23 : c. 130, s. 21.); for exempting members of Friendly Societies from forfeiture (c. 105., s. 24.; c. 130 , s. 22.); for paying over deposits of intestates under £20 without expense of probate (c. 105., s. 26 ; c. 130., s. 24.); for indemnifying the banks against future claims in such cases (c. 105., s. 27.; c. 130., s. 25.); for exempting all documents from stamp duty (c. 105., s. 28.; c. 130., s. 26.); and for their recognition as public Acts (c. 105., s. 30.; c. 130., s. 28.).

To the account in the Bank of England the whole of the monies of the English Savings Banks were to be paid in, and no sum, or sums, to be paid or laid out by the Trustees of the bank in any other manner, or upon any

for the establishment of Branch Banks (s. 16.); and that the Rules of Savings Banks must be submitted for the approval of the Justices at Sessions (s. 17.). Another, in 1820, the 1 Geo. IV. c. 83., made regulations as to the calculation of interest (s. 3.); and as to the employment by the Commissioners of clerks and officers (s. 19.); and extending the privileges relating to investments to those made by Friendly Societies (s. 18.). *It allowed charitable institutions to deposit without limit as to amount* (s. 12.); but this was repealed in 1824, by the *5 Geo. IV. c. 62., s. 24., and has since been re-enacted in 1859.

s. 4. (repealed by 7 & 8 Vict. c. 83. ss. 18., 19.).
s. 17.
s. 61.

---

other security whatever (s. 9.), providing, however, that not less than £50 should be paid in at one time. In the Irish Act, on the contrary, permission was given to invest one-fifth of the total funds of every bank in the hands of any banker, at interest, after the rate of £6 per cent. per annum; and the Bank of Ireland was not to receive less, in one sum, than £100. When the Acts were consolidated, in 1828 (9 Geo. IV. c. 92., s. 11.), these conflicting provisions were harmonized by allowing all banks to deposit with the Commissioners not less than £50 at a time, and to retain in the Treasurers' hands such sums of money as may be necessary to answer exigencies. The provision as to Irish investments with private bankers had been previously abolished by 5 Geo. IV. c 62.]

---

* [The following provisions of the Act of 1820 were confirmed and extended to Ireland by the Act of 1824, which applied to both countries.

s. 14.	1.	The appointment of an agent by each bank to receive money from the Commissioners (s. 4.).
s. 18.	2.	Revocation and fresh appointment (s. 15.).
s. 19.	3.	Withdrawals from Commissioners to be made by Trustees' drafts (s. 6.).
s. 21.	4.	Trustees may attend in person for the purpose (1 Geo. IV. c. 83., s. 7.; 5 Geo. IV. c. 62., s. 17.).
s. 20.	5.	Drafts for large amounts to be signed by more Trustees (1 Geo. IV. c. 83., s. 16.; 5 Geo. IV. c. 62., s. 14.).
s. 41.	6.	Sums under £50 to be exempted from probate duty (1 Geo. IV. c. 83., s. 16.; 5 Geo. IV. c. 62., s. 14.).
s. 31, 42.	7.	Payment to the person appearing to be next of kin valid as regards the banks (1 Geo. IV. c. 83., s. 17.; 5 Geo IV. c. 62., s. 19.).

15.—All these Acts were consolidated, with amendments, in 1828, by the 9 Geo. IV. c. 92., and many additional clauses*

The further leading provisions of the Act of 1824 were—

s. 32.	1. That no anonymous accounts were to be opened (s. 20.).
s. 35.	2. Deposits to be limited to £30 a-year (s. 21.).
s. 33.	3. For deposits made on behalf of others (s. 23.).
s. 34.	4. A Declaration to be made on opening an account (s. 25.).
s. 39.	5. For the transfer of deposits to other banks (s. 26.)
s. 46.	6. Savings Banks to make annual returns to the National Debt Office (s 29.).
s. 47.	7. A duplicate to be fixed in the offices of the banks (s. 30.).
s. 49.	8. Interest to be computed to the 20th May and 20th November in every year (s. 31.).
s. 48.	9. Accounts of the Fund to be annually laid before Parliament (s. 32.).
s. 55.	10. In case of pressure the Treasury may issue Exchequer Bills to assist the Fund (s. 33.).
s. 56.	11. The bank may make advances on such Bills (s. 34.).
s. 57.	12. The Bills to be paid off out of the deposits or out of the sinking fund (s. 35.).
s. 57.	13. If out of the Sinking Fund, stock be transferred from the Savings-Bank Fund to make up (s. 36.).
s. 20.	14. Large demands by Trustees of banks not to be paid without notice (s. 37.).
s. 59.	15. All forms &c. to be settled by the National Debt Commissioners (s. 38.).
s. 60.	16. The Commissioners to be indemnified for their deeds under the Acts (s. 39.).]

---

* [1. The sanction of Justices at Sessions and of the Commissioners required to the formation of new banks (s. 2.).

2. Fees to be paid to Clerk of the Peace on enrolment (s. 3.).

3. Rules to be submitted to the Barristers for certificate (s. 4.).

4. No Trustee or Manager to be responsible except for his own wilful neglect or default (s. 9.).

5. Trustees may receive money from Depositors to be applied in any way authorized by the rules (s. 12.).

6. The officer of the Commissioners to pay to no Bank in one day more than £10,000 (s. 21.).

were then introduced. This last Act has given, as it were, their peculiar character to Savings Banks in this country.

In 1833, an amending Act was passed, which provided for the purchase of Government Annuities, through the medium of Savings Banks (ss. 1. to 24., 26., and 27.); for priority of claim on the estates of deceased or insolvent officials (s. 28.); for the publication of the names of banks neglecting to transmit annual statements in the Gazette (s. 30.); and for the extension of the Act to Guernsey, Jersey, &c. (ss. 34., 35.); and, in 1835, the provisions of these Acts were extended to Scotland (5 and 6 William IV. c. 57.).

In 1844, another amending Act (7 and 8 Vict. c. 83.), was passed, reducing the interest to £3 · 5s. as regards the Depositors (s. 2.); limiting the responsibility of Trustees and Managers (s. 6.); providing for the punishment of defaulting Actuaries (s. 4.); the payment of trust accounts (s. 7.); of deposits of intestates (s. 10.); illegitimates (s. 11.), and married women (s. 12.); for the settlement of disputes (s. 14.), and repealing all the provisions relating to depositing the rules with the Clerk of the Peace and Justices (ss. 18., 19.).

---

7. The surplus fund to be ascertained and appropriated (s. 22.).

8. Separate surplus fund to be created (s. 23.).

9. Charitable Societies may invest up to £100 a year, or £300 altogether (s. 27.).

10. No deposits to be received above £150 (s. 37.); no interest to be paid on accounts exceeding £200 (s. 35.); but this provision not to affect any deposits of above £200 at the time of the passing of the Act (s. 36.).

11. No draft, order, or appointment of agent, &c., to be liable to stamp duty (s. 44.).

12. Depositors entitled on payment of one penny to printed copy of annual statement (s. 47.).

13. Commissioners may purchase Exchequer Bills (s. 50.); provisions for the funding (ss. 51., 52.), cancelling (s. 53.), and sale (s. 54.), of the Bills.

14. Provision for payment in England to the credit of the Bank of Ireland (s. 58.).]

Section 4.—As to the Committee of 1858 *of the House of Commons.*

ART. 16.—The next event, in the order of time, in the history of Savings Banks was the discovery of the great frauds in 1848 and subsequently, to the consideration of which we have devoted a Chapter in Part II. From that date to the present time various *attempts at Savings Bank legislation have been made, and suggestions furnished to Parliament, but little good resulted until the appointment of the Select Committee of 1858 to "inquire into the Acts relating to Savings Banks, and the operation thereof."

---

* [For the abortive attempts, see Part 2, art. 30—33. The actual legislation of the period has been as follows :—

On the 5th September 1848, the 11 & 12 Vict. c. 133., was passed as a special Act for Ireland, in consequence of the grievous Cuffe Street frauds.

The 17 & 18 Vict. c. 50. (24th July 1854) continues the special Act for Ireland, and 12 Vict. c. 133., until 1st of January 1858, and until the end of the then next ensuing Session of Parliament. It also enacts that funds of Friendly Societies may be deposited in Savings Banks to any amount.

The Irish Act has since again been renewed for a like term by an Act passed in the Session of 1858, by which Act (21 & 22 Vict. c. 133.),—

Section 1. repeals for Ireland clause of former Act as to the non-liability of Trustees; but

Section 2. allows Trustees and Managers to fix extent from £100 of liability.

Section 3. appoints auditors (for Ireland).

Section 5. Depositors in Ireland must produce books on one of at least two days in the year, or their accounts will be closed.

On the 4th August 1853, the 16 & 17 Vict. c. 45. was passed as the new Act for Savings Bank Annuities,

Since the report of the Committee, a short Act, 22 & 23 Vict. c. 53., has been passed (13th August 1859), by which Charitable and Provident Societies and "Penny Banks" may invest all their proceeds in Savings Banks. *Certain official restrictions, however, have been introduced, which are said to have the effect of depriving the boon of a great part of its value.*]

In determining the course of evidence, the Committee endeavoured to embrace all the material points of the Acts relating to Savings Banks which are or have been in force. In addition to the information which the officers of the Government afforded on this point, the Committee allowed an opportunity to the Trustees and Managers of Savings Banks to give expression to opinions they had long been known to entertain respecting the manner in which the finances of Savings Banks had been managed, and to bring forward various suggestions for an improved system both of central and local administration.

17.—They examined Mr. Tidd Pratt, as to the history and course of legislation; Sir Alexander Spearman and Lord Monteagle as to the mode of investment and the history of the financial operations; Mr. Boodle, the Actuary of the St. Martin's Place Savings Bank, as to the impressions which prevail among persons practically connected with Savings Banks on the subject; fifteen other Actuaries and Managers as to practical details; and Mr. Taylor, of Rochdale, as to the circumstances attending the defalcation there. The report of the Committee was divided into the following heads:—

1st. The course of legislation from 1817 to 1857.
2d. The central authority of the National Debt Office, and the practice with respect to investment and repayment of balances.
3d. The question of Parliamentary guarantee, and the relations between the Central and Local Offices.
4th. The mode of providing for future expenditure.

As to the state of the law, they reported that it was "unsatisfactory and uncertain, diffused through Acts, partially rescinded, which nowhere present a clear and distinct announcement of the duties, liabilities, or rights of any of the parties concerned in the management and welfare of these institutions;" and they recommended that the whole should be amended and consolidated.

18.—On the subject of the investments of the National Debt Commissioners, the report stated:—

"The Commission consists of the Speaker of the House of Commons, the Chief Baron of the Exchequer, the Master of the Rolls, the Accountant-General of the Court of Chancery, the Chancellor of the Exchequer, the Governor and the Deputy-Governor of the Bank of England. The Acts that constitute the Commission require that Boards should be held, and that there should be in attendance a quorum of three Commissioners, 58 Geo. III., cap. 60. sect. 1., and 3 & 4 Will. IV., cap. 14. sect. 22.; it is, however, shewn by a return presented to the House of Commons, that such Board of late years has met only quarterly; and the Speaker of the House of Commons, the Chief Baron of the Exchequer, the Master of the Rolls, and the Accountant-General, having important duties elsewhere, rarely, if ever, attend any meeting.

"It thus appears that large financial *operations have been carried on by means of the capital of Savings Banks which was at the command of the Exchequer, in purchasing, selling, and varying securities.

"It is alleged by several witnesses that such a mode of dealing with that capital is not warranted by the terms of any statute; that it has resulted in a deficiency of assets, as compared with the liabilities of the fund; and that such deficiency might have been materially reduced, if the Commissioners had treated the money of Savings Banks as simple Trustees.

"It was shown to your Committee, that since the time when public attention was drawn to the existence of a deficiency in the aggregate funds, great dissatisfaction has been felt throughout the local banks; and that, owing to the complicated form in which the annual returns are laid before Parliament, though doubtless they are strictly correct, yet local Managers have been unable to check them, and the loss incurred by the nation upon the general results has been naturally exaggerated, and supposed to be even greater than in fact it is.

"Your Committee is therefore of opinion it would be advisable to repeal all the sections of the Savings Banks Acts which relate to the conversion of Exchequer Bills into Stock, leaving that question to be dealt with separately.

"Your Committee propose that in future the Commissioners of the National Debt shall be relieved from the office of investing the monies of Savings Banks; that this duty shall be confided to a Commission of five persons, of whom the Chancellor of the Exchequer and the Governor of the Bank shall always be members, and that the other three shall be nominated by the Crown.

"Your Committee believe that ample control and margin will thus be reserved to the Executive Government in directing the choice of securities, in which that part of the balances shall be invested, which it is necessary

---

* [See Chap. VIII. for a detailed examination of these operations.]

to keep in such a state that they may be easily convertible into money on demand; and, on the other hand, that by the provisions which they recommend Parliament to adopt, a sufficient check will be imposed upon the facility of dealing in the Public Funds, by shifting the money of Savings Banks from one kind of security to another."

(For Legislation since 1859, *see Part VII. et seq.)*

Section 5.—As to the present condition of Savings Banks.

ART. 19.—Notwithstanding legislative conflicts and internal frauds, Savings Banks have progressed; and it is desirable that the following facts should be recollected: —

That during the seventeen years from 1840 to 1857, 116 millions of money have been *received* from Depositors by the Trustees; and 119 millions (including interest) returned to them.

That 36 millions remained (1858) to the credit of 1,400,000 Depositors in the 600 banks, exclusive of nearly two millions received from Friendly Societies direct by the Commissioners.

The following Table is interesting, as shewing *to how large an extent* the number of persons holding small accounts preponderates over the number of larger Depositors, and is increasing.

Table A.		No. of Depositors.		Increase in 8 years.	Total Deposited 1858.
		20th Nov. 1850.	20th Nov. 1858.		
	£				
Not exceeding	20	677,969	870,987	193,018	4,994,909
	50	251,131	307,008	55,877	9,523,255
	100	106,510	131,869	25,359	9,111,763
	150	35,609	45,281	9,672	5,452,660
	200	18,914	26,560	7,646	4,511,645
Exceeding	200	2,448	1,497	1,049	327,644
		1,092,581	1,383,202	290,621	33,921,881
Add for Char. Inst. and Fr. Socs. depositing in Savings Banks . .		20,418	25,362	4,944	2,292,241
		1,112,999	1,408,564	295,565	36,214,122

Such is the history of Savings Banks in the United Kingdom, presenting a record of industrial prosperity and progress unequalled by any other country in the world, and of an elasticity sufficient to surmount obstacles and disasters, which anywhere else would have been fatal. None the less necessary is it, however, that these dangers, of which we shall shortly speak, should be guarded against for the future; for such precautions will render all the more hopeful any sound attempt at still further improvement.

(*For later statistics, see other parts of this Treatise.*)

Section 6.—*As to Military and Naval Savings Banks.*

ART. 20.—The law relating to Military Savings Banks has been recently consolidated into one Act, the 22 & 23 Vict. c. 20. (passed 13th August 1859). The funds of these banks are deposited by the Secretary at War with the *National Debt Commissioners, but in a separate account, called "The †Fund for the Military Savings Banks;" and they are expressly ‡exempted from the operation of the Savings Bank Acts. The amount that may be deposited is unlimited; but sums in excess of £30 received in any one year will §not bear interest for that year, except in the case of gratuities awarded for good conduct or otherwise; and when a deposit amounts to £200, it ceases to bear any interest. The rate allowed to the Depositors is not to exceed £3. 15s. per cent. The dividends received by the Commissioners from their investments are ‖exempted from Stamp Duty.

The regulations of the banks are settled from time to time

---

* [Sect. 7.] † [Raised under the 8 & 9 Vict. c. 27. (1845).]
‡ [Sect. 14.] § [Sect. 4.] ‖ [Sect. 8]

by the Secretary at War, with the concurrence of the Horse Guards and the Lords of the Treasury. These banks were first established in 1842, by the Act 5 & 6 Vict. c. 71.; and in 1849, the old Regimental Benefit Societies were finally dissolved, and incorporated with the Military Savings Banks (12 & 13 Vict. c. 71.). Returns of the transactions of these banks are annually laid before Parliament.

From a return by the War Office it appears, that on the 31st March 1857, the sum of £161,354 was accumulated in the various Regimental Savings Banks. In the Seamen's Savings Banks, established under the Merchant Shipping Act of 1854, and the 19 & 20 Vict. c. 41. (1856), there is already £12,444 deposited.

Section 7.—*As to Penny Banks.*

ART. 21.—The establishment of Penny Banks may, almost, be called a recent event, and is one of the most gratifying further developments of the economical organization of labour, which may be made to carry into hundreds of thousands of homes the excellent advantages that have attended the establishment of Savings Banks; for the shillings of the skilled artisan can be multiplied ten thousand fold, " when the *unskilled labourer in field and street comes to learn the power of pence to meet the 'rainy day,' which he cannot avoid anticipating in full knowledge of all its chill realities."

---

* [For a history of Penny Banks the reader is referred to two admirable papers—admirable for the generous sentiments exhibited in dealing with the economics of labour—one in *Household Words*, vol. i. page 464, and the other in *All the Year Round*, vol. i. p. 334. A very good draft of a plan has been published by Mr. Clarke of Southampton.]

22.—The Penny Bank movement originated some ten or a dozen years ago in one of the poor parishes of East London, through the practical benevolence of its clergyman. It has already acquired goodly proportions.

"In evidence of the fact that poor people want to put by savings, too small to justify the opening of an account with the ordinary Savings Bank (says a writer in "All the Year Round") let these results be taken.

"At the Birmingham Savings Bank, seventeen pounds is the average balance owned by each Depositor; at the Birmingham Penny Bank it is not seventeen shillings; and a sum now rapidly growing towards a hundred thousand pounds has passed through that Penny Bank in deposits of small savings averaging less than three shillings a-piece. At Halifax, the average amount paid in at once has not been two shillings. At Scarborough it has been only eightpence, and the average balance kept in the bank by its customers is six and fourpence. At Shenstone, near Lichfield, threepence halfpenny is the average sum paid in by each customer. Yet on such terms throughout the country many thousands of accounts are opened."

23.—It may be mentioned, further, that—in a Penny Bank established by Mr. James Crocker at Gateshead in October 1859, open for two hours every Saturday evening—1150 deposit accounts were commenced in the first month, and £170 lodged by the humble investors—an average of 2*s.* 11½*d.*

The constitution of a Penny Bank is very simple; and the following rules have been adopted by several that have already been established:—

I. The Bank to be open every Friday Evening, from Seven till Eight. Deposits may be made from 1*d.* to 2*s.* 6*d.*; or 10*s.* for the first deposit.

II. Any sum reaching £5 will be transferred to the Savings Bank, but deposits may be continued.

III. Persons wishing to withdraw any sum to give a week's notice, unless the Treasurer has funds in hand.

IV. Three per cent. per annum will be allowed half-yearly, on all sums exceeding 5*s.* 6*d.*

V. One penny will be charged for the Deposit-book, also 1*d.* for a copy of the rules, and 1*d.* for the annual statement, if they are required.

VI. The production of the Deposit-book will authorise any person, if known, to deposit or withdraw.

VII. All expenses to be paid out of the surplus interest allowed to the Bank, and from donations.

VIII. The Managers of the Fund will be at liberty to refuse or discontinue the receipt of deposits from any individual.

CHAPTER II.

PRESENT CONSTITUTION.

Section 1.—As to the Formation of Savings Banks.

ART. 24.—The account we have given of the origin of Savings Banks will have shewn that they are, in general, formed at the suggestion of benevolent persons of influence, who unite together in the locality of their residences, and agree to become Trustees and Managers of the Bank.

They themselves make, perhaps, a deposit, by way of advance towards the preliminary expenses, and as an encouragement to humbler classes to join the infant institution.

25.—To give it a legal existence, application is made for the sanction of the Commissioners for the Reduction of the National Debt (according to 9 Geo. 4. c. 92. s. 2.), or, on their behalf, of the Comptroller-General (Sir A. Y. Spearman) or the Assistant Comptroller (Mr. Higham).

The power to give or withhold consent* to the establishment of a Savings Bank has been reserved to the Commissioners, from the proper desire to prevent the formation of

---

* [The Acts do not require the Commissioners to give a reason for withholding their consent, *and, of course, it is only required for Savings Banks that desire to be entitled to the privileges of the Act.*]

opposition Savings Banks in small localities,* and thus to avoid a system, which would act prejudicially to both, by preventing the concentration of the expenses of management in either institution.

26.—The permission of the Commissioners for the formation of the new bank having been obtained, a set of rules is prepared, embodying the main regulations provided by the Acts of Parliament in force, and the personal laws deemed advisable for its management. These rules require (by 7 & 8 Vict. c. 83. s. 19.) the certificate of the Barrister-at-law appointed to carry out the purposes of the 9 Geo. 4. c. 92. (at present Mr. John Tidd Pratt) that they are strictly in accordance with the Statutes: and Mr. Pratt examines a rough copy (for which service a fee of one guinea is allowed by the 9 Geo. 4. c. 92. s. 4), supplies such statutory clauses as he conceives to have been omitted, and then returns the draft to the promoters, that they may make two fair copies, and send them up to him (signed by two Trustees) for his final certificate. The certificate being granted, one copy is returned to the bank; the other is kept by the National Debt Commissioners, under whom Mr. Tidd Pratt acts, for the purpose of reference. The copy, returned to the bank, must be kept open for the inspection of depositors.

Section 2.—*As to the Rules.*

Art. 27.—The rules may contain the following provisions:—

1st. To enable the Trustees to receive sums of any amount from Depositors for investment either in the purchase of stock or otherwise, or for any other purpose, except to be paid in to the account with the Commissioners; in other words, to

---

* [It is not necessary, however, that all the Depositors should be resident in the locality of the Bank.]

act as agents for the working classes in their investments* (9 Geo. 4. c. 92. s. 12.).

2nd. As to making new rules and alterations of rules (s. 3.).

3rd. To pay salaries to officers, not being Trustees, Treasurers, or Managers (s. 6.).

4th. To dispose of surplus funds (s. 22.).

5th. To provide for payment to representatives of deceased Depositors, whose effects do not exceed £50, without Probate or Letters of Administration (s. 41.).

6th. To fix a time for payment of deposits by General Receivers (7 & 8 Vict. c. 83. s. 4.).

7th. To direct as to the disposal of monies received by Trustees and Managers (7 & 8 Vict. c. 83. s. 6.).

28.—The following clauses are *required* by the Acts to be inserted in the rules of a Savings Bank:—

1st. That no person or persons, being Treasurer, Trustee, or Manager, or having any control in the management of the bank, shall derive any benefit from any deposit made in the bank, save only and except such salaries and allowances, or other necessary expenses, as are provided in these rules for the charges of management, exclusive of the Treasurer or Treasurers, Trustee or Trustees, Manager or Managers, or other person having direction or management of the bank, who shall not, directly or indirectly, have any salary, allowance, profit, or benefit whatsoever therefrom, beyond their actual expenses for the purposes of the bank (9 Geo. 4. c. 92. s. 6.).

2nd. That no †Trustee or Manager of the bank shall be

---

* [This has not been done in more than three or four instances, of which the only English one is the Exeter Bank, where stock is bought for Depositors to any amount. (See Tidd Pratt's Evidence, Rep. Com. H. C. 1858, qu. 18—26, and Part VI.)]

† [See the next section of this Chapter, and Part IV., as to Trustees.]

liable to make good any deficiency which may arise in its funds, unless he shall have declared, by writing under his hand, deposited with the Commissioners for the Reduction of the National Debt, that he is willing so to be answerable; and he may limit his responsibility, or the Trustees and Managers may limit their collective responsibility to any sum specified in such instrument; but every Trustee and Manager is personally responsible and liable for all moneys actually received by him on account of, or to and for, the use of the bank, and not paid over and disposed of according to these rules (7 & 8 Vict. c. 83. s. 6.).

3rd. That when deposits shall be made by a *trustee on behalf of another, the sum must be invested in the name of such Trustee and the name of the person on whose account such sum shall be so deposited; and repayment of the same, or any part thereof, will not be made by the Trustees or Managers of the bank without the receipt and receipts of the said Trustee, and the person on whose account such deposit may have been made, or the survivor or survivors, or the executors or administrators of such survivor, whose receipt and receipts, either in person or by agent appointed by power of attorney, which power of attorney is valid if executed by an infant of or exceeding the age of fourteen years, are alone a good and valid discharge to the said Trustees and Managers, except in case of the insanity or imbecility of the party on whose behalf the deposit has been made; upon proof of which to the satisfaction of the said Trustees or Managers, repayment will be made to the said Trustee (7 & 8 Vict. c. 83. s. 7.).

29.—The other provisions vary according to local circumstances and the views of the promoters. If, at any time, the rules are amended, the same proceedings as to registration are necessary.

---

* [By this is meant, not a Trustee of the Bank, but any person acting as Trustee for another. See *Part IV., respecting future regulations for Minors.*]

Section 3.—*As to the Officers.*

ART. 30.—The gentlemen who have constituted and enrolled themselves as *Trustees* and *Managers*, or who may be subsequently appointed, have different powers and liabilities which we will briefly explain. The first act of their authority is to appoint a Treasurer, Actuary, or Secretary, and clerks, who give such security as *two* of the Trustees and three of the Managers decide to be sufficient (7 & 8 Vict. c. 83. s. 17.). The security is made by bond to the Comptroller-General of the National Debt, and lodged in his office. It is endorsed in the following manner:—

"*We, two of the Trustees and three of the Managers, hereby approve of the within bond being given as good and sufficient.*"

The amount of security given by the various officers (except the Treasurer, who is always an honorary officer) depends very much on the amount of their respective salaries, and varies from £5 to £3000.

31.—The Treasurer is, in large towns, usually a banker; in others a clergyman or person of similar position, to whom the Manager of the day, who attends at the office to superintend the receipts and withdrawals, pays over all monies; either taking it himself, or sending it by the Actuary, with a notice-paper, which he has signed, informing the Treasurer how much he is to receive.

The Treasurer from time to time lodges at the Bank of England or Ireland, in the names of the Commissioners of the National Debt, the sums received by him; usually retaining under his care such a sum as he is desired by the Managers to keep available for the current requirements of the bank. In every annual statement he has to sign a certificate that the amount mentioned in the accounts is in his possession (3 Wm. 4. c. 14. s. 32.); and, upon demand made by two Trustees and three Managers, he has to give up all property of the Bank that may be in his hands (9 Geo. 4. c. 92. s. 10.).

32.—The Savings Bank is thus under the control and management of a body of Trustees and Managers, an Actuary or a Secretary, aided by the requisite number of clerks. The Trustees are usually noblemen or persons of high standing; in large banks about twelve in number, who alone have the power to draw out money from the hands of the National Debt Commissioners: and it may be mentioned incidentally, that when they are appointed, each Trustee signs his name to a form, which, being duly witnessed by two Managers, is forwarded to the National Debt Office, in order that the signatures may be ready for verification, before orders for the paying in or drawing out of money are acknowledged by the Comptroller of the National Debt.

The Managers are usually drawn from the superior tradespeople of the locality, and from clergymen and private gentlemen. They are very often forty or fifty in number, and in some cases much more: for instance, in the case of the Exeter Bank, there are 203.—(Return 55, 1858, p. 165).

Section 4.—As to the Rate of Interest allowed.

ART. 33.—By the Act 9 Geo. IV. c. 92. s. 11. all monies belonging to the banks—not wanted for immediate purposes, and not intended by the Depositors to be otherwise invested (s. 12.) under some special provision of the rules (a power which has been exercised in England in only a single case)—are required to be paid over to the credit of the Commissioners for the reduction of the National Debt; and by the 15th section of the same Act, the investment of such monies by the Commissioners is restricted to the purchase of Bank Annuities and Exchequer Bills.

By the 7 & 8 Vict. c. 83. the rate of interest paid by the Commissioners to the Trustees of the banks, was reduced* from 20th November 1844, to £3 · 5s. per cent. per annum; and the rate payable to the Depositors was not to exceed £3 · 0s. 10d. per cent. per annum, or 2d. per diem.

Very few banks, however, give to their Depositors the full rate of £3 · 0s. 10d. per cent.†

34.—The allowing a rate of interest of £3 . 5s. per cent. is attended with loss to the nation, unless the average price of the Savings Bank Stock be bought by the National Debt Commissioners at a price not exceeding 92⅜, since £100 worth of stock bought at that price would pay the purchaser £3 · 5s. a year.

Section 5.—As to the Balances in Treasurer's hands.

ART. 35.—The *Savings Banks* in general keep a balance in their Treasurers' hands for current purposes, and in some cases the amount is large, the average for each bank being now

---

* [By the 57 *Geo. III.* c. 105. s. 11., and by the 57 *Geo. III.* c 130. s. 11., one relating to Ireland and the other to England, the interest payable to the Trustees was at the rate of 3d. per cent. per diem, which was £4 · 11s. 3d. per cent. per annum, but there was no fixed interest payable to Depositors.

By the 9 *Geo. IV.* c. 92., the interest payable to the Trustees was 2⅛d. per cent. per diem, of which the interest payable to the Depositors was not to exceed 2¼d. per cent. per diem, and the *Savings Banks* were required to compute the interest half-yearly or yearly.]

† [See Sect. 10. of this Chapter for statistics as to the *rates of interest allowed by the various banks.*]

nearly £590. As a rule, these balances* are totally unproductive of interest, and hence arises a small loss to the banks, which has to be made good out of the margin between the interest received from the Commissioners and that paid to the Depositors.

In some Scotch cases, it is stated that the banks receive interest on the portion of their funds returned as " in the Treasurers' hands," but this is exceptional.

36.—In his evidence before the Committee of 1858 (Qu. 507), Sir A. Spearman stated that, in his opinion, these balances are sometimes left in the hands of the Treasurer, with the view of compensating him for the trouble he is put to in connection with his office. We concur with the able Comptroller in considering that this is an improper principle to proceed upon.

---

* [Amount of the balances remaining in the hands of the Treasurers and officers of *Savings Banks* on 20th November of the years

Table B.	1852	1857
England . . .	£222,000	£240,913
Scotland . . .	14,900	65,667
Ireland	15,900	48,499
Channel Islands .	1,500	755
	£254,300	£355,834

The loss of interest to the banks from this cause (at £3.5s. per cent.) is nearly £11,565 a year.]

Section 6.—Limitation of Deposits.

Art. 37.—Since the 20th November 1828,* deposits cannot exceed £30 in any year ending the 20th November, nor £150 in the whole; and when deposits and interest amount to £200, the interest is to cease, except with respect to deposits amounting to or exceeding £200 on the 28th July 1828, but no such Depositor is allowed to make a further deposit so long as his deposits amount to or exceed £150. Depositors were allowed to withdraw their deposits, and again subscribe, provided the amount did not, in any one year, exceed £30, but this provision was repealed by the 3 *William* IV. *c.* 14., and now no money, whether such money shall have been previously withdrawn or not, can at any time be received from any

---

* [By the 57 Geo. III. c. 105. (1817), *Friendly Societies* might subscribe the whole or any part of their funds, but no individual Depositor (in Ireland) was allowed to deposit more than £50 in any one year, and there was no limit as to the total amount. By the 57 *Geo.* III. *c.* 130., *Friendly Societies* were allowed to subscribe the whole or any portion of their funds, but no individual Depositor (in England) could deposit more than £100 in the first year, and £50 in every year afterwards. By the 58 *Geo.* III. *c.* 48., no person, after the 1st October 1818, was to deposit any sum exceeding £10 in a year by ticket or number, or otherwise, without disclosing his or her name. By the 1 *Geo.* IV. *c.* 83., *Charitable Societies* were allowed to subscribe any portion of their funds to a Savings Bank. By the 5 *Geo.* IV. *c.* 62., the deposits of any one Depositor were not to exceed £50 in the year ending 20th November 1825, and £30 in any subsequent year, and were not to go beyond £200 in the aggregate, exclusive of interest. Depositors having made their full deposit might withdraw the whole, and again subscribe to a like amount. By the same Act, the provision that no person should deposit more than £50 in any one year in Ireland was repealed.]

Depositor, which shall in any one year ending the 20th November, exceed £30.

38.—By a recent Act (1859) the 22 & 23 *Vict. c.* 53., the funds of *Penny Savings Banks, Charitable and Provident Institutions,* and all charitable donations or bequests for the maintenance, education, or benefit of the poor, are allowed to be invested in *Savings Banks;* thus the Act is a recurrence to the legislation of the 1 *Geo.* IV., which was *repealed in 1828. *Friendly Societies,* if duly enrolled, were allowed to invest any amount; but if enrolled after the 28th of July 1828, the deposits were limited to £300, until the passing of the 7 & 8 Vict. c. 83., which repealed the limitation.

Section 7.—*Separate Surplus Fund.*

ART 39.—The 4*s.* 2*d.* or more per cent. per annum—arising out of the difference between the £3 . 5*s.* paid by the Commissioners to the Trustees and that credited to the Depositors by the bank—is applied, in the first place, to the payment of the expenses of the institution, and if any surplus remain, it must (under the †9 *Geo.* IV. *c.* 92. *s.* 23.) be paid over within six months from the 20th November in each year, to the Commissioners for the reduction of the National Debt, it being

---

* [This is a notable illustration of the way in which important provisions in Acts of Parliament are frequently cancelled from an insufficient appreciation of their effect. It is to be hoped that such an error will be avoided in the approaching consolidation of the Savings Bank Acts.]

† [By the 1 *Geo.* IV. *c.* 83., Trustees were authorized to make rules for the application of increased stock or property, and by the 5 *Geo.* IV., *c.* 62, no application of the surplus fund of any Savings Bank in England or Ireland was to be made until ten years after the establishment of the bank: one half of such surplus was always to be reserved to provide for deficiencies, and thirty days' notice of the intention of making any application of the surplus was to be given to the Commissioners for the re-

provided that the Trustees and Managers might claim and receive from the Commissioners for the purposes of the institution (upon such certificate as the Commissioners should appoint) any sum of money equal to the whole or any part of the *principal monies* which might have been discharged from the account of the Savings Bank as surplus; but no mention appears in this or other clauses as to the National Debt Commissioners being liable to pay interest.

40.—Hence the amounts so paid in by the banks are carried by the Commissioners to a separate surplus fund account, and cease to bear interest. Many banks have large credits in this fund, and they could afford, therefore, to allow the full rate of £3 . 0s 10d. to their Depositors. The rate of interest actually allowed by the Commissioners on the general funds is reduced, by the non-payment of interest on the surplus fund, from £3 . 5s. to £3 . 4s. 1d. per cent.

The wisdom of this system—viz. the non-payment of interest on the separate surplus fund—is open to question. The payment would assist the future expenses of the banks; for although they have saved in the past, a like saving is not to

---

duction of the National Debt; then, by the 9 *Geo.* iv., *c.* 92., it was declared, that within six weeks after the 20th of November 1821, the Trustees were to ascertain the amount of the surplus fund, and to distribute or appropriate the same in the manner provided by their respective rules; and in the event of no provision being made, then in such manner as the Trustees or Managers, or a major part of them assembled at a general meeting, should think fit and proper. The surplus fund does not seem to be increasing in amount. On the 20th November 1848, 582 banks possessed a separate surplus fund of £358,436, or an average of £616 to each institution: now (20th Nov. 1858) the banks exceed 600 in number, but the surplus fund is only £346,792, or less than £572 on an average. *The largest credit in the Separate Surplus Fund is held by the Worcester Bank, which has £15,118 surplus on its £300,000 of deposits. Only two banks in Scotland have any amount in this Fund, viz. Dunfermline and Dundee ; this, of course, arises from the practice of the Scotch Joint-Stock Banks in allowing interest.*]

be calculated upon for the future. The non-payment of interest causes complication and difficulty, and opens the door to error in the Government accounts.

Section 8.—*Profits of Savings Banks.*

ART. 41.—Savings Banks obtain a margin applicable to their expenses, and to the creation of a surplus fund, from the circumstance that when deposits amount to £200 they cease to bear interest in favour of the Depositor, while interest thereon is still credited to the bank by the Commissioners.* Again, a margin frequently arises from the small † fractional advantages in the calculation of interest on each deposit account.

---

*[The number of such accounts was 1497 on the 20th November 1858, and the amount of cash, not costing the Savings Banks any thing for interest, was £327,644, on which the banks received £10,648 a-year.]

†[The lowest amount bearing interest ranges from 1s. up to 30s. as the following table, made out from a return printed by order of the House of Commons, will shew:—

			s.	d.
1	Bank allows interest on		1	0
10	,,	,,	2	6
1	,,	,,	4	0
49	,,	,,	5	0
4	,,	,,	7	6
32	,,	,,	10	0
1	,,	,,	12	6
1	,,	,,	14	0
1	,,	,,	14	7¼
12	,,	,,	14	8
2	,,	,,	14	9
321	,,	,,	15	0
1	,,	,,	15	4
1	,,	,,	15	6
1	,,	,	16	8
72	,,	,,	20	0
39	,,	,,	30	0

2 allow on those fractions of £1 which produce exact pence of interest.

In a great many Savings Banks the interest is computed by weekly or fortnightly intervals. In other instances, however, * monthly periods of time are adopted. In the latter case the 20th is usually taken as the commencement of the month; and if the 20th has just passed, the computation is made from the 20th of the following month, so that if the deposit be withdrawn before that date, no interest whatever is allowed.

42.—As Savings Banks are credited with interest from the day each investment is made with the National Debt Commissioners, and up to the day of withdrawal, there is derived by these means a trifling compensation for the trouble attending deposits and repayments. Several banks, however, credit interest in advance continually throughout the year, on what is termed† "*the prospective plan*," and amalgamate it, with the principal upon every transaction.

It will thus be seen that the rate of interest nominally given according to the returns is not the same thing with the real rate actually received by the Depositors. For example, a bank declaring £3 per cent. interest, computed by the month, on even pounds, gives in effect within a fraction of £2.18s. 4d. per cent.; so that it would retain as much as another bank with precisely the same capital, paying the latter rate, computed by the day, on a small amount of principal.]

* [See DIVISION II., or *Treatise on Building Societies*, for various Tables, shewing the remarkable effect of interest being allowed monthly or weekly, and the equivalent rates for a year. Our readers will, also, find therein several practical and mathematical chapters on the Doctrine of Compound Interest].

† [*For Explanation of the "Prospective Plan," see Part* IV. The accounts of the Bishopsgate Savings Bank for the year 1857 shew that, whilst the interest paid to Depositors is only £2.17s. 6d. a separate surplus fund of £5000 has been accumulated out of the margin.]

Section 9.—*As to Deposits unclaimed.

ART. 43.—These are not much to be depended upon as a source of profit, as the banks are in general liable to be called upon for the amount standing to the credit of any Depositor, however long ago it may be that the last transaction took place on his account.

The following is from a return recently published, "shewing the number of accounts, and the total amount at the credit of such accounts, in Savings Banks, in respect of which no withdrawal has taken place, nor any payment been made in, by Depositors during the ten years ending the 20th day of November, 1858."

TABLE C.

TOTAL, UNITED KINGDOM.

Male.		Female.		Trust Accounts.		Total.	
No.	Amount.	No.	Amount.	No.	Amount.	No.	Amount.
35,691	264,306	27,643	269,717	8,620	114,329	71,954	648,352

In the returns from some of the Savings Banks to the order of the House of Commons it is stated, that although on some of the accounts no payment has been made in, nor any money withdrawn, during the ten years, yet in many cases the Depositors have produced their deposit-books, in order that the interest might be written therein to the credit of the accounts.

44.—It has, however, been contended that a period should be fixed when *future interest* on deposits unclaimed may go towards liquidating the expenses of the bank;—reserving

---

* [See Section on American Banks in the Introduction for some curious particulars respecting unclaimed deposits.]

intact not only the principal, but all interest accrued up to the date specified.*

This is done in the *Stockholm* and other foreign Savings Banks.

Section 10.—*As to Expenses.*

ART. 45.—The figures given† below shew that the total expenses of all the banks in the United Kingdom (except fifteen, which have made no returns) amount to £119,790 a-year, which, compared with the capital invested on 20th November 1857—£34,377,392—is equal to 7s. per cent., thus reducing the available interest allowed by the Government to £2.18s. per cent.

This is the average rate, but many banks are obliged to give less interest to their Depositors, in consequence of their expenses exceeding considerably the amount which the 7s. per cent. would produce. In only thirty-eight banks is the full rate of £3.0s. 10d. allowed to the Depositors.

46.—Sir Alexander Spearman remarks that by some means or other it happens that all the Savings Banks in the country are self-

---

* [In some banks it is provided "that a deposit, if unclaimed for six years after the *death* of the Depositor, shall be forfeited." In the Chichester and Coleraine Banks, all sums unclaimed for seven years after notice given in the county papers, are transferred to the Surplus Fund.]

†

Table D.	No. of Banks 20th Nov. 1857.	Number of Accounts. 20th Nov. 1857.	Amount due to Depositors on 20th Nov. 1857.	Total paid for Salaries during year ending 20th Nov. 1857.	Average to each Bank.	Total Expenses for year ending 20th Nov. 1857.	Average to each Bank.	Aver. to each Deposit Acct. s. d.	Per centage of amount due to Depositors. s. d.
England and Wales.	504	1,165,350	30,850,911	75,750	150	104,194	207	1 9	6 9
Scotland	46	114,735	1,776,901	5,270	115	7,364	160	1 3	8 3
Ireland	51	57,723	1,749,580	5,782	113	8,232	162	2 10	9 5
Channel Islands	2	15,023	403,203	1,005	—	1,205	—	—	5 11
Total, United Kingdom	603	1,352,834	34,780,595	87,807	145	120,995	201	1 9	7 0

The Expenses of management of the Paris Savings Bank amount to 17s. 10d. per cent. of the capital. *See Report of its operations,* 1859.

supporting; but it does not of course follow that the power of self-support is derived in all cases from the difference of interest received and paid.

In some instances they are able to make both ends meet by obtaining gratuitous assistance, and thus economizing in the way of salaries; parties who have other occupation in the immediate neighbourhood accepting smaller stipends for the performance of the duties. Sir Alexander Spearman testified, from his own knowledge, that there were more banks than one in the United Kingdom in which the arrangement with their officers was, that they should receive for remuneration just the amount of the difference of interest, whatever that might be, and themselves pay the bank expenses of management. (Qu. 555, 556.)

In other cases the excess of expenditure is met by certain casual sources of profit, such as—the interest accruing on all sums under £1, and upon the shillings and pence in sums exceeding £1; the interest upon deposits exceeding £200, which cease then to be credited with any by the bank; the fractional parts of a penny, &c. (See Art 41.) In the Moorfields Bank, according to the testimony of Mr. Saintsbury* the Actuary

---

* [His Expenditure for the year 1857 was 10s. 10d. per cent. on capital; of this 1s. 3d. was exceptional. Reserve kept for expenses 7s. 6d. per cent. the difference between this and the 10s. 10d. being supplied from sundry small and casual sources of profit. Interest paid to Depositors, £2. 17s. 6d. The surplus of interest received over that paid in 1857 was reserved to meet the current expenses of 1858, and in the same way a year's income is always kept in advance. Number of open accounts not exceeding £1, on 20th November 1857, 16,555.—The St. Martin's Place Bank pays £2.18s. 4d.: its average of deposits is £30; that of the Moorfields Bank is under £18. Number of dormant accounts 7421. (Qu. 1823, 1832, 1860, 1861).

Mr. Boodle, Comptroller of the St. Martin's Place Institution, states that there, as in the majority of Savings Banks, although deposits of 1s. are received, no interest is allowed except upon even sums of pounds. The interest is calculated by a weekly rate, from printed tables. (Qu. 737—740.)]

(Qu. 1798—1803), these items produced no less than 3s. 4d. per cent. on the capital in the year 1857.

47.—The question of expenses is one very difficult of adjustment. *Cæteris paribus*, large banks are proportionately less expensive than small ones, and country banks than town ones. But there are many circumstances which vary this rule in practice. The number of operations of deposit and withdrawal upon equal amounts of capital have been vastly different in different banks, and it is under this head that the inequality of the present Government fixed allowance per cent. principally arises; the returns, however, shew that, when they are compared with the expenses, every transaction, on the average, costs rather more than 1s. Thus by the return for 1857 (published Oct. 1859) it appears that the total number of receipts from Depositors in Great Britain and Ireland, during the year, was 1,559,607; the total number of withdrawals by the Depositors, 812,488; making the aggregate number of operations, 2,372,095; while the total expenses of management of the banks, during the year, was £120,995.4s. 9d., giving an average cost for every operation of 1s. 0¼d. This arises from the fact that, whatever be the amount of deposits in a bank, a *large portion of the annual expenditure must remain the same irrespective of the number of accounts operated upon in the year, in order to keep together a proper staff.†

---

* [Mr. Craig of the Cork Bank remarked to the Committee that, "if you allow a man to deposit a shilling, which costs the bank a shilling, it amounts to this, that the manager might as well say to him, 'There is a shilling for you; pray do not come here again.'" Even if the deposit were £30—the highest amount allowed to be lodged in a Savings Bank within twelve months—the 4s. 2d. per cent. would only amount to 1s. 3d. in the year; and if the £30 were withdrawn at the end of the twelve months, with 18s. 3d. interest (*i. e.* at the rate of £3.0s. 10d. per cent.) the bank would still be a loser to the extent of 9d.]

† [In the Moorfields Bank out of 50,000 accounts, 30,000 do not pay the expenses of working (Evidence of Mr. Saintsbury, Qu. 1861).

Mr. Meikle, of the Glasgow Bank, says (Qu. 2295—2297), that in nine

48.—The foregoing is the cause of the desire of bank managers that the annual and total limit of the amount of deposits should be fixed as high as possible, *because the profit margin on the interest available for expenses is thereby increased.* For Example, on £5000 of deposits, the margin at the rate of 4s. 2d. per cent. is only £10 . 8s. 4d., whereas, on £100,000 it is £208 . 6s. 8d., or twenty times as much; in other words, 1000 Depositors of £100 each produce to the bank £208 a-year towards the payment of its staff and other expenses, while the same number of £5 depositors would contribute only £10. Moreover, on large deposits there is not so much trouble given to the officials, in the shape of frequent payments in and payments out, as is found to be attendant on the smaller: so that if, as has been proposed by some, the limit were reduced, with the view of keeping out those who are in more easy circumstances, the allowance for expenses would be very much lessened, whilst the labour and efficiency of the office staff could not be relatively diminished. The trouble of attending to each entry, in and out, for the £5 Depositors, is at least as great, if not greater, than that for the £100 ones; and when, as is too often the case, those who make the lesser deposits possess a minor

---

of the principal Savings Banks the Depositors whose balances do not exceed £30, occasion a loss to the banks of £11,000 a-year, while the other deposit-accounts contribute an annual profit of £14,000.

Sir Alexander Spearman stated in his evidence (Qu. 550—552) :—

"The profit in a Savings Bank is mainly derived from the higher class of deposits. There is very little doubt, that if a reduction were made in the amount of deposit, it would affect the difference of interest in the hands of the Trustees to enable them to pay their officers. I dare say many of the smaller banks in the kingdom have stated that, if the limiting amount of single deposits were to be seriously reduced, they would, in all probability, be compelled to close their banks."

In the St. Marylebone Bank (Evidence of Mr. Douglas Finney, Actuary), the expenses of management are 12s. 8d. per cent., or 1s. 10d. per account, in consequence of the number of small Depositors. (Qu. 2977—2979, 2986.)]

degree of information and intelligence, more time is taken up in explaining to the Depositors the regulations of the bank than when the amounts are larger.

49.—From this it will be seen that the present mode of providing for the expenses is open to the grave objection that it starves the most useful class of banks, viz. those which attract numerous small Depositors, while it unduly rewards those which attract large Depositors; and unless the cost of managing the banks can be otherwise provided for, some other system should be adopted, such as that proposed by Mr. Meikle, of making the margin for expenses dependent, not only on the amount of capital, but on the number of accounts open—and that in the proportions of $\frac{1}{2}$ and $\frac{2}{3}$—by allowing the bank, say 2s. 2d. per cent. (instead of 4s. 2d.), of capital, and 1s. 1d. per account.

Mr. G. Saintsbury (Qu. 2042, 15 April 1858) also said: -

"The per-centage upon the capital is not a safe criterion as to the comparative economy of management, for this obvious reason, that if we or any other bank had a run upon us which reduced our capital from £900,000, which it is, to £450,000, the per-centage, at present 10s., would immediately become a per-centage of 20s.; and it would not even stop there, because a run like that would involve probably the doubling of our establishment, in order to enable us to pay everybody that came. Seeing, therefore, that there is that fallacy in testing the expenses by capital, I have looked to find a more legitimate test; and it does appear to me that a more legitimate test is that of the expense per account. Looking at the expense per account, a deposit of 5s. is as expensive to us as a deposit of £30; and, indeed, it is considerably more expensive. Now it is obvious that the expense we should incur with a 5s. account, and the amount which a 5s. account would contribute to the general capital, is so disproportionate to the £30, that those banks that enjoy a higher average receipt than we do must of necessity show a lower per-centage of expense.

I have looked into two other banks' accounts. The Manchester Bank was especially mentioned at the last meeting of the Committee. I find that their average of deposit accounts is £25.1s. 6d.; the St. Martin's Place average is £27.17s. 2d.; our own (Blomfield Street) average is £17.13s. 11d.: the difference of average is therefore so great, that to compare an expenditure as against £17 with an expenditure as against £27, must be unfairly to the disadvantage of the smaller amount. Looking, then, to see what test would be fair, it does appear to me that the expense per account is very much nearer to a just standard, because there as many accounts as you have to work on, so much labour you have, and so many persons you have to keep to work them. I find by that test it comes out thus: the Manchester Bank shews an average expense of 1s. 3¾d. per account; the St. Martin's Place Bank, 2s. 0½d. per account, and peculiar circumstances, with reference to a recent great change there, ought, for fair comparison, to make it 2s. 3d.; the Blomfield Street Bank, 1s. 9d. I find, also, that Liverpool is 2s. 5¼d.; Cork is 3s. 2d. per account, and the Cork Bank, though standing deservedly high, does not give to its Depositors the material guarantee which we give of a contribution to the separate surplus fund, which is so much capital yielding us no interest."

In the St. Marylebone Bank the plan is adopted of allowing only 2 per cent. interest on deposits under £30, and £2.17s. 4¾d. on higher sums: the number of accounts in the first class is 19,454, average £4.9s. 4¾d.; and notwithstanding the difference of interest, there is a loss of 8¾d. on each of the smaller, and a gain of 5s. 0¼d. on each of the larger accounts. (Evidence of Mr. Douglas Finney, qu. 3026—3036).

50.—*Expenses of National Debt Commissioners.*—A certain amount of incidental expenses, as postage, salary to barrister and clerk, &c., are annually paid out of the Savings Banks Fund by the National Debt Commissioners, and have been included since 1850, in the returns presented to Parliament.

The following are the annual amounts:—

		£	s.	d.
1850	paid	814	13	6
1851	,,	704	2	1
1852	,,	648	19	6
1853	,,	626	7	1
1854	,,	821	7	3
1855	,,	738	6	9
1856	,,	616	12	2
1857	,,	626	16	3

From a statement put in by Sir Alexander Spearman, it appears that the total since 1817 (to 20th November 1857) paid under the head of " Incidental Expenses" is £15,243 · 2s. 2d.

51.—*The particulars in the annexed Table E are extracted from the Returns to the 20th November, 1856, relating only to 590 out of the 597 in existence at that date, the remaining seven not having sent in the information required by the House of Commons.*

It is the only complete return relating to the expenditure of Savings Banks.

Additional partial information is furnished by the returns to 20th November 1858, published 31st December 1859, giving a total of 606 Banks, 9 of which have sent no information. It appears that:—

St. Martin's Place retains its position at the head, with 53,735 Depositors and £1,524,839 deposits. Bishopsgate has 50,293 Depositors and only £932,484 deposited.

Manchester 41,398, accounts amounting to £1,030,705. Exeter 37,476 Depositors and £1,007,572 deposits, besides £21,587 Consols, bought under the powers of 9 Geo. IV. c. 92. s. 12.

Liverpool rises to the seventh place on the list, and Marylebone sinks to the tenth, the number of accounts being returned as only 20,774, although the amount in deposit has increased to £351,878.

(46)

TABLE E.

From Returns to the 20th November, 1856.

No. of Accounts remaining op. 20 Nov. 1856.	Name or Number of Bank.	Total Amount owing to Depositors.	Average for each Bank.	Av. Salary of chief officer of each Bank.	Annual Expenses.				Separate Surplus.			Rate of Interest paid.
					Total.	Average.	PerAccount.	Per ct. of Capital	Total.	Average.		
		£			£	£	s. d.	s. d.	£	£		£ s. d.
49,209	St. Martin's Place.	1,411,741		770	5,864		2 5	8 2	(b)8,500			2 18 4
48,799	Bishopsgate	916,911		491	4,038		1 8	8 8½	5,000			2 17 6
38,239	Manchester	952,856	with more than 20,000 Depositors. £749,015	700	2,181		1 1	5 0	7,000	£3,994		3 0 0
36,602	Exeter	1,014,497		400	2,700	£2,749	1 6	5 0	2,713			3 0 9½
33,287	Glasgow	680,485		500	1,956		1 2	6 5	..			3 0 0
26,435	Edinburgh	437,148		300	2,123		1 7	6 11¼	600			3 2 17
24,457	Birmingham	438,131		500	1,524		1 3	12 5¼	..			3 (a)
23,423	Marylebone	346,410		604	2,164		1 10	7 7	14,726			3 0 0
23,282	Liverpool	739,485		408	2,846		2 5	7 8	1,400			2 18 4
21,956	(Montague St. Bloomsbury.)	552,490		650	2,096		1 11	7 5				
10,000 & und.	12	3,774,954	314,579	293	12,161	1,013	1 7	6 5	55,614	4,634		
20,000												
5,000 & und.	29	5,040,129	173,797	248	14,955	516	1 6	5 11	67,907	2,342		
10,000												
100 & und.	528	18,457,466	34,957	..	63,295	119	1 11	6 10	179,145	339		
5,000												
99	Bermondsey, opd.July 7,1856	127	with less than 100 Depositors, £749	30	1		0 4	16 2	..	(a)		2 10 0
91	Ballinasloe	2,337		14	20		4 3	5 9½	111			2 15 0
84	Gorey	1,886		4	5		1 4	13 8				2 15 0
83	Tenby	1,383		5	19		4 8	0 1¼				2 15 3
80	(Nuneaton opd.Ap.7, 1856)	602		20		£5	..	..	(a)			
65	Melbourne	591		5	7		2 4	..	..			2 18 4
52	Newton	530		..	1		0 5	..	..			2 17 0
51	Seaham Harbour	274		..	..		..	..	..			3 0 0
27	Staveley	200		..	..		..	..	..			3 0 0
25	Bedlington	115		..	..		..	..	..			2 18 4
13	Kilrea	195		..	..		..	..	..			2 18 4
Total	590	34,760,933	58,226	..	117,956	198	1 8	6 9	312,716	574		

(a) See art. 40, and note thereto, where the figures are brought down to 1858.
(b) This bank also possesses £5411 in 3 per cents (reduced), and £200 in the Bank of England.

PART II.

OF

FRAUDS IN SAVINGS BANKS;

THEIR EVIL CONSEQUENCES

AND THE REMEDIES.

CONTENTS OF PART II.

CHAP. III. *Defects in the Management of Savings Banks.*

	PAGE
§ 1. Remarks upon the Frauds on Savings Banks	49
§ 2. Extent of the Frauds	55
§ 3. As to the Remarkable Cases of Fraud	59
I. The Cuffe Street Fraud	60
II. The Tralee Fraud	64
III. The Rochdale Fraud	65
IV. The Brighton Fraud	68
V. The Reading Fraud	69
§ 4. Belief of the Public that the Banks had Government Security	70

CHAP. IV. *The Remedy*—In the appointment of Government Inspectors and Auditors, with the guarantee of the State for Sávings Bank Deposits

§ 1. As to what is really desirable	76
§ 2. As to the attempts at Legislation, 1850 to 1857	78
§ 3. As to Government Inspection	81
§ 4. As to Government Treasurers	84

CHAP. V. *As to Improvements in the Internal Management of Savings Banks* - 90

CHAP. VI. *As to sundry points of Internal Management* - 101

CHAPTER III.

DEFECTS IN THE MANAGEMENT OF SAVINGS BANKS

Section 1.—Remarks upon the Frauds on Savings Banks.

ART. 1.—The title of this chapter brings us to the consideration of those painful frauds, which, following close upon each other, have been discovered during the last ten or twelve years to have been perpetrated in so many Savings Banks, and have caused so much distress in various parts of the kingdom. The system of internal management and supervision which was applicable to these institutions, during the early years of their existence, has been found in many respects inadequate for their safe guidance, now that they have progressed to a gigantic maturity.

With the detection of the frauds which we shall proceed to describe, came the discovery of the disheartening fact, that the zeal and earnestness of the promoters of these excellent institutions—as too frequently is the case in voluntary benevolent associations—had become slackened by degrees, and that no such regular and continuous attention had been bestowed upon their inner management, as would be indispensable for the security of the depositors; so that many unfortunate persons, without any fault of their own, have been, in consequence of the reliance they had placed on the stability of the Savings Bank, reduced to a state of destitution.

2.—The earliest important cases, that awakened public indignation, came to light in the years 1848 to 1851.

It was then ascertained that a great number of Actuaries, both in this country and in Ireland, had appropriated to their private uses the funds entrusted to the Savings Bank, instead of placing them, as the law requires, in the hands of the proper Government Receivers in London or Dublin. Numbers of poor and industrious persons found themselves thus suddenly deprived of the savings they had set aside with much patience and self-denial, and were informed that their ruin was caused by the dishonesty of those very officials whom they had been taught to trust with implicit confidence, and whom, from the countenance given them by Honorary Trustees and Managers of influence and high position, they seemed in every way justified in so trusting.

From these cases it became known to the dismay of many, and to the surprise of all, that the Trustees of these Savings Banks,—these gentlemen of wealth, distinction, or repute, to whom, by the rules, the sole control had been reserved,—were in no way *legally* responsible for the money which they had undertaken to receive through their Actuary; and that the Government of this country, which was popularly supposed to have guaranteed the safety of all the deposits the moment they were paid into the Bank, was really answerable only for the sums that might have been paid over to its custody.

The Actuary was discovered to be the only party practically charged with the safe keeping of the money; and he was the very man who had made away with it. It is true that he had (under 7 & 8 Vict. c. 83. s. 17.) to find sureties before obtaining his appointment; but these sureties were bound for very much smaller sums than* the defalcations

---

* [In the Dublin case, the Actuary embezzled £20,000, (which increased afterwards to £56,000), but the security he had given was only for £1000. In the Tralee case, the defalcations amounted to £36,000; and in Killarney, to £20,000; and the securities given by the defaulting Actuaries were trifles in comparison with these amounts.]

amounted to; arising as they did from continuous and systematic fraud.

3.—Since the year 1817, it was found that the Government had made itself responsible for the safe custody of such monies as were transmitted to the National Debt Commissioners, but for nothing more. It did not under the then existing law, (nor could it under the present) take upon itself any losses which might occur from the misfeasance or neglect of parties whom it did not appoint, and over whom it had no control. Moreover, *by the Act of* 1828, *the liability of the Trustees of the Banks, was confined to instances of wilful neglect or fraud on their part, and in* 1844,* *even that liability was removed,* unless they should specially sign an undertaking to be liable for an agreed amount.

4.—This great defect in the Law only added to the increasing tendency of Trustees and Managers to neglect their duties. In the majority of instances they soon ceased to give any

---

* [Section 6. of the Act of 7 & 8 Vict. c. 83. is as follows:—

"Be it enacted, That no Trustee or Manager of any Savings Bank shall be liable to make good any Deficiency which may hereafter arise in the Funds of any Savings Bank, unless such persons shall have respectively declared, by writing under their hands, and deposited with the Commissioners for the Reduction of the National Debt, that they are willing so to be answerable; and it shall be lawful for each of such Persons, or for such Persons collectively, to limit his or their responsibility to such sum as shall be specified in any such Instrument: Provided always, that the Trustee and Manager of any such Institution shall be, and is hereby declared to be personally responsible and liable for all monies actually received by him on account of, or to, and for the use of such Institution, and not paid over or disposed of in the manner directed by the Rules of the said Institution; and an Abstract of the above Provisions shall be enrolled as one of the Rules of the Institution."

IN IRELAND THE MINIMUM OF RESPONSIBILITY is fixed by the Act of 1848, at £100 to each Manager or Trustee. This, of course, is inadequate to provide for any extensive fraud. In the present Dublin Savings Bank (Abbey Street) there are forty-eight Trustees and Managers, and the whole £4800 to which their responsibility amounts is not 10 per cent. of the loss in the Cuffe Street Bank.]

regular attention to the Banks, and left them wholly to the Actuary or Clerk, so that any real check upon his conduct came to an end, and—as if such laxity needed any extension—the Trustees in certain establishments, which enjoyed the reputation of being by no means ill-managed, were in the habit of signing blank forms and Cheques, to be filled up by the nominally acting Manager at his sole discretion, without providing any restraint upon his conduct with reference to them.

5.—The Legislature, in addition, as if to encourage one fruitful source of fraud, actually gave its express sanction to irregular practices,* by inserting in the 7 & 8 Vict. c. 83. s. 4. the following clause—

> "*If any Actuary or other Officer shall receive money out of Bank hours, and shall not, the next time the Bank is open, pay it over to the Treasurer or proper Officer, he shall be guilty of a misdemeanour.*"

Thus, instead of public prohibition under some severe penalty, of the Actuary's receiving any Deposits whatever out of Bank hours, here was a positive recognition and distinct sanction of the very practice by which the largest and longest-undetected systems of fraud† have been carried on.

6.—The discovery of these frauds has created a feeling of distrust in the minds of Depositors in all Savings Banks, and

---

* [See remarks on Trust accounts in Part IV.]

† [In the case of the *Ongar* Savings Bank, "unbounded confidence had been placed in Richardson, the defaulting Actuary, both by the Managers of the Bank and by the public, and it was from the shelter which this afforded him, that he was enabled to escape that rigid and zealous examination, which must otherwise, in an early stage, have detected his nefarious proceedings. After the banking hours were over, many persons paid him their savings with as much sense of security as if they had been placed in the hands of the Receiving Manager during the banking hours, and with these he had, of course, an almost unlimited scope for fraud."]

has greatly shaken their credit. It has elicited, moreover, strong and general expressions of opinion that the working-classes have not been quite fairly dealt with in the matter; and that the nominal Managers and Trustees, on the faith of whose character for vigilance and integrity the poor had committed their little property to the Banks, had no moral right to be thus exempt from all legal responsibility. In the forcible words of Mr. *Greg, the Depositors naturally asked, "To whom did we entrust our money, if not to the " gentlemen whose names were published as Managers of the " Institution, and to the Government, which, we are told, " had, by the Act of Parliament, constituted itself receiver of " the funds? As to the Receiving Clerk, we did not appoint " him; we know nothing of him; and we never conceived " that we were to look upon him as our banker."

7.—The practical discouragements to the virtue of economy, which have resulted from these disasters, can be appreciated only by those who have come into close contact with the operative poor. Every defaulting Savings Bank has been a sermon on the folly of frugality not easily to be forgotten;† and these lessons have multiplied with a fearful rapidity, and been delivered with a most mischievous emphasis.

---

* [See his admirable pamphlet on *Industrial Investments*, 1852.]

† [Mr. Justin Supple, of Tralee, in his evidence before the Committee of 1848, in answer to the question, "Can you state, from the general feeling of the country, what evil consequence will be the necessary result of this failure?" said, "Taking this failure in connection with the fears of famine, which have been upon the people for the last two or three years, I think the consequence will be to drive the class, which have been hitherto industrious and economical in their habits, into vice and wickedness, because the dissipated characters who have saved nothing, now look upon the poor industrious creature who has been cheated, laugh at him, and tell him they have spent their own money, while the industrious man has had somebody else to spend his for him."—Report No. 21, 1849. qu. 878.]

"Why should I save?" asks the jovial footman in Mr Greg's pamphlet; "my fellow-servant, the butler, pinched "himself in every conceivable fashion, earned the character of "a niggard and a miser, that he might store up a couple "of hundred pounds to set up a shop and marry upon. "He invested it in the Rochdale Savings Bank: the Manager "made away with £70,000 of the funds entrusted to him; "the Trustees, it seems, are not answerable for the defalcations; "and I have now the satisfaction of knowing that my fellow- "servant is as poor as myself, and that all his long years "of self-denial have been thrown away." Such cases as these are neither imaginary nor few. They come before us in scores and in hundreds, and are terribly eloquent in the praise of self-indulgence and improvidence.

8.—Little evidence is required of the frauds having been productive of distress of the most serious kind.*

The Depositors of the St. Peter's Parish, or *Cuffe Street Savings Bank*, Dublin, stated, in an address to the Lord Lieutenant, in 1849, that "in consequence of its failure, the

---

* [In the debate on the Savings Bank measure of 1850, Mr. H. A. Herbert, a Member of the Parliamentary Committees on Savings Banks in 1848 and 1849, in alluding to the case of the Tralee Bank, said—" Here was a case where a number of industrious persons had been reduced to the most deplorable state of beggary and destitution, not through any fault of their own, but actually owing to their possession of those qualities which it was the duty of every good Government to foster and encourage, in consequence of their habits of temperance, industry, and self-reliance. What was the use of preaching to the poor the duty of being honest, industrious, and self-dependent, if the fruits of their hard earnings were thus to be swept away? He had witnessed the sufferings of these people; he had seen in the workhouse people who had spent a life of toil, and never dreamed of being compelled to seek parochial relief; he had seen one who, with a hardy spirit, asked if there were any chance of justice being wrung from the Government; and another who had lost his intellect in consequence of the shock occasioned by the failure of one of these Banks."]

Poorhouse had become the reluctant asylum of the industrious mechanic and his family; that many a heart had been broken; and, in not a few instances, even premature death had been the result."

Section 2.—*Extent of the Frauds.*

Art. 9.—From the Parliamentary returns, which were published in the Sessions of 1852 and 1857 respectively, and from communications addressed to us through the Friendly Societies' Institute, we have been enabled to obtain an estimate that may be relied on, as to the amount of loss that has been sustained by Savings Banks, not only through those defalcations which have come to the knowledge of the National-Debt Commissioners, and thus been made public, but through others that would have been equally losses had they not been made good by the Trustees and Managers. The frauds made *public* amount to £229,482.

The first of the above returns includes a period of seven years, namely, from 1844 to 1851, and contains the following statement :—

" The Commissioners for the Reduction of the National Debt, having no authority by law to examine into the accounts of the transactions of Savings Banks with Depositors therein, nor any legal title to call for and compare the books of Depositors with the ledgers and account-books of Savings Banks, there are no records in this department from which any account could be prepared, so as to shew whether in any of the cases deficiencies had occurred, and losses been sustained, by the Depositors, and if so, to what extent.

* [Return 1852 . . .	£159,557
,, 1857 . . .	13,925
Cuffe Street . . .	56,000
Total Frauds . . .	£229,482]

" To procure such information, however, as far as was possible, a copy of the order has been addressed to some one or other of the Trustees formerly connected with the discontinued Banks."

10.—This return shews that, although the amount of voluntary subscriptions towards the relief of the Depositors amounted to £26,220, there still had arisen, during the short period of seven years, a net loss to the Depositors of £109,452, exclusive of the gigantic Dublin case, which exceeded £56,000.

The average *discovered* annual loss by defalcations, as far as could be ascertained by the Commissioners, during the seven years from 1844 to 1851, was upwards of £27,000.

The following is an abstract of the 1852 return:—

Name of Bank.	Total ascertained Defalcation.	Loss sustained by Depositors.
	£	£
GREAT BRITAIN:		
Woolwich Dockyard	2	0
Highgate	700	0
Spilsby	3,213	2,436
Mitcham	5,600	0
Rochdale	71,715	37,433
Monquhitter	336	0
Poole	6,221	5,663
St. Helen's	12,932	6,680
Reeth	230	147
Upper Albany Street (about)	250	0
Newtown	180	160
Carried forward	101,379	52,539

---

* [The following is the Balance Sheet of the Poole Savings Bank, on the 12th August 1850, as prepared by the eminent Accountant, Mr. Grey, who was one of the Commissioners appointed to apportion the Parliamentary Grant in the Cuffe Street case:—

LIABILITIES.

Amount due (including interest to 20th May 1850) to
862 Depositors, whose pass-books have been produced, £34,860 18 5
Ditto to 56 Depositors, whose pass-books have not
been produced 634 2 1

Total Liabilities £35,495 0 6]

Name of Bank.	Total ascertained Defalcation.	Loss sustained by Depositors.
Brought forward	£ 101,379	£ 52,539
IRELAND:		
Kilkeel	976	976
Tralee	36,000	36,000
Killarney	20,370	19,105
Nenagh	832	832
Mallow	No Returns.	
Castle Townsend	No Returns.	
Cuffe Street, Dublin	See forward.	
	159,557	109,452

In Ireland there are about 50 Banks, and 4 have failed. In Scotland the only known defalcation has been at Auchterarder.*

ASSETS (POOLE SAVINGS BANK).

Amount invested on General Account
  with the N. D. C. (including interest to 20th May 1850 . £28,513 8 11
Amount invested as *Surplus Fund*,
  on which no interest is payable . 535 3 3
                                    ─────────────
                                    £29,048 12 2
Amount in the Treasurer's hand . . 224 19 6
                                    ─────────────
Total Assets £29,273 11 8

Deficiency . . . . . £ 6,221 8 10

In the Parliamentary Blue Book there seems to have been omitted the special report of Mr. W. H. Grey on the affairs of the Poole Savings Bank, although it was one of those ordered by the House of Commons to be printed. We have, however, been favoured by that gentleman with a copy, from which the above is taken.]

* [This was a Branch of the Perth Bank. The frauds amounted to between £1300 and £1400, and were effected by short entries in the books of monies received of Depositors, and by overentries in the same books of monies paid to Depositors, spreading over a period of two years, (qu. 2943.) By a subscription among the local Trustees, the deficiency was reduced to £430; and eventually, in 1848, the Depositors were paid off at the rate of 18s. in the pound. (Evidence of Mr. Jameson, qu. 2901—2906.)]

11.—The second return, dated 4th June 1857, describes 11 defalcations, discovered during a period of 6 years, as follows:—

Name of Bank.	Total ascertained Defalcation	Loss sustained by Depositors.
	£	£
Ongar (Branch of Romford Bank)	690	0
Dunmow	16	0
Isle of Wight	8,156	7,850
Runcorn	98	0
Bradford, Wilts	400	0
Southport	200	0
Yoxall and Barton	200	0
Rugby	1,438	0
West London	1,106	0
Bromley	932	0
Leicester	689	0
	£13,925	£7,850

From this return, it appears that in the 6 years (1851—1857) £2715 was voluntarily subscribed to meet the defalcations of Actuaries, &c., and that the total embezzlements *discovered* averaged £2321 a year. In the instances of Dunmow, Bradford, Southport, and Leicester, the sureties of the defaulting Actuary paid up the deficiency.

12.—Numerous instances of fraud, originating in the absence of a proper system of audit and inspection, have escaped publicity through unwillingness on the part of the Trustees or Managers to destroy the confidence of Depositors in their Bank; and they have very naturally preferred the personal sacrifice necessary to make good the deficiency, to incurring the censure that would justly have been passed on the laxity of management which had rendered such frauds possible.

The sums so contributed by Trustees have occasionally been very large. In one instance, Mr. Hoare, the brewer, paid £7000; others have paid, some, £1000, some, £500.

In all cases but those returned to the Commissioners, and included in the Parliamentary Papers, as far as we have ascertained, whatever deficiency has taken place has been provided for by the voluntary subscriptions of the Trustees or their neighbours. The word *voluntary* is not applicable to the case of the Bank at Carnarvon, which failed in 1824, as at that time the Trustees were liable under the law for the whole amount of the Deposits.

To our own knowledge, however, more recent large defalcations in Wales have been made up in this manner.

Section. 3.—As to the Remarkable Cases of Fraud.

ART. 13.—In consequence of the public belief in Government responsibility to Savings Banks Depositors, various attempts were made to obtain indemnity at its hands. These were repeated in Parliament, but were of no use, except in one instance. The case of the frauds on the Cuffe Street Bank, in Dublin, partly from their extent, and partly because they were among the earliest that became known, caused such an expression of feeling and opinion on the subject, that the legislature made a special grant of £30,000 to assist the unfortunate Depositors, so as to return them about 10 shillings in the pound of their loss.

The extent of the frauds in this Bank, and the false position of the National Debt Commissioners with reference to it, gave rise to Committees of Investigation in the House of Commons upon the subject (in 1848 and 1849), and to the introduction of a Bill by the Chancellor of the Exchequer, Sir C. Wood, in 1850, for the better regulation of Savings Banks. The peculiarity of the Cuffe Street defalcations will, at all times, be worthy of special study, as a complicated instance of neglect and peculation, which may be said to comprise every species of individual fraud that has taken place in other institutions; nor will a study of the other cases prove to be without interest or advantage to Savings Bank officials, as an accurate knowledge of the circumstances of past frauds must be the first step towards preventing future ones.

It will also help our readers to discern the defects in the constitution of Savings Banks in general, and to follow our discussion of the most appropriate remedies, if we narrate the manner in which they became insolvent, beginning with the case in Dublin.

I.—*The Cuffe Street Fraud.*

Art. 14.—In 1818, according to an account given by Dr. Hancock, "the *St. Peter's Parish* Savings Bank was established in Cuffe Street, Dublin, and a Mr. Dunne, the parish sexton, was appointed cashier and book-keeper, at a salary of £5 a year. The Trustees and Managers of the Bank included some of the most influential and respectable of the inhabitants of Dublin. The late Archdeacon Torrens was a Trustee, and a surety for Mr. Dunne; the late Judge Johnson was also a Trustee; and the present Lord Chief Justice, then Sergeant Lefroy, was another.

"Under such influential patronage the Bank rose in importance, and large sums of money were lodged which must have amounted in 1831 to upwards of £100,000.

"In 1826 one of the Managers began to suspect that all was not right, and that Mr. Dunne was making away with some of the money. A dispute then commenced in the Committee of Management as to Mr. Dunne's character, and it took the Committee exactly five years to ascertain whether Mr. Dunne was worthy to be trusted or not.

"In February 1831, the defalcation was finally discovered, in a manner described by one of the Managers thus:—'I think the Board came to the decision that Mr. Dunne should not be continued, after an immense deal of battling for a year or two, and I think Mr. Dunne was got to resign. He had not many days resigned before an account came in, a pass-book was presented for payment, and on investigating and comparing it with the ledger, this account was found to be closed in the ledger though open in the pass-book, and Mr. Dunne then suddenly absconded.' The first step the Managers took on this event was a very proper one; they issued a notice of the Actuary having absconded, and called on the Depositors to produce their books. A number of claims at once appeared. They at first thought the defalcation would not amount to more than £1000: they soon found it to exceed £20,000.

"The Managers then proceeded to consult the Commissioners for reducing the National Debt, as to what they should do. They drew up a statement of what had happened; asking the Commissioners for advice and assistance; suggesting that a Commissioner should be appointed to inquire into the management of the Bank, and the cause of the frauds; and either remodel or close the Bank. This statement one of the Managers took to London, and on waiting on the Secretary of the Commissioners, was referred by him to Mr. Tidd Pratt, the barrister appointed to certify the rules of Savings Banks, and to act as arbitrator in all disputes between Depositors and Managers.

"This gentleman then filled, and still fills, an office in which judicial and executive functions are mingled. The Managers applied to him in his executive capacity, as law adviser of the Commissioners in matters relating to Savings Banks. He entertained their application in his judicial capacity; and offered to decide any disputes between the Managers and the Depositors, many of which had arisen as to the rights of parties who had entrusted their money to Mr. Dunne, but which had not been duly lodged by him. Mr. Pratt, accordingly proceeded to Dublin, in his judicial capacity, and awarded £7500 to be paid by the Managers. He also awarded that £4274 claimed was not a legal charge against the Managers, as that amount had been lodged with Mr. Dunne out of the Bank, and out of Bank hours. Taking a strictly judicial view of his duties, Mr. Pratt did not decide whether the Managers had been guilty of wilful neglect or default, as that question was not directly raised. But though, in this matter, he confined himself to acting in his judicial capacity, he offered advice in his executive capacity; firstly, that the £4274, which was not a legal charge on the funds of the institution, should be paid out of the future profits; and secondly, that the Managers ought to carry on the Bank, as the future surplus would realize enough to pay all deficiencies. The Bank was accordingly carried on; and the Managers, no doubt with a view of gaining confidence, did not wait for the future profits, but at once paid out of incoming deposits the £4274, which Mr. Pratt had decided was not a legal charge. They also, with a view to keep up their credit, omitted to post in the office the yearly statement of accounts, as required by the Act of Parliament, from 1831 till 1848. These accounts they furnished annually, however, to th Commissioners for the reduction of the National Debt; shewing, after 1832, in every year a deficiency. The Managers had asked Mr. Tidd Pratt whether the Commissioners would receive the accounts short, and he said they would."

The result was, that when the evil day at last came, in 1848, the deficiency, which had its origin in the £20,000 appropriated by Mr. Dunne, had grown to the enormous sum of £56,000.

15.—It also transpired that, in this Bank, the Acts of Parliament for the guidance of Savings Banks, and the Rules of the Bank founded on the same, had been violated to a very considerable extent:—

1. In receiving from individuals sums exceeding £30 (in some cases even more than £200) in one year.
2. In receiving sums exceeding £150 in the whole.
3. In allowing interest on accounts exceeding £200.
4. In receiving re-lodgments of a large amount.
5. In opening accounts without calling upon Depositors to sign the Declaration required by Act of Parliament.
6. In opening second accounts for the same individuals.
7. In failing publicly to affix and exhibit in the office, as directed, the annual statement of the bank, with a list of the Trustees and Managers.

8. In refusing to supply to Depositors a copy of the said annual statement, and list of Trustees and Managers.
9. In failing to observe the requirements of 7 & 8 Vict. c. 83. s. 6., by omitting to place an Abstract thereof amongst the Rules of the institution.
10. In receiving from a charitable institution, in a period of four years, sums exceeding £2000 in the whole, (the legal limits at that time being £100 *per annum*, and £300 in the whole.)
11. In paying money to Depositors without taking any receipt whatever for the money so paid; thus opening a door to fraud, without supplying any adequate means for detecting it.

16.—It may be mentioned further—and to this we draw the special attention of our readers—that in the returns of Depositors in the Cuffe Street Bank, supplied from year to year to the National Debt Office, there were numerous absurd discrepancies that can have escaped notice only because it was nobody's business to attend to them; for instance—

Year ending 20th Nov., 1831.

Depositors *above* £20 and not exceeding £50—
  Number 1066
  Amount £16,835
when the amount must have been at least £21,320.

1840.—Depositors *above* £200 . . 4
  Amount £793

1847.—*Above* £100 and not exceeding £150—
  Depositors 320
  Amount Deposited . . £13,173
instead of £32,000, at least!

II.—*The Tralee Fraud.*

ART. 17.—In the case of the Tralee Savings Bank Fraud, which was discovered in 1848, the deficiency amounted to £36,000, and the defaulting Actuary was prosecuted, and sentenced to fourteen years' transportation.

Here, according to the Parliamentary evidence, fraud was committed—

"By representing certain accounts as closed that were not so; by receiving money in the absence of the Honorary Manager; and by falsifying the entries in the books. Thus—Supposing there were three depositors, A, B, and C. A would be put down as having paid £3, B as having paid £5, and C as having paid £7. By the close of the day there would have been a great many other Depositors, and perhaps the receipts would amount to £260. The fact is, A had paid £30, B had paid £15, and C had paid £27. It appeared that the books had been kept by the Actuary, with the proper amounts, that is, he had entered the proper amount in the ledger; but after the Manager had gone away, he had put a figure 0 after the 3, a figure 1 before the 5, and a figure 2 before the 7; so that on coming to cast up the total, if they had been properly audited, this fraud would have been discovered."

In this Bank the law regulating the amount of Deposits was entirely disregarded. The sum of £5000 was received in one amount from a Society called the *Irish Reproductive Loan Fund*.

18.—There was also a case of "a poor woman, who had £900 accumulated by the sale of old clothes: she had actually given notice for her money, and it was provided for her, and sent down to the Bank among the notices of the day upon that occasion; but Mr. Lynch, the Actuary, advised her to leave it where it was, and she lost it all."

It is also stated that "the Manager of the day used to tell the Depositors—

"'You cannot pay more than £30 in your own name,

but have you not a wife, or a child, or some relation?' and he would receive any amount they chose to invest, it being really and truly, and he knowing it to be, the money of the Depositor."

Very nearly the same remarks will apply to the Killarney Savings Bank, and to many others.

III —*The Rochdale Fraud.*

ART. 19.—In 1818, the Rochdale Savings Bank was established, and Mr. John Haworth was elected Actuary. At his death, his son, George Haworth, was appointed to the office, and he died in November 1849, having held the situation more than twenty years.

His character for honour and integrity was high in the estimation of all his employers.*:—

" He managed to deceive everybody by an appearance of wealth; he kept a carriage ; and any thing scientific or charitable, or any matter of that sort, he always patronised as far as he could, though not himself a particularly talented man.

" He did an extensive business in wool (the staple trade of the town) by selling it on commission : he was agent for Guinness, and one of the London houses, for the sale of porter. At the time of his death he was also agent to the Sun Fire Office ; he likewise acted as agent for two very large estates in Rochdale, and for sundry minor estates ; he was the valuer and receiver of rents for the Lancashire and Yorkshire Railway Company ; he was also a land agent, and he had a large cotton-mill.

" For honesty, probity, and wealth, there was no man in Rochdale who stood higher : and when surprise was expressed that he should officiate as Actuary to the Savings Bank, he represented that he did it merely as a matter of charity, and this was believed by everybody."

[* Evidence of Edward Taylor—qu. 3114.]

20.—Till his death there was not a suspicion of fraud or deficiency in the funds of the bank, but it was then immediately discovered that he had kept two sets of books—one set, purposely to deceive the Trustees and Managers. The deposit books were called in, and the claims by Depositors amounted to £100,403, to meet which there was only £28,686, in the Government Funds and the Treasurer's hands: *the Actuary having appropriated no less than* £71,717. His property, when sold, realised £16,000, and the Trustees and others subscribed £17,430, so that the loss to the Depositors is still £38,287.

Of the Depositors, 1014 were women; 191 sick clubs; 37 trust accounts; 539 labouring men; and 1184 under 21 years of age.

From a report in this case, it would appear that the fraud had been accomplished in the following manner:—

"Haworth, (according to an account published at the time,) acting both as Manager and Actuary, entered in one of the two sets of books the monies which he took to Mr. Royds, as Treasurer, while in the other set he entered those deposits which he appropriated to his own use; so that he became the treasurer of nearly two-thirds of the Deposits. Haworth picked the depositors, and generally entered in his private book those who had the largest sums invested, and who were generally bringing in money, and taking little out. In his ledger account, when he took any money from a Depositor, he wrote 'withdrawn,' naming the sum, and debiting himself in his cash-book with that amount. In Haworth's book, all the items which were not entered in the Trustee's ledger were distinguished by a mark, by which the eye might easily separate them from the other items. Had the Managers acted in rotation, as is the custom in other banks, to receive and repay Deposits, it would have been difficult to accomplish his purpose. It should, however, be stated that the Bank opened for four hours (an unusually long time) on Mondays and Saturdays, viz. from three to seven o'clock.

"The following is another instance of Haworth's cunning and

duplicity. A friendly society of ploughboys deposited on a given day £30, which was properly entered in the book, and laid before the Trustees, but shortly afterwards the Actuary erased the word 'deposited,' and substituted 'withdrawn,' at the same time placing the figure '1' before the '30,' thus making it appear that the Society, instead of depositing £30, had withdrawn £130. In one case, in which a lodge of Odd Fellows had deposited £30, the item was not carried into either of the Trustees' or Actuary's private ledger. The reason of this, it is supposed, was, that the Actuary was aware that such a Society is not recognised by law, and could have no legal claim upon the bank."

21.—Upon the discovery of the frauds the Depositors were called together* and informed of the position of the bank. They very generously resolved to make no distinction between the deposits which had been properly made and those irregular ones in respect of which the bank had no legal liability, to return in full those sums which had been paid in during the two days that the bank was open after the death of Haworth, and to wind up the Institution without litigation.

The result was a dividend of 12s. 6d. in the pound on all the Depositors' money. The deficiency was afterwards made up by the Government to those of the Depositors who had served in the *army* or *navy*, but to no others.

The moral effect of this distressing case is described by Mr. Taylor to be lamentable even yet in the case of young men and young women. "We will spend our money," the expression is, "rather than a George † Haworth shall have it."

---

* [Evidence of Mr. Edward Taylor, Chairman of the Depositors' Committee.—Qu. 3094—3106, Report of 1858.]

† [Haworth's astonishing proceedings in respect to the appointment of Managers cannot be passed over.

Mr. Taylor says (Qu. 3114 to 3120, 3179 to 3182):—

"The original Trustees and Managers being dead, he slowly introduced

No attempt has since been made to establish a new Savings Bank in Rochdale: and that at Heywood, in the neighbourhood, was closed entirely from the panic caused by this fraud.

IV.—*The Brighton Fraud.*

ART. 22.—The Frauds in this Bank amounted to between £3000 and £4000, and were discovered in the following manner:—

"At the annual meeting, one of the Managers rose, and said he was not satisfied with the balance-sheet; and he moved that the meeting should adjourn, for the purpose of examining the balance-sheet more thoroughly. This alarmed the Actuary (Mr. Buckoll), so much, that when he found the Managers were becoming active in the matter, and that they were going into the accounts, he decamped, leaving a letter stating that he had been

---

people—elected them himself in fact; and the manner in which he did it was, he put their names down in an Annual Report, but never let them know that they were made Managers. To take my own case: I have a Report here for 1838, in which my name is printed as a Manager; but I never was aware of the fact that I was a Manager till the bank failed. I never was at any meeting, and I was never called upon to attend any meeting, and I can name several others in the same way. I will take another case, which occurred to a gentleman named Chadwick. George Haworth said to him as he was passing, 'I want thee,' (he was a member of the Society of Friends): wilt thou come in and sign a return?' Mr. Chadwick said, 'I cannot, I have nothing to do with the bank.' 'Oh, but thou art a Manager,' said George Haworth, shewing him his name: he then got him to look at the accounts, which Mr. Chadwick verified, and put his initials to every item; and when he had done that, Mr. Haworth said, "Now, if thou wilt take that paper, I will call over the items,' which he did from another paper. Having done that, 'Now,' he said, 'thou wilt have to sign this;' and Mr. Chadwick did it, and believed he was signing the duplicate paper of that which he had examined; but it was discovered afterwards that Haworth had substituted a falsified return."

"I know of another instance, in which he waited on a gentleman with a view to get him to be a Trustee: the gentleman said, 'I do not like it:

unworthy of the position he had filled. The frauds were committed by means of false entries in the pass-books, and corresponding false entries in the ledgers, extending over a period of seven years: the Actuary would also call upon his friends, and represent that a poor Depositor wished to withdraw so much money from the bank that he himself could not act as agent for the Depositor, and would Mr. So-and-so oblige him by attending to receive the money for the Depositor who could not attend."—(Evidence of Mr. W. Hatton, qu. 3236 to 3278).

Ultimately the deficiency was made up, £3000 having belonged to the "Separate Surplus Fund," and £600 being obtained from Mr. Buckoll's sureties.

V.—*The Reading Fraud.*

ART. 23.—In 1842, suspicions were excited among the Managers of this bank as to the conduct of their Secretary and Accountant, and an investigation was set on foot, revealing a deficiency of about £3000.

" A portion of this the Secretary was allowed to refund; the remainder was raised by subscription among the Trustees and Managers, Mr. Richard Benyon de Beauvoir giving £1000. This occurred before 1844, while the Trustees and Managers had still a personal responsibility."—(Evidence of Mr. Hatton, qu. 3299 to 3314).

I do not like my time to be taken up with business I cannot attend to, and I do not like the responsibility of it.' He said, 'Thou knowest there will be no responsibility by and bye, for the Government are passing an Act to take away the responsibility;' and afterwards waited upon him and shewed him the Act, which convinced him there was no responsibility. Then the question was, 'What is my work?' Haworth said, 'All thou hast to do is to sign the orders for withdrawing the money invested with the Government which have been audited and looked at by the Managers: thou wilt have to send thy signature, as a sort of check against the Managers: the Managers manage the Bank.'"]

24.—The high reputation of many of these defaulting Actuaries, before their frauds were discovered, is a circumstance worthy of notice.

In reference to one case, that of Mr. William Wheeler Yelf, Actuary to the Isle-of-Wight Savings Bank, whose defalcations extended to £8156, out of deposits amounting to £60,000, it is stated that he was—

"Generally much respected in the island: for many years he was distributor of stamps, and had a large printing establishment, and was a *Wesleyan preacher!*"

In similar instances of fraud, at Scarborough, at Ongar in Essex, and elsewhere, the defaulters were persons in equally good repute.

Section 4.—*Belief of the Public that the Banks had Government Security.*

ART. 25.—We have before stated that, under the existing statutes, starting from the year 1817, it has not been competent for the Government, without a special vote of the Legislature, to make itself responsible to the Depositors for the amount of their savings. It is, nevertheless, a remarkable fact, that until the Report of the Committee upon the great Irish frauds, the almost universal belief, not only of the Depositors themselves, but of persons of high standing and wide information, was, that for the sums lodged in Savings Banks they had the security of the nation. In that report it was, however, correctly stated—" That the *only powers vested

---

* [*The law is more stringent in the State of New York. By the Savings Bank Act,* 20 *March,* 1857, *it was enacted that:*—" If any

by law in the Commissioners for the correction or repression of misconduct in the management of Savings Banks, appeared to be:—

" 1. That of giving notice in the Gazette, in the event of irregularity in furnishing the annual accounts.

" 2. Closing the account of the bank in default with the Commissioners; in other words, refusing to receive further monies on account of such bank." Sect. 46. 9 Geo. IV. cap. 92.

26.—On the important subject of this section, we propose to bring forward the opinions of eminent persons, partly for their historical value, but chiefly because we believe that to establish the fact that men of acknowledged standing and judgment considered it a matter of course that Savings Bank Depositors had a National Guarantee, is to furnish an irresistible argument in favour of an Act being now passed to secure such Guarantee. That the public mind was not at all prepared for the disclosure, that the Government had no control over and was not responsible for the internal management of Savings Banks, is perfectly manifest from the speeches of Mr. Hume and Colonel Thompson in debates in the House of Commons on the subject, (Hansard, 3d Series):—

I. Mr. Hume said (1850), " He thought the public had a right to complain of the Government in this matter, because it was always understood that the Government were pledged to the Depositors, and thus the public were deluded. He said deliberately, the public were deluded, because they had been led to believe that

---

Savings Bank, or institution for savings shall fail to furnish to the Superintendent of the Bank Department, its reports at the time herein stated, it shall forfeit the sum of *one hundred dollars per day* for every day such report shall be so delayed; and the said Superintendent may maintain an action in his name of office to recover such penalty, and when collected, the same shall be paid into the treasury of the State."]

their money was safe from the moment it was paid into the bank; whereas it appeared that the Act of Parliament only enabled the Government to receive the money from the Trustees, and they were only responsible for the sum which was received. Now, this was a matter which the unfortunate Depositors did not know, and they believed that all the money deposited was placed under the control of the Government from the moment it was placed in the bank. It appeared to him that the Government ought to undertake one of two things, either to leave Savings Banks altogether alone, or else to insure perfect security to the Depositors, which he saw no difficulty in doing."

Previous to the above, March 14, 1828, Mr. Hume observed:—

"The money of the Depositors in Savings Banks was vested with Government."

II. General Thompson, in 1848, said:—

"It had struck him with profound astonishment to hear that the Savings Banks were not what in popular parlance was called as 'good as the bank.' He should as soon have dreamed of having payment of dividends at the Bank of England refused because a clerk had gone to America. On the numerous occasions where he had advised servants and others in the less wealthy classes to invest their savings in the Savings Banks, he would assuredly have done no such thing if he had had the slightest conception they had any thing but Government security for their money."

III. On April 17th, 1833, in reply to Mr. Pease, Lord Althorp stated:—

"That the accounts of all Savings Banks were annually laid before Government; and where any bank neglected to do so, the Commissioners exercised the power (one or two instances of which had occurred since he came into office) of closing such bank, till its accounts were sent up."

IV. On July 26th, 1844, Mr. Goulburn said:—

"They (the Savings Banks) were established by benevolent individuals, to encourage habits of economy and industry among the humble classes in their neighbourhoods, and when the Government determined to legislate on the subject, it was with the view of giving greater encouragement to Depositors, by giving *greater security* for deposits."

V. That generally accurate writer, so often quoted by public speakers, the late Mr. G. R. Porter, said in his "Progress of the Nation:"—

"The Savings Banks, on the contrary, can never involve those who there deposit their savings in any risk or expense: the safety of the money is guaranteed by the State."

VI. A distinguished writer in the "Quarterly Review" has said:—

"But the grand bonus was the privilege, to the poor man, of being enabled to place, without trouble or expense, every single shilling, as he could save it, in the strong box of the nation, with the hundred arms of Government to protect it from others."

VII. In that widely circulated periodical "Chambers' Journal," we have:—

"Remember this, that as soon as you place money in a Savings Bank, you become, by the possession of your deposit book, the creditor of the nation."

VIII. The Irish School-books published by the Commissioners of National Education for Ireland, in the fourth Book of Lessons, at Lesson 8, "On Taxes," state—

"When a poor man deposits his money in a Savings' Bank, he is then one of the Government creditors, and receives his share of the taxes."

The above quotations speak so plainly, that it is needless to produce further evidence of the obvious fact, that the one impression on the public mind was that the nation, through the Government, was responsible for the money of Savings' Bank Depositors. Nor is it at all surprising that such an impression should have existed, seeing that the Legislature gave rise to the mistake by the very *language used in the Act of Parliament—"That it is expedient to give protection to such institutions, and the funds thereby established." (9 Geo. 4. c. 92. s. 2.) This, coupled with the provision for the investment of Savings Bank funds in Government securities, and the power, although limited, that was vested in the N. D. C., caused the misapprehension; excusable in the poorer classes, since it prevailed amongst highly-educated persons also. It should not, moreover, be overlooked that, however much the latter have now been undeceived, the uneducated Depositors in localities where frauds have not yet occurred or have not yet been detected, still labour under the impression that their money is safe—"having been placed in the Government Bank."

27.—In concluding this Chapter, we urge upon our readers to consider the cruelly unfair position, in which the defrauded Depositors in the various banks have been left. The year, in which the Cuffe Street failure happened, was, apart from such a calamity, one of considerable distress; and the labouring classes of Dublin were ill prepared, after the disastrous years of 1846 and 1847, to meet with a further loss of nearly £60,000.

It is true that £30,000 was voted by the House of Commons

---

* [On the Depositors' pass-books of *the Moorfields Bank* the words are printed, " *Under Government control.*" See evidence of Mr. Saintsbury, qu. 1837. The Glasgow and other large banks in Scotland bear the title of " National Security Savings Bank."]

towards the deficiency, but even this was not done till the year 1851; and the remaining £30,000 is still unpaid, the House having since distinctly negatived a further vote. This case is one of peculiar hardship, inasmuch as for seventeen years previously the representatives of the government in London had been made aware that a deficiency existed, yet had taken no steps to arrest its progress; and although in 1845 informed of the utterly insolvent state of the bank, yet, *contrary to law*, they allowed it to continue its ruinous operations.

In the cases of Rochdale (deficiency £37,433), Tralee (£36,000), Killarney (19,000), &c., nothing whatever has been done by the Government to repay the losses.

---

* [It is right to say that this occurred before the administration of the present comptroller, Sir A. Y. Spearman, who, applying the results of his large financial experience, has endeavoured, with the most watchful care, to improve the system of Savings Banks ever since they have been placed under his control.

Nor is it easy to know where to fix the blame; for, as remarks a member who has given much attention to questions of public finance, Sir H. Willoughby, M.P., " What was the government in these cases? Why, it was supposed to be the Commissioners for the Reduction of the National Debt, who held their offices *ex officio;* but the Commission being composed of persons like Mr. Speaker, the Master of the Rolls, and the Chief Baron of the Exchequer, they were never called upon to perform any active duty. All they had to do was to meet about four days in the year, for the purpose of adjusting the surplus income applicable to the reduction of the national debt. Now, how was it possible for these gentlemen to attend to the interests of 600 Savings Banks?"—Hansard, vol. cxxix, 3rd series, p. 541.]

CHAPTER IV.

THE REMEDY—
IN THE APPOINTMENT OF GOVERNMENT INSPECTORS AND AUDITORS, WITH THE GUARANTEE OF THE STATE FOR SAVINGS BANKS DEPOSITS.

Section 1.—*As to what is really desirable.*

ART. 28.—It is manifest, from the circumstances described in the previous chapter, that the whole success of Savings Banks, as a means of encouraging a habit of saving, depends on their affording a perfectly safe place of deposit, and on their being so managed as to warrant the labouring classes in believing that their money is faithfully preserved for them.* It is equally plain that Savings Banks will not make the poor more careful of the public credit, unless the public credit is strictly observed towards themselves: in other words, unless their deposits, in institutions where the Government has assumed a share in the management, are perfectly safe. The whole success of Savings Banks, the probability of their attaining the objects for which they have been established, the benefit that they can possibly confer on the community, all depend on the security which the Depositors have for their money.

---

* [See Dr. Hancock on the Cuffe Street Bank frauds.]

In the words of the Right Hon. Sotheron Estcourt, M.P., to whose perfect knowledge of the requirements of the industrious classes in their associations, we owe many improvements in Friendly Society legislation :—

"It is difficult to maintain that Parliament, having released local Trustees from their liability, should not be bound to provide some other guarantee for the money of Depositors, who have no share themselves in the management of the bank."

29.—For this anomalous state of things, *if Savings Banks are to remain, in any way, connected with the Government,* there is but one remedy, viz. *National security;* for Depositors require, not an exorbitant rate of interest, such as can only be given at the cost of the public exchequer, but an adequate amount of profit from the investment of their funds, combined with perfect security: and none can so nearly approach to perfection as that of the nation.

This should be extended to all deposits in Savings Banks from the moment of their being committed to the custody of the Managers and Trustees, or their officers. Those who support this view, urge that such a guarantee is easy of comprehension to the industrious classes: that it relieves them from the task they are unable *adequately to fulfil, of inquiring into the responsibility of the persons who receive their money, and that it offers that encouragement to them, in the exercise of provident habits, which it is fit the nation should afford, and no more.

---

* [An eminent writer remarks, "If the banks were either private or joint-stock concerns, and the Depositors had a share in their management, they would find perhaps more favour, for a time, with many among the working-classes. But it requires no prophet to foresee that from such a state of things mismanagement and frauds would ensue, and the establishments share the fate of many other schemes founded on appeals to the prejudices, ignorance, and cupidity of the people."]

On the other hand, there are some who contend that the establishment of banks with a State guarantee is not only unsound in principle, but might tend to foster in the minds of the mass of the people those erroneous ideas of the nature and functions of Government which have proved so injurious to the peace and welfare of society in other countries. They recommend, instead, *independent 'Banks of Deposit,'* such as we shall discuss in Part VI.

Section 2.—As to the Attempts at Legislation, 1850 to 1857.

ART. 30.—It is a strong proof that great need was admitted for some decisive step being taken by the Government with regard to the management and conduct of Savings Banks, that we find Bills introduced to Parliament on the subject in the years 1850, 1853, 1854, and 1857. The first of these Bills, introduced by the Russell Ministry, was, " To amend the law relating to Savings Banks." The leading feature of this Bill was, that the Commissioners should appoint a Treasurer to each Savings Bank, who should be at liberty to appoint an Agent or Clerk to act on his behalf. Such Treasurer (or deputy) was to attend at the office of the Savings Bank, and to receive and pay all moneys. The Act provided, also, for the appointment of Auditors by the Trustees, and empowered the Commissioners to send their own Inspector at any moment to audit and examine the accounts of any bank.

In bringing forward the Bill the Chancellor of the Exchequer said—

" It was not surprising that new regulations should be called for, or that a scheme which had answered when the transactions of these establishments were of small amount, should be found to re-

ATTEMPTS AT LEGISLATION, 1850 TO 1857. 79

quire further adjustment when they had attained their present gigantic extent. Much of the necessity of legislation arose, in his opinion, from these causes; but there was another circumstance which he thought had contributed to the same result in these institutions, and he believed that the same cause operated in all voluntary establishments. Although, in the formation of benevolent and other institutions like these, the zeal of philanthropic individuals might be successful in founding and starting the infant institution, he was afraid that, after the warmth of the first feeling had cooled, parties were not willing to give that constant and regular attention to the working of the system which was indispensably necessary to its continued usefulness and prosperity. He must observe, with regard to all persons who had taken part in the management of the affairs of those institutions, that, however active and energetic might have been the zeal of individuals in forming the establishment, it was exceedingly difficult to insure their regular attention to its concerns for any length of time. Without being disposed to attribute blame to individual Trustees for the management of Savings Banks—for if he were to do that, he believed he should himself come in for a fair share of it—he was afraid that, with some exceptions, the general practice was, that no very regular attendance was given, and that the affairs of the bank were left very much to the management of the Secretary, Treasurer, Clerk, or by whatever name the person left in charge was called, and that that salutary check was not exercised by the Trustees or Managers, which was perfectly indispensable to the proper management of the establishment."

The Bill, however, at a subsequent stage, was ordered to be postponed, and was eventually lost.

31.—The next movement made by the Legislature in the cause of Savings Bank reform was in 1853, when the Aberdeen Government introduced "A Bill to amend the laws relating to Savings Banks, and in certain cases to give the guarantee of the Government to the Depositors for the repayment of the sums legally deposited." Among the distinguishing characteristics of this Bill may be mentioned the following:—That every Savings Bank established after the passing of the Act, if the Government were to be responsible to the Depositors, should have a Treasurer appointed by the National Debt Commissioners for receiving and paying all moneys That if the Trustees and Managers were not willing to have a Treasurer, so appointed, they should themselves be answerable for all deposits paid into the bank. That with respect to Savings Banks existing at the time of the passing of the Act, if the Trustees and Managers did not within three months avail themselves of the offer of a Government Treasurer and Government security, they should, *ipso facto*, themselves become jointly and severally liable for all deposits entrusted to their care. These provisions formed the substance of the Bill in question, which, like its predecessor, was postponed and lost.

32.—In the Session of 1854, also, a Bill was introduced " To make further provision for the investment and security of the moneys received by the Commissioners for the Reduction of the National Debt, from Savings Banks and Friendly Societies." This Bill, however, did not become law.

33.—Another Bill was prepared in 1857, of which the main object was to provide for the establishment of " Government Security Savings Banks." The existing Banks were to be allowed, on proof of their solvency, to use this title. As regards those who did not, no alteration was to be made in the present law : but all Government Security Banks were to provide for the annual production of every Depositor's book, on penalty of loss of interest. They were to be entirely under the control of the National Debt Commissioners, who were to be empowered to close any bank in which a deficiency was found to arise. This Bill also was withdrawn.

Section 3.—*As to Government Inspection.*

ART. 34.—The guarantee of the nation may be safely accorded to Savings Banks if a proper control over their internal management be in exchange allowed to the Government, a control which would be sufficiently secured by the appointment of efficient Inspectors, possessed of practical experience in the examination of accounts, acting independently of the Trustees, and empowered to enter the banks at any time, without previous notice, for the purpose of examining into every detail and of making frequently recurring audits.*

They should become the visitors of these institutions, and be invested with ample power for †inspecting the books and accounts,—enforcing the strict observance of their own regulations, and for seeing that the staff of each institution is pro-

---

* [Burwood Godlee, Esq., Chairman of Lewes Savings Bank, 4th August 1858—Mr. W. W. Heathcote, Secretary, Hackney Savings Bank, 21st April 1858—Mr. David Prain, Actuary, N. S. Savings Bank, Brechin, 14th May 1858—Mr. Anthony Gibson, Keswick S. B., 8th May 1858—Mr. James Hall, Enniskillen S. B., 15th May 1858—Mr. A. Johnson, Leigh S. B., 24th May 1858—Mr. James Mudie, Actuary, N. S. Savings Bank, Montrose, 29th May 1858—Mr. Edward P. Southall, Leominster, April 23rd, 1858—Mr. Henry Stocks, Rye Savings Bank, and the Officers of St. Clement Danes, Stockport, Congleton, Belfast, and other banks, have expressed to us their concurrence in this view.]

† [Audit, without inspection, is not a security to be relied on. The experience of numerous Joint Stock Companies has shewn that Auditors are too apt to act in a perfunctory way, forgetting the real spirit of their duties. From a desire to prevent a shock that would ruin "the credit of the Company," they have been known to abstain from reporting on improprieties or irregularities in the management, and to have said nothing respecting deficiencies in the funds,—sometimes from a species of foolish sympathy,—sometimes from a *bona fide* sort of idea that the concern could recover itself. Had the Auditors properly discharged their duties, or been possessed of sufficient powers of inspection, the Royal British Bank, and other grievous frauds would not have been perpetrated. See *Part* VI. *on the Audit of Public Institutions.*]

perly maintained, that the *law has not been disobeyed—that the respective duties of each officer are efficiently discharged—that their salaries are proportioned to their respective services—and that no larger sums remain in the Treasurer's hands than are requisite for the ordinary working of the bank: in short, to adopt a phrase used in the Report on Savings Banks in France, they should examine " toute la gestion," that is, the whole of the management of each bank, as well as its financial condition.

By the arrangements proposed in Section 4, page 97, further on, a gradual detailed examination of every Depositor's Book would be made, and a check at once put upon any course likely to lead to inaccuracy or fraud. Even though some months may elapse before all pass-books are examined, the regular inspection at random of such books as are presented by the Depositors for payments in or withdrawals, and of those books called for in their order, would suffice to make it a probability approaching certainty, that by the operation of

---

* [The Savings Banks accounts, ordered by law to be published, afford no check which can be applied by an individual Depositor, and therefore no guarantee against falsification. The present system of publication, moreover, is not adequate ; and in many cases the provisions of the Act are entirely disregarded, no accounts being published at all. The Cuffe Street Bank published no accounts for seventeen years !

That some inquiry into the legality of the proceedings of the banks is necessary, may be illustrated by two facts :—

In one Savings Bank (although the Rules themselves are correctly drawn), at page 11 of the Abstract it is said :—

" No sum, knowingly deposited under a false name, or description, shall bear interest ; and such sum *shall be returned to the Depositor.*"

Whereas the Act provides that the money shall be 'forfeited' to the Sinking Fund.

In another institution—although, according to law, all Savings Bank monies are to be invested with the Commissioners for the Reduction of the National Debt—their Balance Sheet shews that they have more than four times as much invested at interest in certain Joint Stock Banking Companies as in the legal securities.]

the "Law of Average" the others still to be examined are equally accurate.

To each Inspector should be attached one or more accountants and clerks, to assist him in the inspection of the pass-books.

The Inspector should be the general medium of communication between the Commissioners and the Trustees and Managers of each bank; and their reports should be collated together into an abstract, for the purpose of an annual report to Parliament. They should have the power of taking evidence on oath.

35.—In addition, a Local Professional Accountant appointed by the Government Commissioners, should be attached to each bank which is too small to keep a proper staff of officials. His duty should be to audit its operations, quite independent of the supervision to be exercised by the Travelling Inspectors.

A statement of the business transacted each week, and of the disposal of the balance, countersigned by the Auditor, should be transmitted weekly to the Government office.

36.—If this plan be adopted, then, where the accounts were found incorrect, the system of book-keeping imperfect, the state of the bank unsatisfactory, or the management lax, notice thereof would be given to the Trustees and Managers by the Inspector; and, if in all or any of these respects the necessary remedies were not applied without delay after such notice, the Government guarantee should be withdrawn. On the other hand, the *approval* of the Inspector would be found greatly to promote the welfare of that bank which he reported as conducted with good and careful management.

37.—*As to Appointment of the Bank Officials in Guaranteed Banks.*—The Trustees and Managers of each Guaranteed Bank should be allowed to elect their chief officer, subject to the confirmation of the Government; the other officers and clerks being appointed by them as at present. All the officers and clerks should give security to the satisfaction of the Government Commissioners. The Trustees should be required to adopt the method of business prescribed as likely to insure the good management of their bank, and should be expected to afford the voluntary check of attending during bank hours in rotation.

Section 4.—*As to Government Treasurers.*

Art. 38.—The preceding propositions will, perhaps, not at first sight be approved by those members of the Legislature, who supported the various Bills which have been brought into Parliament since 1850, by successive Chancellors of the Exchequer, for, as we have stated in Sect. 2., these Bills made it a condition, precedent to the assumption by Government of further responsibility in respect to Savings Bank funds, that the safe receipt of deposits should be delegated to paid Treasurers, * resident in each locality, appointed by and acting as the agents of the Commissioners. It was proposed that the Treasurer, by himself or deputy, should attend during the business hours of the bank to receive and pay money—and that the Government should then become liable for the amount paid in by Depositors during such hours, to be verified in the pass-books by the signature of the acting Treasurer.

39.—One of the most eminent members of the present Government, the Right Hon. W. E. Gladstone, used the following forcible language upon this point in relation to the Bill of 1853:—"The great evil with respect to the present condition of Savings Banks is not so much any gross, or

---

* [In his explanatory speech of 1850, Sir Charles Wood stated that a local banker would generally be preferable for this office.]

flagrant, or glaring abuse connected with them, as the want of that perfect security which every one must feel that they ought to afford. If we look at the enormous amount of money deposited in the various Savings Banks, and then take the mere figures which represent the total losses that have been incurred by Depositors, no doubt the amount of those losses, in relation to the total deposited, is very insignificant; but the evil that is done in particular cases is, unfortunately, not to be measured by the actual amount of money loss. There is an amount of evil* such as figures can convey no idea of; and besides, it is impossible that the public confidence in those institutions can be that which it ought to be while those losses are liable to occur at all. What Parliament should desire to secure is, not that those losses should be rare, but that they should be altogether unknown—that no such thing should be allowed to take place. That being so, the question arises, how can that absolute security, which is so essential, be given? There is no doubt that where a body of Trustees, such as most of the bodies of Trustees of Savings Banks are, could be induced to give their own unlimited personal security, that would afford safety to the Depositors. But it is hardly

---

* [An intelligent artisan, who was examined before the Select Committee on the savings of the middle and working classes, thus stated the effect produced by the Rochdale catastrophe:—" I was in Lancashire " some time ago, meeting with large bodies of working men, at the time " of the failure, and I shall not soon forget some remarks that were made " about the Government as to the want of security. One man said, " ' Doctor M'Dowall, came here, and told us that the Government was a " ' set of robbers, that they did not care about the property of the work- " ' ing men.' " He said, ' I did not believe M'Dowall then, but when I see " ' that there is no security for the savings of the working-men in the " ' Savings Banks, and we supposed that the Government had them " ' under their protection, I believe now that M'Dowall was right, and " ' that the Government cares nothing about either the poor men or their " ' savings.' " This distrust is evidenced by the fact that the aggregate increase of annual receipts in Savings Banks, during the last twelve years, has only been 7¼ per cent. of what they were previously.]

reasonable to expect that they should be found willing to give that absolute security. If it were, Parliament might be glad that there should be no further intervention of Government, and I need not then trouble you with minute details, or endeavour to introduce any sensible degree of Government control. That, however, is not be looked for as a general rule. There is then but one other way of giving an absolute security to the Depositors, and that is by affording them that which is the best that can be given in this country—namely, the guarantee of the Government. But it will be admitted on all hands, that if the guarantee of the Government should be given to those Depositors, it could only be upon very distinct and definite grounds; and *I am bound to express at once my dissent* from the proposition which has been put forward by the Managers of Savings Banks—not generally, but in certain cases—that the Government guarantee should be given to Depositors, the security taken by the Government in return being the appointment of auditors to the Savings Banks. *I do not hesitate to say that I believe, if I were to make such a proposition to the House of Commons, the House of Commons would reject it, but at the same time I must frankly and openly say that nothing would induce me to make such a proposition.* It is absolutely necessary, if the guarantee of the State is to be given to the Depositors in Savings Banks, that the State should have a sufficient control over the receipt and payment of the money itself—not merely the power of calling for accounts at certain intervals, but control over the receipt and payment of the money itself; and that cannot be had without the full control of the Government over some person in the banks who shall be a party to every receipt and every payment."

40.—Notwithstanding these remarks of Mr. Gladstone, we yet venture to affirm from our experience, that, (even assuming that the appointing of Government Treasurers would produce no serious inconvenience,) yet such a measure is unnecessary and inexpedient, and that it is not clear that any appreciably greater security against fraud would be obtained by the appointment of such officials than exists under the present system. It would be *inexpedient*, because utterly inconsistent with the continuance of Honorary Trustees and *Managers, whose connection with the bank is productive of so great *indirect* advantage to industrial interests, that their resignation would be a subject of just regret; and *unnecessary*, because a sufficient guarantee can be otherwise provided, viz. by the plan of Government †Inspectors. As regards this last point, there can be no doubt that the moral and practical effect of a system of unapprised inspectoral visits would tend to the complete prevention of fraud: they would supply that additional check which has been hitherto wanting in the organization of Savings Banks.

41.—We concur entirely with Mr. Gladstone's remark that "the amount of the losses is very insignificant, but the evil .... is not to be measured by the actual amount of money loss;" and we deduce from it a subsidiary argument, of no mean weight in a financial point of view, in favour of the guarantee of the State for Savings Bank deposits. For, even on the assumption that the future defalcations will, on the average, be equally large with those of past years, their magnitude, although *fatal to the particular bank* in which they might occur, would be a mere trifle to the national resources, even if the whole liability were from this moment adopted by the Govern-

---

* [*The following Resolution was adopted by a meeting held at the St. Martin's Place Savings Bank:*—

"That, in the opinion of this meeting, the proposed introduction into the Savings Banks of a Treasurer and clerks, not under the control of Trustees and Managers, and the consequent existence, in the same establishment, of two sets of officers and clerks, with divided and undefined responsibility, and acting under different heads, must lead to great confusion, and eventually to the disruption of these valuable institutions."]

† [Particularly, if combined with the measure proposed in Art. 7.]

ment. From the Parliamentary Returns we have quoted, it appears that during the 13 years, from 1844 to 1857, the total frauds in Savings Banks in the United Kingdom, (exclusive of Ireland,) were £115,304, or, on the average of the 13 years, £8870 per annum. In previous and succeeding years, (of which we have no official return,) they were undoubtedly much less, and the annual average was probably below the half of the sum above stated.

With respect to Ireland, the three cases of Dublin, Tralee, and Killarney were so audacious in their defiance of the law, and were obviously caused by so great negligence, that they could not possibly recur under any organised system of *external* inspection, however desultory. We may therefore venture to anticipate (and the experience of the last 6 or 7 years bears us out) that a margin of †£8000 per annum on the £38,000,000 invested would be amply sufficient to cover the risk of fraud on the part of Savings Banks officials; in other words, that it would pay any Guarantee Society to insure the safety of the whole £38,000,000 deposited in Savings Banks, at a premium of sixpence per cent. per annum.

---

* [This diminution in the number and amount of frauds may be attributable partly to the greater attention now bestowed by Trustees and Managers on the affairs of Savings Banks, and their more regular attendance during the receipt and payment of deposits, and partly to the kind of lull that usually follows any signal exposures of mismanagement and defalcation.

Should the watchfulness of the public become slackened, or some system of regular inspection not speedily be adopted, it may be confidently predicted that, ere 10 years more are passed, cases of extensive fraud will recur.]

† [The above figures refer to the average amount of fraud, before the assets and security of the defaulting Actuaries are taken into account. The average of the actual *frauds* committed in the period specified is in fact double the average annual *loss*. But even £8000 a-year would be less than a farthing in the pound, or one pound in a thousand of the Poors Rates.]

42.—When it is considered (as we shall shew at length in Chap. 9.) that the State is at present paying, in the form of excess of interest, the sum of £69,000 per annum for the encouragement of deposits in Savings Banks, it will seem unnecessary to urge further a point involving so trifling an expenditure of public money. And when we observe the praiseworthy readiness of the Legislature to make large grants for the benefit of the industrious classes, the spread of education, and the encouragement of provident habits; when we remember that eight millions a year are paid for poors rates, thirty-seven for army and war, and two millions for the administration of justice and repression of offences—we can scarcely believe that they will hesitate to incur an infinitesimal annual risk, in order to give absolute security to the savings of the poor.

CHAPTER V.

AS TO IMPROVEMENTS IN THE INTERNAL MANAGEMENT OF SAVINGS BANKS.

		PAGE.
SECTION 1.—As to Uniformity of Accounts in Savings Banks,		90
,, 2.—As to Actuaries	- - - - - -	92
,, 3.—As to Trustees	- - - - - - -	93
,, 4.—As to production of Pass Books	- - -	97

Sect. 1.—As to the Uniformity of Accounts in Savings Banks.

ART. 43.—In order to facilitate the inspection of accounts, a uniform system of book-keeping should be adopted by all Savings Banks.*

It is well known that, in this country, as it was in France until of late years, the endless diversity in the books and in the mode of keeping them is the great obstacle in the way

---

* [In a future part of this Treatise will be given precedents of the forms to be adopted for this purpose, as well as a set of model rules for Savings Banks. They have been revised after comparison with the forms obtained from Paris, Germany, and the United States, &c. (See also Art. 62, further on.)

In France, we are informed by M. Dupin, that "M. Emile de Girardin, l' un des plus eclairés et des plus zélés promoteurs de l' Institution des caisses d'epargne, proposa d' ajouter à l' art. 7 la disposition suivante: ' Les livrets ainsi que tous les registres, bordereaux et impressions necessaires à la comptabilité des caisses d'épargne, seront fournis annuellement

of a systematic inspection of Savings Bank accounts, by which alone fraud is susceptible of detection, and what is still more vitally necessary, of prevention. The great importance of a uniform system of account-keeping, therefore, cannot be too highly appreciated, and is confirmed from the benefit that has resulted from the recent *French regulations, which render compulsory the adoption of uniformity in the books and accounts.

To see how the adoption of such a plan would produce advantage, it should be remembered, that, under the present system, there is no check on the paid officer, if (as is still occasionally the case, in spite of public indignation at the mischief caused by the frauds) the rotation Manager fails to attend in his regular turn to superintend the receipt and payment of deposits. The Actuary may, as we have seen was done at Rochdale, receive double the amount accounted for, and that, too, without any fear of detection, if he falsified, as under such circumstances he probably would do, the ledger accounts, so as to make them agree with the Depositors' books. He might also draw upon the funds of the bank, as was the case at Brighton and at other places, by means of created accounts in the ledger, and false pass-books to correspond with such accounts, even though a Manager should be in attendance.

---

par l'imprimerie royale, sur une allocation speciale portée à son budget.' Ce serait à coup sûr, dit il, une immense économie que de produire tous les imprimés nécessaires à près de cent caisses autorisées maintenant, et bientôt nous l'espérons, à deux cents autres qui manquent encore, avec la seule dépense d'une composition unique, et d'un tirage uniforme, dans une même imprimerie. Si le gouvernement voulait accorder un tel bienfait aux caisses d'épargne, la somme totale ne serait pas exorbitante, et l'économie relative, nous le répétons, serait considérable pour chaque caisse prise en particulier."]

* [*Decret du* 15 *Avril* 1852, *Article* 6.]

Section 2.—As to Actuaries of guaranteed Savings Banks.

ART. 44.—No Actuary of a Savings Bank (or like official, by whatever name he be designated, such as comptroller, registrar, secretary, or clerk,) should be allowed to follow any other occupation, in which capital is required; or to become responsible for the actions, debts, or obligations of others, except with the consent of the Trustees and Managers.

From the smallness of the remuneration* that can be afforded by the lesser banks, it necessarily arises that their Actuaries depend on some other source of income for support; and the case of Rochdale shews that, where their other business is one requiring capital, the temptation is great to appropriate the funds of the bank. Such employments as that of an accountant or clerk, or those of a professional character, should therefore alone be allowed to be entered upon by the Actuary.

There are a variety of Government appointments, such as for example, *Registrarships of Births, Deaths, and Marriages*, &c., and many others that do not involve *the receipt of money*, to which Savings Bank Actuaries might be appointed where their income is insufficient.

They should be reckoned civil servants of the Crown, and be entitled to superannuation allowances, like other Government officials. (*See Part IV. as to proposed grants for expenses.*)

If a uniform system of accounts were adopted, it would (as remarked by Mr. Porter) prove not only a stimulus to ambition, but a check against fraud, to give the officials promotion from one bank to a larger.

To give an idea of the amount of work done by them we may mention, that the returns shew that the number of transactions in Savings Banks, during the year 1857 was 2,372,095, of which 1,559,607 were payments in and 812,488 withdrawals.

---

* [It is desirable that something should be done to place the salaries of Savings Banks Actuaries on a better footing. The Inspector should have power to recommend an increase of salary, or a gratuity, to the Actuary, where he finds the accounts satisfactorily kept and the bank efficiently managed.]

Section 3.—*As to Trustees and Managers.*

ART. 45.—**Trustees, or others, signing blank orders of investment or withdrawal* should be *ipso facto* disqualified from holding office, and their appointments should become thereby void, and the fact be notified in the offices of the Bank.

---

*[Nearly all the various frauds, which have been practised upon the depositors of Savings Banks are traceable, directly or indirectly, to the Legislature permitting persons to assume the authority and invest themselves with the character of Trustees, without attending to their duties, when it had, previously, released them from that responsibility which the Court of Chancery, consulting the best interests of society, had for more than 300 years inseparably attached to that office.

The mischievous consequences, which the Court of Chancery foresaw and foretold would inevitably result from such a practice, have been realized in this particular instance. Experience has shewn that it would be better to have no Trustees at all, than that they should be inefficient or neglectful.

Indeed, if approaching changes in the law of Savings Banks should deter individuals from lending their names to institutions of this kind, without previously counting the cost, without deliberately determining that their patronage and superintendence shall be not nominal or illusory, but real and effective, we believe that a very beneficial result will have been attained.

On this subject the State Superintendent of Banks, New York, remarks, in his report for 1859, p. 3 :—" The responsibility resting upon those gentlemen who manage this great trust fund should be well considered before entering upon their duties; and it should call forth a careful attention to them, not less than they apply to their own private interests. The result of careless management, bad investments, or defalcations of officers, that should produce a general panic among the Depositors in our Savings Banks, would be more disastrous in its effect, and more wide spread in its results, than any monetary misfortune that could overtake our citizens."]

46.—It does not, however, appear desirable or necessary that the Trustees and Managers should be required to sign undertakings of responsibility, even (as proposed by some of the witnesses) with the provision, " that if any loss arise, which has to be made good by them, then the parties to be first applied to, to contribute to the requisite amount of their undertakings, should be those Trustees or Managers during whose rotation term of office the origin of the loss may occur."

The necessity for their responsibility will no longer exist, when the system of each bank is made subject to the regulations of account keeping and supervision which the Commission shall prescribe, unless the Trustees or Managers *neglect to attend* in their turn at the bank.

47.—It is well, perhaps, to remark that the proposition of requiring Managers and Trustees of Savings Banks to be responsible has been objected to on the ground that none of them derive any benefit from their office, and also that it seems scarcely fair that those Managers who conscientiously discharge the duties they have consented to perform, should be required (as has been the case in several instances of award by the Savings Bank Barrister), to make good, in equal ratio, the loss created by the neglect and omission of brother Managers or Trustees. In reply to this it is argued that any apparent unfairness might be obviated by making the first call on those Trustees or Managers to whose neglect the fraud or loss might be traced. We cite the objection, that the reader may consider how frauds appear to originate wholly in the system of *Rotation-Managers coming into attendance at long intervals, whereby

---

* [See Part IV., on the advantages of an *Executive Committee*. In the Paris Savings Bank, the Committee of Management and the Committee of Supervision each sit twice every week. See Agathon Prévost's *Manuel des Caisses d'Epargne*, p. 15.]

the Actuary is the only person able to explain the working of his books, or to give the clue to a watchful inspection of the accuracy of his entries.

48.—On one point,* all the witnesses before the Committee of 1858 concurred, viz. that *the most effectual restraint upon malversation is to be found in the presence of a †second party in every transaction where money is paid or received;* and that a rule to this effect ought to be imperative in all banks, under a penalty for its infringement.

It is consequently contended that those Trustees or Managers who are absent, after having been duly summoned in their turn, and do not provide substitutes from others of their body, should be fined; and if loss or fraud occur, should be jointly liable with the person who received or paid the money for all transactions on that day.

If this responsibility) which they can avoid by attending) be

---

* [It was, however, stated by Mr. Hatton of the Brighton Bank, that, according to his experience at Reading and at Brighton, and investigation of accounts there, the attendance of the Managers is no check—"since it is difficult for a gentleman attending a Savings Bank only occasionally to know whether the sum appearing to be due to a Depositor is a sum actually due by the bank; and whether the person presenting the Depositor's book is the real Depositor or not." (qu. 3352, 3353.)

He recommended (qu. 3379) that the Depositor's book should be issued by Government, and be uniform throughout the country; and that on the outside of the cover there should be printed in large characters an injunction for the Depositor to satisfy himself that a proper Government receipt stamp was affixed to the entry before he left the office.—*See note to Art. 43 for the views of M. Emile de Girardin on this head.*]

† [In the rules of the Portsmouth and other Banks it is provided that such second party should be an *unpaid Manager.* The Nottingham Bank has an excellent provision, viz. that the certificate for the Treasurer must be made out in the attending Manager's *own handwriting.* The Return of 9th February 1858 shews, however, that in many Banks the attendance of the Managers is very irregular, some of the institutions having been thirty or forty days in the year 1856 without the presence of a single unpaid official.]

objected to, then no alternative would remain, but that a paid officer should attend on each occasion of the bank being open, to check the payments and receipts. This of course would have the effect of causing the Trustees and Managers to cease to take any active interest in the operations of the day, another official being present to do their duty, whose authority would seem to override theirs. *As this cessation of interest would open the door to possible collusion between the paid Auditor and the Actuary, the supervision of Visiting Inspectors would be doubly necessary.*

49.—*As to Payment of Managers.*—Sec. 6. of the 10 Geo. IV., which forbids any Trustee or Manager to derive any personal advantage from the funds of the Savings Bank, is of questionable advantage, and it would be better for the Government to sanction the payment of a fee out of the allowance for expenses (see Part IV.) to the Manager of the day for his labour in what (if really well done) is an onerous duty.

However indifferent some of the Trustees and Managers may be to remuneration, by far the large majority are persons to whom payment for a certain number of hours' work would be but fair and proper. Many accountants and other respectable persons engaged in book-keeping might be invited to become rotation Managers, if payment were offered. It was very justly remarked by the late Sir J. Cross, in a judicial decision, that

"Country gentlemen are willing to lend their names as Trustees in the establishment of banks for the deposit of the savings of the poor, but are negligent, in too many instances, in giving their personal services, by which means the business falls almost entirely under the management of the person appointed as Actuary." *Re Jones*: *Court of Review in Bankruptcy*, 20*th Dec.* 1825.

Section 4.—*As to production of Pass Books.*

Art. 50.—Under sec. 5. of 7 & 8 Vict. cap. 83. it is enacted that every Depositor shall, *once* in every year at least, cause his deposit-book to be produced at the office of the bank for examination, but no penalty is provided in case of omission to do so.

This section has scarcely ever been acted on, and many persons are of opinion that an important check against fraud has been neglected. Hence it has been suggested, that in the new Act a clause should be passed depriving the Depositors of of the State guarantee, and of a portion of the interest to which they are entitled, if they do not once in each year bring in their pass-books for examination. It is held that the risk of loss to the bank from fraud would thus be limited as much as possible, and its range would be reduced to the current year.

The adoption of this suggestion was not decided upon by the Committee of the House of Commons in 1858, for they thought, that however practicable the annual production of pass-books might be in small banks, there would be some difficulty in carrying out the system in those of extensive operations. Some of the Actuaries also urged that there would be harshness in enforcing it " on thousands of Depositors who are at sea, or travelling, or reside at a distance from the bank, or are not at their own disposal as regards time, or are illiterate," and from one or other of these causes* neglect to bring in their books for inspection.

Mr. Ayrton, M.P., however, forcibly contended that " wherever a bank is not carried on upon a scale so large as to admit of a

---

* [The Finsbury Bank (June 1850), the Devonport Bank (June 1853), the Edinburgh Bank (July 1853), urged that it "would inflict a severe penalty upon the Depositors, seriously disturb their confidence, entail continuous audit of the accounts, the annual comparison of the Depositor's pass-book with his account in the bank books, made by some other person than the stipendiary officer of the bank, is the

great labour upon the banks, great obstruction to their other business, and inconvenient and vexatious interference with the Depositors' accounts." The Alford Bank, the Belfast Banks, Mr. W. Gard of Devonport, the Managers of the Glasgow Bank (9th April 1858), and Mr. Alfred Huband, Actuary of the Evesham Savings Bank (24th May 1858), express the same views.

The " Reporter " newspaper (July 1855), on the other hand, argued, "The indifference or ignorance of some few Depositors in almost every bank is perfectly unaccountable, seeing that their pecuniary interests, upon which our countrymen are usually particularly sharp, are involved. Unless incapacitated by distance, idiotcy, or death, Depositors should be compelled to look after their own interests. The provision will regularly bring in the books of all sane people at the appropriate time."

Mr. Henry Stocks, Secretary to the Rye Savings Bank, writes to us:— " The duplicate *cannot* be produced yearly for inspection, as I may say they are all over the world. I know some belonging to Depositors in this bank are in America. Depositors have an objection to produce their books (in the country where they are known) in the day time: they like to slip in and deposit their money, and 'be no more seen' till they want to withdraw or deposit."

The Bury St. Edmund's bank urge that " in the case of country banks the range is very wide, extending often to a distance of fifteen miles," and that it would therefore be impossible to get in the Depositor's books within a limited time.

Mr. James Hall, Actuary to the Enniskillen Savings Bank, writes (15th May 1858), in reference to the law in Ireland:—" We find it to be a great inconvenience and dissatisfaction to the Depositors; there being only one Savings Bank in the county (as is the case in several other counties in Ireland), the Depositors having necessarily to come long distances—many from 10 to 20 miles—often withdraw their sums altogether. Although the Trustees have power, in certain cases of difficulty in attending, to allow interest, the applications are so numerous, that they have determined not to make use of the privilege in any case whatever; so that many persons, such as constabulary police, servants (who often cannot attend), the illiterate, and some removed to distant parts of the world, lose their interest for a long term. The Chancellor of the Exchequer is reported to have told a deputation who waited upon him on the subject, that ' this law worked well in Ireland :' I only wish this gentleman had a

best safeguard against fraud." He recommended that it should be provided, " that whatever loss may arise from the neglect of the Depositor to comply with this rule, should be borne by himself, and not by the funds of the bank. Thus the risk of loss to the Trustees or the funds of the bank would be limited to the current year."

51.—The periodical inspection of the Depositors' books and their comparison with the bank ledgers are, indeed, vital elements in any system of audit, and we cannot but express our opinion that *their production should be required by the Inspectors from time to time,* so that once at least in 18 or 24 months each should be examined, and stamped by him accordingly. And, to prevent any preparation of the office books to correspond with the inspection, arrangements should be so made that the bank officials should not know beforehand in what order they will be sent for or required. There would be no difficulty in devising and organising some satisfactory plan to carry out such a principle.* But it will be useless to make regulations if they are not to be attended to: in the *Bank at Abbey Street, Dublin,* we find that, in the year 1858,

---

personal trial of its working for one year, it would put such a notion out of his head faster than any argument that could be offered. We think, however, that, had Mr. Ayrton's motion been adopted, it would have worked satisfactorily."

Burwood Godlee, Esq., Chairman of the Lewes Savings Bank, writes on behalf of the Acting Committee (4th May 1858), " We know by experience that the annual production of the pass-books, even to a Committee of Managers, *is no check at all to their accuracy.*"]

* [The following anecdote is related by the Actuary of a country Savings Bank:—

" When our duplicates were called in three or four years ago for examination, a poor woman from a neighbouring village came, and when the door was opened by the porter for her admission, she caught sight of the back of a gentleman, and she immediately inquired of the porter if that was Dr. ——. He said, 'Yes.' She then closed the door without entering, and said, 'I shall not go in. If Dr. —— knows I have got money here he will not give me any more soup.' Dr. —— is the Vicar

only £90,000 worth of books out of £208,000 deposited were presented for examination. Of the books only 3279 out of 9727 were produced, in direct contravention of the special statute for Ireland.

52.—In large banks, with a good system of book keeping, and a sufficient number of officers acting as mutual checks, the Inspectors might be satisfied after having examined each year 20 per cent. of the books in circulation; but in banks managed by only two individuals, or on a less satisfactory system the Inspector should continue his examination until he had verified perhaps †70 or 80 per cent.

Mr. Meikle, the able Actuary to the Glasgow Savings Bank, whose testimony is remarkably careful and full of information, states at qu. 2324, in his evidence, " We have done so in Glasgow on three several occasions, and the same practice has been followed in other banks. The first examination at Glasgow was made in the year 1850; the Directors personally attended within the bank office, and with the assistance of an accountant, distinct from their own officers, compared the ledger with the pass-books of the Depositors passing through the usual current of business; and in that year, between the 12th of January and the 15th April, they examined 10,373 books. These books contained £204,087. In 1852 the Directors and Accountant attended from 2nd January to the 18th February, a period of seven weeks, and examined

---

of her parish, and gives soup away in the cold weather to his poor parishioners."

A Depositor, writing to us from Norfolk, says, " I deposit in London, and I live 128 miles from the metropolis. The going to London with my book would be to me an impossibility. The losing the interest would be less than the expense. I should withdraw my deposits if such a Bill were to pass."

Many persons prefer depositing where they do not reside, lest their neighbours should know they have money.]

† [Mr. Shopland, Actuary to the Exeter Bank, stated in his evidence (qu. 1401—1415), that certain false entries in the books of one of their branches at Ilfracombe were discovered by the accidental presentation at the head office of a deposit book for examination.]

9422 books out of 27,160 in circulation; in 1855 that attended from 12th May to the 16th June, five weeks, and examined 10,131 books out of 32,203. In the first of these years they called in the books by public advertisement, but finding that that alarmed the Depositors, they did not advertise in subsequent years, but simply took the books of Depositors as they were presented in the ordinary course of business." Again:—

"To examine 30 per cent. of our books would require a period of about seven weeks. In not a single instance, out of 29,926 accounts examined, was there the slightest discrepancy discovered, and yet our transactions are *forty per cent.* more numerous than those of any other Savings Bank. This arises from the fact that we afford more ample facilities, and have, in consequence, attracted a larger proportion of small Depositors than any other Savings Bank, with the exception of that of Edinburgh. In our bank 76 per cent. of the Depositors belong to the class whose balances do not exceed £30; but in other large Savings Banks that class constitutes only 70 per cent. (qu. 2324-2406.)"

53. The Depositors might easily be saved the trouble of coming to the bank with their pass-books, if they were furnished on the covers of those books, with the printed form of a return which they should be required to fill up each year, and send, addressed

"To the Savings Bank Inspector,

Post-Office,

———————

To be left till called for."

These forms should be kept at the post-office, and not delivered at the Savings Bank, so as to prevent their being tampered with.

There would be no difficulty in filling them up, with the particulars required, viz. the amount of deposit and interest, for if the Depositor could not read, he would easily find some one more capable than himself to do it for him.

They should be transmissible by post to the nearest post-office to the Savings Bank, free of expense, as suggested in Chap I., Part V., which treats of "The Post-office Savings Bank Plan."

If the Inspector found the return did not agree with the ledger, he would address a notice to the Depositor to bring in his pass-book for special examination.

For simplicity, uniformity should be adopted in all pass-books, and the return should be framed so as to exactly correspond with them.

CHAPTER VI.

AS TO SUNDRY POINTS OF INTERNAL MANAGEMENT.

Section 1.—As to Declarations - - - - - - 103
  „   2.—As to Withdrawals - - - - - - 105
  „   3.—As to Money Payments out of Office Hours - - 107
  „   4.—As to the Rules and Annual Statements - - 108
  „   5.—As to Books of Account - - - - 110

We now propose to advert to sundry minor details of internal management, a disregard of which, by a large number of the smaller country banks, has been productive of errors or loss.

Section 1.—*As to Declarations.*

ART. 54.—The* *declaration*, required by the Act to be made by each Depositor on opening an account, should be carefully

---

* [As an illustration of the ambiguity that attends legal phraseology in Acts of Parliament,—in one of the very large Banks, the clause relating to the printing of the Form of Declaration in the Deposit Books (7 & 8 Vict. c. 83. s. 3. which says that the declaration "*shall be annexed to or printed at the beginning of the Deposit Book*")—is understood to mean annexed to the Deposit Book, or printed at the beginning of the Deposit Book; and the declaration is nevertheless printed AT THE END; whereas the Committee read the phrase as meaning "annexed *to the beginning*, if not printed at the beginning !]

kept in a book, and referred to for comparison by the attending Manager and the Actuary before paying out money on withdrawal.

In some banks it has been found that the declarations have been put away in bundles, as of no value.

Mr. Grey, who has had larger experience than any man in England in investigating Savings Bank frauds, writes to us on this subject:—

"A little experience in examining signatures will shew how difficult it is, generally speaking, and especially among the class of persons of which Savings Bank Depositors consist, to imitate the writing of another person; and how great a safeguard, therefore, the handwriting affords against an attempt at personation. It is true that many Savings Bank Depositors cannot write at all; but even in these cases a little precaution affords means of identification which are hardly mistakeable.

"These persons make a mark to their declarations: when this is done, some short description of their person, especially of any peculiarity, should be noted in a space to be provided in the Declaration Book for that purpose, and certain inquiries should be made, such as the age—the birthday—the birth-place—names of parents—and any other points which only themselves are likely to be acquainted with. The answers to these should also be written down; and the correct *repetition of these answers when money is to be withdrawn, affords the next best identification to that of the hand-writing."

---

* ["Il est de la plus grande importance de ne jamais porter sur le livret aucun des renseignements propres à établir l'identité du déposant et qui sont exclusivement réservés aux registres matricules. Il faut surtout s'abstenir de faire signer le titulaire, soit en tête du livret, soit à la mention d'un remboursement quelconque." Agathon Prévost, Manuel des Caisses d'Epargne, p. 24.]

Section 2.—*As to Withdrawals.*

Art. 55.—The rules for this adopted by the best Savings Banks are as follows, and should not be omitted :—

" Depositors shall personally attend to receive whatever sums they may wish to draw out, unless prevented by illness or any other sufficient cause, in which case they shall send an order, signed by themselves in the presence of the officiating Minister of the parish wherein such person shall reside, or of a Justice of the Peace, or one of the Managers of this Institution.

"Deposits fraudulently withdrawn.—The Trustees and Managers, and the Actuary, will diligently endeavour to prevent fraud, and to identify every Depositor transacting business at this bank; but in case any person presenting a Depositor's book, and stating himself or herself to be the Depositor named therein, or producing an order purporting to bear the signature of the Depositor, shall unlawfully obtain any deposit or sum of money from the Actuary, or any Manager, during the hours of business, they will not be responsible for the loss so sustained by any Depositor, nor will this Institution be liable to make good the same."

56.—It is the business of the bank officers to take every precaution that they do not pay away money improperly. The production of the *pass-book* is frequently, however, considered a sufficient authority for claiming the amount deposited, or any part of it; but this is not a very safe mode of proceeding. A pass-book may be lost or stolen, and the deposit may be claimed by some one who has no right whatever to receive it. The application should be made in a given form, and should be witnessed, where necessary, by some known person, to whom reference could be made. If the Depositor cannot write, the particulars required to be stated in making the declaration upon admission (see Section 5), should also be appended and *compared.

The Trustees and Managers of the day should be pecuniarily responsible to the Commissioners for all† loss arising under this head, and for the indemnification of the parties withdrawing, if these precautions be neglected.

57.—In no case when a Depositor is ill, or unable to attend, should a written ‡ order be accepted, unless his signature (or mark if he cannot write) be witnessed by some person of respectability as mentioned in the rules quoted, or by his surgeon, or a substantial householder, whose signature can be identified, and who knows the Depositor; and in such cases the sum withdrawn should not exceed £20 within intervals of seven days.

This limit of £20 might, however, on special application, be extended by the Manager of the day, on his own responsibility, if he should think fit; but an entry of the circumstances should be at once made in the journal or book of orders to be kept at the bank, for reference.

---

* [" Une règle absolue, et qui ne souffre jamais d'exception, est qu'aucun payement, quelque minime qu'il soit, partiel ou total, n'est opéré sans le rapprochement préalable de la signature de la demande avec celle du registre-matricule ou du registre des autorisations." Agathon Prévost, *Manuel*, pp. 30, 31.]

† [Many frauds are stated to have been perpetrated by Actuaries withdrawing money on behalf of real or fictitious Depositors, and appropriating it to their own use.]

‡ [" Les autorisations produites, soit par les représentants qui ont versé pour le compte d'un tiers, soit par des femmes mariées, à l'effet de verser pour la première fois, sont classées dans leur ordre numérique, et reliées pour former des registres, divisés, comme les matricules, en numéros impairs et en numéros pairs." Agathon Prévost, *Manuel*, p. 22]

Section 3.—As to Money Payments out of Office Hours.

ART. 58.—In Arts. 4 and 5, we have adverted to the danger of frauds, arising from the circumstance that, at present, the business in the smaller banks is not unfrequently conducted at the residence of the Actuary, and that larger sums are often received at irregular times than during the prescribed days and hours of business. To prevent this, it should be enacted:—

1. That no money be received, nor business transacted, except in the presence of at least one Officer of the bank besides the Actuary, such as a Trustee or Manager, or other independent official appointed for the purpose. The Actuary should be strictly prohibited from either paying or receiving money in their absence.*

2. That if money be accepted out of office hours or of the bank premises, by any one being, or pretending to be, an officer of the Commissioners or of the bank, he shall be guilty of a misdemeanour, and punishable accordingly, even if he afterwards account for the same.

3. That no person shall have any claim in respect to a deposit, unless it shall have been made at the office during the published office hours; and

4. That any officer encouraging Depositors to infringe the law, shall be held to be guilty of a misdemeanour.

59.—A printed notice of the office hours should be publicly exhibited in every room occupied by the bank, and in the win-

---

* [This has been urged in letters to us from the Rev. W. H. Owen, St. Asaph; R. Wheeler, Esq., High Wycombe; Mr. Stocks, Actuary of the Rye Savings Bank; the Manager of the Hemel Hempstead Savings Bank, and others.]

dow of the office;* and as regards guaranteed Savings Banks in England, the "bank hours" should be registered at the office of the Commissioners.

It is worthy of notice, that in many Savings Banks, the period allowed for transacting business is very limited. By a Parliamentary return it appears that about fifty Savings Banks are open for only *four hours monthly*, that 120 are open for *one hour per week*, and 142 open for *two hours per week*. There are 97 whose total number of receipts from Depositors for the year 1854 were under 300 each, *i. e.* each bank received an average of *six sums per week*. There are 77 banks receiving an average of *eight sums per week*; and 157 banks receiving *fifteen sums per week*: making altogether 331 Savings Banks where receipts from Depositors average about *a dozen per week*.

Section 4.—As to the Rules and Annual Statements.

ART. 60.—The Rules and Bye-Laws of the bank, or an abstract of them, to be approved by the certifying Barrister, should be †printed in every deposit-book, and also suspended together with all notices issued from time to time by the Commissioners, in some conspicuous place in the office of the bank.

An abstract, clearly drawn up, might be preferable to the Rules at length. It should be in large type.

---

* [See the cases of the Cuffe Street, Killarney, and Tralee frauds, where persons were encouraged to deposit more than the limit allowed by the law, and thus to risk the entire loss of their money, with the view of increasing the margin for the expenses of the bank.]

† [The Devonport Savings Bank, and the Edinburgh Savings Bank, among others, in 1853, wrote to support this view. Most Savings Banks act upon it, though not by law required to do so.]

It cannot be too strongly urged upon the Depositors in Savings Banks to make themselves acquainted with their Rules. In the words of Mr. Porter :* " If they have not done so already, it is time they should do it now; and as they pass from Rule to Rule, if it be one imposing a duty on themselves, let them ask have they complied with such duty? and if it be one imposing a duty on the bank, and the Trustees and Managers, have they seen that it is obeyed? If they have been negligent in those duties, and if they have allowed year after year to roll on without passing a thought on so vital a subject, is it fair to superadd the blame which fairly attaches to themselves, to that which belongs to those Trustees and Managers who confidingly believed that, because the Depositors seemed happy and satisfied, therefore all was safe and satisfactory? And as to such Trustees and Managers as now wake for the time under a sense of responsibility, it may be asked, what steps have they taken to see that the Depositors were not allowed to place themselves in a false position, and thus involve themselves and their families in, perhaps, irretrievable ruin?"

61.—A statement should be hung up in the bank, and, if thought necessary, printed for distribution among the Depositors, of the whole† of the balances, at the end of every half-year, referred to by the number of each book, and, if requisite, by the initials of the ‡Depositor's name.

---

* [*Savings Banks: their Defects and Remedies.*]

† [This is supported by Robert Wheeler, Esq., Treasurer, and Mr. W. H. Butler, Secretary, of the High Wycombe Savings Bank (which publishes such accounts annually), Burwood Godlee, Esq., Chairman of the Lewes Savings Bank, (4th May 1858), Mr. Taylor of Rochdale, and Mr. Sikes of Huddersfield, in opinions to the Committee. It is done in the Ely Bank and a few others.]

‡ [Great care should be taken to secure the accuracy of the annual statements. At Rugby, Mr. Grey reported that "the former Actuary has been in the habit of making up the annual statement in a very untruthful manner," and "annually fabricated the classified statement of balances required by the National Debt Office, so as to make it appear

When the transactions are very numerous, so that one sheet would be inconveniently large, progressive groups of numbers might be printed on separate sheets.

The statutory penny (10 Geo. IV., c. 92., s. 47.) should not be demanded from Depositors applying for printed copies of the annual statement, but they should be supplied *gratis*, as is done at the banks at St. Martin's Place, Exeter, Worcester, and many others.

Section 5.—*As to Books of Accounts.*

ART. 62.—There should be an *index to names, whereby the

---

that the liabilities of the Bank corresponded exactly with its assets." The Actuary would, no doubt, have continued to conceal the difference between the assets and liabilities as he had done " before, *by falsifying the classified statement of balances.*" These were in 1853 and 1855 also fictitious. Mr. Grey reported as to the Farringdon Street Savings Bank—" There *is no sign whatever that the ledger entries have ever been called over with the cash journal!* The consequence is that the ledgers are full of errors." " Payments were made on closed accounts, and others on open accounts which have never been posted." In 1854 the balances due to Depositors " were stated at £567 . 2*s*. less than the truth." This reduction was accomplished by dropping £30, £40, or £50, each, from some of the larger balances, until the whole was brought down to the sum which (allowing for the known deficiency) would meet the assets on hand. Mr. Wortley also mentions a case in which Auditors had passed errors of considerable amount: in another he found Auditors and an Actuary who had *never seen* the customary half-yearly vouchers from the Government for money in their hands. He related many other instances in which the accounts never balance accurately, and in which the method of book-keeping was such that it was next to impossible they should do so.]

---

* [" Il arrive fort souvent qu'on a besoin de trouver le compte d'un Déposant sans avoir entre les mains son livret, et sans savoir quel est son numéro : ou a recours alors au *répertoire*.

" Le nombre des Déposants étant trop considérable pour que les

numbers of the corresponding pass-books may be found. Mr. Grey concurs with us, however, in thinking that

"It is quite unnecessary that the current amounts in the ledger and pass-books of any Savings Bank should shew (as many still do) debtor and creditor sides. Savings Bank deposit accounts are never in debt or overdrawn. The balance, if there be one, is always to the credit of the Depositor."

One page consisting of two * money columns is sufficient to shew what that credit is. Further deposits, and † interest on those already in hand, are easily added from time to time to the balance; and any withdrawal is as easily deducted from it when it occurs, still shewing, after each transaction, the balance in hand, without the necessity of totalling two sides of an account, and deducting one from another. This arrangement also greatly economises space in the ledgers; an important consideration when the accounts become numerous.

---

recherches eussent été faciles dans un répertoire établi sur des registres, le répertoire est *mobile*, et se compose de cartes dont chacune porte le nom d'un déposant, ses prénoms, la série et le numéro de son livret. Ces cartes sont placées dans des boîtes où elles sont classées et maintenues dans l'ordre alphabétique le plus exact." Agathon Prévost, *Manuel*, p. 13. This plan is considered in France to be preferable to an Index Book.]

* ["Quant aux comptes particuliers, ils figurent, comme on l'a vu, sur des registres séparés, qui ne sont pas tenus par *débit* et *crédit*, mais par *addition* et *soustraction.*" Agathon Prévost, *Manuel*, p. 12.]

† [See Part IV. for an explanation of the *Prospective Interest* plan.]

⁎ While revising the proof-sheets of the foregoing Part, the idea occurred to us that a *cursory* perusal of it may convey, to some, an impression that we have treated the subject of the requisite limitations and checks on the actions of Savings Bank Managers and Actuaries, on the supposition that they have all been generally negligent in the discharge of their duties—that none of the former duly appreciate their responsibility, and that the latter have manifested (so to speak) a proclivity to the committal of fraud.

We here very earnestly disclaim any opinions which could give colour to such an imputation: they would be altogether at variance with those we actually hold, and have derived from a sufficiently extensive experience: and if the painful *individual* cases we have had to discusss have really given an unfavourable turn to public opinion with regard to men almost universally of personal honour and business integrity, and (in numerous instances) of striking ability, we consider such an effect is to be classed among their most lamentable results.

PART III.

FINANCIAL DEFECTS

IN THE

PRESENT SAVINGS BANK SYSTEM.

CONTENTS OF PART III.

                                                                                            PAGE

CHAP. VII. How the deficiency in Savings Bank Assets has arisen, and as to the loss experienced by the Nation - - - - - - - 115

CHAP. VIII. The operations of Chancellors of the Exchequer, and their effect on Savings Banks - 135

CHAPTER VII.

HOW THE
DEFICIENCY IN SAVINGS BANK ASSETS HAS ARISEN,
AND REMARKS ON THE
LOSS EXPERIENCED BY THE NATION.

CONTENTS OF CHAP. I.

§ 1. Preliminary Considerations as to the correct principles for *Valuing* Securities - - - - - - - - 115
§ 2. Statement of the *Deficiency* in Savings Bank Securities, and of the Errors of the System - - - - - - 118
§ 3. Statement of the *Causes* of the Deficiency - - - - 122
§ 4. Remarks on the Loss arising from the rate of *Interest* allowed to Savings Banks by the Nation - - - - - - 128
§ 5. Remarks on the Losses attending Purchases and Sales of *Stock* for Depositors' purposes only - - - - - - 131

Section 1.—*Preliminary Considerations as to the correct principles for valuing Securities.*

ART. 1.—*The Government Plan.*—The rule prescribed by the annual order of Parliament for the valuation of the securities, held by the National Debt Commissioners on behalf of Savings Banks and Friendly Societies, consists in adopting the price of stock (whatever it may happen to be) on the 20*th November* in each year as the basis of every estimate. The application of this unsound principle on the 20*th November* 1858, when Consols were high, viz. 98⅛, made the cash deficiency to appear to be only £3,099,714 in their value as compared with the amount due on deposits.

2.—It is evident, that as the estimated value of the securities depends solely on the price of stock, it must be materially lessened if there be any fall, consequent on a panic or an unexpected demand for money; and the estimated deficiency of assets is thus liable at any time to be greatly increased. Thus, for instance, if the funds were to sink to what they were, no longer ago than January 1856 or October 1857, namely, £86 per cent., there would be an apparent cash deficiency of £6,182,594 in the amount of stock Government has in hand to meet its liabilities to Depositors.

3.—The result of the plan of valuation adopted by the National Debt Commissioners has been, that in the successive Parliamentary returns to the 20th November of each year the *deficiency has sometimes appeared greater than it really was, and at other times less—just as the funds have happened to be either low or high on the day of valuation.

Thus, in 1847, stock was only worth $83\frac{3}{8}$ on the 20th November, and, although the deposits were then but thirty-two millions, the deficiency was returned to Parliament as being £5,462,300.

---

* [Those, who prepared the order of the House, do not seem to have reflected that any investments, made at one price, will shew a deficiency if valued when the market has fallen lower. In illustration of this we may mention a case of a purchase of £10,000 stock made by a Society in July 1857, which cost £9600. On a valuation being made in November 1857, when the funds had temporarily fallen to about 88, it would have appeared, if that reduced price had been adopted in the calculation, that the stock was only worth £8800, and a loss of £800 would have been shewn. In the same way with the Savings Bank funds: if the whole £38,372,090 had been invested in the funds at the *price of safety*, viz. when they were at £92 . 6s. 2d (which *is the price at which* £100 *cash invested in* 3 *per cent. stock would produce* £3 . 5s. *a-year, and thus enable the Commissioners to pay the present rate of interest without loss to the nation*), the stock bought would have been £41,569,761. This amount, if valued afterwards when the funds were at 85, would shew a deficiency of £3,037,793, and this without any "dabbling" by Chancellors of the Exchequer, on whom many seem by this word to desire to throw the responsibility of the greater part of the existing deficiency. (See c. 8. in this part. On the *Operations of Chancellors of the Exchequer.*]

4.—*As to an Average Period.*—It requires, therefore, little argument to shew that a deficiency or surplus, as the case may be, in Savings Banks securities cannot be fairly deduced from an estimate based on the price of stocks on a particular *day of the year, but must be taken on such a principle as will allow for fluctuations of successive years. This is complied with by taking for basis the average of the prices, that stock has borne during a sufficiently long period of time (such as twenty-five years) to allow for compensating influences in the money-market. The results of a valuation, so made, would undergo but little alteration, though considerable fluctuations of price might occur in the course of a subsequent equally lengthened interval, and a variation, in any particular year, would only affect the average price of the stock by one twenty-sixth of the difference between the *average* price of stock for the whole twenty-five years and that for the twenty-sixth year alone. In respect to Savings Banks stock there is a peculiarity, that it has in general to be bought when the funds are high, and sold when they are low (see sect. 5.); hence the average result of their operations differs from that of the public funds generally. Again, although the claims of Savings Banks and Friendly Societies on the National Debt Commissioners amount to more than £38,000,000, represented by securities, which are nearly all in the 3 per cents., yet of this the average amount sold for the requirements of Depositors, in the course of twelve months is but small, and judging from the †past, not likely in any year, to exceed five millions; hence the prices

---

* [Of the £786,801,000 of the National or Funded Debt, but a very small portion, in the course of each year, is exposed to the fluctuations of value by sales; the remainder resting for series of years in the same hands, and passing at death to the heirs without a sale.

Hence the price of the day is no guide to the value of the nation's liability to its creditors for the public debt. See *Appendix on the National Debt*, at the end of this Treatise.]

† [See Art. 18, where the real average is shewn to be much lower.]

realised by the sale of these few millions are no guide to the value of the whole thirty-eight.

Savings Banks deposits being subject to exceptional influences, the corresponding securities must be measured by the average of such influences, so that the value of the portion, *not likely to be called for* at depreciating periods, will be measured properly by taking the average prices of the *funds generally* for twenty-five years, whilst the *value of the extreme amount—say seven millions—likely to be *withdrawn*, should be measured by the average of the prices of *past sales* during a similar period.

Section 2.—Statement of the Deficiency in Savings Bank Securities, and of the Errors of the System.

ART 5.—Having determined the principles upon which Savings Bank securities should be valued, we will now consider the financial condition of the Savings Banks and Friendly Societies of the United Kingdom, depositing with the National Debt Commissioners, and the state of their †funds in the Commissioners' hands on the 20th November 1858. From the absence of sufficient published data for ascertaining the exact proportion liable to be thrown upon the market in each year by withdrawals on behalf of the Depositors only, we have taken the whole value of the stocks at the *average price of* 3 *per cent. Consols for the last twenty-five years.* This, according to the Journal of the Statistical Society, happens curiously enough to be £92⅞, almost exactly the price that will produce ‡£3 . 5s. a-year interest per cent. on the money invested.

---

* [The proportion of the actual sales to the total deposits differs very largely from year to year: for instance, in 1855, it was ¼; in 1858, ⅟₇].

† [Exclusive of the Deferred Annuities account, for which see further on, Part V. c. 14. s. 3.]

‡ [See Table B, and remarks on this point in note to Art. 16.]

ACCOUNT OF DEFICIENCY.

Dr. LIABILITIES OF THE COMMISSIONERS.	£	£	£	ASSETS OF THE COMMISSIONERS. Cr.	£	£	£
*1. Total amount of *Principal Money* paid in by Trustees of Savings Banks since 1817	44,578,271			1. *Stock* held, viz. :—			
Aggregate amount of interest paid and credited to Savings Banks since 1817	29,981,860			Consolidated 3 per Cents.	5,979,334		
		74,560,131		Reduced do.	3,419,310		
Deduct amount repaid by the Commissioners to the Trustees, viz.				New do.	17,291,821		
Principal	37,621,859			New 2¾ per Cents. (value 81½ per Cent.),	31,900		
Interest	546,864			New 3 per Cents. (Irish)	1,031,589		
		38,168,723				27,743,954	
Balance due to Savings Banks			36,391,408	*Value* of above Stock, at a mean average price of 92¾ per cent.			25,628,476
viz.—Bearing interest	36,040,914			2 *Exchequer Bills* held (taken at par)			7,000,000
Separate Surplus Fund not bearing interest	350,494			Interest on Exchequer Bills then to be received			76,112
2. Total amount of *Principal Money* paid in by *Friendly Societies* established under Act 59 Geo. III.		2,951,233		3. *Cash Balance* waiting investment			653,585
Interest paid and credited to such Societies at rates of £4. 11s. 3d. and £3. 16s. 0½d. per cent. since 1817		1,688,620		Total Assets			33,958,173
Principal Money paid in by Societies under Act of 13 & 14 Vict.		100,957		*Balance deficient*			4,413,917
Interest credited to such Societies, £3. 0s. 10d. per cent. per annum		10,623					
		4,751,433					
Deduct amount repaid by Commissioners to Friendly Societies		2,770,751					
Balance due to Friendly Societies			1,980,682				
Total Liabilities			£38,372,090				£38,372,090

* See Art. 19. of this Part.

In other words, on the 20th November 1858 there remained due by the National Debt Commissioners to the Trustees of Savings Banks, for deposits received in cash and for sums credited by way of interest:—

Great Britain - - - -	£34,577,011
Ireland - - - - -	1,814,397
Friendly Societies, direct - -	1,980,682
Total - -	38,372,090
Deficiency (See Art. 19) - -	4,413,917

6.—To appreciate the causes that have given rise to this £4,413,917 deficiency of assets, we will ask our readers to suppose a case, viz. that a banker had received, at various times, sums amounting to £10,000 altogether, on the understanding that he was to pay a high rate of interest thereon, and yet to invest the money in securities, for the benefit of the Depositor:—such securities to be restricted to a particular kind, viz. the public funds, and yet to be available for repayment of the amount deposited on demand, and at par.

Suppose that, in lieu of investing the amount received, the banker retained various sums, amounting in the whole to £920, and only invested £9080, purchasing with it 3 per cent. stock at a price of 94¾ per cent., by which he obtained £9583 stock.

Suppose that, some years afterwards, the Depositor were to inquire into the value of the securities held by the banker for his money, he would find that it depended upon the price at which they could be realized.

Suppose, by that time it happened to be 92⅜, so that the value of the £9583 stock was only £8852, shewing a deficiency of £1148 on the £10,000 which he had entrusted to the banker to invest.

Suppose the banker were asked to account for this deficiency, and he acknowledged that it arose partly from his having kept back £920 of the money entrusted to him, and partly from the unavoidable fluctuations in value that attend public securities.

Suppose that, when asked why he had kept back the £920, he answered that he had done so by degrees, mainly because he had undertaken to pay the Depositor a higher rate of interest than he had been able to realize on the money, which, therefore, he had paid out of capital, and partly because he *wanted to take up the bills of another customer of his, so that too many of them might not come into the market and be depreciated in value.

Suppose he also added that a portion of the loss had arisen from the Depositor having drawn some of his money out and paid it in again, when the funds were at various prices.

Suppose he concluded by saying, that, after all, the apparent deficiency was of no moment to the Depositor, as he, the banker, was able and willing to acknowledge his liability to repay in full all the money that had been entrusted to his care.

7.—Now, in the preceding illustration, if we put, for £10,000, £38,372,090, the amount of Savings Bank and Friendly Society deposits; for the banker, the National Debt Commissioners; for the other customer, the nation; and for the bill discounting, the operations of the Chancellor of the Exchequer in Exchequer Bills, &c.; we shall obtain a clear perception of the causes of the financial position of Savings Banks at the present time. It appears, in fact, that out of the £4,413,917 deficiency in the Savings Bank and Friendly Society assets, on the 20th November, 1858, as shewn by the preceding balance sheet, no less a sum than £3,476,330 was a *cash* deficiency, arising from the fact of the National Debt

---

* [*See, in Chapter* VIII., *the remarks of the Right Hon. Mr. Disraeli on this question.*]

Commissioners not having been able to lay out or keep invested in stock on behalf of the Depositors,* inclusive of the money in hand, more than £34,895,760 out of the £38,372,090 they had received from the Trustees, which is equivalent to a loss of £9 in every £100. The remaining £937,587 of the deficiency is to be accounted for by the fact, that when the stock is valued by the average price for twenty-five years, viz. £92⅞ per cent., it is worth even less than the cost, from the purchases having been made at a higher price.

Section 3.—As to the Causes of the Deficiency.

ART. 8.—If the origin of the deficiency of £4,413,917 be traced in its minute details, we arrive, without difficulty, at three main causes why the amount of Savings Banks and Friendly Society securities in the hands of the National Debt Commissioners is insufficient to meet their liabilities. As they are fundamental errors in the present system, and several general principles will be evolved by a discussion of them, we commend them to the attention of our readers. They are:—

I. *The granting by the nation to the banks of a higher rate of Interest than the securities produced.*

		£
* [*The amount invested in stock* up to 20th November 1857 (according to the return 193, Session 1858), Savings Banks only		32,283,662
Transactions of 1858 (return 262—I., 1859):— £		
Paid for Purchases 1,134,586		
Less received for Sale 692,075		442,511
Friendly Societies (return 262, 1859):—		
Amount due 1,980,682		
Less loss by interest 440,558		1,540,124
Balance of cash in hand		629,463
		34,895,760

II. The *restriction which limits the investment of Savings Bank money to Government securities, such as stock and Exchequer Bills.

III. *The undertaking to repay all deposits on demand, and at par, whatever be the price of the funds.*

It has been alleged that there is yet another cause of considerable loss, viz. the dealings with Savings Banks funds by successive Chancellors of the Exchequer for national purposes. These transactions are so intricate and important as to require a separate Chapter for their consideration. (See chapter 8.)

9.—The three errors stated above have been allowed to exist in consequence of a disregard in the past administration of Savings Banks of the simplest axioms of sound practical finance; one of the most elementary of which is, *that it is impossible for any, who receive money for investment, to pay to Depositors, without incurring loss, the full amount of interest they themselves realize, while simultaneously guaranteeing the repayment of the deposits on demand, and at par.*

In the succeeding sections of this chapter we have given an estimate of the actual loss resulting from each of these causes: we may here, however, offer some remarks to confirm what we have asserted.

10.—It is a well understood principle that, down to a certain limit, with, *cæteris paribus,* equally good security, the rate of interest payable by banks or investment institutions on deposits must be less, the † shorter the notice that is cove-

---

* [By Sect. 15 of 9 Geo. IV., c. 92.]

† [At present, sums under £10,000 can be demanded by the Trustees from the Commissioners at five days' notice (9 Geo. IV. c. 92. s. 19.), and sums exceeding £10,000 at the expiration of fourteen days' notice (s. 20.); but no Savings Bank can receive, on any one day, from the Commissioners, more than £10,000 (s. 21.). The following is the clause

nanted to be given before a withdrawal can be made; in fact, Savings Banks are the only Investment Societies which pay out money *on demand* and yet allow to Depositors the full interest realised after paying expenses.

By way of illustration: From 4 to 5 per cent. are the ordinary limiting rates of interest obtainable upon mortgages, on which six months notice of withdrawal is required; whilst banks, which allow interest on deposits with only a few days' notice of withdrawal, usually limit their rates to a range from 1 to $2\frac{1}{2}$ per cent. per annum, and pay *no* interest on by far the larger part of their accounts, which being withdrawable on *demand*, are termed *" current."* In certain cases (such, for instance, as the public funds), where a rate between the extremes already quoted is obtainable, the power of withdrawal is virtually restricted, since the stockholder is exposed to the loss of a portion of the principal, if, on selling, the market price should be lower than that at which he bought. (*See note to Art* 6, *Part* VI.)

11.—Generally speaking, in times of peace and plenty,

---

adopted by most Savings Banks in reference to the notice of withdrawal required by them from their Depositors :—

" Deposits of £5 and under will be paid on demand to those found entitled or duly authorized to receive them, on any of the days appointed for receiving deposits; and deposits above £5, and not exceeding £15, will be paid on seven days' notice; and deposits above £15 will be paid on fourteen days' notice; but such payments can only be made to the Depositor personally, and on his or her receipt, or to the bearer of the book, with an order signed by the Depositor. Provided, however, that in cases of urgent necessity, such as illness, or death in the family, or sudden removal of a Depositor to a distant part of the country, a sum not exceeding £15 may be withdrawn without notice, on production of evidence, satisfactory to the Actuary, of the existence of such necessity."

The notice required is so short as to amount, practically, to payment on demand. In some first-class banks, however, as, for example, the *Leeds Savings Bank*, a *month's* notice is required before withdrawing any sum above £10, and a fortnight for any sum from £3 to £10.]

when money is abundant, trade brisk, and the price of the funds *high*, deposits in Savings Banks increase, and thus necessitate *purchases* of stock at a high rate; *but in periods of financial difficulty, when the labouring population do not obtain good wages, the funds fall to a *low* price, and yet that is the time when the necessity for †*withdrawal* arises. Thus the Commissioners, under the present system, *are compelled continually to buy in the dearest, and sell in the cheapest market.*

12.—At an early period (before the year 1844), when these

---

* [An extraordinary notion was suggested by one or two of the witnesses before the Committee, viz. that the Depositors withdraw their money when the funds are low for the purpose of " buying in stock." Any one with the least experience in industrial investments would know, that while Building Societies, and other similar associations, are in operation, purchases of stock are about the last thing they would think of. (See Part IV., Chap. xii.)]

† [There is, however, a restorative element at work on the prices of public stock; for when the poorer classes are compelled to withdraw, and stock is sold for them, the richer classes buy, because men experienced in money matters are in the habit of advising people who seek to make a profit by speculating in the funds, to buy in when the price of stock is 89 or under, and to sell when it passes 96. This is one of the causes why—apart from political considerations or monetary fluctuations—the funds tend to recovery when they get below 89, and tend to fall when they pass 96. The converse takes place with regard to persons of limited means, like the Depositors in Savings Banks. "I do not include in the general loan fund of the country, (Mr. Stuart Mill, Pol. Econ., vol. 2, p. 184, remarks) "the capitals, large as they sometimes are, which are habitually employed in speculatively buying and selling the public funds and other securities. It is true, that all who buy securities add, for the time, to the general amount of money on loan, and lower *pro tanto* the rate of interest. But as the persons I speak of buy only to sell again at a higher price, they are alternately in the position of lenders and of borrowers: their operations raise the rate of interest at one time, exactly as much as they lower it at another. Like all persons who buy and sell on speculation, their function is to equalize, not to raise or lower, the value of the commodity. When they speculate prudently, *they temper the fluctuations of price.*"]

errors had not yet excited public attention in England, they were ably pointed out in an eloquent speech by Baron Dupin, as follows:—

"The British Parliament has not feared to establish in favour of Savings Banks a legal interest of £3.16s. per cent., which, compared with the interest on the public funds and Exchequer Bills, is equivalent to an annual loss of £120,000. From 1817 to the present time, the funds having always risen, the loss sustained upon the interest may have been compensated by the profit on the capital. But let adverse circumstances occur—a war, or great social commotion, which will depress the price of stock— then the profit will vanish, at the very moment that the panic will cause a simultaneous rush upon the Savings Banks for repayment. It is an error to place the Savings Bank funds in the funded debt by means of purchases at the price of the day. *The operations of the Government are then nothing else than speculations for a rise.* .... Since 1817 circumstances have been prosperous, but the system itself can only exist by these favourable circumstances..... Let them change, the system crumbles and perishes; for it is exclusively founded upon a rise; it cannot survive a fall..... If war should arise —an event which certainly ought to enter into the calculations of every Government—the funds will fall, and the present Savings Bank system in England will be annihilated..... Another will replace it, and the State will have to bear the *expense."

---

* [M. Dupin, however, congratulated his countrymen that they had avoided the financial error of the English Legislature, by placing the deposits in the *Caisse des Dépôts et Consignations* (or floating debt), instead of the funded debt. This would be the same thing as if the investments in England were made only in Exchequer Bills, which are payable at par. M. Dupin overlooks, that if a demand were made upon the French Government to return a very large amount of deposits on short notice, they could only obtain the necessary money by selling other securities or borrowing at a loss. (*See Section on France, in the Introduction.*)

It was remarked by the Committee of the Corps Legislatif in France, of which M. Louvet was president, in their admirable Report in 1852:—
" L'Angleterre, il est vrai, n'absorbe pas les capitaux de ses caisses d'Epargne dan sa dette flottante, comme nous le faisons en France pour

This prediction, made in the year 1843, is practically being verified at the present day.

13.—The effect of rises and falls of the public funds on the purchases or withdrawals for Savings Bank Depositors is shewn very clearly in Parliamentary Paper, No. 441, 1858, p. 35:—

By way of example, we see that, in the quarter ending April 1844, about £650,000 more was deposited than withdrawn, the stock being at 97¾. On the other hand, in July 1848 the Savings Bank money was reduced, by an excess of withdrawals over receipts of (about) £1,420,000, the price of stock being but 83½.

In the previous quarter, the price of stock had fallen as low as 80⅓, which may perhaps indicate that the necessities of the Depositors in Savings Banks require some short period of time to be acted upon by the circumstances that produce a fall in the public stocks, to such a degree as to cause the *withdrawal* of deposits. This leads to the reflection that a prudent administration of Savings Bank deposits might, in times of crisis, prepare for withdrawals.

---

le majeure partie de ces capitaux ; elle les fait administrer par une commission spéciale, appelée *commission de la reduction de la dette nationale*. Cette commission emploie les capitaux qui lui sont versés par les caisses d'Epargne en achats de rentes sur l'Etat ou en negociations de bons de l'échiquier, mais presque toujours en rentes sur l'Etat. Ce mode de procéder a ses avantages. Beaucoup de bons esprits désirent qu'il soit appliqué en France : mais il a aussi ses inconvenients. En définitive c'est toujours l'Etat qui est le seul véritable debiteur dans les deux pays ; et si tous les remboursements étaient demandés, l'embarras de l'Angleterre ne serait guère moins grand que le nôtre."

M. Gustave du Puynode remarks, in his learned work before quoted (p. 388) :—"Les dépôts des caisses d'epargne constituent, sous notre législation actuelle, un grave, un énorme péril pour le trésor ; ils le soumettent sans cesse à des demandes innombrables de remboursement. C'est une lettre de change de plusieurs centaines de millions tirée sur lui, et chaque jour à échéance. Personne, sans doute, ne contesterait, depuis notre dernière révolution, le danger qu'ils créent."]

Section 4.—As to the loss attending the rate of Interest allowed to Savings Banks by the nation.

ART. 14.—From the subjoined Table A* it will be perceived, that a very large portion of the deficiency has arisen from the great excess of *interest paid and credited to the Trustees of Savings Banks,* including *direct Friendly Societies,* over that received by the Commissioners from their investments. This excess amounted on the 20th November 1858 to :—

£2,845,968 for Savings Banks,

440,558 } for Friendly Societies making their investments direct with the National Debt Commissioners,

£3,286,526

15.—Apart from the question of the rate being too high, a loss in interest annually arises from the total securities

---

* *As to Savings Banks only* :—

TABLE A.

Year ending 20th November.	Annual loss of Interest.	Rate per cent. of Interest granted by the Nation to Trustees of Savings Banks.	Total Interest paid in excess during the whole period when such rate was allowed.	Average loss of Interest for each year of the period.
1818—1828	...	£4 11 3	£744,363	£67,669
1829—1844	...	3 16 0½	1,435,567	89,723
1845	£20,185			
1846	17,277			
1847	17,664			
1848	29,251			
1849	36,857			
1850	36,684			
1851	43,149			
1852	46,227	3 5 0	666,038	47,574
1853	58,097			
1854	26,363			
1855	101,819			
1856	100,791			
1857	59,755			
1858	71,919			
			£2,845,968	£69,414

held by the Government being *short of their liabilities to the banks. As a natural consequence, the dividends which the partial investments yield, even if the rate of interest paid were the same as realized, would be inadequate to the payment of the interest on the larger sum due to the Depositors.

Thus the interest made by the Commissioners in the year 1858 was only about £2 . 19s. 1d. per cent., while they credited to the banks £3 . 5s. (see *Table B, next page.*)

---

* [*Future deficiencies will accrue if the present system be continued,* even although the present deficit be made up by a public grant, for loss of interest on the present rate of £3 . 5s. per cent. must arise unless two separate events concur in their average results :—
 1. *That the average price of the future purchases of stock by the Commissioners shall not exceed* 92¾ *per cent.*
 2. *That the average result of the future sales made for Depositors shall not be below* 92¾ *per cent.* (See the last paragraph of the next note.)

This has never been the case, for the average of *past* purchases has been at least 2 per cent. above 92¾, and the results of the sales have always been below 92¾. Sir Alexander Spearman stated (Qu. 3868), that—"Taking the average price of Government securities for each year since 1817, the only years in which the prices appear to have been such as to have produced a rate of interest equal to that at the same time paid to the Trustees, were the years 1847 and 1848 ; but those were years in which, instead of having to invest stock, they had very largely indeed to sell. Those were years in which the drafts of the Trustees were of enormous magnitude."

When the National Debt Commissioners were paying £4 . 11s. 3d. per cent., as from 1817 to 1828, they should have been able to buy £100 stock for £65 (see Table B. page 130), whereas the average price of stock for the years 1817 to 1828 was 78¾. Again, from 1828 to 1844 the rate of interest allowed was £3 . 16s. 0½d. per cent., so that the price of stock, in order to escape loss, should not have exceeded £78 ; whereas for the years 1828 to 1844 the average price was 89¾.

By far the largest portion of the interest allowed is credited to the banks and made capital. The reader will observe, that if the deficiency arising from the interest which the National Debt Commissioners were crediting had been made up from the first by an annual deficiency grant from Parliament, as it should have been, the system would have been objected to long ago ; but as the interest is only credited, and the actual liability deferred, the subject has escaped the attention it should have received.]

TABLE B.

Shewing the rate of Interest obtainable from 3 per cent. Stock for £100 cash invested according to the price of the day.

Price of Stock. (1.)	Interest which £100 cash obtains. (2.)			Amount of Stock £100 will purchase, or amount of Stock required to be sold to produce £100. (3.)			*Most recent years in which the average price of the 12 Months was that of (1.)
	£	s.	d.	£	s.	d.	
60	5	0	0	166	13	4	1815
61	4	18	9	163	18	9	1813
62	4	16	9	161	5	10	1816
63	4	15	3	158	14	8	
64	4	13	9	156	5	0	1811
65	4	12	3	153	16	11	
66	4	10	11	151	10	4	1808
67	4	9	7	149	5	1	1814
68	4	8	3	147	1	2	1820
69	4	7	0	144	18	7	
70	4	5	9	142	17	2	
71	4	4	6	140	16	11	
72	4	3	4	138	17	8	1819
73	4	2	2	136	19	9	1817
74	4	1	1	135	2	9	1821
75	4	0	0	133	6	8	1788
76	3	18	11	131	11	7	1793
77	3	17	11	129	17	5	
78	3	16	11	128	4	1	1777
79	3	15	11	126	11	8	1826
80	3	15	0	125	0	0	1831
81	3	14	1	123	9	2	
82	3	13	2	121	19	0	1760
83	3	12	4	120	9	8	1827
84	3	11	5	119	0	11	1832
85	3	10	7	117	12	11	1848
86	3	9	9	116	5	7	1847
87	3	9	0	114	18	10	1773
88	3	8	2	113	12	9	1833
89	3	7	5	112	7	2	1841
90	3	6	8	111	2	3	1855
91	3	5	11	109	17	10	1856
92	3	5	3	108	13	11	1842
93	3	4	6	107	10	7	1849
94	3	3	10	106	7	8	1744
95	3	3	2	105	5	3	1843
96	3	2	6	104	3	4	1853
97	3	1	10	103	1	10	1850
98	3	1	3	102	0	10	1851
99	3	0	7	101	0	3	1852
100	3	0	0	100	0	0	1751
101	2	19	4	99	0	2	1743

* [The average price of stock for the whole of the last 100 years (1759 to 1858) is about 78½. During that period the average price for the whole

Section 5.—*As to the losses attending the Purchase and Sale of Stock for Depositors' purposes only.*

ART. 16.—The investigation of this part of our subject is replete with difficulty, from the imperfection of the Parliamentary returns; and there are no means of measuring the actual loss that has attended the operations for purchase and sale. It can, however, be traced indirectly as follows :—

We have already estimated the total deficiency on the 20th November 1858, (Art. 5,) at . (*a*)£4,413,917
And we have shewn that the items constituting this deficiency are of two kinds:

1st. *Cash losses* (arising from the amount actually invested by the Commissioners being less than that due by them to the Trustees,) to the extent of (See Art. 7) . . (*b*)3,476,330

---

of a year has never been at or above par. The average for several months of the year 1852 was above 100. It is curious, however, that during several years previous to 1759, the average price for the whole of the year was at or above par: thus, in 1733, '42, '50, and '51, it was 100; in 1739 and '43, 101; in '36, 102; '54, 103; '38, '52, and '53, 104; and in 1737 it was as high as 106. On the other hand, between 1781 and 1815, there were ten years in which the average fell below 60. Between 1822 and 1831, a medium price of about 80 was kept to.

Loss of capital stock on sales produces an annual loss of interest:— let the double operation be taken of £1,000,000, (a portion of several millions on which £3 . 5*s*. per cent. per annum has to be paid) invested in, say July 1856, when the funds were 96, and a like amount realized in October 1857, at a price of 86½. The purchase caused a first loss of £1250 a year in interest, because £31,250 only was received, and £32,500 agreed to be paid: but this loss in interest was raised to £3432 a-year through £1,156,069 stock having, subsequently, to be sold to pay out the £1,000,000 in full. On these operations, the loss of Capital stock was £114,402.]

2d. *Depreciation* arising from the fact that the investments actually made have cost more, either in fact or in effect, than 92¼ for £100 stock: forming the remainder of the deficiency, [or (*a*) less (*b*)] . . . (*c*)£937,587

Now, we have seen that a portion of the first, or Cash loss, has arisen from the interest paid and credited to the Trustees having been greater than that received by the Commissioners on their investments, to the amount of (See Art. 14.) . (*d*)3,286,526

The remainder must therefore be attributed, principally, to the selling of stock at a lower rate than that at which it was purchased, making the *loss under this head [or (*b*) less (*d*)] . (*e*)189,804

Again, the second *Depreciation*, or loss, likewise originates in two ways, viz.

1st. Through the money invested having been placed on securities less productive than stocks. We shall shew in Chap. 8. that this is acknowledged by the National Debt Office to amount to £342,146 stock, which is equivalent in cash to (*f*)315,801

2d. Through the purchases of stock, or the *funding* of Exchequer Bills (which we shall shew in Chap. 8. to be the same thing) having been effected at a higher price than 92¼. (the *valuation average price* taken in the Balance Sheet). . (*g*)621,786

It would thus appear *by adding* (*g*) *to* (*e*) that a deficiency of more than three quarters of a million may be fairly estimated as having arisen from the purchase of stock for Depositors' purposes at high prices, and its sale at lower rates.

---

* [In his return, p. 329 Committees' Report, Sir A. Spearman estimated this item at £178,915 to 20th Nov. 1857.]

17.—The loss may be appreciated better by one illustration, selected from the last official returns (1858) from which it appears, that during the year ending 20th November 1858, the stock

 Bought amounted to £1,170,000, and cost £1,134,586
 Sold „ „ 755,250, realized 692,075

 Difference: Amount £414,750 Price £442,511

In this year the purchasing prices ranged from $95\frac{3}{8}$ to $98\frac{1}{4}$ and the selling prices from $89\frac{3}{8}$ to 94 per cent. Thus we see, that so disadvantageous were these rates, that the balance of stock remaining in hand from the year's transactions, namely, £414,750 had cost £442,511, or, which amounts to the same thing, £106 . 13s. 11d. in cash had been virtually paid for every £100 of this remaining stock.

18.—*Direct evidence* of a large portion of the *three quarters of a million* loss, shewn in Art. 16, is afforded by the following Table C, which exhibits the excess of receipts from, over withdrawals by, Trustees (or the reverse, as it happened to be) from 5th January 1840 to 5th January 1858, grouped, for the sake of brevity, into periods of six quarters each, *in which corresponding prices prevailed—the quarters, of course, not being consecutive.* Nothing can be more conclusive than the evidence which this Table affords, that the position we have advanced is abundantly supported by facts, viz. that it is the peculiar fate of Savings Bank securities that they in general have to be purchased when the funds are high, and to be sold when they are low, and that no compensating operation can be made to neutralize the result:—

134   LOSSES ATTENDING PURCHASE AND SALE OF STOCK.

TABLE C. Average price of 3 per Cent. Stock during six separate quarters of years. (Col. 1.)						Excess of Receipts over Withdrawals in the six quarters when the average price of 3 per Cent. Stock was as in Col. 1.	Excess of Withdrawals over Receipts in the six quarters when the average price of 3 per Cent. Stock was as in Col. 1.
£	s.	d.	£	s.	d.	£	£
£80	10	10 to	87	1	6	. . .	4,043,247
87	9	8 to	89	0	0	. . .	1,096,523
89	9	7 to	90	9	8	. . .	1,583,659
90	11	5 to	90	16	6	. . .	518,240
90	17	10 to	91	17	0	. . .	1,090,482
92	1	9 to	93	8	11	. . .	301,102
93	17	7 to	94	10	7	. . .	53,457
94	12	11 to	95	12	6	384,350	
95	15	0 to	96	10	11	223,653	
96	11	10 to	97	15	10	920,486	
97	16	9 to	99	10	5	485,005	
99	13	8 to	101	8	3	1,312,268	

Thus an excess of—
£4,043,247 was *withdrawn* when the funds were at an average of £83 17 5
and £4,643,463,   „   „   „   „   90 6 1
While an excess of—
£2,013,494 was *purchased* „   „   „   „   96 0 10
and £1,312,268   „   „   „   „   100 1 10

The average price realised on the balance of sales over purchases in the 18 years was only £80.18s.

19.—It is, consequently, manifestly unsafe to guarantee the repayment of deposits at par, and to invest them in securities which fluctuate in price, unless a reserve fund be accumulated or provided for out of the interest received, or from some other sufficient source.

⁎ *Since the preceding was put in type we have received the following information for the year ending 20th November* 1859:—

Total due to Trustees of Savings Banks and Friendly Societies by the National Debt Commissioners (instead of 38 millions) - £41,180,832

Deficiency in total securities to meet the above (valuation being made on the same principle as in the Balance Sheet, Art. 5) - 4,496,088

Increase in deficiency between 20th November 1858, and 20th November 1859, £82,171.

CHAPTER VIII.

THE OPERATIONS OF CHANCELLORS OF THE EXCHEQUER, AND THEIR EFFECT ON SAVINGS BANKS.

CONTENTS.

§ 1. As relates to Savings Banks . . . p. 135
§ 2. As regards the Nation 147

Section 1.—As relates to Savings Banks.

ART. 20.—As we have stated in Art. 8., some portion of the deficiency in Savings Bank securities has arisen from the following cause, viz. the dealing with the deposits for national purposes by Chancellors of the Exchequer. Singular exaggerations, however, both as to the actual amount of the loss created and its effect upon the fund, are current among even persons of intelligence and practical experience, from an imperfect apprehension of the results of these financial operations; these erroneous statements were taken up, doubtless without mature consideration, and shaped into positive denunciations of the conduct of the Chancellors, by some of the members of the Committee of 1858. Their opinions were founded on various elaborate memorials published during the last fourteen years by several of the banks in England and Scotland, in which it was attempted to be proved, by an extensive array of statistics, that the nation had experienced a loss of several millions by the purchases and sales referred to. As injurious effects might result from such statements, if left uncorrected, we propose to subjoin, at some length, the details of the actual transactions, so that our readers may have an opportunity of judging for themselves how little cause existed for the popular clamour on this subject, and how even intelligent persons may embrace conclusions which have been too hastily drawn. Indeed, a certain amount of ill-feeling and an impression of injustice have already been created in the minds of the industrious classes by these ill-judged assertions, and a notion has spread amongst them that their savings have been made a means of gain to the State, and that irresponsible persons connected with the Government have been allowed to tamper with the funds placed for safe keeping in their hands.

21.—One of the principal witnesses before the Committee in 1858 was Mr. Boodle, Comptroller of the St. Martin's Place Savings Bank, who stated in his evidence:—

"I have given my attention very much to the subject of investments. I consider that they have been so made as to realize (I will not say to the country, but to the Savings Banks) a very considerable loss—some millions. The system is one of very long standing; but in the year 1844 the managers of our institution protested against it. They stated that the National Debt Commissioners had been in the habit of selling out large amounts of stock when the funds were low, of buying Exchequer Bills, and then funding those Exchequer Bills again when the funds were very high; so that, up to that period, there was a considerable depreciation in the value of securities held by the Commissioners on account of Savings Banks. *Within the last six years* I should say there has been between £2,000,000 and £3,000,000 lost. I think the provisions of the Act 9 *Geo.* IV. *c.* 92. as to investment, have been wholly disregarded." (Parliamentary Report, Qu. 858—873.)

22.—This witness, in common with some of the others,

appears to have derived this opinion of the magnitude of the deficiency caused by the operations of the Chancellor of the Exchequer, from its appearing that a very much greater number of purchases and sales of Savings Bank stocks were made by the Commissioners than would answer to the payments and withdrawals made by the Trustees of Savings Banks. This is admitted, and readily appears from the following return to 1857 (*Parliamentary Report*, pp. v. & vi.)

I. Total receipts since the establishment of Savings Banks, not including Friendly Societies . . £43,283,915
Total amount of interest paid and credited . . 28,851,993
                                                72,135,908
Total investments in stocks of all kinds, Exchequer Bills and Bonds 81,966,006

Investments more than could have been required by the deposits and dividends . . . . . . 9,830,098(*a*)

II. Total withdrawn by Trustees 36,880,197
Stocks of all kinds sold . . . 23,795,252
Exchequer Bills sold . 4,067,700
    ,,   ,, funded   8,090,550
    ,,   ,, paid off, 16,238,800
                          ─────────── 28,397,050
                                                52,192,302

Sales more than were required to meet the withdrawals . . . . 15,312,105(*b*)

Total amount of operations* (*a*) and (*b*) not possibly required for the purposes of the Savings Banks . 25,142,203

---

* [The investments and withdrawals did not, in all instances, require to be met by purchases or sales of stock. Hence the amount of the operations *not* required for Savings Bank purposes would be represented by a larger sum than £25,142,203. In reference to these variations in Savings

23.—The Committee seem to have been deeply impressed with the necessity of making a thorough investigation into the truth of the complaints which had been made as to the effect of the operations of the Exchequer. They found that the ordinary annual and other returns, furnished to Parliament in reference to Savings Banks, afforded no means of ascertaining the actual effect of such operations. They, therefore, requested the Comptroller of the National Debt Office, Sir Alexander Spearman, Bart., to furnish them with a distinct and categorical statement of what would have been the actual position of the public stocks, standing to the credit of Savings Banks, if no dealings had occurred with them except to meet the requirements of Depositors.

This statement appears to have been readily furnished, and Sir A. Spearman disposed of the charges in a very clear and satisfactory manner, shewing, by the information he gave in elucidating what had taken place, that although a portion of the Savings Bank money might perhaps appear to have been placed, at various times, at a disadvantage, by having securities transferred from other Government creditors, yet neither the Savings Bank fund nor the nation were damnified thereby to any large extent. (See Art. 25, forward.)

24.—The witnesses, indeed, can scarcely have reflected, that it, by no means, followed that the average result of the above purchases and sales, although so extensive and numerous, would be attended by any great loss in respect to the aggregate amount of stock resulting at the end; as, from the very num-

---

Bank securities, Lord Monteagle remarked (20th May 1858) that "the power vested in the Commissioners to change their securities, and thus to become active agents in the stock market, with a power limited only by the enormous amount of Savings Bank stock placed at their disposal, is a larger power than ever was possessed, I believe, by any branch of the community, or any combinations of individuals, and affecting, in proportion to that power, the public credit and the interests of private parties." (qu. 4394.).]

ber of the operations, the law of *'averages' comes in, and prevents any important effect either way arising.

A deficiency of £342,146 is acknowledged by Sir Alexander Spearman, which is attributable rather to the insufficiency of interest, arising from the difference of the rates receivable on Exchequer Bills and stock respectively, and to the loss of interest for portions of a year that attends and affects all dealings with the public stocks. The deficiency from these sources could not, therefore, be expected to prove the "millions" suggested by the witnesses. He stated distinctly (qu. 3890) that no such loss had occurred, and added, that it was a marvel that any such statement should have been made to the Committee: *there was no truth in the statement that during the last six years there had been a loss of between* £2,000,000 *and* £3,000,000.

ART. 25.—*The amount of the Loss.*—From the returns furnished by Sir Alexander Spearman, we are able to ascertain, for two periods of time, the amount of the fund that would have been in the hands of the National Debt Commissioners, if no portion of the monies received by them had ever been applied to the purchase of Exchequer Bills or Bonds, or to any operations in stock not required for Savings Bank purposes; and we gather from them the extent of the loss to the fund.

First, in reference to the whole transactions since 1828,

---

* [If a sum of money were invested in the funds, starting when they are below par, and, for a sufficiently long period, sales and purchases were made, then it would be found that the investor would be in pretty nearly the same position at the close of the transactions as when he started. This principle of the law of average, though true of ordinary purchases and sales, such as were effected by the Chancellor of the Exchequer for national purposes, does not, however, (as we have shewn in Art. 18) apply to those made for the requirements of Depositors, which are peculiar, and have created (as shewn in Art. 16), a portion of the estimated deficiency exceeding three-quarters of a million.]

it appears from the subjoined *return, that if no Exchequer Bills had been bought and no operations in stock had taken place except for Savings Bank purposes, the fund would have been, on the 20th November 1857 - - £34,794,428
Whereas it was only - - - - - 34,452,282

Shewing a deficiency of securities equal to - £ 342,146

---

* [ACCOUNT shewing the several CAPITALS of ANNUITIES standing, on the 20th November 1857, to the credit of the Commissioners for the reduction of the National Debt, on account of the fund for the BANKS for SAVINGS; and shewing also the several CAPITALS of ANNUITIES which would have been standing at their credit on the said 20th November, on account of the same fund, supposing that no transaction relating to Exchequer Bills or Exchequer Bonds had taken place between 6th August 1817 and 20th November 1857, but that all monies received for dividends, together with all monies received from Trustees during that period, had been regularly applied, week by week, to the payment of Trustees' drafts, or the purchase of annuities, as the case might be, at the prices of such annuities, during each week, in the market, *and no stock had been sold at any time over the period, unless the money was required to pay drafts by Trustees.*

	Stock standing in the name of the Commissioners at the 20th Nov. 1857.	Stock which wou'd have been standing if no part of the Cash Balances had been applied to the purchase of Exchequer Bills or Bonds, between the 6th August 1817 and 20th November 1857.
	£ s. d.	£ s. d.
Consols	14,386,611 9 6	5,955,000 0 0
Reduced 3 per Cents. .	2,921,610 9 4	5,913,000 0 0
New 3 per Cents. . .	16,027,371 7 10	21,845,000 0 0
Irish New 3 per Cents.	1,031,588 13 7	1,031,588 13 7
2½ per Cents. . . .	31,900 0 0	
	34,399,082 0 3	34,744,588 13 7
Uninvested Balance .	53,200 2 0	49,839 5 7
	34,452,282 2 3	34,794,427 19 2

In the account of Capitals of Annuities standing to the credit of the Commissioners on 20th November 1857, the Exchequer Bills held by the Commissioners are assumed to be converted into annuities, under the provisions of the Act 9 Geo. IV. c. 92. s. 50. & 51.

National Debt Office, 28th April 1858.]   A. Y. SPEARMAN.

which is therefore the *Stock loss* suffered by the Savings Bank fund in consequence of the transactions of the Commissioners in Exchequer Bills and stock not required for Depositors' purposes, the worth of which estimated in present cash, according to the principle laid down in Art. 5., is £315,801.

26.—The second *return, given below, is also very interesting, as shewing that the more recent operations of the kind—namely, those since 1853—have been attended with actual advantage to the fund; for it amounted, on the 20th November 1857, to - - - - - £34,452,282
Whereas it would have been - - - 34,249,102

Shewing a profit on the Exchequer operations
as regards the period of 4½ years, of - - £203,180
instead of the two millions or three millions loss represented by the witnesses as having occurred in the same period.

It would appear from these figures, that whilst the earlier transactions, namely, those which terminated in 1849, were un-

---

* ["Stock which would have been standing if no part of the cash balances had been applied to the purchase of Exchequer Bills or Bonds, between the 5*th April* 1853, and 20th November 1857, but if all monies received for dividends, together with all the monies received from Trustees during that period, had been regularly applied, week by week, to the payment of Trustees' drafts or the purchase of annuities, as the case might be, at the prices of such annuities, during each week, in the market, and if no stock had been sold at any time over the period, unless the money were required to pay drafts by Trustees:—

		£	s.	d.
Consols		11,118,656	2	11
Reduced 3 per Cents.		5,128,105	14	2
New 3 per Cents.		16,897,121	7	10
Irish 3 per Cents.		1,031,588	13	7
2½ per Cents.		31,900	0	0
		34,207,371	18	6
Uninvested Balance		41,730	3	8
		34,249,102	2	2

"A. Y. SPEARMAN.

"National Debt Office, 20th April 1858."]

favourable, and attended with a *loss to the Savings Bank fund of £545,326, a very considerable †profit was obtained from similar operations between 1853 to 1857, and thus the earlier losses were to a great extent made good, and the ultimate deficit reduced to £342,146. From 1849 to 1853 there were no transactions of the kind.

27.—Having shewn that the Savings Bank deficiency from Exchequer operations is very much less than the witnesses imagined, Sir A. Spearman explained that the effect on the Savings Banks themselves has not been any whatever. They have neither risk nor interest in the mode in which the funds are invested, whether at a profit or a loss; for the whole risk of the fluctuations of securities rests upon the Government itself.

The Government, in relation to the Trustees of Savings Banks (for it has none to individual Depositors), stands in precisely the same position as a banker to a customer who deposits money with him, on which interest is to be allowed, under two simple conditions:—1st. That the customer may draw it out, in whole or in part, at any moment he pleases, or on giving an agreed notice; and 2ndly, That, for whatever time it remains, he shall receive interest at a given rate.—The banker has these two obligations, and no other. He is left with perfect freedom to employ the funds thus committed to his charge as he may think best. He may discount bills—he may make advances to his customers on cash credit—he may invest in Consols, Exchequer Bills, Exchequer Bonds, or Railway Bonds, just as he pleases, subject only to the obligations to his customers already named. It is, indeed, quite

---

* [Namely £342,146, added to £203,180.]

† [See Art. 40., where Sir Alexander Spearman estimates that, even if the fund nominally lost, the nation at large gained. He mentioned one transaction, in 1833, as having given one-half of £53,000 a-year profit to the nation, equivalent to £883,000 gain in stock.]

plain, that if the banker had not the liberty thus to invest and use his deposits, he could neither pay interest to his customers, nor obtain a profit by his business, nor even discharge the expense of conducting it;—and the whole art of banking is so to arrange these investments, that they may yield to the banker the largest possible interest, consistently with their character of easy and immediate convertibility in order to enable him to meet the demands of his Depositors. A banker, therefore, apportions his investments among various securities. While he holds a certain amount in cash to meet immediate demands, he invests some in the discount of Bills of Exchange, which are daily falling due and supplying him with cash if required; he invests another portion in Exchequer Bills or Bonds, which, though giving less interest, are easily converted without risk, at any moment; another portion he invests in Consols or Railway Bonds, which are subject to greater fluctuations and risk, but which pay him a higher profit. In all this the banker has the sole and absolute discretion. The customer has no interest whatever in the matter, so long as the banker is able to fulfil to him the simple conditions of payment of his deposits, with interest, when and as he calls for them.

28.—The relation of the State to Savings Banks is precisely the same. The engagement is to receive deposits to any amount, to keep them for any time, short or long, and to be prepared to repay them, with interest, at a moment's notice. To these conditions the whole credit of the State is pledged. It is plain, therefore, that so far as the interests of Savings Banks are concerned, if the present system be continued, it is a matter of entire indifference in what way the Government invest or appropriate these deposits: in any case the simple obligation, as stated, remains.

No injury of any kind is done to the Savings Bank account, inasmuch as, whatever use the State may choose to make of the monies, it is liable to the Savings Banks for the actual, return in cash—even ultimately in gold, as Lord Monteagle remarked—of the full amount received by the National Debt Commissioners. On the other hand, it is equally clear, that the only considerations in respect to these deposits, which ought to influence the Government, are, the performance of their obligations to the Depositors with least cost, and the most profitable employment of the deposits thus placed in their hands. For investments, the Government confines itself to State securities; but with that limitation, it is plain that the same rule applies to the case of the National Debt Commissioners, for the management of Savings Banks deposits, as applies to bankers. They should hold the securities which are most profitable; but also with a view to their easy convertibility to such an extent as is likely to be required; and it is obvious that the best management would consist in holding a variety of securities, so that, in case of need, those might be sold which, at the moment, would yield the most profit to the nation. According to such a plan, certain amounts would be held in Exchequer Bills, Exchequer Bonds, and Consols, and those securities might from time to time be held in very different proportions,* according as it suited the public interest, as distinct from that of the Savings Banks.

---

* [This view was advocated also (1859) by Mr. Gladstone:—

"In my opinion there cannot be a more gross delusion than to think that the funds in the hands of the Commissioners of the National Debt are the funds of the Depositors in Savings Banks. They are not the funds of Depositors in the Savings Banks any more than £50 remaining in a banker's till belongs to me if I happen to have deposited £50 with him. It does not belong to me: it is his money, to use it as he thinks fit, subject to its repayment to me. To say that the Depositors in Savings Banks, after placing their money in the hands of a public body, were to be responsible for the prudent use, or gross misuse, of their funds by that body, would be doing them any thing but a kindness. It would be impossible to lay down a rule that would be more ruinous to the Depositors themselves. What do you do? You take the money of these Depositors, and you give them the entire security of the public for their money.

29.—Accordingly, the Chancellor of the Exchequer, under his official power as one of " The Commissioners of the National Debt," has exercised an absolute discretion in the mode of investment in public securities of Savings Bank money; and had the operations of the Chancellor been confined to a mere change of securities, no complaint could have arisen: but something more has been done which strikes at the very root of Parliamentary control over the public debt. According to existing Acts of Parliament, Ways and Means Bills, or Deficiency Bills, —to make good the charges on the Consolidated Fund—may be issued to the Commissioners of the National Debt, in exchange for Savings Bank monies, which bills need not be redeemed from the growing produce of the revenue, as they would ordinarily be, but are *allowed to be funded and so to increase the national debt. The Chancellor of the Exchequer for the time being, without the authority of Parliament, thus indirectly provides by his own will for an excess in the current expenditure of the year by the †creation of additional stock.

They cannot have a better security; and if you give them that, they have no interest in the employment of the money: it does not signify to them if you fling it to the bottom of the sea. So long as the treasury of the country is sound, it does not matter one rush what the Chancellor of the Exchequer does with the money. If he invests it well, they are no richer; and if he plays all the tricks of the mountebank, or disposes of it with the artifices of the swindler, they are none the poorer. The Depositors in Savings Banks have nothing to do with the question, and it is only weakening and impairing their position to make them depend upon the prudence of the Minister, instead of upon the credit of the British public."]

* [Sections 50, 51 of the Act.]

† [The conversion into *stock* of Exchequer Bills bought from the public was the main ground of complaint. Such bills, however, as Sir Cornewall Lewis justly remarked in a recent debate, are practically as much a debt for future posterity as the public stocks:—

" It is quite true," said he, " that according to the theory of Exchequer Bills they are charged only upon votes of *supply*, and they may be paid off at certain short periods; but we know that, practically, the vote for

30.—This power has fortunately not been much resorted to, but it cannot be disputed that the command over so *large a sum as arises year by year from the deposits of Savings Banks may be a material relief to the Exchequer at critical moments, and facilitate the ordinary transactions of the Treasury in regard to Exchequer Bills. Without affecting the character of the deposits, or the claim of each Depositor, these balances may enable a Chancellor to postpone demands which he cannot meet without loss, and to obtain his supplies without submitting to exorbitant interest.

---

the renewal of Exchequer Bills is taken annually as a matter of course; that Exchequer Bills are just as much a portion of the permanent debt as Consols; that precisely the same obligation lies; and that, although there is a power of varying the interest, we should, for all practical purposes, regard Exchequer Bills as being as much a portion of the national debt as the Three per Cents."—*Speech of Sir C. Lewis, March 9th,* 1859.

Mr. Hankey, in moving, on the same day, "That in future no funding of Exchequer Bills held by the Commissioners of Savings Banks be made without the authority of an Act of Parliament," remarked, "About £4,000,000 of Exchequer Bills were, he believed, funded in 1853 or 1854. The effect of that operation was to take a certain amount of Exchequer Bills out of the market, whereby the price of Exchequer Bills was enhanced, they being, perhaps, at the moment, at a discount. Now, that operation was in effect neither more nor less than a war loan. He was afraid that the present Chancellor of the Exchequer regarded that operation as a very convenient one, and would have resorted to it if he had been in office during the late war. About £16,000,000 of stock had been added to the funded debt within the last twenty years by means of the existing arrangements between the Government and Savings Banks. That involved a permanent charge of nearly £500,000 a-year. The House ought to watch these operations very jealously. He believed it had never been contemplated that the Savings Bank Act should be a means of permanently increasing the funded debt. He hoped to hear from the Government that they had no intention to make use of this power. At the same time it was desirable that Chancellors of the Exchequer should

---

* [On the 20th November 1859 the Savings Banks and Friendly Societies deposits in the hands of the National Debt Commissioners were over forty-one millions; more than double the amount of the unfunded debt.]

In any alteration of the law, therefore, the Chancellor of the Exchequer should still retain the power of availing himself, at his own discretion, of the facility which idle monies in the hands of the Commission would always offer, of relieving the Bank of England of Deficiency Bills, subject to his being required afterwards to redeem them out of the growing produce of the revenue, in the same way as he now redeems those Bills in the hands of the Bank. He should also be prohibited from funding such bills. If these measures were adopted, Savings Bank deposits could not be infringed upon in the slightest degree, and the permanent debt of the country would not be increased by indirect means, as at present.

Section 2.—*Effect as regards the nation.*

ART. 31.—*The Law relating to transactions in Exchequer Bills, &c.*—To enable our readers to trace further the opera-

---

have no authority to fund except by making special application to Parliament for that purpose; and if such an understanding were come to, the Government would very seldom put this power into execution."

Sir H. Willoughby said, that if it were required to raise £7,600,000 with the Three per Cents. at 95, it would be necessary to create £8,000,000 of stock. In this case, however, "the amount of stock created had been £8,469,237: therefore, at the first blush of the transaction, the public appeared to have lost £469,237 by the transaction. In the year 1847 Mr. Goulburn was compelled to have recourse to the same system. He created £7,627,000 of stock, and he (Sir H. Willoughby) believed, that during a series of years nearly £16,000,000 had been added to our funded debt. He hoped a measure would be introduced to limit the action of the Chancellor of the Exchequer in creating funded debt to cases where the interests of the Savings Banks were alone concerned. It was never intended to make the money of the Savings Banks an engine for creating new debt, except in some great emergency, and he trusted the practice now in vogue would be put an end to at once and for ever."

tions, that really did take place on the Savings Bank funds, and to fully understand how far they affected the nation (as distinct from the interests of the banks), we will state how the law at present (1859) stands in relation to the change of securities, and the purchase of Exchequer Bills, &c., adopting (where the meaning is doubtful) the construction put upon the clauses of the Act by the authorities at the National Debt Office :—

I. The Commissioners are authorized to lay out the whole, or any part, of the monies, which shall be standing in their names in the Banks of England and Ireland respectively, in the purchase of Exchequer Bills, and they are entitled to receive for the sums thus laid out in Exchequer Bills such an amount of Three per Cent. Consolidated or Reduced Annuities* as the same sums would have brought if they had been so applied. It being understood, in all these conversions of Exchequer Bills into Annuities, that the price of the latter is to be taken at the sinking fund average for the quarters in which the Bills were purchased. The amount of stock placed to the credit of the Commissioners to be notified by the Accountant-General of the Bank within five days from the time the entry is made.

It is also provided that :—

II. The Comptroller-General of the National Debt Office shall certify to the Treasury, at the end of each quarter, the amount of principal and interest paid for Exchequer Bills.

III. The Commissioners may sell any annuities they may

---

* [Section 51. appears to require that this conversion should take place every quarter, but the Commissioners do not interpret it as compulsory. Section 53. enables them every quarter to exchange for new bills, if they like, instead of cancelling, but this they have not done. In the words of Sir Alexander Spearman, "the Act of 9 Geo. IV. had given them a power to sell stock and purchase Exchequer Bills. The Act of 3 Will. IV. gives them the power to sell those Exchequer Bills, and to buy other stock or other Exchequer Bills."]

have at any time standing in their names, and appropriate the proceeds of such sales to the purchase of Exchequer Bills.

IV. The Commissioners may give notice at any time to the Treasury of the amount that may be required for satisfying the demands of Savings Bank Trustees; and it is lawful for the Lords of the Treasury, or any three of them, to cause Exchequer Bills to be made out for the whole, or any portion, of such sums, and advances may be made to the Commissioners upon these Exchequer Bills by the Banks of England and Ireland to any extent that may be agreed upon between the Commissioners and the Banks.

V. The Commissioners may discharge, from time to time, as they think fit, the principal sum of every such Exchequer Bill, together with all interest thereon, by any Savings Bank or Friendly Society deposits, or by the sale of Bank Annuities, or out of the Sinking Fund. It is provided, however, that

VI. Immediately upon such payment being made, the Commissioners shall receive Exchequer Bills to the like amount from the Bank, and shall deliver them over to the Paymaster of Exchequer Bills to be cancelled.

VII. Should the liquidation of any of these Bills be effected by monies from the Sinking Fund, the amount drawn from that fund is to be replaced by a transfer of such an amount of some other stock, standing in the Commissioners' names, as may be necessary; and a certificate of every such transfer shall be transmitted by the Accountant-General of the Bank to the Commissioners, specifying the amount and description of stock transferred.

32.—In the subjoined summary in Tables D and E of the transactions in Exchequer Bills and Bonds, during each year from 1828, when the Act of 9 Geo. IV. was passed, we give the rates at which the fundings were effected. (See cols. 6 and 8 of Table D):—

TABLE D.

Year ending 20th Nov.	(1.) Amount of Exchequer Bonds purchased in each year.	(2.) Amount of Exchequer Bills purchased in each year.	(3.) Amount of Exchequer Bonds sold in each year.	(4.) Amount of Exchequer Bills paid off in each year.	(5.) Amount of Exchequer Bills sold in each year.	(6.) Amount of Exchequer Bills funded in each year.	(7.) Total of columns 4,5,6, being amount of Exchequer Bills disposed of in each year.	(8.) Interest funded on Exchequer Bills in each year.	(9.) Balance of Exchequer Bonds held by the Commissioners at end of each year.	(10.) Balance of Exchequer Bills held by the Commissioners at end of each year.
1828	....	500,000	....	....	....	....	....	....	....	500,000
1829	....	1,281,800	....	1,000,000	....	....	1,000,000	....	....	781,800
1830	....	2,147,000	....	368,000	....	....	368,000	....	....	2,560,800
1831	....	174,000	....	117,000	254,000	....	371,000	....	....	2,363,800
1832	....	....	....	....	100,000	....	100,000	....	....	2,363,800
1833	....	3,750,000	....	2,600,000	....	....	2,600,000	....	....	3,413,800
1834	....	2,500,000	....	2,450,000	1,200,000	....	3,650,000	....	....	2,263,800
1836	....	1,174,000	....	700,000	300,000	1,075,000	2,075,000	4,430	....	1,362,800
1837	....	1,545,750	....	29,150	1,039,200	1,513,500	2,581,850	20,378	....	326,700
1838	....	1,942,100	....	688,000	....	600,000	1,288,000	1,790	....	780,800
1839	....	1,489,300	....	1,101,750	....	500,000	1,601,750	782	....	668,350
1840	....	1,476,100	....	722,050	....	500,000	1,222,050	164	....	922,400
1841	....	1,900,050	....	283,900	....	1,574,600	1,858,500	712	....	963,950
1842	....	390,000	....	....	....	1,026,250	1,026,250	37,463	....	327,700
1843	....	168,050	....	23,150	....	40,200	63,350	1,442	....	432,400
1844	....	32,200	....	121,700	....	14,000	135,700	658	....	329,900
1845	....	82,500	....	139,150	....	....	139,150	....	....	272,250
1846	....	33,700	....	275,250	....	....	275,250	....	....	30,700
1847	....	....	....	2,700	....	....	2,700	....	....	28,000
1849	....	....	....	28,000	....	....	28,000	....	....	....
1853	....	1,247,000	....	1,900,000	....	1,247,000	1,247,000	8,072	....	30,700
1854	1,600,000	2,458,000	....	3,690,000	500,000	....	2,400,000	....	1,600,000	58,000
1855	250,000	7,316,500	85,000	....	563,500	....	4,253,500	....	1,765,000	3,121,000
1856	....	2,470,000	....	....	111,000	....	111,000	....	....	5,480,000
1857	....	2,120,000	1,765,000	....	....	....	....	....	1,765,000	7,600,000
Total...	1,850,000	36,198,050	1,850,000	16,239,800	4,067,700	8,090,550	28,398,050	75,891		

EXCHEQUER BILLS.

TABLE £.

Year of Funding.	Amount of Exchequer Bills and Interest funded.	Three per Cent. Consols	Three per Cent. Reduced.	Total Amount of Stock created to meet Exchequer Bills funded.	Equivalent to a price per cent. of
1836......	1,079,430	1,177,878	....	1,177,878	91 12 10
1837......	1,533,878	806,971	896,018	1,702,989	90 1 5
1338......	601,790	....	648,264	648,264	92 16 8
1839......	500,782	....	541,386	541,386	92 10 0
1840......	500,164	546,627	....	546,627	91 10 0
1841......	1,575,312	1,758,996	....	1,758,996	89 11 2
1842......	1,063,713	807,629	383,547	1,191,176	89 6 0
1843......	41,642	26,252	18,595	44,847	92 17 1
1844......	14,658	15,217	....	15,217	96 6 6
	6,911,369			7,627,380	90 12 3
1853......	1,255,072	891,662	383,098	1,274,760	98 9 1
					Equivalent to an average price of
	8,166,441	6,031,232	2,870,908	8,902,140	91 14 9

No fundings were effected between 1844 and 1853, or between 1853 and 1859.

34.—In addition to the transactions detailed in the preceding Tables, the following " Consolidated Fund Bills," which are securities altogether of a temporary nature, and distinct from Exchequer Bills, were funded during the years 1838—1841, and thus became a permanent addition to the National Debt.

£600,000 on September 5, 1838.
500,000 ,, October 2, 1839.
500,000 ,, April 25, 1840.
700,000 ,, March 25, 1841.

35.—In considering these various transactions, it is evident—

1st. That the funding can have produced no effect on the ultimate amount of the Savings Bank stock-fund, because it always took place under 9 *Geo.* III. *c.* 92. *s.* 50., at the price of the original quarter in which the Bills were purchased, *i. e.* in which the Savings Bank monies were handed over to the National Debt Commissioners.

2d. That the fundings have been safe for the nation, taken on the aggregate, because they happened to be at an average price of 91¾, which is but a little below the price per cent. at which stock produces £3.5s. per cent. interest. (See Table B, Art. 15).

3d. That if loss has arisen from the sale (as distinct from "funding") of Exchequer Bills, &c., it has been occasioned by a lower price being realized than was paid for the purchase of them.

4th. That a temporary loss, during the period Exchequer Bills are held, has, at times, been experienced from the lower rate of interest receivable on some of such securities than on stock.

We will now proceed to give an account of the transactions in detail, for the purpose of proving the further important fact that they have been productive of a considerable *gain* to the nation.

I.—*Transactions prior to the Year* 1833.

ART. 36.—These do not appear to have been anywhere spoken of as having been unadvisable. At the beginning of 1833, the Commissioners held £2,263,800 in Exchequer Bills. Lord Monteagle (then Mr. Spring Rice) was Comptroller of the Treasury.

II.—*Years* 1833 *to* 1836.

37.—The transactions of these years have been impugned by various witnesses, as follows:—

1. "On the 28th March 1833, there were £574,712 Three per cents. sold at 87; £10,000 was sold every transfer day at prices varying from 89 to 90." (*Boodle,* 945, 946.)

2. "In the course of eighteen months, between February 1833 and July 1834, £2,348,401 of stock was sold out at comparatively low prices, and £6,250,000 became invested by the National Debt Commissioners in Exchequer Bills yielding, as those securities did,

a considerably lower rate of interest than might have been derived under a more profitable state of investment. The expediency of these transpositions could not be accounted for by any circumstances connected with Savings Banks, inasmuch as by reference to the annual returns made to Parliament, it is shewn that the total amount of payments to Savings Banks and Friendly Societies collectively, in the course of the two years ending the 20th November 1834 (comprising the whole of the period in question), amounted only to £1,087,962, whilst their investments in the course of the same two years amounted to £3,219,173." (*Statement of Facts issued by St. Martin's Place Bank*, 1844.)

In a document emanating from one of the largest Savings Banks in Scotland it is also stated " that the Commissioners, either through ignorance or from some sinister motive, have employed the Savings Bank deposits in the purchase and sale of stock, wholly irrespective of the requirements or interests of the Savings Banks. The object of these incomprehensible transactions has never been disclosed to the public. Their effect on the Savings Banks funds, however, was most prejudicial, as an instance or two will shew. Three per cent. stock, to a large amount, was sold out in 1833, when its average price was £84 . 7s. 5d., and the same stock was replaced in 1836 at an average price of £91 . 12s. 10d; thus causing a loss upon this particular stock of £7 . 5s. 5d. per cent."

38.—In explanation of the item 1., or the sale of £574,000 stock at 87, it was stated by Sir Alexander Spearman that

" That sum was not sold in the market; that it was transferred from the Savings Banks account, under the arrangements that were made by Lord Althorp for reducing the rate of interest payable by the State on a part of the public funded debt, bearing interest at 4 per cent. per annum, from 4 to $3\frac{1}{2}$ per cent. The stock itself of £574,000 was cancelled, and the Savings Bank fund received money in exchange for it at the price of 87; the money was lying at the account of the Commissioners for the Reduction of the National Debt, upon the account of annuities for terms of years. The Commissioners for the Reduction of the National Debt are authorised, under the Act 10 Geo. IV., to grant annuities for terms of years. Very large speculative purchases of annuities for terms of years were made at that time, and £500,000 was paid in by two or three parties on the Stock Exchange for such annuities. The money received, instead of being sent into the market to purchase stock and so raise the price of stock very considerably, was applied to the cancelling of the £574,000 of stock held on account of Savings Banks, the money being transferred to the Savings Bank account, to be employed in Deficiency Bills until required to pay off the 4 per cent. dissentients."

An analysis of the returns shows that transactions 2, as well as 1, were required to complete the provision for paying off these dissentients.

39.— The circumstances of this transaction were still further detailed and warmly defended by Lord Monteagle, as follows—

"I give the Committee, as an example, (and there are others,) that which was done by my late noble and respected friend Lord Althorp in a case in which he accomplished a great financial operation in which the public were largely interested—I allude to the reduction of the interest of the 4 per cents in the year 1834. Lord Althorp could not have accomplished that object except by having funds at his disposal by which he could meet with punctuality the demands of the dissentients, or of those parties who would not accept the terms he proposed for reducing the interest of that debt. The Committee will observe here, that the object was one in which the public at large had a great interest, namely, the reduction of the debt. That and similar operations have been the great causes of our effecting a saving in the charge of the debt, through the means of our public credit, independent of any real, and still more of any fictitious Sinking Fund investments. What did Lord Althorp do? On the 9th of June 1834 (see Hansard, vol. xxiv. p. 340), Lord Althorp, by realizing and laying by funds out of the Savings Banks, had money enough provided when the Act of Parliament was passed for reducing the interest of the 4 per cents. to enable him to pay off the dissentients, whoever and whatever they might be. That was the best arrangement that could have been made for all parties. The amount taken was nothing that endangered the real security of any Depositors in the Savings Banks. This fund was employed for an important public object. The public wanted this fund: how else could you have got it? If your income had been close run, and you had no surplus, or no adequate surplus, you would have had to go through the formality of entering into a loan, the amount of which might be, perhaps, in itself above what you wanted to meet those Depositors, the number of, or the extent of whose claims you were not acquainted with. But the Savings Banks in a time like that became, as it were, a credit which you had at your bankers to be used to the amount that you yourself required. Lord Althorp stated to Parliament the whole of the case, and Parliamentary authority was obtained for the operation. There was no concealment: it was not the mere *arbitrium* of the Finance Minister, but it was the Finance Minister acting with a fund which he could employ without danger to the parties primarily entitled to it. In explaining the operation to the House of Commons, he stated that he was fully prepared to redeem such portions of the 4 per cents. as the holders might dissent from, according to the proposal he had made. A greater number of dissentients than he had anticipated came in, amounting to 469 persons, and representing the sum of £4,600,000. The House of Commons thereon resolved that the dissentients should be paid off out of such monies, stock, or Exchequer Bills, as might be deposited in the names of the Commissioners of the National Debt, or monies which might be invested on account of Savings Banks. There was thus a resolution of the House of Commons passed: it was done by just and legitimate authority. I should be sorry indeed to see the Finance Minister prohibited from meeting similar cases by similar means."

40.—From the evidence of Sir Alexander Spearman, it further appears (Qu. 4330, 4331, 4431), that "the profit to the public upon Lord Althorp's reduction of the 4 per cents. was about £53,000 a-year, effected mainly by these operations directed by him upon the Savings Bank funds:" the amount of Savings Banks fund applied for carrying into effect his operation was very nearly, if not quite, one-half the whole amount of the capital reduced.

In other words, the saving to the nation on this one transaction, by the employment of Savings Bank money, was equivalent to the gain of one-half of £1,766,667 stock.

III.—*Transactions of the years* 1836—1843.

41.—In respect to these, the St. Martin's Place Committee alleged :—

"That it also appears, upon reference to another Parliamentary return (pp. 150, 1844), that at various subsequent periods between the 10th of October 1836 and the 5th of July 1843, these, or some other substituted Exchequer Bills, amounting together to £6,022,115, held by the Commissioners on account of Savings Banks, have been funded at greatly increased prices, whereby, as it appears from the return now quoted, an increase (without any special interference or consent of Parliament) has been occasioned to the permanent debt of this country, by the stock thus created, of £6,631,740, with an annual charge, in respect of dividends and expenses of management, of £200,941; to which may be also added, as the result of these and other similar operations by the said Commissioners, a heavy loss to the public in the deterioration in the value of the securities; and, as will be more fully explained in another part of these observations, a vast proportion of the loss accruing annually on the interest account."

42.—In reference to the point raised in the above paragraph, it is necessary to explain, that under the interpretation fixed by the Commissioners on the 50th and 51st sections of the Act

9 Geo. IV., as we have seen, they very properly hold themselves bound, at whatever time the funding may be effected, to go back to the average prices of stock in the quarters in which the Bills were purchased. The period of sale, therefore, and the price of stock at that period, would not affect the transaction. The following is from the evidence of Sir Alexander Spearman, and it is confirmed by Lord Monteagle:—

" My opinion is, that Exchequer Bills purchased with Savings Banks monies can be funded at the Sinking Fund price of the quarter in which they are purchased, and that these Exchequer Bills can be held for any length of time; and if they have been held, say six years, you are able to go back to the price of the quarter in which they were bought if you wish to fund them." (Qu. 4255 to 4258.)

IV.—*Transactions of the year* 1844.

43.—The next transaction deserving our attention, as one in which Savings Bank money was employed by the minister of the day for national purposes, took place in 1844, when Mr. Goulburn, then Chancellor of the Exchequer, reduced the interest upon stock to 3 per cent., at which it at present stands; thus effecting an *annual* saving to the State of £1,300,000. The amount of Savings Bank money employed for this purpose was not more than two or three millions, or about 2 per cent. of the total capital of the debt reduced; but the knowledge that the whole of the Savings Bank funds were at his disposal must have contributed very much to the feeling of security with which Mr. Goulburn proposed so gigantic an operation. In this case, as in Lord Althorp's, Parliamentary sanction was afterwards given to the transaction, (qu. 4330, 4331).

V.—*The time of the Crimean War.*

44.—At the period of the Crimean war, moreover, Sir A. Spearman estimates that "very considerable gain accrued to the public, when the supplies granted by Parliament for the army and navy were required far more rapidly than the revenue came in, and when, in point of fact, if the Chancellor of the Exchequer had not availed himself of the power he possessed of issuing Ways and Means Bills, the public service must have come to a stop: he issued those Ways and Means Bills to the Commissioners for the reduction of the National Debt, and was thus enabled at once to apply money paid into the Exchequer to meet those heavy demands. The Ways and Means Act authorises the issue of such bills, and unless money had been raised in that manner to a large amount, the public service would have been brought to a perfect stand still."

VI.—*The years* 1853—1858.

45.—Although from 1849 to 1853 no Exchequer Bills or Bonds were held by the Commissioners, yet during the next four or five years large quantities were purchased, causing a balance of £7,600,000 in Exchequer Bills to remain in their hands on the 20th November 1858. These operations are thus explained in Sir Alexander Spearman's evidence:—

"My belief is, that for several years past the Exchequer Bills we have held could not at any time have been all floated in the market. A very small portion of the Exchequer Bills which we hold were taken from the market; of the bills we now hold probably in round numbers something like £1,300,000 may be said to have been bought in the market, and that amount was a pressure on the market; but the great mass of the bills never were upon the market: they passed straight to the Commissioners from the Exchequer, through the Bank of England, and have never been held in any other hands whatever. If we had funded them at the times they were taken, we should have received the same amount of stock that we shall do now, and in that sense there has been no loss whatever in postponing the funding. There is a loss in another sense, namely, that the Savings Banks fund has been receiving a higher rate of interest than it would have received on the funding. We receive £3.16s. on these Exchequer Bills up to the present time, whereas if we had funded them we should have had only the interest on the stock. I believe that the Savings Bank fund has gained somewhere about £28,000 by not funding at the time."

VII.—*The year* 1859.

46.—In January 1859 the abovementioned balance of £7,600,000 was funded by Mr. Disraeli, and this operation being criticised in the debate to which it gave rise in March 1859, Mr. Disraeli replied as follows:—

"I have been called on to state why the Government funded an amount of £7,600,000 in Exchequer Bills. I will tell the reasons that induced me to take that course. During the autumn my attention was very much called to this subject, by complaints on the part of the Commissioners of Savings Banks that they were losing on the securities in their hands—that they did not receive that interest on them they would receive from another form of investment. It may be said that the Chancellor of the Exchequer and the Commissioners for the reduction of the National Debt are the same parties, but that is not so. There are two accounts—one of the Savings Banks, the other the general account of the country. Not wishing to see a loss regularly occurring in the Savings Bank account, we closed it altogether. But although that was a reason, it was not the main reason which induced me to sanction this operation. My attention was called to that to which no person in my position could be insensible, namely, the very delicate state of the Exchequer market, in consequence of the great amount of Exchequer Bills then in existence. I had to consider what might be the effect of having so large an amount of Exchequer Bills in the market. I naturally inquired what was the reason that the Savings Bank Commissioners were in possession of so unusually large an amount of Exchequer Bills as between £7,000,000 and £8,000,000.* It

---

* [He further added: "Suppose such a state of affairs as prevailed at the end of the year 1857 had suddenly arisen, the minister would have found that the Savings Banks could not give him any assistance, inasmuch as their resources would have been entirely absorbed by their holding these £7,000,000 or £8,000,000 of Exchequer Bills. That state of things was very unsatisfactory, not only to the Chancellor of the Exchequer, but to the Commissioners of Savings Banks themselves. It was thought necessary to sanction a change which would put an end to that system, but that sanction was not hastily given. My hon. friend, the member for Huntingdon, talked of needy Chancellors of the Exchequer who availed themselves of these changes for their own benefit; but I would impress upon the House, and remind him, that in this instance the change was made for the benefit of the Savings Banks themselves, because the Savings Banks, insead of holding a security which they viewed with distrust and suspicion, received for that a security with which everybody is satisfied. And that is the real reason which prevailed with me in sanctioning the funding of this large amount of Exchequer Bills held by the Savings Banks. I believe I took a course very much for the advantage of the Savings Banks, but in it the Government were really not at all interested, because they were not affected by the floating of these Exchequer Bills in the market. They were practically in the possession of the Government. I was obliged to look to the circumstances which had arisen from this gradual, but at the same time rapid increase of Exchequer Bills in the hands of the Savings Bank Commissioners, and it appeared that these circumstances had arisen in a very legitimate and proper manner. I do not for a moment question the propriety of the course which occasioned them, but they arose in consequence of a very exceptional and extraordinary state of things, namely, the occurrence of a war, to carry on which this House voted that the Chancellor of the Exchequer might raise money by the issue of Exchequer Bills. Well, that transaction was closed. I looked upon the funding of these Exchequer Bills as a virtual completion of the transaction, and I have no hesitation in employing a phrase used by the hon. gentleman opposite,—no doubt it was the virtual completion of a loan which the

appeared to me that that was a very dangerous state for us to be placed in. The Exchequer Bill market being a very delicate market, it occurred to us to fund a portion of the Exchequer Bills to prevent the possibility of our being liable to pay them at a moment when there was a great scarcity of money."

47.—*As to the Exchequer Bill Market.*—The preceding remark, as to the delicate state of the market for Exchequer

---

country had obtained to carry on the war. But the transaction was completed legally, and also most satisfactorily to the Savings Bank Commissioners. If the assertion of the hon. member for Lambeth, that Chancellors of the Exchequer have never interfered in transactions of this kind except for their own benefit, be correct, I can assure him that at least this transaction was of no advantage whatever to the Government. This funding was necessary, and strictly in consonance with the law."

Mr. T. Baring, who had been a member of the Committee of 1858, said that one question for the Committee to consider was, to what extent the Government was a security to the Depositor, and the result of the inquiry was, as he believed, that all these changes of securities were not made always for the benefit of the Savings Banks, but sometimes to aid a needy Chancellor of the Exchequer in his operations. That was the ground on which the Committee ventured to recommend that some limit should be placed on the power of the Commissioners of the National Debt, or in other words, of the Chancellor of the Exchequer; for every one knew that in reality they were the same. It had always appeared to him to be most objectionable to vest in the Chancellor of the Exchequer the power of secretly, without the cognizance of the public, and without that notoriety which was essential for the credit of the country, transferring the unfunded debt into funded debt, thus throwing a mass of funded debt upon the market without previous notice. He did not say that the transfer from Exchequer Bills into Consols was an increase of the debt of the country; but it was an increase of one portion of the debt without notification to the public, and it was this which made it objectionable. Under the present system, the Commissioners had authority, whenever convenient, to fund Exchequer Bills, so that there was, as it were, a kind of mill, into which Exchequer Bills being put came out funded debt, and this went round and round as long as it suited the convenience of the Chancellor of the Exchequer. He had no doubt that the power was honestly and conscientiously exercised by Chancellors of the Exchequer, but he contended that it was one which could not exist with safety to the credit to the country. (Hansard, 1859.)

Bills, is justified by the fact, that it is very different now from what it was fifteen or twenty years ago. During that time, other large openings for temporary investment have arisen, from the practice in *Joint Stock Banks* of allowing interest on deposits. *Railway Debentures* and *India Bonds* have also been much used for the same purpose, and some effect was produced on the market by the *Exchequer Bonds* of Mr. Gladstone. *Sir Alexander Spearman* remarked (qu. 4116), that "It is *not* the practice of the Commissioners to hold *Exchequer Bills* for the purpose of meeting any sudden demand of the Savings Banks, and that he should not think it a good practice if it were." When asked (qu. 4138), Why the Commissioners, having seven millions and a half of Exchequer Bills in their possession, sold stock when the amount of money required *between the 30th of September and the close of the year* 1857, was very nearly a million beyond the amount applicable to pay the drafts, he replied, that, at that time, it would not have been possible to sell *a million of Exchequer Bills*, without producing such a derangement in the market as would seriously have affected the value of all those securities held by individuals, by the Commissioners themselves, by the Bank of England, and by all parties holding Exchequer Bills. He added, "We should, therefore, if we had sold Exchequer Bills in proportion as we wanted the money to pay the drafts, have been operating very injuriously against a security at that time rather depressed, and that would in all probability have *rendered it necessary for the Government to raise the rate of interest*, not upon the amount of Bills sold, but *upon the whole sum of twenty-one millions issued from the Exchequer.* It was that consideration which led to the sale of stock instead of the sale of Exchequer Bills."

(*For Legislation on Exchequer operations since* 31*st December* 1859, *see Part* VII., *et seq.*)

PART IV.

FINANCIAL REORGANIZATION

OF

SAVINGS BANKS.

CONTENTS OF PART IV.

CHAP. IX. *Fundamental Principles for Financial Reorganization.*

	PAGE
§ 1. Preliminary Considerations	165
§ 2. Of the Field for Savings Banks	168
§ 3. Of Securities for Savings Banks Investments	171
§ 4. Further Preliminary Considerations.—How a Deficiency is to be prevented in future	177

CHAP. X. *As to the Alterations that are desirable in the Government connection with Savings Banks.*

§ 1. General Reorganization suggested	184
§ 2. Of the Commission	186
§ 3. Modes of Investment	187

CHAP. XI. *Recommendations.*

§ 1. Plan recommended for Payment of Savings Bank Expenses	191
§ 2. Of the interest recommended to be allowed to Depositors	193
§ 3. Recommendations respecting Notice of Withdrawal	194
§ 4. Changes recommended in the Annual Limit	196
§ 5. Of Investment direct with the Savings Bank Commissioners	198

CHAP. XII. *Subsidiary Recommendations.*

§ 1. As to the Conversion of Deposits into Stock	200
§ 2. Trust Accounts.—Changes recommended	203
§ 3. As to Privileges relative to Estates of Deceased Depositors	206
§ 4. Uniformity in the Calculation of Interest recommended.—The "Prospective Plan"	207

CHAPTER IX.

FUNDAMENTAL PRINCIPLES
FOR
FINANCIAL REORGANIZATION.

Section 1.—Preliminary Considerations.

ART. 1.—Before proceeding with our subject, we will very briefly recal the attention of our readers to what has been done in the foregoing Parts II. and III.

We have pointed out that the present system of Savings Banks is defective in two distinct ways: first, in relation to internal management; secondly, in relation to finance. The former class of defects, or those of *management*—which gave opportunity for the frauds we have described, and to which, therefore, the losses of Depositors are ultimately attributable—we have discussed in Part II., where we have also suggested what

---

* ["Il n'en est pas moins incontestable que le chiffre toujours croissant de cette dette instantanément exigible ne doive être pour le Gouvernement un juste sujet de préoccupation et de vigilance.

Mais, en revanche, quels précieux avantages le Gouvernement ne recueille-t-il pas de cette grande et populaire institution des Caisses d'Epargne ? A part la moralisation des classes ouvrières par l'esprit d'économie et par le bien-être, à part le lien étroit qui rattache les déposants à la cause de l'ordre et à la stabilité du pouvoir, les Caisses d'Epargne n'exercent-elles pas une salutaire et notable influence sur le crédit public, par l'abondance des capitaux qu'elles accumulent ?

La France s'enorgueillit à juste titre des grands travaux publics qu'elle exécute depuis plusieurs anneés ; mais où a-t-elle pris les fonds nécessaires à l'exécution de ces travaux ?

Est-ce dans ses seuls revenus budgétaires ? Ils auraient été insuffi-

we believe to be their appropriate remedies. The latter class, or those arising from *financial* errors—which do not directly affect Depositors, but importantly concern the nation at large—we have analysed and explained in Part III. The treatment of this portion of our subject will be completed, when we have explained the principles by which the re-organization of Savings Banks should be guided, in order that the errors of the present financial system may be rectified, and a recurrence of their ill effects permanently obviated.

This explanation must, however, be introduced by some preliminary considerations on the possible and desirable extension of the Savings Bank system, and on the manner in which this extension would affect the financial dealings with the deposits.

---

sants, s'il n'était venu s'y joindre cette accumulation des petites épargnes, qui, moins exigeantes que les gros capitaux, se contentent d'un intérêt modeste et sont pour l'Etat un auxiliaire puissant."—Rapport de M. Louvet au Corps Legislatif, pp. 44, 45.

In a valuable Mémoire, "Sur le developpement progressif des Caisses d'Epargne," read by M. Dupin before the Academy of Sciences, Nov. 6th, 1843, he remarked in reference to the fear entertained as to Government losses by a panic:—

"Alors même qu'on serait contraint d'accorder qu'en temps de paix, disette ou non, les libres remboursements des caisses d'épargne ne peuvent occasioner aucun embarras serieux au trésor public, on se récrie sur les dangers du passage de l'état de paix à l'état de guerre.

"On se figure le peuple entier des déposants saisi tout à coup d'une terreur panique, venant en masse *réclamer le remboursement de ses épargnes;* on se peint aussitôt le trésor de l'etat mis dans un danger imminent par le retrait obligatoire et soudain de centaines de millions. . . . .

"Voilà l'objection presentée, je l'espère, dans toute son énormité.

"Si le danger d'un retrait subit et complet de trois cent millions, de cinq cent millions, d'un milliard d'épargnes, si dis-je, ce danger existe, je l'affirme, ce n'est pas alors aux petites et miserables mesures, qu'ont proposeés certains esprits meticuleux, qu'on doit s'arrêter. *Il faut supprimer les caisses d'épargne.*

"C'est aussi ce que demandait le journal intitulé le *National,* qui trouve que l'institution des caisses d'épargne ne peut, ni ne doit, être ni défendue ni maintenue."]

2.—The design and proper aim of a Savings Bank is the encouragement of provident habits among the working classes; and it is therefore evident that those whose savings are sufficiently large to be capable of being made productive in the ordinary channels of trade and commerce should not be sharers in its advantages, and that the prime object of the Government snould be to give an impulse to the augmentation of the number of Depositors of *small sums,—of Depositors whose occupation is so uncertain and necessities sometimes so urgent, that, in the absence of a little fund upon which they can fall back, they are liable, in the case of inability to labour, to a change—as rapid as it is great—from the enjoyment of a fair worldly means of support to destitution and the poor-house.

That this class is at present far from being fully repre-

---

* [Some hostility to these institutions has arisen from an idea, pretty generally circulated, that, forgetting their destination, (viz. to render productive the savings of the *poor*,) they have received the deposits of persons in easy circumstances, who have invested partly for convenience, and partly for the sake of the rate of interest allowed to Depositors.

This idea has probably arisen from the impression that the deposits as an aggregate are large in amount. This, like all prejudices, cannot withstand the attentive examination of facts, and the evidence resulting therefrom.

On the 20th of November 1858, out of 1,409,135 accounts (including Friendly Societies) in Great Britain and Ireland, the large proportion of 870,987, or 62 per cent. were for deposits under £20.

The greater part, in fact, are for very small sums, which do not average quite £5 . 15s. for each. Only 7 out of every 100 Depositors are entitled to balances over £100, while the aggregate of their savings alone is nearly one-third of the total deposits.]

† [The Table of classes given in the Introduction shews that the chief Depositors in Savings Banks are domestic servants of both sexes, and females of other occupations or position; a large proportion are clerks, shopmen, and minors; and of actual 'working-men' the number is about 36 per cent.]

sented in Savings Banks is manifest from the Table, Art. 19, Part I., which shews that out of the thirty millions population of the United Kingdom, there are only 1,309,864 Depositors for sums under £100.

There are at least two millions of families among the working classes, consisting of an average of five persons each, with regard to whom it would be the most satisfactory feature in social economy, that they should be in possession of such a small sum of money as £100; and that alone would make up in Savings Bank Deposits 200 millions of money.

3.—Could so large a number of Depositors be obtained, very great would be the moral and pecuniary advantage to the State, and the attention of the Government cannot be directed to a more useful channel than to give due encouragement to an extension of Savings Bank operations.

But we repeat, that, in reorganizing their financial system so that no loss to the rest of the community may arise in the future, all possibility should be removed (for the reasons indicated above, and on account of the financial difficulties to be presently described) of advantage being taken by Depositors of superior means to fructify their larger savings by the aid of institutions designed for their poorer neighbours.

Section 2.—Of the Field for Savings Banks.

ART. 4.—The evidence before the Select Committee of 1858 shews abundantly that there is a wide field upon which the Savings Banks might operate in populous districts,[*] especially if the duty of the officials and their advantage went hand in hand, and the banks were rewarded and subsidized, less ac-

---

[*] [The number of places in which no Savings Banks exist is about 3500, of which nearly 150 have a population exceeding 10,000.]

cording to the amounts accumulated, and more according to the measure in which the masses* of the people might be attracted.

The system has not been extended sufficiently into the smaller villages and parishes.† If a knowledge of the advantages of Savings Banks should become more widely diffused, and if the re-organization of them should receive the confidence of the country, the *annual deposits,* which now average in amount but seven millions, and form so small a proportion of the aggregate income of the working classes, would in a short time be trebled.

5.—It is estimated that at least 25 persons out of every 100 of the class, of which the members should be Depositors in Savings Banks, are debarred from exercising a provident spirit through the ‡absence of Savings Banks in their localities.

This was prominently set forth in 1857 by the Managers of the Huddersfield Savings Bank, who stated that the total amount *withdrawn* from Savings Banks by Depositors during the *seven years* preceding, exceeded the total amount received by £134,689, and that the only increase of the aggregate capital arose from the interest accumulating thereon. They pointed out the non-establishment, for some years past, of new Savings Banks, and the great disproportion between the relative number of the population and of the Depositors in different counties—a difference ranging from one in eight to one in thirty-six. They stated that " in a large number of populous localities, from there being no Savings Bank, the labouring and industrious classes are without any suitable

---

* [Meikle, qu. 2303.]

† [" With any thing like sensible and provident habits, 20 millions a-year might be deposited in the Savings Banks of the United Kingdom.' (Sikes, qu. 2716.)]

‡ [See on this head the Post Office Suggestions, Part V.]

institution in which they can place the surplus out of their wages. This is to be regretted, as the general prevalence of employment, at remunerating wages, has given a great power to save if a place of security were within reach."

From the recent Returns, it appears that there is a whole county in England (Rutland) in which there is no Savings Bank; and that in Scotland there is none in the counties of *Ayr, Clackmannan, Haddington, Kinross, Linlithgow, Orkney and Shetland, Peebles, Sutherland, and Wigtown; nor in Ireland* in the counties of *Carlow, Donegal, Kerry, Leitrim, and Longford*. The aggregate population of these Scotch counties is no less than 430,707, and of those of Ireland 755,735.

6.—From these various facts and the known increase in the resources of the industrious classes, it cannot but be concluded that the amount at present deposited, large as it may appear, and important as are the interests which it represents, is not as much as could have been accumulated in Savings Banks in the fifty years that have elapsed since they were first established. If their income be taken (according to the best estimate) at £180,000,000 a-year, the total amount deposited in Savings Banks is not much over one-fifth of that amount, or *eleven weeks *wages*: the annual produce of these savings is but £1,140,000 at 3 per cent., or not half a week of their income. When, however, the savings are taken in connection with the actual number of Depositors, satisfactory results appear as far as they are concerned. If the income of this number be taken as being 75 millions a-year, their savings are equal on the average to about half one year's income.

---

* [The whole of their savings would only pay one and a quarter year's interest of the National Debt. It is but about five years' poors' rates.]

Section 3.—*Of Securities for Savings Banks Investments.*

ART. 7.—It will doubtless be admitted, that from the investment in Government Securities of so large a sum as the probable amount that Savings Banks deposits will attain in the future, serious inconvenience, if not loss, is likely to arise. It also becomes important to consider whether it is possible to obtain a higher rate of interest than is given to the Depositors or required for Expenses, so as to provide a marginal fund to meet losses on sale for withdrawals, and thus obviate, in the future, such a deficiency as that which, in Part III., has been shewn to exist already in Savings Banks assets.

The question in fact resolves itself into an inquiry into the practicability of media for investment being found, which would so distribute the people's savings as to release the nation from the defects of the present system.

In respect to interest, the subject is replete with difficulty, for all experience shews that a high rate of interest is only obtainable on small sums of money. As soon as a society or company has millions to invest, it cannot expect to find investments, which in any period will produce, on the average, much more than the public funds.

As, therefore, Savings Bank deposits advance in amount, the difficulty will increase. Yet, in future arrangements it is necessary to provide for the contingency of the fund to be invested becoming, not 41 millions as at present, but, with an increase of savings and of population, some 100 millions. Indeed, should a Government guarantee be accorded to Savings Banks, and a high rate of interest be still allowed, these institutions would be more than ever applied to as places of safe and advantageous deposit.

8.—Moreover, in dealing with large deposits, (apart from the question of interest,) the case of public institutions is the same as that of individuals: they must not have all their investments on one security, otherwise a depression in value will take place when sales are desired. A variety of investments is required; and the principle (as explained in Art. 27, Part III.) is fully recognised by bankers under similar circumstances, who hold securities of different kinds, so that in meeting withdrawals no great depreciation can arise, and the money likely to be required in any year may be realized not from any particular class of investment, but from several. As far as Savings Banks are concerned, if their operations be closely exmained, it will be seen that not more than one-fourth need continue in what are termed readily-convertible securities, as that greatly exceeds the extent ever likely to be withdrawn in a year without a corresponding replacement, and is far beyond the largest amount that would be required, under ordinary circumstances, to conduct the accounts, and to make the payments required by the banks. This sum of one-fourth might be invested in such Government Securities as might appear the most eligible, in order that, when the Commissioners require to sell, they may dispose of that description of security which at the moment may appear the most marketable. The remaining three-fourths are available for general investment. It is not probable, however, that safe and productive securities can be obtained to any sufficient extent, and periods must be anticipated to arise when large sums of money will be returned upon the hands of the Commission, and have to be placed in the public funds.

This is confirmed by the experience of all the great Assurance Societies. The Actuaries of those important institutions, in valuing their affairs, do not now consider that a higher rate than 3 per cent. on large investments for a long period can be relied upon. Although they can and do accept a variety of profitable securities for money that is not required to be withdrawable on demand, but may remain out for almost any term of years, experience has led them to the practical recognition of the principle, that while a single million may be placed out at 4 or 4½ per cent., the investment of several millions cannot be so made as to produce (when an average of a term of years is taken) very much more than the public funds. This is accounted for by the fact that certain unavoidable expenses and delays, which produce loss of interest for a time, accompany general investments, whereby the actual profit-interest is reduced.

9.—Again, there are not many securities, except investments by way of loan on mortgage or debenture, which return the money at par,* or without some risk of losing a portion of the capital on the realization. On this account, Assurance Companies do not refuse to invest even at a low rate per

---

* [Mr. Stuart Mill has very properly pointed out that the rate of interest on good security, which alone we have here to consider, (for interest in which considerations of risk bear a part may swell to any amount,) is seldom, in the great centres of money transactions, precisely the same for two days together, as is shewn by the never ceasing variations in the quoted prices of the funds and other negociable securities. Nevertheless, there is, as in other cases of value, some average rate which (in the language of Adam Smith and Ricardo) may be called the natural rate, about which the market rate oscillates, and to which it always tends to return. The rate of interest derivable from the public funds is the weather-gauge of the market rate. These depend partly on the amount of accumulation going on in the hands of persons, who cannot themselves attend to the employment of their savings, and partly on the comparative taste existing in the community for the active pursuits of industry, or for the leisure, ease, and independence of an annuitant. In fact, fluctuations in the rate of interest depend almost entirely upon the portion of the capital of the country, which is in the hands of bankers and others who desire to lend for short terms only, and who are continually in the market seeking for short investments. The capital of those who live on the interest of their own fortunes has generally sought and found some fixed investment, such as the public funds, mortgages, or the bonds of public companies, which investment, except under peculiar temptations or necessities, is not changed.]

cent. when the full capital is secured, or receivable by way of an annuity which produces a gradual repayment of the capital at par.

Indeed, it is the practice of the richer companies to advance large sums, such as £200,000 or £300,000 at a time, at $3\frac{1}{4}$ or $3\frac{1}{2}$ per cent. interest, in consequence of the difficulty of obtaining a higher rate for money with the certainty of receiving back at par. They would be the very last to do so if it were possible always and readily to obtain more productive investments, especially as in the majority of cases such companies have on their direction men of great experience in finance and in business matters, receive the best legal advice, and are managed by officials possessing a familiar knowledge of every kind of security that the market offers.

If Assurance Companies find this difficulty with funds which are but small as compared with Savings Bank deposits, it can scarcely be anticipated that the Commissioners will be able to obtain advantageous investments for so large an amount as they will be entrusted with, especially as it is obvious that one effect—a fall in the average rate of interest—would be likely to arise from so large an amount of money being known to be in the market.

10.—Nor should the evidence be overlooked of the Joint Stock Banks, which experience difficulty in obtaining more than a trifling rate of interest on large sums of money, that are liable to be called back on demand or with short notice. If our readers will refer to the remarks on non-Government Banks or Banks of Deposit in Part VI. they will see that *the actual bona fide profits on safe banking do not exceed 2 per cent per annum, although identically the same business is transacted as by Savings Banks, which are receiving from the Government £3 . 5s. per cent.*

To the difficulty that all Banks feel in procuring much interest for large sums of money, an able witness, Mr. Sikes, of the Huddersfield Joint-Stock Bank, bore testimony before the Committee. He remarked—

"Some of the wealthiest bankers in England are only allowing 30s. per cent. for deposits under £300 or £400."—Again, "the fact is that, as a rule, the *safer* and the higher the position of the Bank, *the lower the rate of interest they allow.*" (Qu. 2702.)

The obvious reason of the better class of Banks or Banking Companies allowing only 30s. per cent. interest on their deposits being that they cannot pay more without loss, or without giving up the small margin (10s. per cent.) they keep for their own remuneration.

11.—In estimating the relative merits and advantages of different classes of investments for very large sums of money, care is necessary when we come to the consideration of the Public Funds, the convenience of which as a medium of investment is undeniable, but the public, accustomed for more than thirty-five years past to hear Consols quoted

---

* [Mr. Stuart Mill has suggested one medium of investment which presents some novelty, viz. a *National Bank of Deposit and Discount*, with ramifications throughout the country; which he considers might receive any money confided to it, and either fund it at a fixed rate of interest; or allow interest on a floating balance, like the Joint Stock Banks, the interest given being of course lower than the rate at which individuals can borrow in proportion to the security of a Government investment, and the expense of the establishment being defrayed by the difference between the interest which the bank would pay, and that which it would obtain by lending its deposits on increased landed or other security. "There are (he says), no insuperable objections in principle, and I should think none in practice, to an institution of this sort, as a means of supplying the same convenient mode of investment now afforded by the public funds. It would constitute the State a great Insurance Company to insure that part of the community who live on the interest of their property, against the risk of losing it by the bankruptcy of those to whom they might otherwise be under the necessity of confiding it."]

at high prices, are apt to look upon these prices as a fair type of what may be realized at *any time*. Yet the case is far otherwise, and we have but to refer to Table C, Art. 15, Part III., to be convinced that where the sum to be invested is very great, and particularly where larger and larger portions of that sum are likely to be required as the price of stock takes a more and more downward tendency, they become a dangerous mode of investment. During the twenty-five years from 1731 to 1755, the average of the 3 per cent. Consols was 97; for the following twenty years it was depressed to 86; for the forty-eight years next succeeding, it fell as low as 66; and yet during the last thirty-five years it has risen again to over 90. To these facts, if we add the consideration already urged in Part III., namely, that just in proportion as the price of stock sinks lower, the amount of Savings Bank withdrawals increases, the impropriety of investing the *whole* of Savings Bank monies in such securities must be admitted.

12.—The difficulties, we have pointed out in the preceding articles, have led many experienced persons to inquire whether, instead of the investment* of Savings Banks money being cen-

---

* [In France, various curious suggestions have been made, having for their object the obtaining greater interest than the public funds produce. An orator in the Chamber of Deputies, M. Lombard Buffières, 27th February 1835, said—

"Il aurait souhaité qu'on organisât, par l'autorité de la loi, toutes les caisses d'épargne, d'après le modèle d'un établissement qui se combine avec les monts-de-piété, et qui, dans une grande ville de l'Est, produit des résultats admirables.

M. de Lamartine, also proposed, "d'établir une banque universelle, ayant pour capital légal tous les millions accumulés par toutes les caisses d'épargne du royaume."

M. Coquelin also, in his excellent work, " Du Crédit et des Banques," made some suggestions :—" Que pourraient faire de leurs fonds ces établissements, à les supposer complétement libres? Ils remplissent admirablement cette première fonction des institutions de credit, de recueillir les épargnes, les économies disséminées entre toutes les mains, pour en former des capitaux ; mais tout débouché leur manque.

tralized into the hands of Commissioners in London, it might not be possible, by an extension of the principle of Sect. 12. of the present Savings Bank Act, to leave the investment to each individual bank, on the plan which will be found detailed in Part VI. on non-Government Banks.

Section 4.—Further Preliminary Considerations.—How a Deficiency is to be prevented in future.

ART. 13.—*Resumé.*—The circumstances described in the preceding section lead to the following conclusions:—

I. *That, although three-fourths of the Savings Bank funds might be invested without inconvenience in general securities, it is very improbable that sufficient for even one-fourth will be available.*

II. *That, allowing for losses on general securities and expenses, delays in investment, &c., it is highly improbable that the rate of interest that can be made on the whole of the Savings*

["Ils ne pourraient encore, laissés à eux-mêmes, que les porter à la bourse et au trésor.

"Dans mon dernier chapitre, j'ai indiqué une autre voie qui leur sera ouverte bientôt, si l'on ne s'y oppose pas. Mais ce ne serait pas encore suffisant. Il faut après avoir reçu par fractions minimes des mains des travailleurs d'importants dépôts, que les caisses d'épargne les renvoient par filets plus larges au commerce, aux manufactures comme à l'agriculture, les versent à tous les canaux de la production, afin, d'une part, de féconder chaque travail industriel, et de l'autre, qu'il n'y ait plus d'engorgement à redouter. Alors aussi les travailleurs économes seront vraiment devenus les commanditaires de la production et ils profiteront doublement de l'emploi de leurs fonds, puisque toujours, où quelque branche de l'industrie se développe, les salaires montent. Je pense, à la vérité, que les prêts des caisses d'épargne aux banques agricoles presenteraient le plus d'avantages; mais pour cela encore qu'elles soient libres et agissent selon leur interêt de chaque jour. Et s'il en était ainsi, loin de craindre de voir la masse des dépôts s'élever à de trop fortes sommes, ne serait-on pas assuré que plus elle serait considérable, plus elle serait féconde?"]

Bank deposits, when the average of a number of years is taken, will much exceed 3¼ *per cent.**

III. *That, as a first step, it will not be wise to assume a higher rate than* 3½ *per cent. to be realizable, when the reorganization of Savings Banks shall be considered by the Legislature.* (See note, page 192.)

14.—It is also perfectly clear, that, whatever investments be found for Savings Bank deposits, and whatever be the annual rate of interest obtainable by the Commissioners, the repayments and withdrawals must be so managed as to tally, if possible, with the receipts from the securities; and somewhat less interest than is realized by the investments must be allowed, so as to provide a †margin for the rise and fall in the securities when purchased or sold, and for the expenses of the banks, in order *that the business may be made self-supporting.*

---

* [It should be noticed, that although every legal restriction on interest has been removed by the final repeal of the Usury Laws in 1854, yet a comparison of the rates, through a period sufficiently long to eliminate the effect of fluctuation, shews a progressive diminution, which will probably continue, as a fall of profits and interest naturally takes place with the progress of population and production; the cause of this decline in the rate being the increased cost of maintaining labour, the larger amount of capital competing for employment, and the greater security afforded by the absence of troubles in the State. The repealed laws themselves indirectly shew the fact, for in the reign of Elizabeth an Act was passed limiting the rate of interest to 10 per cent.; in the reign of James I. it was limited to 8 per cent.; in that of Charles II. to 6 per cent.; and in the reign of Anne, the Act, which until recently was the basis of the law, limited the rate of interest to 5 per cent.]

† [The plan adopted by the "Bank for Savings in the City of New York," (under the Act 23 April 1831) appears to be based upon sound principles :—

"The Board of Trustees of the Bank for Savings in the City of New York, are hereby authorized to accumulate gradually, and hold invested, a surplus fund, not exceeding three per cent. on the amount of the deposits,

The margin required will not be produced, unless a large portion of the 41 millions be invested in general securities; it would be derived only from that portion, and then only after the contingencies discussed in *Part III. have been provided for. Any aggravation in the circumstances referred to therein during the coming twenty-five years will prevent any reserve being accumulated. Should it be a period of peace and high prices, the rate of interest received for investments will be low, and little margin will be obtained. If the converse, the rate realised may be high, but the cessation of speculative investments, and of the formation of new companies to any extent, would bring

to the end that, in case of a reduction in the market price of the public stocks and securities, held or to be held by the said Bank, below the par value thereof, any loss to the Depositors, by reason of such reduction, may be prevented or made good by means of the said fund." The necessity for some such margin is admitted by continental authorities. A learned German economist urges that "under the most exemplary organization and administration, losses can never be otherwise obviated."]

* [There is an impression, that if the present Deficiency be recouped, the rate of interest £3.5s. per cent. may safely be continued for the future, even if all investments be made in the public funds. This is, however, erroneous, *because the average of the purchases is always likely to be above, and the averages of the sales below* 92¾, the *price of safety*: hence (as we have explained in Art. 15, and the note thereto, of Part III.,) a fresh deficiency in Savings Bank assets must arise, while no restorative element exists in their operations, nor compensating influence to recoupe the annual loss.

The necessity of some margin, as referred to in the text, will be appreciated by considering the transactions of 1858, which are set forth in Art. 17. of Part III. It appears that £755,250 stock was bought at the average price of £96.19s. 6d per cent., costing £732,391, by which an interest of £3.1s. 10d. was produced (See Table B, p. 130); and on an equal amount sold to meet withdrawals, only £692,075 was realized, or £91.13s. per cent.

This difference, £40,316, produced a deficiency of £5.6s. 6d. in every £100, and it would take more than nine years before a margin, say of even 10s. per cent., would enable the Commissioners to recoupe the loss made by the sales of that one year.—*See No. 9 of the Compound Interest Tables in the Building Society Treatise.*]

other capital into the mortgage and parliamentary securities market to compete with the money of Depositors waiting in the hands of the Savings Bank Commissioners for investment.

15.—This question of the rate of interest that should be allowed to Savings Bank Depositors has been discussed by different persons from directly opposite points of view. On the one hand, there are those who, arguing from the considerations into which we have entered at length in the Section on Expenses, Part I., as to the greater costliness of small accounts, and the large amount of unremunerated trouble they occasion, would reduce the rate of interest on the smaller deposits, such as those not exceeding £20, to £2.10s. per cent., giving to the Depositors of larger sums a rate of £3.

On the other side, there are many who object to the Government guaranteeing so large an annual rate of interest as £3.5s. per cent.,* and who urge, with perfect justice, that Depositors, whose savings are large, are not of the class of persons who require the aid of the nation in encouraging provident habits: and that, if a premium is to be offered to provident habits by the Government of the country, its advantages should be confined to those who really belong to the poorer classes.

They argue, therefore, that a low rate of interest, such as 2 per cent., is all that need be allowed to the larger Depositors, while the full rate of 3 per cent. should be credited to those accounts which do not exceed £20.

16.—To decide between these two opposite views, it is not

---

* [" En outre," observes M. du Puynode, " on ne peut douter, que dans un temps, plus ou moins prochain, l'intérêt de la rente ne diminue (cela est arrivé)—et dans ce cas l'Etat, continuant à employer les dépôts comme il le fait, ne recevrait plus ce qu'il devrait remettre, ce qui donnerait aux caisses d'épargne le caractère d'établissements d'aumône." (*Des Lois du travail et des classes ouvrières.*)]

unimportant to consider that although, in principle, Depositors desire the advantage resulting from compound interest, it does not appear that the *rate* itself has an appreciable influence on the amount of their deposits. The Legislature has, by successive enactments, lowered the interest allowed, yet the deposits have, notwithstanding, continued to increase from year to year. Many Savings Banks in Scotland have, for a long time, allowed only 2½ per cent.; and yet their deposits, when added to those of the like class in Joint Stock Banks, are, in proportion, more numerous and larger than for a similar population in England. Interest is, no doubt, a premium to economy, which it encourages, rewards, and thus contributes to maintain; but a high rate need not be looked upon as a condition indispensable to the prosperity of Savings Banks.

The Superintendant of the banking department of New York remarks, in his Report relative to Savings Banks, that " The primary motive which induces deposits in these banks is entire security of the sum deposited; the secondary motive, the accumulation of interest. The first overrides the second, and is the main condition. The difference between the legal rate of interest and that allowed by these institutions is of little or no importance to the Depositors individually. The *eventual return* of the *sum deposited* is the object sought, and the *controlling idea of the Depositor.*"*

---

* [The opinion of that practical philanthropist, the late *Dr. Chalmers*, may be cited on this point. " He often spoke to me on the subject," (said one of the witnesses before the Committee, Mr. Maitland), " and his argument used to be, that the ready receipt and payment of small sums of money and their safe custody were every thing, and the rate of interest quite unimportant; and that the result of high interest had been to swamp our Savings Banks as a national system. That the care taken of the small amounts for investment was the main question."

Mr. Deaker also says (Qu. 3627), " I think Depositors of small amounts look more to the safe keeping of their money than to the actual amount of interest they may receive."]

17.—It is, indeed, idle to suppose that interest is the attraction which makes the poorer classes come to the Savings Banks, for it is only an attractive element to the recipient when measured in large quantities: 3 per cent. per annum is only one-fifth more than a halfpenny in the pound per month; so that a Depositor having £5 in the bank for six months would only receive 1s. 6d. If the rate were £2.10s. per cent. his interest would be 1s. 3d.

Where, however, the savings are £100 or more, the owners begin to think of the profit they can make for it; and with the feeling of having capital at command they seek for investment in some more lucrative medium than a Savings Bank. Some go into business, others invest in various associations, fancying that they will get at least 6 or 7 per cent. per annum interest, possibly (they think) much more. Once comparatively well off, they do not care for a Government investment, from which, according to their ideas, no such chance of gain can arise.

18.—*As to withdrawals.*—The difficulty with regard to the investment of the funds, and, at the same time, the necessity of obviating the inconvenience which would follow upon an unexpected demand for large repayments, has given rise to a proposal for modifying the existing rules, and for substituting a proportionate delay, according to the amount to be withdrawn, between the demand and the repayment. It has been proposed to leave to the Depositor the free disposal of a portion of his deposit, either by fixing a certain amount beforehand, such as a fourth, or taking a proportional part, which might be withdrawable at pleasure and on demand, leaving the remaining three-fourths subject to a longer notice.*

---

* [The necessity for such a provision has been long admitted in *Prussia*. A ministerial rescript on 31st May, 1849, recommended that not more than £1.10s. should be withdrawable on demand; £7.10s. a-fortnight

It has been urged that the working classes themselves are not so unreasonable as to expect both profit on their subscriptions and also immediate repayment of their money on demand. This appears to be sustained by the fact, that if an Investment and Building Society, an Industrial Partnership Association, or a Friendly Society, be established anywhere, money pours in from members, anxious to avail themselves of the advantages offered, who readily recognise the propriety of proper notice before withdrawal, or, at all events, the necessity of allowing immediate withdrawals only of a very small fraction of the money deposited.

19.—The liability to *withdrawal of the many millions deposited with the National Debt Commissioners is undoubtedly a difficulty in the Savings Bank question, which could be overcome by the Trustees having power to require longer notice for sums over a certain amount. With sufficient time, there would be no difficulty in providing funds to meet calls, and securities might be accepted which are not readily negociable, since, during the currency of the notice, withdrawals would be provided for, in most cases, out of the incoming deposits, and no operation of sale would be required.

---

afterwards; but larger sums should only be repaid after three months' notice. This is acted upon in the majority of the Prussian Savings Banks. The previous regulation (promulgated in 1838) was little less stringent: two months' notice being required for all sums exceeding £3.15s.]

* [It is remarkable that the amount of Savings Bank Deposits appears to have *doubled* in about 22 years, ending 20th November 1859. This happens to be the time in which the Deposits on hand 22 years ago, would have doubled themselves by the mere addition of compound interest at £3.5s. per cent., if undisturbed: that is to say, the *withdrawals* during the period by Trustees of Savings Banks have just equalled the *new deposits, and the accruing interest thereon.*

The number and extent of withdrawals from Savings Banks each year is exceedingly great (see Art. 44, Part II.). Independently of the large sums occasionally withdrawn from the Government by the Trustees, there is required annually, on the average, £11 of every £13 that is deposited, to provide for repayments, and not more than £2 passes into the hands of the Commissioners.]

CHAPTER X.

AS TO THE ALTERATIONS THAT ARE DESIRABLE IN THE GOVERNMENT CONNECTION WITH SAVINGS BANKS.

Section 1.— General Reorganization suggested.

ART. 20.—The fundamental principles, described in the previous Chapter, lead to the legislative alterations necessary. The changes we suggested in 1851 in the Government connection with Savings Banks, without reference to a national guarantee to the Depositors, are as follows:—

1st. The appointment of a Commission to superintend and manage the general funds of Savings Banks, and the investment of the deposits received by it.

2nd. A grant to be accorded by the Legislature to make up the present *deficiency in Savings Bank securities, estimated on the principle laid down in Part III., on the understanding that,

---

* [It should be remarked, that, in measuring the Deficiency, the object is not to ascertain what amount of grant should be made to enable an immediate sale of the whole stock in hand to be effected, and the Depositors in Savings Banks paid off in full out of the produce. For it is evident, that in such case the price of stocks would at once fall through so large an amount being thrown upon the market.

If handed over to a Commission, the Deficiency grant should be measured by the average price for twenty-five years. Any proposal in the coming session to make up the deficiency by a grant at the price of the present year will prove largely insufficient, as the Funds happen now to be at very near the highest price for the last twenty-five years. (See Table B, Art. 12, Part III.)

should any surplus arise on the future conversion of the stock into cash, it be applied to recoupe the nation for the deficiency grant; but should the Stock voted prove insufficient, then a further grant to be made.

3rd. The funds of Savings Banks to be left by the Commission, in the present securities, until more advantageous investments present themselves, and then to be gradually withdrawn to the extent of one-half, and placed (if possible) in others producing a better rate of interest.

4th. The Commission to receive for the deposits exactly what interest their investments realize.

5th. The Commission to have power to replace any amount of the deposits in Government Stock in case other satisfactory investments cannot from time to time be found.

6th. Any financial necessities of the public exchequer (such as are discussed in Chapter VIII. Part III.) to be provided for by allowing the Chancellor to borrow such money as he may require from the Savings Bank Commissioners, and to replace the same with interest.

7th. The *Commissioners to be instructed to encourage the formation of new Savings Banks in places where none exist.

---

* [In Art. 18. Part I. we have described the constitution of the National Debt Commission. It is, as Lord Monteagle justly remarked, impossible for the high officials who compose it, even with the utmost diligence, consistently with their other avocations, to attend to the affairs of Savings Banks. The narrative contained in previous Parts sufficiently proves that ex-officio Commissioners cannot pay attention to important financial business when they are so fully occupied with other and more direct duties. Even should some very important question require their presence, it will be as easily understood how unequal to the business a member of any board would be who does not attend its meetings regularly. He can but try to take up the fragments of a question, of the antecedents of which he is ignorant, and with respect to the future results of which he must likewise be very uncertain. The magnitude of capital involved, and the probability of the further extension and developement which Savings Banks will yet acquire, render it absolutely necessary that there should be some official responsibility answerable to Parliament for due attention to the business to be transacted in connection with them.]

8th. A modification of *Mr. Whitbread's Post Office Plan* to be adopted as a feeder to local banks in large towns from small places where none exist, or where it is not yet expedient to establish independent branches. (For fuller details, see Art. 5, Part. V.)

Section 2.—Of the Commission.

ART. 21.—That Savings Banks business may be effectually conducted, the Commission ought to be paid.

There is no way of enforcing real responsibility, unless there be the power of saying to a man, "I give you so much for a certain duty, and I therefore demand, and shall enforce, the proper discharge of it." No money could be so well expended as in paying a proper remuneration to a well-constituted and effective Board.

It should consist of five members, three * to be nominated by the Crown, and to be paid, the others to be *ex-officio*, viz. the Chancellor of the Exchequer and the Governor or Deputy-Governor of the Bank of England.

---

* [The Committee of 1858 recommended that only *one* of the five Commissioners should be paid; but all experience shews that it is unadvisable to commit large interests to the keeping of one paid Manager, controlled only by honorary officials.

No supervision is ever effectual unless performed as a duty, and not as a voluntary act.

If the dignity of some of the contemplated Commissioners be so high, that the remuneration would not be of importance to them, let there be a sufficient number on the Commission to whom proper and adequate remuneration would be an object, and who will discharge their functions as the business of their life, just as is the case with County Court Judges, or any other public stipendiary officials.

If only one Commissioner were salaried, he would be practically as powerful as if he were sole uncontrolled Manager. The only unpaid members of the Commission should be those who, like the Chancellor of the Exchequer, are *ex-officio*, entitled to a veto upon its proceedings, and who, by having the right to be present at the Board meetings, could make suggestions.]

Although the Parliamentary Committee of 1858 did not refer to it, we cannot but think that the Comptroller of the National Debt Office should be one of the Commission—whether *ex officio,* or not, is, however, a question. It would be, in every way, important to secure to the future administration of Savings Banks the benefit of the experience he must necessarily possess.

Section 3.—*Modes of Investment.*

ART. 22.—In Art. 8 of the previous chapter we have said, that of the £41,000,000 deposited (1859) by Savings Banks and Friendly Societies with the National Debt Commissioners, a very considerable amount might with strict prudence be invested in securities of a less marketable nature than the public funds, but calculated to yield a higher rate of interest, (*assuming they can be found to a sufficient extent*), such as ' *Parliamentary securities* ' having the guarantee of the State, and others like the following (some of which are chargeable under the authority of statutes), viz. :—

> 1st. On the security of *County or Borough Rates* authorized to be levied and mortgaged by any Act of Parliament.
>
> 2nd. On the security of *Rates, Tolls, Duties,* Assessments, Bonds, Debentures, or other securities of any body or company *incorporated* by Act of Parliament or charter, which such body or company is authorized by such Act or charter to raise, levy, or mortgage.

Under this head would come advances under the *Land Drainage Act,** which it is stated would be attended with no

---

* [*Of Land as security for advances.*—The value of land as security for advances is yearly augmenting, and if, as we have discussed elsewhere, facilities be given for an inexpensive mode of

risk, because, whatever mortgages or incumbrances there may be upon the lands, the money for drainage is made a first charge. Also, first class *Railway Debentures*, and the Bonds of the greater dock companies and other corporate bodies of ample revenue.

3rd. In Bank of England Stock.
4th. In India Bonds, stock, and loans.
5th. On mortgage of freehold, leasehold, or copyhold property (such leasehold being for a term of years absolute, of which not less than thirty years shall be unexpired, and such copy-

---

dealing with real property, the Savings Bank Commissioners may have a field for profitable loans opened to them.—[See Treatise on the Enfranchisement of Copyhold and Church property, pages vi. to ix. and Appendix.] An elaborate writer on the history of money (Mr. Hodge) remarks, that should the same rate of increase continue for as long a period as it has already been in progress, the annual value of an acre of land in England three hundred years hence will be nearly £20 sterling; the revenues of some existing entails, if they can be maintained unbroken, will be reckoned by millions; and the rental, for a single year,[2] of the whole landed property of the United Kingdom, will exceed the present amount of the national debt.

Towards the end of the seventeenth century,[3] rent in England was about six shillings the acre; and as the average in 1843 was

---

[2] The total rental of England and Wales is estimated to have been—

In 1600, £6,000,000 } By Davenant, vol i., p. 362 (*including houses*
    1680, £14,000,000 } *and mines*).
    1771, £16,000,000..By Arthur Young: *Northern Tour*, iv. 366 (land only).
    1806, £25,900,000 ⎫ By McCulloch: *Statistical Account of the British Empire*, i. 558 (land only). These
    1815, £34,230,000 ⎬ numbers having been deduced from the
    1843, £40,167,000 ⎪ property-tax returns, are probably correct;
    1852, £41,118,000 ⎭ the accuracy of the others is necessarily very doubtful.

[3] *Usury, &c., examined by T. Morley*: Lond. 1682; p. 11.

hold being copyhold of inheritance in Great Britain or Ireland.)

6th. On security of heritable property in Scotland.

7th. In any chartered or other public Joint-Stock Bank in Scotland.

This last-mentioned medium of investment, although included in the Friendly Societies' Act, may perhaps be con-

---

not less than [4] twenty-four shillings the acre, Lord [5] Macaulay is correct in his estimate that it had quadrupled in the interval between the two periods—about a century and a half. It had increased in exactly the same proportion during the nearly similar interval preceding the Revolution : so that, assuming the growth to have been uniform, the annual value of land in England has been doubled once in every period of seventy-five years since the Reformation, being an increase in each year of £0.934, or 18s. 8d. per cent. The writer quoted adds that :—

"It seems probable that, in the reign of James I., the value of land was from twelve to fourteen years purchase; and as, according to the scale of progression that has been laid down, the rent would be about 3s. per acre, the selling price average from 36s. to 42s. per acre is not much more than a twentieth part of what, even without any peculiar advantage of situation, is commonly realized at the present time. As the relative improvement must have been greatest in the manufacturing districts, we may readily believe the assertion that the present amount of the yearly *rental* of Lancashire would have bought the *fee simple* of the county in the time of Elizabeth."

[4] In McCulloch's *Statistical Account of the British Empire* (vol. i. p. 553), the average rent of land, in 1843, is given for England only at £1.3s. 2¼d. per acre; but as this result is obtained by dividing the gross rental of the kingdom by the aggregate acreage of the counties, without allowance for roads and wastes, the actual average must be somewhat higher.

[5] *Hist. Eng.* i. 318.]

sidered objectionable, after the recent disastrous failures in Scotch banks. It has been suggested as a readily available, safe, and productive form in which to retain the floating capital, to place it " on deposit at interest among the leading Joint Stock Banks of England, Scotland, and Ireland;" but in this, for the same reason, we cannot concur.

Another eligible kind of investment, as good as many of the above, would be to apply a portion of the Savings Bank capital to assisting Societies for *Improving the *Dwellings of the Poor*, on the plan detailed at length in the Appendix to this Treatise.

ART. 23.—If a †variety of investments be decided on, two accounts should be opened by the Commissioners:

1st. A SHORT INVESTMENT ACCOUNT { In which half of the Savings Bank Deposits would be invested in the public funds or any easily convertible securities producing a low rate of interest.

2nd. A LONG INVESTMENT ACCOUNT { In which the other half of the money would, if possible, be invested on general securities.

---

* [This was very ably urged by Mr. Christopher Bushell, in his capacity of Chairman of a Section at the 1858 Meeting of the Social Science Association.]

† [The money required for *Exchequer Loans*, to assist public and private improvements, &c., might be obtained from Savings Banks at interest, instead of (out of the produce of taxation) from the Consolidated Fund. This would include the operations of the *Public Works Advance Commission*, (created by Act 57 Geo. III. c. 34., subject to numerous amending Acts, the last being 20 and 21 Vict. c. 63.). The total sum advanced by them during forty-three years is £13,700,000, on which £4,100,000 principal, and £300,000 interest, remained due on the 31st March 1859. It would also include the similar fund created for Ireland by the Act 1 and 2 Wm. IV. c. 33., which has made advances amounting to 5 millions. (Return No. 30, sess. 2. 1859, p. 65—67).]

CHAPTER XI.

RECOMMENDATIONS.

Sect. 1.—Plan recommended for Payment of Savings Bank Expenses.

ART. 24.—In Art. 15, we have adverted to the diversity of opinion, that prevails as to the selection of the rate of interest which shall be right as between small and large Depositors, when regard is had to the question of expenses.

The difficulties under which Savings Bank reformers labour, owing to that question, can only be properly obviated by an *annual grant from the Commissioners, *out of a fund to be created for the purpose* (see note below). This, if taken at £140,000 a-year for the amount of Savings Bank deposits, would not amount to more than 7s. 6d. per cent. out of the interest realized, and would suffice to defray the expenses attending the conduct of one Savings Bank, or branch thereof, in every town of the kingdom; such grant to be taken out of the produce of the investments as an aggregate, and not out of the per-centage of the profits of each bank. By this arrangement the Government would be able to say to the Managers, " What matters it that the larger Depositors withdraw, and

---

* [The total expenses, according to Sect. 10. Chap. II., are at present £119,790. (Returns to 20th November 1857.)

The fund for the grant, which will probably have to be increased, can be measured thus :—the aggregate annual interest that the Commissioners would have to pay is shewn below, supposing £3 per cent. to be

thus produce deficiency in the fund available for expenses? they are not the class that require the aid of the nation to encourage them to save money, and we will guarantee your expenses." The Commissioners would thus enable the Bank Managers, who at present are crippled from want of resources, to give an impulse and activity to the transactions of the bank, and to fairly proportion the remuneration to the labour and duties of their staff. (See Art. 44, Part II. Of Actuaries).

---

allowed on so much of each deposit as amounts to £100, and £2.10s. on the excess, as recommended in Sect. 2 of this chapter. The figures are taken to the 20th November 1858, as no sufficient details are yet published for 1859.

Individual Depositors.	Number of Depositors.	Total amount due.	Annual Interest.	
			Amount.	Rate Per cent.
Not exceeding £100	1,309,864	£23,629,932	£928,912	£3 0 0
Over £100 for £100 worth	73,338	7,333,800		
Balance over £100		2,958,149	73,954	2 10 0
Total Individual Depositors . .	1,383,202	33,921,881	1,002,866	
Add for Charitable Institutions, and Friendly Societies . .		2,292,241	68,767	3 0 0
		1,080,682	59,420	
Total . . .		£38,194,804	1,131,053	
Expenses . .		(say)	140,000	
			1,271,053	

Now, if on the 38 millions 3¼ per cent. average interest be obtained, ... =£1,336,818
there will be a Balance of 65,765
as a yearly RESERVE FUND FOR LOSSES ON WITHDRAWALS.

But if, as we ourselves believe, 3¼ *per cent. only be obtained*, there will be a *large annual deficiency*, instead of a margin, and it would be necessary to lower still more the rates of interest allowed to Depositors.]

Sect. 2.—*Of the Interest recommended to be allowed to Depositors.*

ART. 25.—When the expenses of each guaranteed Savings Bank are defrayed by a grant out of the general fund from the Savings Banks Commissioners, the interest allowed to them can be reduced to that which they shall offer to their Depositors. Supposing that £3.10s. per cent. be the average interest produced on the investments (see Art. 23, p. 190), and 7s. 6d. the average annual per centage for expenses, it would be necessary to reduce the rate of interest to Depositors, in order that a proper margin may be provided. That this reduction may be effected in a manner most in accordance with the proper object of Savings Banks, viz. to encourage the smaller deposits, the rate should be £3 per cent. on sums* not exceeding £100, and on so much of larger deposits. For the surplus, up to £200, it should be £2.10s. These rates are preferable to any other, from the facility they afford in calculations. *(See Sect. 5 of this Chapter.)*

† With this change in the rate of interest, a change in the

---

* [In the American Banks a distinction is also made between the benefits afforded by way of encouragement to provident habits among the really poorer classes, and those facilities for investment which are opened to persons of better means. Clauses like the following are generally adopted :—

"The said Board of Trustees may also regulate from time to time the interest to be allowed to Depositors, so that the interest, allowed to Depositors having five hundred dollars or more deposited with the said bank, shall be at least *one* per cent. less than the interest or dividend allowed to Depositors having less than 500 dollars deposited therewith."]

† [Mr. Sikes, in his evidence, recommended a greater reduction, viz. that " interest should be allowed at the rate of 3 per cent. up to £100; and with respect to any balance that exceeded £100, 2 per cent. on such excess over the £100 ; that is, if there be a balance of £140, 3 per cent. would be allowed on the £100 portion, and 2 per cent on the surplus, that is, on the £40." (qu. 2676.)

Mr. Porter considered that the interest should be reduced to "2 per cent., or even lower."]

power of withdrawal should be made, as explained in Sect. 3.

A check on withdrawals would be created if the rate were made £2 . 10s. per cent. on *all* deposits, and if the balance of the £3 for the Deposits not exceeding £100 were awarded half-yearly in the shape of a *bonus of 10s. per cent. per annum to those accounts, upon which no withdrawal had taken place for six months previously.

Thus, while encouraging the keeping up of a provident spirit, the †check on withdrawals would diminish the trouble of the bank, and, consequently, the expenses referred to in Part I.

Sect. 3.—Recommendations respecting Withdrawal.

ART. 26.—To obviate the liability to sudden withdrawals in Savings Banks, and to check their being taken out uselessly,

---

* [The calculation of the bonus would be simple, viz. one-fifth would have to be added half-yearly to the interest credited for the past six months.]

† [*EXTRA DIVIDENDS to those who permit their Funds to remain in the Institution.*

" At the end of every five years, the first to be computed from the   day of   18   , there shall be declared a dividend of all the profits which may have accrued within the said five years (after deducting the dividends already made, the necessary expenses of the Institution, and the sums necessary to keep good the capital stock), to and among all such Depositors, whose deposits exceed the sum of five dollars, and which shall have remained in the said Institution for the space of one year at least, next preceding the time of declaring the said extra dividends, in proportion to the interest which may have accrued on their deposits during the preceding five years; and the said dividends shall be disposed of in the same way as ordinary dividends."—*From the By-Laws of the* LOWELL INSTITUTION FOR SAVINGS.

Similar regulations are in force in the banks at Boston, Chelsea, Newburyport, and in most other Savings Banks in the State of Massachusetts.]

it is desirable that some modification should be made in the existing system, which is equivalent to a payment on demand. While fourteen days' notice should suffice for sums under £25, the plan (customary in Building Societies) should be adopted for larger withdrawals, and one month's notice should be required for the repayment of £50 additional, and six weeks for sums over £75. Thus a person giving notice to withdraw £120 would receive £25 in a fortnight, £50 more in two weeks afterwards, and the balance, £45, in another fourteen days.*

There are no circumstances under which a working man can require a larger sum than £25 so unexpectedly that he could not give a month's or six weeks' notice; and even if a special contingency should arise, it should be met by a provision that, in such case, the Trustees of the bank should, if they deemed it right and had funds in hand, pay the applicant the money required without insisting on the full notice or time elapsing previously.

---

* [Mr. Porter considers the above notices as scarcely long enough. He says (p. 41), "To prevent a senseless run on those institutions at the bidding of some misguided individual, the Bank should require one week's notice for all sums under £20; one month's notice for all sums ranging between £20 and £50; and three months' notice for all sums over £50."

There is no doubt that large sales of stock have been caused by the want of longer notices.

Sir Alexander Spearman stated that "in the three months beginning with the 1st of October and ending with the 31st of December 1857, we commenced with a balance of £20,800. We received from Trustees £110,000. We received dividends on stock, on the 10th of October, £290,000, and in that period we paid to Trustees £1,170,000. To enable us to make these payments, we had of course to sell stock, *and we sold £909,000 at an average price of* 91¼. We did not sell much more than was requisite to balance the account, and at the close of the year the Trustees were still drawing. *We are now* (May 1858) *purchasing back that stock at* 96 *and* 97, 97½, and probably it will be *at par* before we have done with it. These are the circumstances which shew that the transactions between the Trustees of Savings Banks and the National Debt Office may and do occasion loss to the fund."]

Section 4.—Changes recommended in the Annual Limit.

ART. 27.—The amount that may be deposited in a year should not be limited to £30, as it is at present under the 35th section of the Act of 9 Geo. IV. c. 92.; but it should be left open to the Depositor to place in any sum that does not raise his account beyond £200, without reference to whether such amount consist of interest or deposit.

There is something contrary to common sense in the existing regulation, tending as it does to check that provident spirit which makes the industrious classes willing to invest in Savings Banks.

It not unfrequently happens, that, by the sale of a little property, as in the case of members of Building Societies, or by a legacy or gift, a working man comes into possession of a larger sum than £30; and it would be well for him, by depositing it at once, to place himself beyond the temptation of spending it.

28.—A case occurs to our mind of an industrious mechanic, who withdrew a somewhat large sum of money from a Savings Bank to add to the amount, which he had borrowed from a Building Society, for the purpose of purchasing a small house. Just as he was about to complete the transaction, a defect was found in the title, which caused the whole affair to fall through. He returned to the Savings Bank, but it declined to receive more than £30 in one year; and as the Building Society was not empowered to accept single deposits, he had no investment for the money thus thrown upon his hands, and was led, as might be expected, to play ducks and drakes with it. The check to provident habits, which he thus received from the Legislature, led to results from which it would take him a very long time to recover.

Mr. Wortley, (qu. 1567), said—

" It would be, I think, a very useful thing, if the limits which are now so troublesome to Depositors were entirely removed, retaining a maximum: those impediments are often injurious to the poor, preventing their depositing the whole of any particular sum which they may have in their possession by legacy or otherwise, and causing them in some instances to carry money about with them for a long time for want of an opportunity of getting it into a bank. What I mean is, that supposing the maximum to be fixed at £150, a Depositor should be allowed to put in the whole £150, or so much as he conveniently could, without limiting him to £30 a-year."

It seems to be a general opinion among persons of experience that the limit should be either raised or abandoned. (See the evidence of Messrs Boodle, Wortley, Maitland, Jameson, Finney, Deaker, &c., in proof of this.) Mr. Porter, indeed, urges, that to the existence of the limit are traceable the frauds perpetrated in respect to trust accounts. (See Sect. 2. chap. 12. in this Part.)

29.—Moreover, the annual limitation punishes the poor man, whose necessities may require him temporarily to withdraw, by forbidding him to reinvest when he recovers himself; and the supporters of the limit, who argue that, if it be removed, too great facilities would be offered for withdrawal, overlook the following important points:—

1. That their object—of checking withdrawals—would be better attained by a system of longer notice (such as we have described in Section 3 of this Chapter).

2. That Savings Bank Depositors are in general very prudent, careful people, and rarely withdraw money except for their actual requirements.

3. That the existence of the limit would not *prevent* a person from withdrawing who had resolved to do so.

4. That when the proposed Commission is in operation, there is every probability that, if they introduce a system of gradual notices, they will be able to pay any amount likely to be demanded, without so great a loss through depreciation of securities as has occurred in the past, and that the objection therefore to frequent withdrawals will be to a large extent removed.

5. That the disadvantages, which the limit occasions, are greater than any advantages that could be expected to arise from the discouragement of withdrawals.

30.—The regulation in Military Savings Banks (see Art. 20. Part I.) is, that deposits of any amount may be received, but (except in special cases) sums in excess of £30 in one year bear no interest for that year.

Section 5.—*Of Investments direct with the Savings Bank Commissioners.*

ART. 31.—Should it be thought expedient for the State to give to Depositors over £100 the opportunity of making more than £2.10s. per cent. on their surplus, they might be permitted to remit sums of not less than £50 to the Savings Banks Commissioners for investment in the *Long Investment Department;* the local Savings Banks transacting the business as the Depositors' agents. The Commissioners might on such investments guarantee £3 per cent. per annum interest, provided a notice of two months on withdrawal were required, and no withdrawals were allowed within four months from the date of the deposit; and provided that power were reserved to the Commissioners to refuse Deposits in the Long Investment Department, or to inform the Trustees of the Savings Bank, to which the Investors belong, that the amounts at their credit would be returned, or the interest reduced to $2\frac{1}{2}$ per cent., should continued opportunity for long investment not be found.

Power should rest with the Commissioners to authorise the Trustees to pay withdrawals without notice, even from the Long Investment account, in urgent cases (such as the Depositors' leaving the country or dying, &c.) proof of which should be given to the satisfaction of the Trustees, and a drawback of 1d. in the £ should be made in favour of the bank, by way of compensation, on the continental plan. (See Introduction).

In respect to the expenses incurred by the Commissioners in conducting their investments, it may be observed that they are unlikely to exceed the present annual £300 per million of Savings Bank stock (or £12,000 a-year) paid to the Bank of England under the existing Statutes.

CHAPTER XII.

SUBSIDIARY RECOMMENDATIONS.

Section 1.—As to the Conversion of Deposits into Stock.

ART. 32.—In order to diminish the amount for the safe investment of which the commission would be responsible, it has been suggested that all *Depositors should have the option of buying stock, in small quantities of £20 at a time,* through the

---

* [As far back as 1822, the French Government sought by this measure to provide against the danger that might arise, during an extraordinary fall in the funds, of a general demand for the reimbursement of deposits. The minimum of stock any person might hold was reduced in favour of Depositors. At various periods the law has been amended: its present operation is thus described by M. Prévost, in his *Manuel,* pp. 39, 40, article, "*Achats de rentes d'office*":—

"En execution de la loi du 30 Juin 1851, il y aura lieu chaque année, après la capitalisation des intérêts sur tous les comptes particuliers des déposants, à faire acheter d'office 10fr. de rentes pour chacun de ces comptes dont le solde excédera 1000fr. Cette operation ne devra se faire qu'après le 1er Avril."

In countries like France—where co-operative associations for profit do not exist to any great extent among the working-classes, it may happen that stock is frequently bought and sold for them in very small quantities. This will, however, never be the case in England while societies for all kinds of industrial investment abound. Even in France there are many who question the desirability of Savings Bank Depositors being induced to purchase Government stock. A long debate took place in 1844, in the Chamber of Deputies, relative to a modification of the measure, and much opposition was offered to the resolution that Depositors should not be permitted to hold in a Savings Bank more than 1000fr. (£40), and that the surplus should be applied to the purchase of stock. One of the most vigorous opponents of the measure was M. Dupin, who exclaimed—"Quoi! nous avons supprimé la loterie pour soustraire le peuple aux dangers, à la passion funeste du jeu des numeros, et nous lui

Savings Bank, and should be credited with the dividends free from charge for income tax. It has, also, been proposed to apply such a measure *compulsorily* to accounts exceeding £150, in the manner adopted in France and *Prussia.

33.—There do not appear sufficient grounds for believing that the industrious classes would care to avail themselves of

---

donnerions en échange le triste jeu de la rente? Nous estimons peu l'épicier qui, non content des profits honnêtes de sa légitime industrie, spécule, agiote et joue sur le *trois six*, et l'on voudrait lui donner le jeu du *trois cinq*." Again, when, more recently (in 1852), the expediency of affording even greater facilities for the purchase of stock was under discussion, the Committee of the Corps Legislatif reported thus (p. 47) :—
" Les facilités nouvelles qu'on accorderait aux deposants consisterait à les autoriser à se faire acheter, sans frais, des rentes par la Caisse d'Epargne, pour toutes sommes facultatives *en dehors* de leur livrets.

" Cette compensation serait bien faible pour eux, puisque déjà ils peuvent faire acheter, par l'intermédiare gratuit de la Caisse d'Epargne, des rentes sur l'Etat pour le *montant des sommes inscrites à leurs livrets* : mais cette mesure entraînerait surtout à sa suite beaucoup d'inconvénients et de dangers. Les déposants, ayant souvent besoin de retirer des sommes supérieures à 500fr. seraient obligés de faire vendre frequemment une partie de leurs petits coupons de rente, sauf à les faires rachether ensuite.

" *N'est-il pas à craindre, dès lors, qu'ils ne prennent insensiblement le goût et l'habitude de la speculation et de l'agiotage?* Puis les ordres de vente en province ne s'exécutent pas avec la même rapidité qu'à Paris. Enfin, le cours de la rente est variable; et l'ouvrier qui a amassé, deniers par deniers, quelques modestes épargnes, éprouve des craintes à l'endroit d'un placement qui peut lui rendre, à certains moments, son petit capital amoindri."

No one who has watched the speculative character of industrial investments in France during the last seven years can say that this result has not already taken place.]

* [It is provided by the Prussian law (stat. of 1838), that when deposits reach an amount to be fixed by the rules of each bank, (in no case higher than £75 sterling), they may be invested in stock, without the consent of the Depositor, up to the limit prescribed in the law relating to *pupillarische* securities, as a " *Separate Fund.*" From the valuable " Statistical Review of the state of the Savings Banks in the Province of Branden-

such a privilege, and it would only be accepted as a boon by those who have no opportunity of otherwise making profit for their money. We concur with the foreign writers (quoted below), in considering that the plan is objectionable in every way, but chiefly because it exposes the Depositor to risk, since, on such purchases of stock, he would not have any claim upon the Government for repayment of the principal at par in case a loss should arise on a subsequent sale.

34.—A compulsory measure would be unpopular and inexpedient, and productive of inconvenience to individual Depositors. A preferable course would be to *allow a reduced rate of interest (£2 . 10s. per cent.) on accounts that had attained £200, and permit the Depositor not only to leave that sum in the bank as long as he should desire, but to add to its amount, if he wished, without receiving any interest on the excess.*

---

burg," referred to in the Introduction, comprising the important cities of Berlin, Potsdam, Frankfort-on-the-Oder, &c., besides the districts of Neumark, and the lower Lausitz, we find that the provisions relating to separate funds were discovered, in the years 1847 and 1848, to have been very generally neglected. The result of this was, that in those years, when the price of the public funds fell very low, on account of political disturbances, and the withdrawals of large accounts were very numerous, the Savings Banks experienced great difficulty in meeting them. A circular-rescript was therefore issued on the 31st May 1849 by the provincial authorities, under the sanction of the Government, (although the State has no responsibility or financial connection with the Banks,) to enforce attention to the law in future. It is still, however, very unpopular. In many Savings Banks no separate funds exist: the amount so invested, for the whole of the province, (31st December 1857), is only £8412; although there are 18,191 accounts exceeding 100 thalers (£15), which should be so treated, if the Government recommendation had been carried out. The reason of this is, that although the Depositor is charged with all the loss that may arise on the realization of his stock, he only receives the ordinary Savings Bank rate of interest; and it has been found that any attempt, to carry into effect the " Separate Fund " regulation in a Savings Bank, has been met by immediate demands for withdrawal.]

Section 2.—*Trust Accounts. Changes recommended.*

ART. 35.—The subject of *Trust Accounts* has been much discussed of late years. Until the Act 7 & 8 Vict. cap. 83. was passed (in 1844), the advantages offered by Savings Banks for the investment of small sums were greatly abused by persons who, having an amount larger than any one individual was allowed to deposit, divided it into a number of parts, each being within the restricted limit, and invested each portion in a different name.

Facilities were offered for such practices by the very law itself, as it then stood, which, while it provided that all monies paid in by one person as Trustee for another should be entered to an account in their joint names, yet authorized the receipt of the *Trustee alone* being taken as a valid discharge for any portion of such monies, when withdrawn.

36.—This provision was modified by the Act passed in 1844, and it is now compulsory on the part of Savings Banks —before paying away any portion of a trust account—to require a receipt signed both by the party for whose benefit the investment was made, and by the individual who had acted as his Trustee. It is averred, nevertheless, that even now there are Depositors who open accounts in the names of various members of their family for money which in reality belongs exclusively to themselves—regardless of the declaration they are required to sign, under the 34th section of 9 Geo. IV. c. 92., and of the penalty—of the forfeiture of the deposits—to which they are liable.

37.—By some experienced bank officials it is believed, on

the other hand, that the Act of 1844* has for the most part answered its intended purpose, and that the additional restriction it imposes has been the means of preventing the mischievous practices referred to. They consider that there is little unfair advantage to be taken of trust accounts which might not be prevented by the exercise of reasonable caution on the part of the bank officials.

It is a defect, however, in the present system that—even where the person, on whose behalf the deposit is made, is old enough to sign the declaration when the account is opened—the signature of the Trustee only is required. Thus there is no provision of any kind made for identifying the real owner of the money, either by his signature or otherwise, when at some future time he attends with his Trustee to withdraw the deposit and sign the receipt.†

---

* [In the evidence given before the Select Committee of the House of Commons in 1848 by Mr. Tidd Pratt, he stated that, within his own knowledge, the power of depositing in the names of other persons as Trustees had led to very considerable frauds. He mentioned several instances; one of a Savings Bank which had issued 354 pass books to 105 Depositors; and another, where 72 Depositors held 207 pass-books. He referred also to the case of a man, "who, on going to a Savings Bank at a time when money bore a very low value, and the funds were consequently very high, was told that he could not put in more than £30 in his own name, but that, if he had a wife and children, and friends, the matter could be arranged by receiving £30 in each of their names. Their names were accordingly given, and in that way the sum of £510 was deposited in one day; the man receiving as many as 17 pass-books, and having the power of doing what he pleased with them." Mr. Tidd Pratt's evidence went to shew, further, that " people would go to Savings Banks with children in arms, and enter deposits in their names, they themselves keeping the pass-books, and, though acting nominally as trustees, acting really for their own benefit."]

† [A case of fraud is said to have been successfully carried through at one of the principal Savings Banks in consequence of this defect. "A party, having been intrusted with some money by another person, deposited it in the bank in question in his own name, as trustee for the

38.—*The proper way to prevent Trust accounts being used disadvantageously is to remove the incentive thereto by reducing the rate of interest, allowed to them, below that credited to ordinary Depositors, viz. to $2\frac{1}{2}$ per cent. per annum.* In the case of lunatics, or like incapable persons, however, the full rate should be allowed. A like exception might be made in favour of *minors, where the deposit is made for a specified term of

owner, and the transaction was entered in the office-books in due course. Subsequently the trustee applied at the bank for the repayment of the money, and, proceeding there to receive it, took with him a fictitious person instead of the absolute owner, and both parties signed the receipt for it. The fraud could not at the time be discovered, because, according to the existing law, and the regulations of the bank, there were no means of testing the accuracy of the signature of the pretended owner of the money; that of the trustee alone having been appended to the usual declaration at the time when the account was opened."

In the Worcester, Massachusetts, Five Cents Savings Bank " deposits may be made by any person in the name and for the benefit of any other person, but cannot be withdrawn *except by such other person*, and, if it is a minor, except by a guardian legally appointed."]

* [It has been suggested that every facility should be given to minors to open accounts, but that they should not have the power of withdrawal before the age of fourteen.

In the St. Martin's Place Savings Bank, London, the age of withdrawal is fixed at twenty-one.

Rule 19 provides—" Money is received from or for the benefit of children, but it will not be repaid to them until they attain the age of twenty-one years, unless the Managers (on satisfactory proof of its being intended for the children's benefit) shall otherwise allow; but, in the event of death before attaining the age of twenty-one years, the money will be payable (on a month's notice) to their personal representatives, or relatives, in the same manner as the deposits of a deceased adult Depositor."

In most of the Saving Banks in the State of Massachusetts, where the Law (Stat. 1855, Chap. 361) is similar to that in England, the provision is as follows:—

" Any Depositor may designate, at the time of making his deposit, the period for which he is desirous the same shall remain in this Institution, and the person for whose benefit the same is made; and such Depositor

years. The privilege of opening trust accounts for *minors is of service to executors and administrators, as, in the division of property, small sums frequently become payable to infants, which, being too small for investment in the public funds, can only be secured advantageously in a Savings Bank.

Section 3.—As to privileges relative to estates of deceased Depositors.

ART. 39.—Under *Sect.* 41. *of the* 9*th Geo. IV. cap.* 92, it is provided, that where the estate of a Depositor dying intestate does not exceed the value of £50, no duty shall be charged on any of the documents necessary for taking out letters of administration, or the Trustees of the Savings Bank may pay the amount, standing to the credit of the Depositor, without

---

and his legal representatives shall be bound by such condition by him voluntarily annexed to his deposit."

(*Rules of the Institutions for Savings and Five Cents Savings Banks at Boston, Worcester, Newburyport, Salem, Lowell, &c., Mass.*).

Some of the " Five Cents" Savings Banks provide that, "*Deposits made for, and in the name of minors cannot be withdrawn by a parent unless legally appointed and qualified as a guardian, evidence of which will be required.*"]

* [The following is the regulation in Paris :—

" Pour les mineurs qui ont été assistés, lors du premier dépôt, par leur père, mère, ou tuteur, le quittance dont être souscrite par la personne qui a fait le premier versement, tant que le mineur n'est pas devenu majeur ou n'a pas été émancipé."—Agathon Prévost's Manuel, p. 32.

In the Rapport of M. Louvet, au Corps Legislatif (1852), it is urged— " Ne perdons pas de vue d'ailleurs que les femmes mariées et les mineurs ont généralement besoin, plus que d'autres, qu'on leur facilite l'accès de la Caisse d'Epargne : les mineurs afin de s'habituer de bonne heure à l'economie, les femmes mariées afin de se prémunir, elles et leur famille, contre les prodigalités malheureusement trop frequentes du chef de ménage."]

letters of administration to the parties entitled thereto under the Statute of Distributions.

It has been *suggested, that in the case of Depositors, whose accounts at death do not *exceed* £100, their families might be saved the attornies' charges for taking out letters of administration, by substituting for them a declaration before a magistrate that the deceased "had no other property except clothes, or a small quantity of furniture, not exceeding in value £ ." This declaration, or any other requisite document, to be supported by two competent witnesses, and to be passed by the Actuary through the Stamp Office of the town where the Savings Bank is established; the duty to be paid by him out of the deposit before the balance is handed over to the representatives. It is said that cases are not unfrequent in which, although the duty does not amount to £1, the law expenses are very heavy, and that they might be avoided without material increase to the labour of the Actuary.

Section 4.—As to Uniformity in the Calculation of Interest, and the Prospective System.

ART. 40.—To complete the system of uniformity in the book-keeping of Savings Banks (which we have recommended in Chap. VI. Part. II.), and as a further means of preventing

---

* [Mr. J. Jacob, of the Weymouth Savings Bank, Letter to the Friendly Societies Institute, 10th May 1858. Mr. Sturrock, in his Evidence, June 1858, said—" At present the law allows the representatives of Depositors to draw their money, without making up any legal title, to the extent of £50. That should be extended to £100, as the expenses of the title make a heavy burden generally on children, and at a time when death causes other expenditure."]

fraud, it is desirable that a *uniform *method* of *calculating and crediting interest should be adopted.*

Nothing can tend more to create errors and confusion than the diversity of the rates of interest at present allowed, which, in Part I., are shewn to vary from £2 . 8s. 6d. up to the maximum of £3 . 0s. 10d. per cent. authorized by the Statute.

The interest should be calculated by †months, not by days. No money should begin to bear interest till the twentieth of the month following the date of the deposit. We recommend the calculation by months, because it enables the interest (if £2 . 10s. per cent., or $\frac{1}{2}d$. in the £ per month be allowed), to be ascertained without reference to a table.

Interest should be allowed on each 10s. of the deposit, but not for any time less than a month.

---

* [In the Report of the *Paris Savings Bank for* 1856 (page 7) the Managers stated, "Le Gouvernement anglais—ému de quelques événements graves dans les Savings Banks dont il veut, à tout prix, prévenir le retour—a présenté, à cet effet, un bill au Parlement. De tous les moyens auxquels il pourrait recourir, le *plus simple et le plus efficace*, à nos yeux, serait d'imposer aux Savings Banks un mode *uniforme de comptabilité* qui rendrait leur marche plus sûre, et plus facile, et permettrait à l'autorité de contrôler aisément, et sans gêne pour ces établissements, le détail de toutes leurs opérations."]

† [Were the date up to which interest is calculated the same in all banks, and sums less than 10s. not to bear interest, the Savings Banks Commissioners would be always able to ascertain, with the greatest degree of approximation, what are the total liabilities of the banks.

Although we do not recommend interest to be calculated by days, it may be agreeable to some of our readers to know the following easy rule to calculate interest *in pence*, at the rate of £2 . 10s. per cent. per annum for any number of days :—

Multiply the pounds by the number of days and divide by 6, cutting off the last figure. The error is $+\frac{1}{3000}$.

If the rate of interest be £3 . 0s. 10d. per cent. divide by 5 instead of 6, cutting off the last figure, as before. The result is exactly correct.]

THE PROSPECTIVE INTEREST PLAN.

ART. 41.—THE easiest mode of capitalizing interest is that called the PROSPECTIVE SYSTEM. It consists in crediting the Depositor at the time of each new deposit with interest, *in advance*, in a separate column, for the unexpired portion of the financial year, and accounting for it as the year proceeds.

This plan, which is of the highest value as much facilitating the ready checking of accounts involving interest calculations, is of ancient use in foreign book-keeping, particularly in France and Belgium. It seems also to have been early introduced into the Continental Savings Banks; the Paris Bank having adopted it, as *M. Prévost informs us, in the year 1829.

The system is not yet in operation in many banks in the United Kingdom, although Mr. Craig, of the Cork Savings Bank, introduced it into that bank in 1843 (see his evidence, qu. 3755—3757), and endeavoured, by a very valuable pamphlet, to make it generally known. According to M. Prévost :—

Whenever a deposit is made, interest (calculated in *advance* from the date of the deposit to the end of the financial year) is added in a separate column in the books of the bank, entitled *"Prospective Interest,"* which is treated as if the sum

---

* [" Rue de l'Echiquier, Paris, 15th December, 1859.

" In reply to your queries, M. Prévost says—that the system of interest account-keeping, to which you refer, has been known here for so long a time that all trace of its origin is lost. He himself introduced it into the Paris Savings Bank in 1829, and made mention of it in the 1832 edition of his *Manuel*.

" The same system is generally employed in ordinary banking-houses here, and has been so from time immemorial. The provincial Caisses d'Epargne have, to a great extent, adopted the same plan on the model of the Savings Bank in Paris."]

invested were to remain intact to the end of the year. In like manner, every time a *withdrawal* is made in the course of the year, that withdrawal is charged with what is called "Retrograde Interest," that is to say, interest on the sum withdrawn, from the date of withdrawal to the end of the year, is calculated and placed in another column (as under) bearing that name.

A personal examination of the working of this plan in the Paris bank satisfied us that its advantages are considerable. It facilitates the ultimate capitalization of interest and the preparation of the annual statements, and thus enables the amount of the bank's liabilities for deposits and interest, at any time, to be separately ascertained by deducting interest on the whole amount of the deposits for the unexpired portion of the financial year. The following example will illustrate the system (Rate of interest allowed being 2½ per cent., or ¼d. on each 10s. per month):—

Date 1859.	Operations in words.	Retrograde Interest.	Number of months.	Principal.	Prospective Interest.*
		£ s. d.		£ s. d.	£ s. d.
4 January.	Received Three pounds 14s.	...	10	3 14 0	0 1 5¼
8 April.	„ Four pounds 13s.	...	7	4 13 0	0 1 3¾
				8 7 0	
12 July.	Repaid Two pounds 10s. . .	0 0 5	4	2 10 0	
				5 17 0	
16 October.	Received Four pounds 3s.	...	1	4 3 0	0 0 2
					0 2 11¼
	Interest capitalized . .			0 2 6¼	
20 November.	Balance			10 2 6¼	

If the interest be allowed weekly, and at a rate more difficult to calculate than 2½ per cent., another plan may be adopted, viz. to enter in the interest columns merely the

---

* [The Prospective interest is to be taken from the 20th of the month next following the date of the deposit, and the Retrograde interest from the 20th immediately preceding the date of the withdrawal.]

product of the number of half-sovereigns by the number of weeks, and to convert the *balance*, at the end of the year, when the account is made up, into the corresponding shillings and pence of interest.

M. Prévost considers it to be of great importance that the entries for 'Retrograde' interest should be made in a separate column from those for the 'Prospective,' and not by subtraction only. It is also according to his *arrangement that the retrograde column in the above form is not placed on the same side of the cash-entry as the prospective; the object being, thus to avoid the chance of a clerk posting into the wrong column by mistake. The blending of the cash and interest columns, or the amalgamation of the interest with the capital, as practised by some banks in the United Kingdom, is deemed objectionable, because it would be an †impediment to an Inspector's testing the accuracy of the books.

42.—The preceding only applies to the entries in the bank account-books. The interest is not transferred into the Depo-

---

* [The following are the regulations issued by the French Government:—

"Les versements, les remboursements et les achats de rentes sont portés aux livrets par addition et par soustraction.

"Quant aux intérêts, ils n'y sont pas indiqués avec detail; on se borne à y inscrire, soit au moment des *remboursements totaux*, soit en fin d'année, les intérêts acquis aux déposants.

"Les intérêts sur les versements sont calculés jusqu' à la fin de l'année, sans qu'on ait à se préoccuper des remboursements qui pourraient les interrompre. Ils prennent le nom d' *intérêts anticipés*.

"Les intérêts sur les remboursements sont également calculés jusqu'à la fin de l'année, et comme ils réagissent sur ceux dont il vient d'être question, ils sont dénommés *intérêts rétrogrades*."

† [M. Prévost considers—and in this almost all the witnesses examined before the Parliamentary Committee concurred—that in banks of numerous operations much inconvenience and delay would arise if the Prospective or Retrograde interest were entered in the pass-book, or amalgamated with the principal on each occasion of receipt or repayment; and

sitor's book until the end of the financial year, unless complete withdrawal takes place previously, in which latter case the Retrograde interest is deducted. Hence in the French pass-books only one column is used, as when the interest is credited it is treated as capital and placed underneath the deposits.

In the Belgian pass-books the interest is shewn in a separate column (as below)*; this, they consider, enables the Depositor, at any time, to ascertain how much he has paid in for deposits, and how much profit he has made by way of interest.

---

that so far from advantage in respect of checking being furnished by such a plan, it would be likely to give rise to confusion and misunderstanding in the minds of the Depositors.]

* [It is a good illustration of the facility for calculation that a decimal coinage affords:—

Column 4 (which is merely the number of francs in col. 3 divided by 4) multiplied by the number of months (col. 5), gives accurately the interest at 3 per cent., in centimes.]

No. 1859.	Recettes ou Payments en toutes lettres.	En Chiffres Fra. c.	Division par 4.	Nombre de mois.	Taux de l'intérêt	Intérêts Fra. c.
Janvier 21.	Cent francs . .	100 | 0	25	11	3 p. ct.	2 | 75

PART V.

THE
"POST-OFFICE SAVINGS BANK" PLAN,
AND THE
EXTENSION OF LIFE ASSURANCE AND SICK BENEFITS AMONG THE INDUSTRIOUS CLASSES THROUGH THE AGENCY OF SAVINGS BANKS.

CONTENTS.

	PAGE
CHAP. XIII. The "Post Office Savings Bank" Plan	215
§ 1. Mr. Whitbread's Plan	216
§ 2. Remarks in favour	223
§ 3. Objections	224
§ 4. Recommendations	227

CHAP. XIV. On the Extension of Life Assurance and Sick Benefits among the Industrious Classes by the aid of Savings Banks, and Mr. Whitbread's Plan of a Poors Assurance Office 231
  § 1. As to Life Assurance 231
  § 2. As to Sick Benefits by Parish Friendly Societies, in connection with Savings Banks 234
  § 3. Mr. Whitbread's Plan of a "Poors Assurance Office" . 239
  § 4. Of Government Life Assurance 247
  § 5. Of *Deferred Annuities, and provisions for old age* . . 251

CHAPTER XIII.

THE "POST-OFFICE SAVINGS BANK" PLAN.

ART. 1.—A plan for the extension of the benefits of Savings Banks, by the agency of the Money-Order Offices, among classes and in localities where they have not been hitherto introduced, has been widely promulgated during the present year through the leading journals. The plan (according to the "History of Savings Banks" by the learned Registrar, Mr. Tidd Pratt) is that proposed by Mr. Whitbread, M.P., in 1807, and seems to have lain dormant and almost forgotten to the present time; until by the efforts of Mr. McCorquodale,* Dr. Hancock, and †Mr. Sikes, (and more particularly by the writings of the latter gentlemen,) the views of that enlightened philanthropist, Mr. Whitbread, have been rescued from half-a-century's oblivion. (See Art 11. Part I.).

Mr. Whitbread's objects were twofold :—

1st. To enable the poorer classes to obtain investment for their savings, or to buy *stock or Bank annuities* in small sums, by payments transmitted through the General Post Office, *at an expense of one penny in the pound.* (See pp. 216 to 223.)

2d. The establishment of a "*Poors Assurance Office,*" to enable persons subsisting wholly or principally by the wages of their labour to make provision by Assurance for their families. (See Chap. XVI.).

In order that our readers may understand these plans, which were passed as "approved in Committee" of the House of Commons in 1807, and appreciate how much their proposer

---

* [*Paper on Savings Banks. By W. Neilson Hancock, LL.D.,* 1852. See also Art. 7, Part VI.]

† *Letter to the Chancellor of the Exchequer. By C. W. Sikes,* 1859.]

was in advance of his time in knowledge of the requirements of the industrious classes, we think it right to reproduce the clauses of his Bill at length.

Section 1.—*Mr. Whitbread's Plan.*

ART. 2.—The following is Mr. Whitbread's *Bill:—

" A BILL (as amended by the Committee) for establishing a Fund and Assurance Office for investing the Savings of the Poor.

"Whereas such of the poor as are desirous of making out of their earnings some savings as a future provision for themselves or their families, are discouraged from so doing by the difficulty of placing out securely the small sums which they are able to save, and it would tend to promote habits of industry and frugality, and to encourage the poor to make a provision for themselves and their families if an establishment were formed in which they might invest their money with security and advantage.

" [*Offices of the Poors Fund and the Poors Assurance to be established, in which limited Sums may be invested and assured.*]— Be it enacted by the King's most excellent Majesty, by and with the advice and consent of the Lords Spiritual and Temporal and Commons in this present Parliament assembled, and by the authority of the same—

I.—" That within Six calendar months after the passing of this Act there shall be established in the City of London, or within the City of Westminster or the liberties thereof, an office for receiving and investing the savings of the poor to be called ' The Office of the Poors Fund,' and an office of Assurance to be called ' The Poors Assurance Office.'

" Such offices shall respectively be under the management and direction of such and so many Commissioners as His Majesty, his heirs and successors, by warrant or warrants under his sign manual shall nominate and appoint, for the management and direction of the said

---

* [*For convenience, only the important clauses are printed in full-sized type.*]

offices respectively; and the persons so to be nominated and appointed by His Majesty, his heirs or successors, shall respectively be and continue Commissioners for the respective purposes for which they shall be so appointed as aforesaid, so long as they shall respectively behave themselves well in the execution thereof; and on every vacancy by death, resignation, or misbehaviour of any such Commissioners, it shall be lawful for His Majesty, his heirs and successors, by warrant under his Royal signmanual, to nominate and appoint such person as he may think proper to supply such vacancy.

"And every Commissioner so to be appointed shall, before he shall enter upon the execution of the office of a Commissioner, take and subscribe in open Court, in some of His Majesty's Courts of Record at Westminster, an oath to the effect following (that is to say)—

Oath of Commissioners.—I (A. B.) do swear That I will faithfully and honestly, according to the best of my ability, execute the powers and trusts reposed in me by an Act passed in the forty-seventh year of the reign of His Majesty King George the Third, intituled (the title of this Act to be here set forth) according to the tenor and purport of the said Act.

"So help me God."

"And be it further enacted,

"II. That all powers, authorities, trusts, and duties, which the said Commissioners of the Poors Fund are by this Act required or enabled to execute, and all sales and transfers authorized to be made by such Commissioners, shall and may be exercised, executed, and made by any two of such Commissioners of the Poors Fund; that all powers, authorities, trusts, and duties which the said Commissioners of the Poors Assurance Office are by this Act required or enabled to execute, and all sales and transfers authorized to be made by such last Commissioners, shall and may be exercised, executed, and made by any two of such Commissioners of the Poors Assurance Office.

III. [*"Commissioners of the Poors Fund to appoint an Accountant (to be approved by the Commissioners of the Treasury) and other Officers"*].—And be it further enacted, That the said Commissioners of the Poors Fund to be so nominated and appointed as aforesaid shall, with the approbation of the Commissioners of His Majesty's Treasury, appoint some person properly qualified to be the principal conductor of the business of the office of the Poors Fund, who shall be called "the Accountant of the Poors Fund," and shall be removable by such Commissioners of the Poors Fund with the approbation of the Commissioners of the Treasury, and upon such removal, or on the death or resignation of such Accountant, some other person properly qualified shall be by such Commissioners of the Poors Fund, with such approbation as aforesaid, appointed to succeed him in the manner hereby directed for the original appointment of such Accountant, and so from time to time in like manner as often as any such removal, death, or resignation shall take place; and the said Commissioners of the Poors Fund shall, and they are hereby empowered from time to time to appoint such Cashiers and other officers, clerks and servants as they shall find necessary for the despatch and execution of the business of their said office.

IV.—[*Persons entitled to the benefit of the Office of the Poors Fund.*]—" And be it further enacted, That every person in Great Britain, who shall subsist and shall be certified by one of His Majesty's Justices of the Peace acting for the County, Riding, City, Town, or Division in which such person shall reside, *to subsist wholly or principally by the wages of his or her labour,* shall be entitled to the benefit and advantages of the said office of the Poors Fund, under and subject to the Rules and Regulations in the articles thereof which shall be deemed to be part of this Act, as if the same had been inserted therein under special enactments, viz—

Articles for the Regulation of the Office of the Poors Fund.

1.—" That every person entitled to the benefits of this office may remit to the Accountant thereof, by the GENERAL POST or otherwise, or pay to such Accountant or to the proper officer or clerk in such office in a Promissory Note, or in Promissory Notes of the Governor and Company of the Bank of England, or in Cash, any sum not exceeding Five pounds to be laid out and invested in the manner hereinafter directed.

2.—" That no person be allowed to remit or pay more than Twenty pounds in any one year, nor more than Two hundred pounds in the whole.

3.—" That when any sum shall be remitted to this office by the GENERAL POST in a note or notes of the Governor and Company of the Bank of England, the postmaster of the place from which the same shall be so remitted, being thereto required, shall for the greater security of the person remitting the same, enter in a book to be kept by such postmaster for

(*Articles of the Poors Fund, continued.*)

that purpose the name of the person remitting such note, and the day on which the same shall be brought, and the date, number, and amount of such note; and such postmaster being thereto required, shall also write or stamp legibly and plainly on the face of every such note so remitted the name of the place and the day on which such remittance shall be sent by the post, and the office to which the same shall be directed, in such manner as His Majesty's POSTMASTER GENERAL shall from time to time direct: and every postmaster shall be entitled to receive for his trouble in entering and marking every such note, from the person bringing the same, one penny in the pound upon the value thereof.

4. *As to the purchase of Bank Stock.*—" That every sum so paid or remitted be forthwith carried to the credit of the person remitting the same in a Cash Account to be raised with him or her in the books of this office.

" And that on some one or more days in every week, to be appointed by the said Commissioners of the Poors Fund, and to be from time to time varied as they shall see occasion, all the money which shall have been remitted in the preceding week shall be laid out in the *purchase* of some of the *perpetual Annuities** transferable at the Bank of England; and all the Annuities so to be purchased shall, in the books of the Governor and Company of the Bank of England, be transferred to the said Commissioners of the Poors Fund by the description of ' The Commissioners of the Poors Fund established by Act of Parliament.'

5. "That after every purchase of Annuities of the said Commissioners of the Poors Fund the proportion of each person from the amount of whose remittances such purchases shall have been made in such *Annuities* shall, in the books of the office of the Poors Fund, be carried to his or her credit in a Stock account to be there raised with him or her, he or

---

* *See Part IV. of this Treatise, on the conversion of Savings Bank Deposits into Stock.*]

(*Articles of the Poors Fund, continued.*)

she being at the same time debited in the Cash Account for the sum expended in such purchase.

6. "That the dividends of all the *Annuities* so to be purchased shall from time to time be received by the said Commissioners of the Poors Fund, or by one of them, and be carried in the books of the Office of the Poors Fund to the credit of the respective persons entitled thereto: AND WHEN THE DIVIDENDS TO WHICH ANY PERSON SHALL BE ENTITLED SHALL AMOUNT TO TEN SHILLINGS AND NOT BEFORE, THE SAME SHALL BE PAYABLE TO HIM OR HER.

7. "That if any person on whose account any such Annuities shall have been purchased shall request the Dividends thereof to be laid out and to accumulate, such Dividends as the same shall amount to Twenty shillings shall be accordingly from time to time laid out until such person shall otherwise request; but in no case shall the money remitted by and the Dividends laid out for any one person be allowed to exceed Twenty pounds in any one year, nor Two hundred pounds in the whole.

8. "That every person entitled to any of the said Annuities so purchased who shall be desirous of selling the whole or any part of the Annuities to which he shall be so entitled, and shall signify such desire personally or in writing to the proper officer at such office shall be furnished with the form of a request for that purpose properly filled up and that such request, being signed by the requesting party at the said office, or being signed by him or her in the presence of and attested by one Justice of the Peace, or by the Minister and one Churchwarden or one Overseer of the Poor of the Parish in which the requesting party shall reside, and the request so signed and attested being left at or transmitted to such office, the Annuities thereby requested to be sold shall be sold accordingly.

9. "That on some one or more day or days in every week to be appointed by the said Commissioners of the Poors Fund, and to be from time to time varied as they shall see occasion, all the Annuities for the sale of which requests properly signed and attested shall have been left or received at the office in the preceding week shall be sold and transferred to the said Commissioners.

10.—"That after every sale by such Commissioners the proportion of each person in the produce of the sale shall be carried to his or her credit in the Cash Account of this office, and shall be forthwith payable to him or her.

11. "That the Accountant or such other officer as shall for that purpose be appointed by the Commissioners of the Poors Fund shall sign a warrant for the payment to every person by name, or to his or her order, of the sum which shall become payable to every such person for any di-

(*Articles of the Poors Fund, continued.*)

vidend, or for the produce of any sale made at his or her request; and that every person entitled to any such payment who shall apply in person at the said office, and shall there sign on his or her warrant a receipt for the amount thereof, shall forthwith receive the sum by such warrant made payable to him or her.

12. " That every person entitled to the money made payable by any such warrant may (by writing under his hand to be attested by one Justice of the Peace or by the Minister and one Churchwarden or Overseer of the Poor of any Parish in England or Wales, or by the Minister and one of the Elders of any Parish in Scotland in which such person shall reside) authorize any other person or persons, to be in such writing for that purpose named, to apply for and receive such warrant, which shall be accordingly delivered to the person or persons so to be authorized, and being endorsed by the person to whom the same shall be made payable (such endorsement being attested as aforesaid by one such Justice or by the Minister and one Churchwarden or Overseer of the Poor of the Parish), shall be payable at the said office to the person producing the same, and shall be accepted and taken in payment by all Receivers and Collectors of the Public Taxes and Duties payable to His Majesty.

13.—" That when any person entitled to the money made payable by any such Warrant who shall reside beyond the limits of the Twopenny Post shall transmit to the said office by the GENERAL POST a request signed by the person so entitled, and attested in the manner directed by the next preceding Article, that such warrant may be sent to him or her by the General Post, the same shall be accordingly so sent, addressed to such person in the manner by him or her requested.

14.—" That upon payment of any sum to any Cashier or other proper officer of this office for the purchase of annuities [*that is, Government Stock*], a receipt shall be given by the proper officer to the person paying the same; and when any sum shall for such purpose be remitted to such officer by the General Post a receipt for every such remittance shall be returned by such Post from this office to the person making the remittance; and after any sum so paid or remitted shall

(Articles of the Poors Fund, continued.)

have been laid out in the purchase of annuities, the said Accountant, or some other proper officer, shall sign a Certificate of such purchase, containing the name and residence of the person for whom the purchase shall have been made, the sum laid out, and the amount and denomination of the annuities purchased therewith; and such Certificate shall, upon application, be delivered to the persons therein respectively named as the purchasers, or to such other persons as they shall direct; or in case where the sum laid out shall have been remitted by the GENERAL POST, the Certificate thereof shall be sent by the General Post, in the manner in which receipts for the money remitted are hereinbefore directed to be sent.

15. "That when the dividends under Ten shillings respectively, and the money which shall have become payable for larger dividends, and for the produce of sales (and which shall not have been demanded), shall amount to such sum as shall, in the opinion of the Commissioners of the Poors Fund, be more than sufficient to answer the current demands for such dividends, and the produce of such sales, the said Commissioners of the Poors Fund shall cause so much of the surplus amount as they shall think proper to be laid out and invested in their names, by their description aforesaid, in the purchase of transferable annuities or other Government Securities, and, as there shall be occasion, shall sell and assign sufficient of such last-mentioned annuities and securities so to be purchased, to answer the demands of all persons to whom any such dividends, or the produce of any such sales, shall be due, and a separate account shall be kept of the annuities and securities purchased by and out of such surplus, and of the interest, increase, and accumulations thereof; and the dividends, interest, and accumulations of such surplus, beyond what shall be sufficient to answer the demands of the principal money laid out in the purchase thereof, shall be applied towards the expenses of the said office of the Poors Fund, and the payment of the salaries of the Commissioners thereof, and of the Accountant and other officers, clerks, and servants, to be therein employed.

16. "That no person employed in the said office of the Poors Fund, or in the execution of the duties or business thereof, shall be entitled to or shall receive from any person taking the benefit thereof, any payment, gratuity, or reward, for any thing done in the execution or performance of such duty or business; nor shall any such person be subject to any charge or reduction for brokage, commission, or otherwise.

V. [*Commissioners of the Treasury to issue from the Consolidated Fund the expenses of the Office of the Poors Fund.*]—"And be it further enacted, That the Commissioners of His Majesty's Treasury shall from time to time cause to be issued and paid, out of the Consolidated Fund of *Great Britain,* to the Commissioners of the Poors Fund, such sum and sums as such Commissioners of the Treasury shall judge to be sufficient, with the dividends, interest, and accumulations of the surplus arising from unclaimed dividends and produce of sales, for the expenses of the management of the said office of the Poors Fund, and for the payment of suitable salaries and rewards to the Commissioners thereof, and the Accountant and other officers, and clerks, and servants to be employed therein."*

Section 2.—*Remarks in favour.*

ART. 3.—It will be interesting to see whether the present generation will adopt Mr. Whitbread's views, in favour of which several arguments are advanced and modifications proposed. It is urged that there are four times as many Money-order Offices in the United Kingdom as there are †Savings Banks; and the Money-order Offices are open every day of the week, except Sunday, from nine o'clock to five, while the smaller Savings Banks are open only for an hour or two hours on a single day of the week. "It is quite obvious that a working man will be much discouraged from saving if he has to walk many miles to reach the bank where he may deposit his small store, and still more if the bank should only be open for an hour or two in a week, at a time when it may not be convenient for him to attend. The number of Money-order Offices is 2360, and they are constantly on the increase. The practical effect of the two systems may in some degree be inferred from the slow increase of the number of deposits in Savings Banks, and the

---

* [For the clauses relating to the Poors Assurance Office, see Chap. XVI.]

† [See remarks in Part IV. of this Treatise on the "Field for Savings Banks."]

extraordinarily rapid increase in the amounts remitted through the Money-order Offices. Within the twelve years the receipts of the Savings Banks only increased $7\frac{1}{2}$ per cent., while the Money-orders increased 90 per cent. in number, and 79 per cent. in amount."

It is proposed, therefore, to establish a *Central Savings Bank* in London, to which Depositors may send their money in sums of not less than £1, through the Money-order Offices; and which shall issue, in return or acknowledgment for the remittances, Savings Bank Interest Notes to the amount remitted, —entitling the holder to receive the amount of his deposit, with the addition of interest at the rate of $2\frac{2}{3}$ per cent. a-year. The deposit to be remitted in the form of a money-order through the Post Office, and the interest-note to be received by the same means in one or two days. " As it would be very undesirable that the interest-notes should come into circulation as a currency, it is suggested that the names of the owners should be written upon them, so as to make them only payable to the owners or their representatives, who might obtain the amount by complying with a simple form at the Post Office."*

Section 3.—Objections.

ART. 4.—On the other hand various strong objections to the modified plan, thus recently brought forward, have been raised by many experienced Savings Bank Actuaries who have written to us on the subject. They appear to consider :—

1st.—That the establishment of a Central Bank in London, as a *centre to the Money-order Offices*, is quite opposed to the Report of the Parliamentary Committee of 1858, which, after hearing the various witnesses, and maturely considering the subject, concluded by recommending merely:—That the connection between the National Debt Commissioners and the Savings Banks should be terminated; and that, in the place

---

* [Pamphlet by Mr. Sikes, page 11.]

of the former, a Savings Bank Commission should be appointed to receive from the Trustees of Savings Banks their aggregate deposits, and to invest them, if possible, in more advantageous securities than those contemplated by the existing Acts of Parliament; and that it should not be any part of their duty to have any thing to do with the receipt of money from individual depositors.—Moreover, it is urged that it would be highly injudicious to adopt any new system that might have the ultimate effect of (1st.) Shutting up the large and admirably conducted Savings Banks at present existing; and (2nd.) *Centralising too much the control of the savings of the working classes in the hands of the Government.*

2nd.—The encomium bestowed on the Money-order system as having already rendered invaluable services to the working classes, is considered overdrawn, as the real cause of the increase in the transactions of the Money-order Offices is the facility which that department has afforded for the transmission of money from various parts of the kingdom, in payment of small business accounts. It is also known to be largely used for the remittance of premiums to Assurance Companies, &c.; and it is natural, that as the commercial transactions of the country increase, those of the Money-order department should be augmented in a corresponding degree.

It is also argued,

3rd.—That it is probable the nation will always have to transact Savings Bank business at some loss, and that it is, therefore, necessary to confine it strictly to the industrious classes, especially as it is estimated that—as the Post Office would deserve liberal remuneration for their very valuable services,—the nation must expect to lose on each entry or transaction on a deposit, by the expenses of officials, the cost of the notes, and the outlay attending the chief Savings Bank.

4th.—That the existence of Trustees and Managers in local Savings Banks is a check on any, but persons of the class intended, availing themselves of the benefits, or depositing more than the permitted amount:—but

5th.—That this would not be the case with an isolated Money-order Officer, especially if the transactions are to pass only through his hands, and he is to sign a declaration of secrecy.

It is suggested further,

6th.—That tradespeople and people with small sums of idle money will be using the Money-order Office for temporary investment at a serious cost to the nation.

7th.—That it will open the door to great fraud.

8th.—That the establishment of some kind of Savings Bank in every town is preferable, because the actual existence of such an Institution on the spot is likely to have more local influence in creating and fostering systematically provident habits, than the mere knowledge that such a Bank is established in a distant metropolis. That the Money-order Office would never secure the same object, and could but be regarded as the medium of transmission to some far-off Institution, scarcely known to the Depositor even by name; whereas, the local Bank, with the familiar and respected names of its Trustees, conveys to the mind of the working man something infinitely more tangible and real, and therefore more attractive.

9th.—That it would be better to establish a Penny Bank under the clergyman of the parish, or some person of like respectability, and to place it in connection with the present Savings Banks; in other words, to give greater extension to the Branch system, as is the case in the Exeter Savings Bank, and is recommended by Mr. W. N. Wortley* of the Finsbury Savings Bank and others.

It is observed that, as 20s. is the minimum sum proposed to be transmissible, Penny Banks would have to be established in each locality as feeders of the Money-order Office, and that it is not more difficult to form a local Savings Bank or Branch for the receipt of large deposits than for the receipt of pennies. †And it is contended that 20s. is a large amount for the majority of

---

* ["In every case, it would be advantageous that the local management should be as influential as possible."—W. N. Wortley, Finsbury Savings Bank, 1849.]

† [Mr. Sikes remarks, "As the receipt of shillings and sixpences would entail an immense amount of writing without corresponding benefits, and those small sums come within the province of the Penny Savings Banks, which are so rapidly increasing, I propose that the Interest Notes shall be for exact pounds."]

working men to lay by at one time. Before they have accumulated the requisite sum a temptation may arise, and the money may be spent.

Section 4.—*Recommendations.*

ART. 5.—Although these objections are advanced to the proposed modifications of Mr. Whitbread's plan, it appears to be generally admitted that the Post Office might be made of great service in places where the Incumbent of the parish will not set on foot a Savings Bank or a Branch, and that until the nucleus of either can be formed, the Postmaster General might be authorised to make some arrangements, whereby the Money-order Official of such locality might receive deposits on behalf of *the nearest Savings Bank*, and transmit them to its head office.

That this should be done at a cost to the Depositor of one penny for any sum not exceeding £5; and that the Savings Bank should pay out of its allowance* for expenses what may be necessary for the remuneration of the Money-order Official for his extra trouble: establishing such a check against fraud on his part, as may be devised for their guidance by the Savings Bank Commissioners.

6.—Although a central bank in London, and a system of *one pound* interest notes are both deemed objectionable, there appears to be good reason to recommend that the Post Office should grant orders at the above charge, *not only* to Depositors, but for Branch banks in the transmission of money *to and from* the chief local banks both for *payments in* and *withdrawals.*

7.—It is, also, very desirable that the valuable privilege of Freedom from Postage, recommended by Mr. Whitbread in

---

* [See Part IV., as to future Government Allowance for Expenses.]

the following clause of his Bill, should be granted for the books and documents required to be transmitted on behalf of Savings Banks :—

"XIII.—[*Letters or Packets to and from the Offices of the Poors Fund and Poors Assurance to be exempt from Postage.*]—And be it further enacted, That no letter or packet which shall be sent by or through the General Post Office, to or from the said office of the Poors Fund, or to or from the said office of the Poors Assurance, solely on the business of the said respective offices, shall be subject to any postage or other tax or charge for the conveyance thereof; so as in every case such rules and directions as may from time to time be established by His Majesty's Postmaster-General, for the prevention of frauds, with regard to the conveyance of such letters and packets, shall be observed and obeyed."

8.—*Of Branch Banks.*—A Savings Bank Actuary of experience, Mr. Wortley, proposed in 1849* that the chief Banks of a district should be constituted " Central Banks," and any other banks, either in or out of their particular district, should be associated with them, and made branches thereof, receiving from the chief, or central banks, a portion of their profits. "At present," he remarked :—

" Savings Banks are only to be found in the larger towns, and are open, in general, for a few hours on one or two days in each week. This, indeed, may be sufficient, under the present system, for they cannot enlarge their business beyond the wants of their own neighbourhood, and are obliged to leave, unused by the public during the remainder of the week, that ample accommodation which was provided with a view to their full business, during those limited hours. Both Managers and Officers would willingly see their offices fully occupied, and are quite aware that their fuller occupation would enable them to administer their affairs at a much less cost per cent."

---

* [Letter to the Right Hon. Sir C. Wood, Chancellor of the Exchequer. 1849.]

For, in a proper use of the superabundance of official accommodation, with which many Savings Banks are at present supplied, Mr. Wortley considered the means are to be found for the economical extension of the system; and he gave as his opinion, that arrangements might be adopted by which every town in the United Kingdom might have its own branch bank, without any large proportionate addition of expenses.*

9.—M. du †Puynode, speaking of the same subject in France, urges that—" Chaque chef-lieu de canton devrait posséder au moins une succursale de la caisse d'épargne, chaque grande ville en devrait ouvrir dans ses différents quartiers.

" A Paris les versements d'un même déposant ne se renouvellent que tous les six mois. . . . . Ce long intervalle résulte avant tout de la distance qu'il y a à parcourir pour se rendre aux bureaux de la caisse d'épargne. La loterie était plus prevoyante, elle avait 100 bureaux seulement dans Paris."

10.—Another writer suggests an excellent plan, viz.— to " take a country district, commanding, say, for example, six different Savings Banks, each opening on different days, once a week, or once a fortnight, for the transaction of business. Constitute the largest, or most central, the head branch of the group, and make the other five contributaries, or sub-branches to it."

---

* [In the Exeter Savings Bank the following regulation is adopted for distant Depositors:—Receivers of deposits are appointed for distant towns, parishes, or districts, where persons of respectability and influence are willing to undertake the same, who will receive deposits, and transmit the same to the Institution at the Depositor's risk. As those receiverships are established for the sole benefit and convenience of persons living at a distance, or unable to attend at Exeter, the receiver will only engage to remit the moneys he receives by his usual mode of conveyance, and the Institution will in no degree be answerable for any sum so deposited till the amount has been paid over to the Actuary, who will give receipts for, and make regular entries of the same in the books of the Institution. Any person may, notwithstanding the appointment of receivers, transmit his deposit to the office in Exeter (Devon and Exeter Savings Bank Rules, P. 13). The Perth Savings Bank has also arrrangements for district Savings Banks.]

† [*De la Monnaie, du Credit, et de l'Impôt*, tom. i. p. 415.]

"Place the head branch of each group under the management of a resident accountant, and an out-teller (with sub-clerks to each where necessary). The duties of the out-teller would be to attend at each of his five sub-branches in succession, one day in every week, or fortnight (as the custom might be), to receive or pay deposits, and to transmit to his head branch a statement of his transactions for the day. The duties of the resident Accountant would be to place these transactions to their various accounts in the ledger, make all interest calculations, and transmit to the Savings Bank Office in London an abstract of the operations of his branch and sub-branches for the week."

By this system of grouping, "the number of chief offices in direct communication with the Savings Bank Office in London would probably be reduced to about 100. If so, the present expense of management would admit of £1000 a-year for the salaries and expenses of each branch." And it is further urged that a "numerical reduction in the host of officials which the present system employs indifferently, and pays worse, would enable this great object to be effected, viz. *to pay a less number of officers handsomely, instead of a greater number badly. It would also enable the system of promotion to be introduced on a large scale, one of the strongest incentives to honesty and good conduct amongst the officers of a large establishment.*"

11.—On the inexpediency of substituting *Money Order Offices* in the place of Savings Banks, an authority of the first eminence, M. Prévost, entertains a very strong opinion. He remarks that:—

"The first condition of the very existence of Savings Banks, is their private character: it would be a sentence of death to them to make them a direct branch, an integral portion of public administration. Not that such administration lacks either benevolence or skill; nor that it is not entitled to the entire confidence of Depositors; but there is in the absolute rules of administrative government, in its unchanging forms, something absolutely contrary to the very essence of a Savings Bank, which is a sort of complaisant servant of the poor man—which lends itself to his wants, even to his caprices—which simplifies proceedings—and which, to reach the desired end, consents to take any road whatever, provided it be the shortest and surest."

CHAPTER XIV.

ON THE EXTENSION OF LIFE ASSURANCE AND SICK BENEFITS AMONG THE INDUSTRIOUS CLASSES, BY THE AID OF SAVINGS BANKS,

And Mr. Whitbread's Plan of a "Poors Assurance Office."

Section 1.—*As to Life Assurance.*

ART. 12.—The tardiness, which the Legislature deems it desirable to manifest before sanctioning improvements of a social character, is exhibited very conspicuously by its continued neglect to provide a law to enable the working classes to avail themselves of the facilities afforded by the Savings Banks for the extension of Life Assurance among them.

It is many years since it was first pointed out to members of both Houses,—who are known to take a special interest in the encouragement of provident habits among the working classes, and who are constantly lamenting the insecurity attending the ordinary Benefit Clubs,—that several of the most respectable London Assurance Companies would be willing to make arrangements for granting Policies, even of very trifling amounts, such as £5 or £10, provided facilities were afforded to them by Savings Banks for the collection of the corresponding small weekly or monthly premiums. It was explained that it would be simply necessary to introduce the following clause into the next Savings Bank Act, subject to such subordinate arrangements as the Commissioners of Savings Banks might approve, viz. :—

"Provided always, and notwithstanding any thing hereinbefore contained to the contrary, that it shall be lawful for the Managers of any Savings Bank to receive from any person or persons, sums of money, not exceeding   per annum, to be placed to the credit of any Life Assurance Society, which shall have registered its name, and deposited its regulations, with the Commissioners of Savings Banks, without its being necessary for the person so depositing, or for the Life Assurance Society to make any such declaration as in this Act required from persons making deposits in Savings Banks, and notwithstanding that such Assurance Society shall have similar deposits in any other Savings Bank or Banks. Provided, nevertheless, that the Commissioners of Savings Banks shall have power from time to time to make such regulations as they may think fit in reference to the receiving and crediting of such deposits."

Such deposits to receive interest in the ordinary way until paid over to the Society, and the Assurances created thereby, to be exempted, up to some prescribed amount, from legacy duty, stamp duty, &c.

13.—Under the above clause, it would be competent for any respectable Assurance Company to have accounts opened in its name in every Savings Bank in the kingdom, and thus to afford to the labourer or artisan of the most humble means the opportunity of insuring his life.

As soon as he had complied with the necessary formalities for giving evidence as to his age and state of health, he would have no further trouble than to make his payments weekly to the Savings Bank; these would be carried to the credit of the Assurance Society, and at his death the bank would act as the agent for settling the payment of the amount assured to the man's family or nominee.

The Directors of the Assurance Company would thus be able to feel infinitely more secure, on the average, against the perpetration of fraud by the assurer or his family, than if they were to grant Industrial Policies through the instrumentality of a private agent.

Moreover, the Savings Bank being permanent, no inconvenience would arise from the removal of its Actuary by death or otherwise, as is the case where a change of *ordinary agents takes place.

That official could, also, be fairly remunerated for his trouble by a per centage (which the Assurance Company would be willing to allow) on the amount of premiums collected through his bank.

---

* [We have received numerous communications on this subject like the following:—

" I am very anxious to see your suggestions carried out, as I am convinced it will be of immense advantage to the working classes; and that it would induce those to effect insurances, who now either know but little of the principles of Life Assurance, or are very careful not to pay their money into the hands of agents."—Wm. Gard, Devonport.

The Rev. William Webster, M.A., of King's College, London, who has published many excellent contributions on the subject, in a recent letter to us on this question, remarks, " A majority of our industrial classes are so wedded to the present system, as to abjure the thought of making social provision in any other manner. Yet I am of opinion that among the million members of the Manchester Unity, and kindred bodies, some 25 per cent. are capable of appreciating the advantages of an improved plan, and have that self-control, as well as self-reliance, without which all the advantages of the wisest possible system will be thrown away. . . . . The intelligent mechanic will buy in the cheapest market. He can obtain more for his money with greater security from a Life Assurance Office, than from any Friendly Society of which the rates have come under my notice, because an Assurance Office, which issues life policies up to and beyond £1000 in amount, can afford to grant industrial policies for £100 at a cheaper rate than any ordinary Benefit Society . . . . But whatever plan is deemed to be most eligible, the greatest difficulty will be to introduce it to public notice so as to secure its general adoption.

" To aid in the dissemination of a wider knowledge of the subject, I

Section 2.—*As to Sick Benefits, by Parish Friendly Societies in connection with Savings Banks.*

ART. 14. *As to Parish Friendly Societies.*—The working-classes, as a rule, are far from improvident; but from the want of correct information as to the principles of management necessary to insure success, and of the exact nature of the operations their societies are undertaking, there arises much of the unsoundness, which has been detected in the condition of thousands of Benefit Clubs. For this reason we have, in another publication, recommended* the formation of large and important societies in the nature of united "*Parish Friendly Assurance Societies,*" to be conducted by practical men, and so established that their operations may extend over wide districts, and their risks be guaranteed by a certain amount of paid-up capital.

Those noblemen and persons of influence, who encourage the formation of isolated local clubs, commit a very grave error.

The insufficiency of the number of members in such petty institutions to form an Average, and the ignorance of the Managers, are fatal obstacles to their prosperity. Sickness

---

would suggest that pupil-teachers should be brought to apply their arithmetical knowledge to the investigation of questions—relating to rates of interest, duration of life, average sickness and mortality—which are essential to the success of Friendly Societies.

"Moreover, I would suggest the propriety of Her Majesty's Inspectors of Schools setting in their examination papers some questions, which may draw the attention of masters and mistresses to the relations, that ought to exist between the liabilities and assets of such societies according to the rate of interest and the age of the assurer. This will prove the most efficient way of extending the practice of social provision, and of establishing its operations on a firm basis."]

* [See the plan of a Parish Friendly Society, in our Treatise on Friendly Societies, 10th Edition, p. 92.]

allowances and old age benefits can only be safely guaranteed by institutions dealing with an aggregate of large numbers.

The proper plan is for each district to have a Branch of some large association, holding its office at the Savings Bank where there is one, under the superintendence of local management for the enrolment of members, the receipt and collection of subscriptions, the distribution of benefit payments &c.; subject, however, to periodic supervision by a Central body meeting in the most important town. The liabilities of the branches and such portions of the receipts as are not applicable to expenses of local management, being made to form part of the Liabilities and Assets of the whole institution. Each Branch to be founded as a Parish Friendly Society under the countenance of the clergy, the expenses of management being defrayed by the parochial authorities, and not by the members.

It is scarcely necessary to point out the immense facilities which Savings Banks offer to the outlying districts—especially in connection with the system of Post-office Branches recommended in Chapter XV.,—for the collection of Friendly Society subscriptions, and for crediting them, at proper intervals, to the Central Institution which undertakes the risk.

The management of the Parish Friendly Society could be intrusted to no better officer than the Actuary of the Savings Bank; and an evening in the week might be set apart for the transaction of its business. One of the great difficulties,—viz. in respect to calculations,—would, by such an arrangement, be provided for, as most Actuaries of Savings Banks are familiar with the operations of compound interest; and by the aid of the *'True Law of Sickness,' which we have deduced from actual Friendly Society experience, the Actuary could readily acquire a competent practical skill in the specialities of the subject.

---

* [Friendly Societies' Treatise, pp. 106—110.]

15.—So long ago as 1817, a Committee of the House of Commons on the Poor Law made the following report:—

"Your Committee are of opinion that it would be expedient to enable parishes to establish Parochial Benefit Societies, under the joint management of the contributors and the nominees of the parish, calculated to afford greater pecuniary advantages than could result from the unaided contributions of the subscribers. They trust, that holding out to the people benefits somewhat superior in amount and security to any which they can now attain by the contributions of their earnings, and adding some which are not generally afforded by voluntary association, they might be made not less popular than advantageous. They are therefore of opinion that parishes should be enabled to afford to the contributors a benefit rather greater than that which a Table formed on mere calculation would yield; and, in order to adapt the new system to the situation of the country under the administration of the Poor Laws, your Committee are of opinion, that, at the outset of these institutions, parishes should be permitted to place, by contribution from the parochial funds, those who had advanced in years, without having made any provision of this nature, on the footing of advantage on which they would have stood if they had commenced their contributions at an earlier age. Your Committee are well aware, that under existing circumstances the incapacity of individuals to make even the smallest deduction from their wages might render this species of institution inapplicable in some parts of the country; but they conceive that it might be safely left to each parish, under the inspection of the local magistracy, to determine upon the propriety of trying the experiment within itself."

16.—Scientific data cannot be depended upon as the means of effecting the regeneration of Friendly Societies. It is necessary to provide in some way for the payment of the Expenses, so as to preserve intact the Benefit funds, and an application of the principle of Mr. Ewart's "Public Libraries Act"

(1850) might be the most convenient form of provision on the part of the nation for this necessity.

Supposing the premiums charged to be fairly calculated, yet not so high as to deter members from joining, and the risks to be aggregated for the whole of the country, so as to distribute them over an immense surface, the Consolidated Fund might, without any risk, be made to guarantee every Parish Society against bankruptcy.

If the principle of universal assurance for the whole kingdom were adopted, it is highly improbable that, upon so large an area of risks, aberrations from the estimated law of sickness and mortality would occur; and even if they did, the deficit would be but trifling, in comparison with the Poor Rates * and Police Rates, which alone amount to £8,655,000.

---

* [It has been urged by some friends to the industrious classes that the exercise of provident habits should not be left entirely a voluntary matter on their part. The Rev. J. B. Owen, M.A., remarks with much force:—" In England, every man produces three times as much as one man can consume within an ordinary life of frugality; and the consequence is, every individual can, if he likes, render himself independent of the Poor Laws. I think it a very hard case that there should be a law in this or in any other country to compel me—and when I mention myself I take the position of any citizen whatever—to pay so much in the pound out of what I may happen to earn for the support of my neighbour, in the shape of a Poor Law, when there is no law to compel that neighbour to lay up so much in the pound for the support of himself. Whether Parliament interfere or not, I do trust that the time is coming when the public opinion of the nation will lead men to feel universally their responsibility in this matter, and induce each to say, ' I will not be guilty of constructive fraud and positive injustice by making it necessary for my neighbour to contribute any thing at any time towards my support, when I can support myself.' Friendly Societies assist to create a large-hearted, comprehensive honesty, not the honesty simply of paying twopence for something worth the twopence, but that honesty which would prevent the spending of twopence to-day lest it should cause a neighbour to-morrow to pay a penny to repair it."

" Many instances, " says Archbishop Whately in his *Lectures on Political Economy,* " might be given to shew how much even charitable

In a word, Friendly Societies can only be rendered safe on the principle of local management and distribution of benefits, with a national area for the risks incurred.

---

relief tends, unless distributed with the most vigilant care and discretion, to paralyse industry, and destroy habits of forethought and self-reliance. Make relief compulsory, give men a legal right to out-door relief, and they will, to a man, be thrown into a state of destitution."

M. Agathon Prévost, of the Paris Savings Bank, also observes, " The poor-rate was established in the reign of Elizabeth, after the suppression of the monasteries, in order to supply the place of the charities afforded by the religious orders. This dangerous system of official charity, the results of which were far from being foreseen, has at last brought forth its fruits. It has brought upon England an enormous tax, which, expended by the overseers, tends only to render the poor degraded, idle, dependent, and miserable. Every year has increased the list of persons seeking relief, and it has become impossible to tell where this deplorable movement will terminate."]

Section 3.—*Mr. Whitbread's Plan for a " Poors Assurance Office," granting Policies with Government security.*

ART. 17.—The following are the clauses of Mr. Whitbread's Bill (see p. 215) which relate to his plan for a Poors Assurance Office :—

VI. *Commissioners of the Poors Assurance Office to appoint an Actuary to be approved by the Commissioners of the Treasury, and other Officers.*—" And be it further enacted, That the Commissioners of the Poors Assurance Office, to be nominated and appointed by His Majesty, his heirs and successors, in manner aforesaid, shall, with the approbation of the Commissioners of His Majesty's Treasury, appoint some person, properly qualified, to be the principal conductor of the business of such Assurance Office, who shall be called " The Actuary of the Poors Assurance Office," and shall be removable by such Commissioners of the Poors Assurance Office, with the approbation of the Commissioners of the Treasury; and upon such removal, or on the death or resignation of such Actuary, some other person, properly qualified, shall be by such Commissioners of the Poors Assurance Office, with such approbation as aforesaid, appointed to succeed him, in the manner hereby directed for the original appointment of such Actuary, and so from time to time in like manner as often as any such removal, death, or resignation shall take place.

" And the said Commissioners of the Poors Assurance Office shall, and they are hereby empowered, from time to time, to appoint such cashiers and other officers, clerks, and servants as they shall find necessary for the despatch and execution of the business of their said offices.

VII. *Tables for Assurances to be calculated*—" And be it further enacted, That the said Commissioners of the Poors Assurance Office shall cause tables to be calculated for the assurance, in consideration of yearly, half-yearly, or quarterly payments during life, or for any shorter period to be limited, of gross sums, upon the death of the party assured, or upon such party, or upon the wife or any child of such party nominated for that purpose, attaining a given age; and other tables for the assurance, in consideration of yearly, half-yearly, or quarterly payments, during any limited portion of a life, of a proportional annuity during the remainder of such life; and tables for the assurance in consideration of yearly, half-yearly, or quarterly payments, during the continuance of any life, or during a limited portion of any life, of an annuity for the life of any other person to be named, if such person shall survive the party during whose life, or during a portion whereof, the consideration for such assurance shall be payable;

" And that such tables shall be calculated upon such rates of interest, and probabilities of the duration of life, as shall be likely to produce, by the sums to be received, sufficient funds to answer the payments to be assured, with the charges and the expenses of the establishment and management of such Assurance Office;

"And such tables, being approved by the Commissioners of His Majesty's Treasury, shall be the tables, guides, and rates for all assurances hereby authorized, and shall be made public in such manner as the said last-named Commissioners shall direct.

Provided, and be it further enacted,

" That it shall be lawful for the Commissioners of the Poors Assurance Office, by the authority and direction of the Commissioners of the Treasury from time to time to cause other Tables, at other rates of interest and probabilities of the duration of life, to be calculated; which being in like manner approved and published, shall thenceforth be the tables guides, and rates for all future assurances; so, nevertheless, that every assurance which shall have been made before the variation of such tables, shall continue in force, according to the terms thereof, as if such tables had remained unaltered.

VIII.—*Persons entitled to the Benefit of the Poors Assurance Office.*—" And be it further enacted, That every such person as is hereinbefore declared to be entitled to the benefits of the Poors Fund, by this Act directed to be established, shall be entitled to make assurances, upon the events hereinbefore described, in the Poors Assurance Office, under and subject to the Rules and Regulations in the Articles thereof, which shall be deemed and taken to be part of this Act, as if the same had been inserted therein under special enactments.

Articles for the Regulation of the Poors Assurance Office referred to.

1. "That every person, desirous of obtaining an assurance upon any of the events for which tables are by this Act directed to be calculated, shall deliver or send to the Assurance Office a proposal for such assurance, setting forth his or her name, place of abode, and occupation, and the names, place of abode, occupation, and age of the person upon whose death, or upon the continuance of whose life, any such assurance shall be proposed to be made.

2. "That in every case, in which any assurance shall be proposed for the payment of a gross sum, or of an annuity upon, or to commence from the death of any person named in any such proposal, there shall, annexed to the proposal for such assurance, be delivered or transmitted to this office an affidavit, by the person proposing such assurance, of the place of birth, age, and occupation of the person on the event of whose death any sum in gross, or any annuity, shall be proposed to be made payable or to commence, and that such person is in good health, and also an affidavit by some physician, surgeon, or apothecary, that he hath known such person for at least one year, and believes him or her to be in good health, and that there is not, to the knowledge or in the opinion of the physician, surgeon, or apothecary, making such affidavit, any thing peculiar in the constitution or habit of such person tending to shorten his or her life, which affidavit shall be sworn before one of His Majesty's Justices of the Peace, who shall certify that he knows the person on whose death the assurance is proposed to take effect, or that he knows the physician, surgeon, or apothecary, making the affidavit, and that such Justice hath no reason to doubt the truth of the representation contained in the proposal annexed to such affidavit.

3. "That in every case where the proposal or affidavit, in order to any assurance, shall contain any untruth or misrepresentation, any assurance which shall have been made in consequence thereof shall be void, and all the money which shall have been paid thereon shall be forfeited to, and remain part of the fund of, the Poors Assurance Office.

4. "That where the person, upon whose death any payment is proposed to be assured, shall be resident within the limits of the Twopenny Post, the Actuary, or other proper officer of this office, may, before such assurance shall be made, require him or her to attend personally at the Assurance Office.

5. "That no payment for any assurance, whether annually, half-yearly, or quarterly, shall be less than Ten Shillings.

6. "That no annual payment, nor the yearly amount of the

half-yearly or quarterly payments on any assurance, shall exceed Five Pounds; and that no person shall be allowed to make an assurance or assurances on one or more of the events, on which assurances are to be made, of more in the whole than a gross sum of Two Hundred Pounds, or than an annuity of Twenty Pounds; or if a gross sum and an annuity shall both be assured to the same person, the whole shall not exceed the value of Two Hundred Pounds, calculating the annuity at ten years purchase.

7. "That if any annual, half-yearly, or quarterly payment for any assurance shall be in arrear more than thirty days, there shall be payable, in addition thereto, one twenty-fourth part of the amount of the sum originally payable; and in case any such payment shall be in arrear more than sixty days, there shall be payable, in addition thereto, one twelfth part of the sum originally payable; and in case any such payment shall be in arrear more than three calender months, the assurance on which such payment shall be due shall be void, unless the Commissioners of the Poors Assurance Office shall, on proof by affidavit, to be sworn before some Justice of the Peace, and transmitted to the Assurance Office, be satisfied that the default of payment arose from accident or mistake, or from the inability of the party; in which case the sum in arrear may be received within such time, and with such addition to the original amount thereof, as the Commissioners shall on consideration of the circumstances adjudge to be reasonable.

8. "That all the money to be received upon and for every such assurance shall, by the Commissioners of the said Assurance Fund, be laid out and invested in the purchase of some of the annuities transferrable at the Bank of England, or in some other of the Government Securities, and all the transferrable annuities so to be purchased shall, in the books of the Governor and Company of the Bank of England, be transferred to the Commissioners of this office, by the description of "The Commissioners of the Poors Assurance Office, established by Act of Parliament;" and any one of such Commissioners shall be competent to receive the dividends of such annuitants; and all dividends and interest to be from time to time received by any of the Commissioners of this office, beyond what shall be sufficient to pay the demands upon assurances which shall have become due, shall be in like manner, from time to time, laid out in such annuities, or other securities, to form an accumulating fund for payment of the sums assured, as the same shall become due and payable, for which purpose a sufficient part of the dividends and interest, and, when it shall be necessary, a sufficient part of the principal funds, shall, by the Commissioners of this office, be sold and transferred to answer such payments.

"And such Commissioners are also empowered from time to time, at their discretion, to sell, assign, and transfer any of the annuities and securities in or upon which the money to be by them received shall be invested; and the money produced by and from such last-mentioned sales shall be by them forthwith laid out in other annuities or Government Securities, in the names of the said Commissioners, in manner aforesaid.

9. "That no sum in gross, or by way of annuity, which shall become due upon the death of any person, upon the event of whose death any assurance shall have been made, shall be payable until after an affidavit of his or her death, and of the time and place thereof, shall have been transmitted to this office, such affidavit to be sworn before one of His Majesty's Justices of the Peace, who shall, in the jurat of such affidavit, certify his knowledge of the person making the affidavit, and his belief of the facts therein sworn to.

"And no sum or annuity, which shall by any such assurance be made payable to any person, in the event of his or her surviving any other person, shall be paid until after an affidavit shall in like manner have been made, sworn, certified, and transmitted, that the person to whom such sum or annuity shall have become payable by survivorship did actually survive the person upon whose death the same was to accrue; and no payment depending on the existence or continuance of any life shall be made without a like affidavit of the existence or continuance of such life, at the time when each such payment shall have become due.

10. "That all the rules and directions in this Act contained, for and in relation to the receipt and payment of any sum to be paid to or by the Commissioners of the Poors Fund, or to or by any of the officers for the management thereof, so far as such rules and directions are applicable to the payments to be made to or by the Commissioners of the Poors Assurance Office, or any Actuary, Cashier, or other officer for the management thereof, shall be observed, practised, and carried into execution by the Commissioners, Actuary, Cashiers, and officers of such Assurance Office, as if the same were here repeated and expressly applied to such last-mentioned Commissioners, Actuary, Cashiers, and officers.

11. "That out of the dividends and interest of the annuities and securities which shall be vested in the Commissioners of the Poors Assurance Office, such sums shall be retained by such Commissioners for the expenses of the management of the Poors Assurance Office, and for the payment of suitable salaries and rewards to the Commissioners of, and the Actuary, officers, clerks, and servants employed in such office as the Commissioners of His Majesty's Treasury shall from time to time by their warrant direct.

IX.—*Commissioners of the Poors Fund and the Poors Assurance may establish Rules.*—"And be it further enacted, That it shall be lawful for the Commissioners of the Poors Fund and the Commissioners of the Poors Assurance Office respectively, to establish such Rules and Regulations for the said respective Offices of the Poors Fund and the Poors Assurance, and for the conduct of the officers, clerks, and servants to be therein respectively employed, and for facilitating the business of such offices respectively, and guarding against frauds and mistakes therein, and to settle and appoint the forms of the instruments to be used in the transactions of such respective offices, and the said respective Commissioners of the Poors Fund and the Poors Assurance Office shall from time to time think meet; so as no such Rule or Regulation to be established by them respectively shall be repugnant to any of the Articles or Provisions in this Act contained.

X. "Provided always, and be it further enacted, That the Commissioners of the Poors Fund and the Commissioners of the Poors Assurance Office respectively, who shall or may be appointed under or by virtue of this Act, or some two or more of such respective Commissioners, shall from time to time transmit or deliver to the Governor and Company of the Bank of *England*, a true and attested copy of the commission or appointment under or by virtue of which they shall respectively from time to time act as such Commissioners, certified under their hands to be a true attested copy of such commission or appointment, two days at the least previous to the Commissioners in such commission or appointment named or appointed, or any of them, demanding or requiring to have transferred to their account any public stock, funds, or annuities, transferrable, or which shall hereafter be transferrable at the Bank of *England*, and also previous to their demanding or requiring to accept or transfer the same or any part or parts thereof, or to receive any interest or dividends which shall become due or payable thereon ; and that such attested copy, certified as aforesaid, of the commission or appointment of respective Commissioners, shall be received and admitted as evidence in all Courts of Law or Equity, and before all Judges and other Magistrates, of the due and legal appointment of the Commissioners therein named to exercise all the powers and authorities given to them by this Act, over the stocks, funds, and annuities, which shall be transferred to their account in the books kept by the Governor and Company of the Bank of *England*, and over the interest or dividends that shall or may become due or payable thereon, either by transferring and disposing of such stock, funds, and annuities, or any part or parts thereof, or receiving and disposing of the said interest and dividends, or any part or parts thereof; any law, custom, or usage to the contrary notwithstanding.

XI.—*Dividends, &c., exempted from the Tax on Property and from the Stamp Duty on Probates and Letters of Administration.*—" And be it further enacted, That no dividend or interest, or other profit or proceed of any of the annuities, fund, or securities, which shall be vested in the Commissioners of the Poors Fund, or in the Commissioners of the Poors Assurance Office, nor any dividend, annuity, or other payment, to any of the persons hereby authorized to make deposits and assurances in the said offices of the Poors Fund, and the Poors Assurance office, shall be liable to any deduction for, nor any dividend, annuity, or other payment to any of the persons hereby authorized to make deposits and assurances in the said offices of the Poors Fund, and the Poors Assurance office, shall be liable to any deduction for, nor shall any person be chargeable in respect thereof, with the payment of the tax or duty to His Majesty on the profits arising from property, possessions, trades and offices, charged and imposed by the Acts passed for that purpose in the Forty-third, Forty-fifth and Forty-sixth Years of His present Majesty's reign, or by any such Acts; nor shall any such dividend, annuity, or other payment, be subject or liable to any of the duties imposed on legacies, or on any share of any estate received by virtue of the statute for the distribution of intestates' estates; and that no probate or letters of administration shall, by reason of any sum payable by the Commissioners of the said respective offices of the Poors Fund and the Poors Assurance, by virtue of this Act, be subject, or liable to any stamp duty, to which such probate or letters of administration would not have been subject or liable in respect of other property of the testator or intestate.

XII.—*Policies and other Instruments to be exempt from Stamp Duty.*—" And be it further enacted, That no policy, certificate, warrant, bill, draft, order, receipt, affidavit, letter of attorney, or other instrument of writing required, or which shall be used for any of the purposes or transactions of the said offices of the Poors Fund and the Poors Assurance, shall be subject or liable to any of the stampduties.

For Clause XIII., *see page* 228.

XIV.—*Punishment of Forgery.*—" And be it further enacted, That if any person or persons shall forge, counterfeit, or alter, or act or assist in the forging, counterfeiting, or altering any warrant, bill, draft, or order for payment of money, or any receipt for money payable by virtue of this Act, or any request or authority for delivering to any person, or for transmitting by the General Post any such warrant or order for the payment of money, or any signature, indorsement, or attestation of or upon any such warrant, order, request, or authority, or any affidavit to be made for any of the purposes of this Act, or the signature, jurat, or caption of any such affidavit, or shall utter or publish as true any such warrant, bill, draft, order, receipt, request, or authority, or any such signature, indorsement or attestation of or upon any such warrant, order, request, or authority, or any such affidavit, or the signature, jurat, or caption of any such affidavit, knowing the same to be forged or counterfeited, with an intent to defraud any person or persons, body or bodies political or corporate, whatsoever, every person so offending, and being thereof convicted by due course of law, shall be deemed guilty of felony, and shall suffer such punishment by transportation for life, or for any number of years, or by whipping, the pillory, fine, imprisonment, or by any one or more of such punishments as the Court before whom any such offender shall be convicted shall adjudge; and it shall be sufficient in any indictment for any such offender, when the same shall have been committed with an intent to defraud the Commissioners of the Poors Fund, or the Commissioners of the Poors Assurance Office, hereby respectively established, to describe such Commissioners respectively, as the case may be, as the Commissioners of the Poors Fund established by Act of Parliament, or as the Commissioners of the Poors Assurance Office established by Act of Parliament, as the case may be, without naming such Commissioners or any of them, or any further or other description of them.

XV.—*Punishment of Perjury.*—" And be it further enacted, That if in any affidavit or deposition authorised by this Act, or in any affirmation under or for any of the purposes of this Act, by any of the people called Quakers, any person shall wilfully and corruptly swear or affirm any matter or thing which shall be false, every person so offending, and being thereof lawfully convicted, shall be, and is hereby declared to be subject and liable to such pains and penalties as by any law now in being persons convicted of wilful and corrupt perjury are subject and liable to."

Section 4.—As to Government Life Assurance through the medium of Savings Banks.

ART. 18.—While recommending the plan, suggested in Section 1. of this chapter, for placing within the reach of the industrious classes the power of obtaining policies from the existing Life Offices, we recognize a very valuable principle as being involved in Mr. Whitbread's proposal, that the Government should be authorized to grant assurances of small amount, viz. up to £200. This would be practicable through the agency of Savings Banks, in the same manner as purchases of annuities are effected under the present *Annuity Act* relating to those institutions.

There is, in fact, a clause in that Act by which the National Debt Commissioners are empowered to guarantee the *payment of sums of money at death,* subject to the following provisions:—

"X.—*Power to grant Payment of Money on Death of persons purchasing Deferred Annuities.*—The said Commissioners may contract with any such person or persons for the payment of a sum of money on his or her death, provided that the party contracting for such payment on death shall at the same time purchase a deferred annuity depending upon his or her own life, as the case may be, and that the money payable on death do not exceed the amount of the sum paid down for the said payment on death and annuity taken together, and shall in no case exceed one hundred pounds in the whole." (16 & 17 Vict. c. 45.)

The condition that an annuity should be purchased concurrently with the assurance is objectionable, and has rendered the clause useless: the more so as the total amount that can be assured is only $3\frac{1}{3}$ years' payment of the maximum annuity of £30.

19.—To a system of government assurance it has been objected, that the State should not entrench upon the industrial portion of the business of those offices which already grant small policies, because it would be impossible for them to compete with Government, either in the security or the privileges that could be offered to assurers.

To the mind of the reader, it is probable that the possibility of so benefiting the working classes, without risk to the State, would furnish a strong argument for disregarding the injury to existing companies, on the principle that the good of the many must take precedence of the advantage of the few.

It is indeed no slight matter that such assurances should be obtainable from the State at a more moderate rate of premium than private companies require.

The larger extent of assurance business, that Government security would induce, would have the effect of rendering the estimate of the probable law of mortality among the, lives accepted more accurate, and, consequently, the corresponding rates of premium could be more correctly assessed.

20.—Assurance companies find it necessary to add to the mathematical rate of premium, deduced from their standard table of mortality, a considerable *margin or per-centage to meet the following circumstances:—

1. The expense of transacting the general business.
2. The commission on obtaining new policies.
3. The margin to provide for the possibility that the table of mortality adopted, although true for the general community, may undergo an unfavourable aberration when applied to assurers of a particular company.
4. A per-centage by way of profit to the shareholders who afford to assurers the protection of their capital.

21.—Those, who support Mr. Whitbread's view, contend that, on the policies granted by the nation, one main advantage might at once be accorded, viz. :—

That the rates could be made lower than are charged by any office, because no expense would have to be incurred on the new business, and no aberrations from the law of mortality need be anticipated or provided for.

In fact, that a very moderate margin over the net tabular premium would be sufficient to realize to the nation a profit,

---

* [See Art. XIII. *of Preliminary Remarks to Division* III., *or the Friendly Societies Treatise.*]

*which, instead of being appropriated by way of bonus to shareholders, could be transferred to the credit of the revenue.

---

* [*As to Deposit Life Assurance.*—During the last fifteen years an attempt has been made to give to policy-holders the power of withdrawal, to a certain extent, of the premiums they have paid in.

Modified forms of the plan of Deposit Life Assurance (which we suggested in the Mathematical Appendix to Division II. or the Treatise on Building Societies), have been adopted by several offices in England and Scotland.

In Division III., Art. 16, p. 21, will be found a full exposition of the plan, which is well adapted to the present requirements of the middle and humbler classes, and is especially suitable to Depositors in Savings Banks.

Sets of deposit tables for Savings Banks are also given at p. 145 of the same work.

In that Division observations have also been made on the obstacles yet attending the extension of the ordinary system of Life Assurance among persons of uncertain and limited means, and remedies suggested for the defects which still exist in the practice of Assurance Companies.]

Section 5.—*As to Deferred Annuities and Provisions for Old Age.*

ART. 22.—In sect. 4. of this chapter we have referred to the clause of the Act (16 & 17 Vict. c. 45.) now in *force in reference to the granting of Deferred Annuities by the National Debt Commissioners, by which it is provided that—

" From and after the said tenth day of October, one thousand eight hundred and fifty-three, it shall and may be lawful for the Commissioners for the Reduction of the National Debt to grant to or for the benefit of any Depositor in a Savings Bank, or other person whom the said Commissioners shall think entitled to be or to become a Depositor in a Savings Bank, any immediate or deferred life annuities depending on single lives, or immediate annuities depending on joint lives with benefit of survivorship, or on the joint continuance of two lives, to any amount not less than four pounds nor more than thirty pounds in the whole, to or for the benefit of any one person, and to receive payment for such immediate life annuities in one sum, and for such deferred life annuities either in one sum or in annual sums payable for fixed periods: Provided always, that no such annuities shall be granted to or for the benefit of any person under the age of ten years." (s. 2.)

---

* [The first Savings Bank statute on this subject was the 3 Wm. IV. c. 14. passed in 1833, and intituled, " An Act to enable Depositors in Savings Banks and others to purchase Government Annuities through the medium of Savings Banks; and to amend an Act of the ninth year of his late Majesty to consolidate and amend the laws relating to Savings Banks."

This was amended by the 7 and 8 Vict. c. 83, passed in 1844, but in 1853 the present Act (the 16 and 17 Vict. c. 45,) was passed, " to consolidate and amend the Laws, and to grant additional facilities in relation to the purchase of Government Annuities through the medium of Savings Banks, and to make other provisions in respect thereof."

This statute repeals so much of the previous acts as relates to annuities.]

23.—This clause, however, has not been acted upon to an extent at all commensurate with the expectations of its framers. A comparison of the returns for 1859 with those for 1854 shews that, during the period of *five years, £4671 was paid in single sums, and £60,359 in annual premiums, making altogether £65,030 (*a*) in the purchase of deferred life annuities—an average of only £13,006 per annum.

The number and amount of the annuities purchased by those payments is not stated; but during the same period £281,073 (*b*) was invested as consideration money for Immediate annuities; and the number of annuities granted in respect to the total of £346,103 [(*a*) *and* (*b*)] is stated to have been 1403, for £28,557 a-year. What proportion of these figures represents Deferred annuities cannot be ascertained from the returns.

Out of the £65,030 received for deferred annuities, £22,673 was applied to the return of the premiums paid by deceased, non-paying, and insolvent Depositors, and the remainder to the purchase of stock, by which means annual dividends amounting to £1440 were cancelled. The £281,073 received for immediate annuities was all invested in the purchase of stock, which was likewise cancelled. No Term annuities were granted, but £209 was received in further annual payments upon four deferred term annuities previously created, and was also invested in the purchase of stock, cancelling dividends of £29 a-year.

---

* [The total since the deferred annuity system was commenced, 26th March 1834 (a period of twenty-five years), has been—

    In single sums - - - - - £ 29,557
    In annual payments - - - - 177,644

Out of these sums, £45,297 has been returned on account of death, discontinuance, or insolvency. Of the annuities purchased, 958, representing an annual State disbursement of £10,570, are still outstanding, to be entered upon at some future time.]

It will thus be seen that a present cash payment, on the part of the nation, of £1469 a-year is all that the operations of the last five years in deferred annuities have cancelled, and that Savings Bank Depositors have not invested more than about £250 a-week in the purchase of these provisions, notwithstanding the supposed advantageous rates of premium at which they are offered.

Objections made by Depositors.

24.—The reason of this aversion to a scheme presented under such apparently favourable aspects is not difficult to divine. The workman reflects that, in case he should survive to the distant period which is fixed for the commencement of the annuity, and actually enter upon the enjoyment of it, it would cease at the instant of his demise, however short might be the interval during which he had received it. In a transaction of this character he will not conceive himself fairly treated unless an equivalent for the money he has paid be given in the only form which he understands—viz. direct cash compensation.

He avoids deferred annuities on account of their *uncertainty.

---

* [Mr. Sikes (qu 2700) remarked—" I do not think that the principle of annuities will ever be popular among the working classes of this country, because it involves so large an amount of risk, partaking almost of the lottery principle; and, personally, I would not recommend the working classes to put their principal in jeopardy. I do not know one single instance of a working man purchasing an annuity; and I speak confidently when I say, that *annuities will never be popular among the working classes*, because there is in them an element of uncertainty, and almost of gambling."

This argument is well urged in reference to Tontines (which are in a

To appreciate this, let the example be taken of a deferred annuity of £30, purchased at age 35, to commence at age 65. For this the charge by the Government tables would be £5. 7s. 6d., with the right to the purchaser to receive back, in case of previous death or of desire to terminate the contract, the whole of the premiums paid, without interest, provided he do so before entering on the annuity.

Now—if the question of survivorship to age 65 be disregarded, and if—instead of buying a deferred annuity for him of the Government—the Savings Bank were itself to accumulate the Depositor's annual premium of £5. 7s. 6d., with compound interest at 3 per cent., there would be a sum of £263. 7s. 9d. standing to his credit at age 65, which he could

---

great measure analogous to the present system of Government deferred annuities) by M. Agathon Prévost, in his paper in the " Cent Traités," as follows :—" It is well known that these societies (named after the inventor, Tonti), were founded two centuries ago (1653), and consist of an association formed by a certain number of persons. These persons, by paying a fixed sum, secure to themselves an annuity which goes on continually increasing, because the reversion of each annuity, void by death, goes to the survivors, until the last remaining member receives the whole. Formerly, on the death of the last member, Government claimed the capital: in all existing societies it is distributed among the heirs or claimants of the original members.

"It is plain that this system has for its object to transform the 'savings' into an annuity. This is the principle of the ' Reserve Office' (*Caisse de Retenue*), which secures pensions to Government employés. Their chance, however, depends on a throw of the dice, and in fact makes a kind of Lottery of it, giving the system the attractions of a speculation. Under whatever form it may present itself, the Tontine cannot be recommended to the operative. In the first place he has not in his possession the capital necessary to enter such a society with advantage, *i. e.* with long chances of survivorship. He must already have found, with great difficulty, the means of raising the sum to be placed in the tontine. Then this temporary alienation of his capital, even if it should make a return at an uncertain and necessarily distant epoch, may be very proper for a bachelor, whose personal well-being it secures, but not for the Father of a family, who by joining a tontine would deprive the rising generation of

either receive in cash at that time, or sink in the purchase of an annuity of £28 . 10s. 9d.; since at age 65 the price of an immediate annuity of £1 is £9 . 4s. 7d.

Moreover, in case of previous death or withdrawal, the Depositor would, without loss to the Savings Bank, be repaid not only the *whole of his deposits,* but compound interest thereon.

The gain to him, in such a case, would be great. Suppose, for example, he withdrew at the end of twenty years, or at age 55.

By the present Government plan he would receive back only twenty premiums, or £107 . 10s.; whereas, if he had what his money had accumulated to, he should receive £148 . 15s. 3d. In like manner, if the extreme case be taken of the withdrawal occurring a year or two before the annuity is entered upon, say in twenty-eight years, he could only claim back from the Government twenty-eight premiums, or £150 . 10s., whereas his accumulations in the Savings Bank would amount to £237 . 13s. 7d.

25.—No further illustrations are necessary to explain why the present Government deferred annuity plan is not popular; for no trifling increase in the annuity can compensate to the minds of the industrious classes for the loss of the compound interest and the capital. Indeed, cases are known where the parties have said, "I had rather reserve to myself the power,

---

the profits of his labour. Those feelings which link families together being among the most powerful auxiliaries to morality, nothing contrary to them should be raised without a prudent distrust." (*See also Chap.* 2. *in our Treatise on Building Societies and Tontines,* Part. II.).

It is worthy of notice that deferred annuities are equally unpopular in France as in England. The returns published in the year 1858 of the Paris Savings Bank shew that only twenty were purchased during that year.]

when I am 65, of doing what I like with my money: I may be in very bad health, and might, then, prefer to buy an annuity on the life of my wife."

Respecting the *Deferred Annuity System* M. Gustave du Puynode remarks (p. 390, 391, tom. i.):—

" Le danger, que recèlent les dépôts des caisses d'épargne, avait frappé les legislateurs anglais avant les notres. Dès 1833, ils décrétaient que les versements aux caisses d'epargne pourraient être convertis, au gré des déposants, en dépôts spéciaux, lesquels, après s'être accumulés par les soins des commissaires de la dette publique, se transformeraient, à un instant déterminé d'avance, en pensions* viagères. Le parlement anglais a fondé pour les ouvriers une véritable caisse de retraites, alimentée par leurs versements voluntaires, en cherchant à diminuer les dettes des caisses d'épargne. Quelque préférable que soit ce système au nôtre—qui, une fois le terme de leurs dépôts atteint, excite trop les ouvriers à acheter de la rente, *et soumet ainsi leurs épargnes, aux chances décevantes, souvent immorales, de la bourse*—ce système renferme de grands inconvénients encore.

" L'État ne peut, en effet, sous quelque forme qu'il le fasse, payer des intérêts qu'à la condition de les prélever sur le capital, et lorsqu'il l'à consommé, il est forcé, pour continuer ce payement d'intérêts, d'augmenter les contributions.

" Ce n'est pas un industriel, il ne paie pas, il dépense, quelle que soit la manière dont il emploie les fonds qui lui sont confiés."

---

* [M. de Lamartine, in speaking on this question in 1835, does not seem to have been aware of the existence of actuarial science, or that the deferred annuity tables were based upon an estimate of the probable duration of human life. He used the English plan as an argument to obtain from the French Legislature some concession to Savings Bank Depositors:—

"L'Angleterre, en 1833, a proposé, par un bill, une mesure qui paraîtra bien plus exorbitante encore : cette mesure consiste à accorder une pension viagère de 20 livres sterling à tout individu âgé de soixante ans, qui, depuis l'âge de trente ans, aura déposé dans les caisses d'épargne une somme de trois schellings par semaine."]

Indeed, although, under certain circumstances, the purchase of a superannuation allowance may be profitable and desirable to an artisan, in the majority of cases he reflects very wisely, that *the capital, which his savings have created, the deferred annuity will *extinguish.* This, indeed, it is the part of the nation to prevent, as far as lies in its power, rather than to encourage; for it is to the accumulations of the capital of previous generations that we have to look for the foundation of national enterprise and prosperity.

Financial Objections.

26.—It is perhaps fortunate that the Government have not done much, for, from the principle of buying up and cancelling stock with the money received for deferred annuities, a largely increased charge upon the revenue would be thrown upon the future, in consideration of the cessation of a small annual charge

---

* [Many consider that the *interest* of a man's savings should be made sufficient to provide for his declining days, and the capital be *preserved* for those who come after him. A writer in the "Quarterly Review," many years ago (when the interest on Savings Banks deposits was £4.11s. per cent.), argued on this ground that the limit of £200 should be removed.—" Certainly, as a provision for helpless age, the interest on £200, or £9.2s. 6d. a-year, is altogether inadequate. We are aware that parochial assistance to a single individual does not often exceed this limit (3s. 6d. a-week), nor would we wish, in general cases, that it should ; as every possible discouragement must be given to a dependence on it: but we deprecate the idea of offering this minimum of pauperism as the maximum for which we will secure support, out of his own funds, to the declining age of him who has spent a life of labour and self-denial, from the hopes of closing it in independent comfort. We think £400, or even £500, might very properly be assumed as the maximum of total deposit. We would prefer the latter sum, because we think it better proportioned to the allowed annual deposit of £30, and because few Savings Banks pledge themselves for more than £4 per cent. to Depositors, from the necessity of reserving something for casualties and general expenses."]

s

now; the effect of which would be to relieve the present generation at the expense of the next. Indeed, the very workman who bought the annuity would have in his old age to submit to a heavier per centage of taxation himself, to assist in the payment of it. For example: Suppose that, by a group of lives, of which the average age is (say) 35 next birthday, £10,000,000 have been withdrawn out of the Savings Bank deposits and invested in provisions for old age, to be received at 65; this £10,000,000 would buy £2,826,855 a-year annuity during the remainder of their lives, and, according to practice, would be invested in the purchase of stock, say at the average price of 92⅜; this stock would be cancelled, and a diminution would at once be effected of nearly £324,760 a-year in the charges of the Funded debt, which the Chancellor of the Exchequer has to provide for.

So much less would have to be contributed by the present generation, in return for which, the next—thirty years hence—would be saddled with an increased payment of £2,826,825 a-year, or about nine times as much.

This example will be immeasurably more forcible if, for £10,000,000, we substitute the whole Savings Bank deposits, and suppose that they had been converted into provisions for old age.

This financial error has proved unimportant, solely because deferred annuities under the existing Government tables are not popular.

Recommendations.

Art. 27.—It appears, then, that the present system is objectionable:—

I. Because the industrious classes find it does not offer them all the advantages they can obtain by simple accumulation, and because they are not willing to part with all control over their money.

II. Because it does not provide for the creation of a fund sufficient to protect future generations from increased taxation in the future.

The objection in II. would be avoided if the principle, laid down in the preceding articles, be attended to, by which the Government would be able to offer to the industrious classes (after a repeal of the present Act) the following privilege, which may be denominated " DEPOSIT ANNUITIES," viz. :—

> That any person, joining the Provision for Old Age Fund, may have his subscriptions—either accumulated with 3 per cent. compound interest by the purchase of stock or investment in other securities, and returned to him in cash at par (Government running the risk of fluctuation), on attaining the given age—or converted then into the annuity which, at that age, it would purchase, according to the Tables for Immediate annuities. In case of previous death, or desire to terminate the contract, then the proportionate accumulated amount to be returned to the Depositor after three months' notice, less a small charge towards the expense fund for the trouble occasioned.

There is nothing new in this proposition: it is, in another form, what the Savings Banks do at present for ordinary deposits, with one limitation—that no Depositor can accumulate more than £200, inclusive of interest, which amount, at the age of 65, would only buy an annuity of about £21.10s. a-year.

28.—The above plan affords the further advantage to the Depositor, that it does not bind him to have his annuity at the age he originally contemplated: he may, if his health fail him earlier, cease his payments, and obtain a smaller annuity.

On the other hand, should he find himself, when the time arrives, able to continue work, he might be allowed to make further deposits, and to defer the commencement of the annuity a few years longer, when, of course, it would be increased.

⁎ The formulæ for such *Annuities* will be found appended to the *Building Society Treatise*, pp. 281 to 296. The corresponding tables are given in the *Friendly Society Treatise*, pp. 145 to 158.

PART VI.

AS TO NON-GOVERNMENT BANKS OF DEPOSIT,

AND THE

AUDIT OF PUBLIC INSTITUTIONS.

CONTENTS OF PART VI.

                                                                                     PAGE

CHAP. XV. As to Non-Government Banks of Deposit, or Independent Savings Banks without State Guarantee - - - - - - 263

CHAP. XVI. As to the Investments of Non-Government Banks, and Section 12 of the Savings Bank Act, 9 Geo. IV. c. 92 - - - - 273

CHAP. XVII. Extracts from Rules of American Deposit Banks - - - - - - - 280

CHAP. XVIII. General Remarks on the Audit and Management of Public Institutions - - - 283

CHAPTER XV.

AS TO NON-GOVERNMENT BANKS OF DEPOSIT;

OR,

INDEPENDENT SAVINGS BANKS WITHOUT STATE GUARANTEE.

Section 1.—As to their Management.

ART. 1.—There are many, as we have said in Art. 29 of Part II., who—disregarding the great advantages (described in Part III.) that accrue to the State from the power of making use of Savings Bank Deposits on occasions of financial emergency—deem it undesirable that the nation at large should become pecuniarily liable for the correct management of any institution which is the agent of the depositors in transmitting their money to the National Debt Commissioners. *They hold that, while every encouragement and facility for

---

* [" Le jour viendra" (remarks a distinguished writer, who objects to Government intervention in Savings Banks) " où avec l'aide de la raison, de l'expérience et de la science, les bons esprits s'ouvriront à cette vérité fondamentale, que l'État doit seulement administrer la part de la fortune publique, qui lui est confiée, pour assurer la marche paisible de la société, et qu'il remplit mal cette grande fonction lorsqu'il se transforme en régisseur, en intendant de qui que ce soit, classes ou individus."—*Article*: *Caisses d'Epargne,* by *M Louis Leclerc, Dictionnaire de l'Economie Politique.*]

investment should be given by the State, it is not expedient to make it actually answerable for the deposits. Few Trustees say they, will continue in office if their management be interfered with or controlled, even if the control be compensated by a Government guarantee. If the soundness of these views were admitted, it would appear—although of the beneficial results of such a course we have doubts (see note to p. 77)—that no other alternative would remain, but to declare such banks as decline inspection to be 'non-Government banks,' and to make up for the want of a guarantee by confiding to the Depositors themselves the watching over the safety of their funds, so as to cause them to feel the same interest in the details of the working of their bank, and in the conduct of its affairs, as the members of other industrial associations feel in theirs.

2.—In 'non-Government banks,' the existing privileges as to investment* with the National Debt Commissioners, or with whatever Commission might be in operation for the purpose, might still be allowed; but with their independence of government guarantee they would have the option of any other form of investment, which the Managers for the time being might deem expedient. The audit of these banks might be properly entrusted to the Depositors, or to a Committee nominated by them, as suggested by us in the year 1851 to Sir Charles Wood, the then Chancellor of the Exchequer. The suggestion derives additional weight from the fact, which has only recently come under our notice, that a similar view of the subject was taken, forty years previously, by one of those who

---

* [*This privilege is at present enjoyed by all Friendly Societies.* See Part VI. and Appendix, as to the other modes of investment that might be adopted by Savings Banks. To facilitate the calculation of interest on their investments, we have appended a set of new *Savings Bank Deposit Tables* at page 145 of the *Friendly Society Treatise*, in which are also to be found the several statutes in force.]

may be considered the founders of Savings Banks. In an early edition of the "Encyclopædia Britannica," the writer of an article on the subject states, that the Rev. Mr. Duncan, at the very outset in 1810, expressed it as his opinion that Depositors should have some voice in the management and supervision of the banks they subscribed to.

The views of Mr. Duncan were founded upon an accurate knowledge of human nature. He appears to have known where to find its springs, and the means which the circumstances of the case afforded for bringing them into action. "It may be observed in general," said he, "that in all those situations where it is *practicable to assimilate the mode of management to that of Friendly Societies, the advantage to be derived from such a circumstance ought not to be overlooked.*"

3.—Those, who are at all acquainted with the history of Friendly Societies, must be aware that they owe much of their popularity to the interest excited among the lower orders by their participation in the management. The love of power is inherent in the human mind, and Mr. Duncan felt that the constitution of Friendly Societies was well calculated to gratify this feeling. In the exercise of their functions the members find a certain increase of personal consequence, which is pleasant to most, and interests them in the prosperity of the establishment. Besides, by having constantly before their eyes the operation of the scheme in all its details, they are better able to perceive and appreciate its advantages, and are thus induced not only to make greater efforts themselves to promote its success, but to persuade others to follow their example. Hence it happens that a great number of active and zealous supporters are to be found amongst the members of every Friendly Society, who do more for the prosperity of the institution than the exertions of benevolent individuals in a higher station can possibly effect.

4.—It is said that for these reasons Mr. Duncan held it to be expedient to give the contributors themselves a share in the management of the Savings Bank. For although the contributors in a body were not fit to be the acting parties, they were qualified to choose those who should act for them. According to his rules, he provided for the holding of a general meeting twice a-year, consisting of all the members who had made payments for six months, and whose deposits amounted to £1. By this meeting were to be chosen the Court of Directors, the Committee, the Treasurer, the Trustees, and the functionaries to whom the executive operations were to be confided. The transactions of such past half-year were controlled and examined by the meeting, and it had power to reverse the decisions of the Committee or Court of Directors; to make new laws and regulations, or alter those already made; and, generally, to provide for the welfare of the institution.

5.—There is, indeed, nothing to prevent the contributors of a Savings Bank from being called together for the purpose of electing either the managing officials, or delegates to whom such election should be entrusted. That there is no very great difficulty in getting the members to meet is proved by the ample experience of large Friendly Societies, the members of many of which do actually assemble and transact business much oftener than once a-year; and that, too, without the assistance of persons of the upper classes, such as would be afforded in a Savings Bank. In London itself there are very many associations, the subscribers to which, though extremely numerous, are annually called together for the election of Committees and other matters. A central or general body, to give unity and combination to the operations of the different banks of a great city, might be formed of delegates chosen by the members of the several district or parochial banks; thus, without any serious inconvenience, that interest, which is the natural result of giving the contributors themselves a part in the conduct of their bank, would be secured.

6.—The arguments in favour of independent Savings Banks are based to some extent on the practice of *similar institutions in the United States, Prussia, Austria, Holland, Sweden, Hamburg, Belgium, &c.

---

* [Their principle of action is rational, and very different from that of certain Deposit Banks in this country, which are understood to give, not only a very high rate of interest (such as 4½ or 5 per cent.) to their investors, but also a commission of 1 per cent. to the agent who brings the business. If any foolish people trust such Companies with their savings, every deposit would entail a cost to the institution of 6 per cent., exclusive of probably another per centage for sundry expenses allowed to the agent: and the deposits themselves must ultimately be lost under such a system. It is a serious matter that noblemen of high standing imprudently lend the credit of their names as Trustees to such associations, without making thorough inquiries into the principles upon which they are established, and the accuracy of the statements circulated by the managers. In order to judge of the safety of a Deposit Bank, returns should be required of

1. The cash in hand to cover ordinary and extraordinary demands;
2. The amount invested in securities as compared with the deposits;
3. The rest or guarantee fund;
4. The bad debts, if any;

with many other points of information, which need not be detailed in this note. The great Joint-stock Banks are not able to pay more than an average of 2 per cent. per annum on their deposit accounts, although the divisible profit arises from investments that are in some cases (by the aid of the current accounts, which bear no interest) about three times as large as the deposit accounts; so that practically the average profit realized is less than 1 per cent. per annum. That portion which the shareholders take away from the Depositors would not make any sensible increase in the rate, for in the largest of the Joint-stock Banks in London, the surplus profit taken by the proprietors as their share for the last half year was but £80,000, which when compared with the total funds of the bank, about 13 millions, is only equal to 12s. 3d. per cent. It is therefore impossible that any Bank of Deposit, receiving money repayable *on demand* can pay 5 per cent. to its customers, in addition to expenses of management, agents, and advertisements.

It behoves the shareholders in these Deposit Banks, for their own safety, to look well into the principles upon which their business is conducted,

Section 2.—*As to Banks of Deposit.*

7.—The extension of Industrial Banking in England has been advocated by several writers. Dr. W. M. Hancock remarked (1852):—

" The business of Savings Banks is really a species of trade, being part of the trade of banking. These institutions are neither more nor less than banks of deposit for the poor; and before the legislature encourages their formation by charitable or Government interference, an inquiry should be made, why this business

while there is time to prevent serious consequences. The writer of an excellent article on Savings Banks in the ' Law Review ' remarks very justly, that " The result of the present imperfect system has been to lead to the establishment by private persons, sometimes publicans, of a species of Savings Banks, which, though generally, if not always, originating in the best and purest of motives, often lead to lamentable results. A time of pressure arrives, and the savings of the poor are too often diverted from their original purpose, to satisfy the wants of the gambler or the spendthrift, or in vain endeavours to stave off bankruptcy by the unfortunate or the imprudent."

A Report of the " Chamber of Commerce " of Glasgow on Banking Laws contains some very useful remarks on this subject:—

" Imprudent banking is at the root of all unsound trading. The great fault of modern banking is the insufficiency of reserves. Bankers, like traders, are bound to provide for their solvency: they must reserve ample means to meet their obligations, and in their case any departure from this rule is the more inexcusable that the proper amount of reserve for them to hold may be ascertained with almost mathematical precision. But the desire of profit, or the urgency of their customers induces bankers, in too many instances, to invest their deposits more closely than prudence warrants, safety is sacrificed for an additional per-centage of profit, the reserve is allowed to fall dangerously low, and when a time of pressure comes the bank has nothing to fall back upon. This insufficiency of banking reserves is the immediate cause of our panics. When pressure occurs our great money-lenders are the first to take alarm: with enormous liabilities and inadequate reserves of immediately available resources, they feel that their solvency is endangered, and their violent efforts to regain a position of safety are the chief cause of disturbance in the money-has not been taken up by private enterprise? When there are Banks of Deposit for the rich, why are there none for the poor? Such an inquiry would show that the present state of the laws respecting pawnbroking, and of the laws of *debtor and creditor,

---

market. Instead of lending to others, they become themselves the most importunate of borrowers. They who should sustain credit are the chief authors of discredit; they who should inspire confidence are themselves panic-stricken. It is not the needy Depositor or ignorant noteholder of the provinces who causes our panics; it is the millionaire money-lender of our great centres of commerce. One great cause of insufficient reserves is undoubtedly the high rate of interest allowed upon deposits. Such rates can only be paid and a profit realized by a close investment of deposits. Our trading credits rest mainly on accommodation from the banks. The provincial banks deposit a great part of their reserves with London bankers on call. The London bankers again invest their deposits closely, and trust mainly to advances from the Bank of England in case of need; while the Bank of England itself allows its reserve in times of pressure to fall to a trifling fraction of its deposits. Thus the vast superstructure of British commerce rests ultimately on a mere trifle of reserved capital. Our whole credit system is an inverted pyramid. Your Committee does not look for any legislative remedy for the abuse of credit. The cure must be found in the more honest and intelligent appreciation of their duties by all who either give or take credit."

A like danger is pointed out by the New York Chamber of Commerce in its last report (p. 278): " When credit is abused for the purposes of speculation, whether to produce artificial scarcity or artificial demand; when banks and bankers employ the capital and credit which should be the sheet anchor of the public to promote speculation and extravagance, for the sake of a temporary harvest; the interests of the community are evidently disregarded, and selfishness stands out in all its marked deformity."

"There is no doubt," remarked the late Mr. Tooke, (*Inquiry into the Currency Principle*, ch. 14) " that banks, whether private or Joint-stock, may, if imprudently conducted, minister to an undue extension of credit for the purpose of speculations, and that they have so ministered not unfrequently."]

---

* [Part of the plan seems to be to give to the promoters of these institutions a limited liability, after the manner of Mr. Headlam's Bank Act of 1858 (21 & 22 Vict. c. 91.). It is remarkable, however, that no Joint-stock Bank has yet ventured to avail itself of the privileges of that Act.]

prevent the formation of banks of discount for the poor, and consequently prevent the formation of banks of deposit; the banks of discount being the banks of deposit for the rich. In like manner, the impediments to the repayment of deposits to parties under disabilities, and to the legatees and next of kin of Depositors where the sums are of small amount, have all been taken away in the case of charitable Savings Banks, but all retained in the case of private banks of deposit; and the Directors of several Joint-stock Banks have stated their willingness to take up the trade of receiving deposits from the poor, if these impediments be removed. In Scotland, where the law is different, the Savings Banks have never made much progress, and the deposits in the Joint-stock banks are more extensive than in this country.

"The laws respecting judgments and loans on personal security, and the laws respecting * mortgages and loans on the security of land, are in such a state as to afford a complete barrier to the safe investment of small sums in the natural Savings' Banks, provided in every country by the existence of property in land, which the owner might be enabled to mortgage for the smallest amount and at the most trifling expense.

"Again, the mode of managing the transfer of the public debt in the Bank of England and Bank of Ireland suggests an inquiry, whether some plan might not be devised for enabling the funds to be transferred, and interest to be paid on them in every large town in the kingdom.

"If it be found, after giving private enterprise a fair trial, that banks of deposit for the poor are not established, then would arise the question, whether the business is one that Government ought to undertake, in the same manner as the money-order business at the post-office. [See Part V., on the Post-Office Plan.] My own impression is, that if our laws were framed with a view to allow of small deposits and small investments, private enterprise is quite

---

* [See remarks on the Land Debenture system of Mr. V. Scully, Q. C. M.P., in our *Treatise on Copyhold and Church Lease Enfranchisements*, and in the Report (1857) of the Registration of Title Commissioners.]

adequate to supply a complete system of safe investment for the poor."

8.—In answer to doubts as to the possible mismanagement of these non-Government Deposit Banks, other writers repeat the argument of the late distinguished economist, M. J. B. Say, that*

"Il est sans doute fâcheux qu'il y ait des gens qui se ruinent et qui nuisent au commerce par de mauvaises entreprises. C'est un malheur auquel il faut cependant savoir se résigner, s'il est une conséquence nécessaire de la liberté de s'enrichir ou simplement de pourvoir à son existence."

9.—Again, says M. †Gustave du Puynode:—

"D'où provient donc le mal, et comment doit-on s'efforcer de le détruire ? Il est tout entier dans l'intervention de l'état. Evidemment, sans cela le trésor n'aurait rien à redouter de l'extension des caisses d'épargne. La seule question est ainsi de savoir si ces établissements peuvent se passer de l'intervention du pouvoir. Or en Allemagne, les caisses d'épargnes ont toujours été libres, sont toujours restées des institutions privées, et cela ne les a pas empêchées de se développer. En Prusse, à la fin de 1849, 261,000 dépôts composaient la somme de 61,000,000 fr. L'intervention de l'Etat n'est donc pas indispensable aux caisses d'epargne, et sa condamnation absolue ne se trouvera-t'elle pas toujours dans la banqueroute qui a suivi à leur égard, chez nous, la révolution de 1848 ?"

10.—On the other hand, Mr. J. M. Cook, the Superintendent of Banks in New York, an official whose great ability gives weight to his opinion, observes:—

"While one association enters upon its business with honesty, capacity, and capital, for the successful prosecution of it, able and

---

* [*Catechisme d'Economie Politique.*]
† [*De la Monnaie, du Credit, et de l'Impôt,* tom. i. p. 420.]

willing to fulfil every obligation it may incur, another, with the same outside presentment to the public, may enter upon a career of fraud: the end of the one legitimate and commendable, the other conceived in fraud and successfully prosecuted to the end originally intended. The personal liability and the capital of the one a sure and perfect guarantee that every obligation assumed, whatever may be its nature, will be freely and promptly paid; the other without the intent or capacity to do the same. Personal character and reputation will do much towards establishing the difference between the genuine and the counterfeit, and will certainly do it with the business community. But we should remember that this is not the class who deposit their surplus money in a Savings Bank. They can, from their vocations and position in life, know but little, if any thing, of personal credit or responsibility. They can only judge from external appearances, and are liable to be deceived and cheated by what would be a warning to the business man, the glitter and show of the spurious banker himself."

CHAPTER XVI.

AS TO THE INVESTMENTS OF NON-GOVERNMENT BANKS, AND SECTION 12 OF THE SAVINGS BANK ACT, 9 GEO. IV. C. 92.

ART. 10.—In some of the quotations in the preceding Chapter we have adverted to the danger that would attend non-Government Banks conducted in an improper manner. The proposition for their establishment, however, as distinct altogether from government institutions, has so many supporters, that it may be advisable to pursue the subject further, and consider the nature of the securities in which their investments can be made with safety.

The question is one which gives rise to several interesting points of finance, some of which we have entered upon in Chap. IX., Part IV., where the possibility is adverted to, that local private banks, making their own investments separately, may be placed in a better position than a Central commission, for finding good and advantageous securities.. In other words, that banks which do not allow withdrawals on demand could, with sufficient notice, perhaps, pay $3\frac{1}{2}$ or 4 per cent. if their capital be not large and their expenses reasonable, but that this could not be done with a fund amounting to 41 millions. This view is warmly supported by Dr. von Stubenrauch, of Vienna, who, in his learned *work, remarks :—

---

* [Statistical Sketch of the Associations existing in the Austrian Empire, drawn from Official Sources, by order of the Minister of the Interior, by Dr. M. v. Stubenrauch, Professor in the University of Vienna.

That "Savings Banks should be formed in the spirit of the local circumstances of the places where they are established, by investing their funds in purposes best suited to the locality, and varying the rate of interest accordingly; they should also consult the will of the Depositor how best to employ his funds, and to determine thereby the rate of interest in proportion to the extent of the risk to be incurred. .... He, who wishes his savings invested in mortgage-property, may reasonably be content with $2\frac{1}{2}$ per cent., and if in the funds and stocks, with 4 per cent."

11.—*As to Section* 12. *of the Act.*—There is one remarkable provision of the Act of 9 Geo. 4. c. 92. (s. 12.,) which allows any Savings Bank to receive sums* of money without limit as to amount, to be applied "for the benefit of the several Depositors, in any other manner" than with the National Debt Commissioners, according to the rules and regulations of the bank; and the Managers are not required to render any account to the Commissioners of the funds so invested. Mr. Tidd Pratt (in his evidence before the Committee of 1858,

---

* [The 12th Sect. of 9 Geo. 4. c. 92. is as follows, "That nothing in this Act contained shall extend to prevent the Trustees of any Savings Bank, already established, or to be established, receiving any sum or sums of money from any Depositor for any purpose except to be paid into the bank to the account of the Commissioners of the National Debt; and that it shall be lawful for such Trustees to apply any such sum or sums of money in any other manner for the *benefit of the several Depositors* according to the rules and regulations of such Savings Banks respectively; any thing in this Act contained to the contrary notwithstanding."

The following statements in reference to this Section were made by Mr. Tidd Pratt in his evidence before the Committee (18th February 1858) :—" The Savings Banks may conduct the business of general bankers under that clause, but it has never been done in England, except in one bank. The rules for the sanction of such a regulation come before me. Under this clause, if provided for in rules, the Trustees and Managers could invest the surplus sum, whatever it might be, in any security which they might wish, other than the Government securities.

"The clause is prospective, and I should be bound to approve of the rules if they contained such a provision."]

qu. 18) states that this clause was devised to enable the Trustees to invest the money of Depositors in any security they might think best, where they had savings exceeding the amount of £200 allowed to be placed in a Savings Bank.

12.—As yet, in only one bank in England—that at Exeter—and in two or three in Scotland, have the privileges of the Section now under consideration been taken; and in the Exeter Bank, the *rules only provide for direct investment in 3 per cent. stock.

This is easily understood, when regard is had to the fact, that the original object of Savings Banks was to give security to Depositors; little or no attention being paid to the question of interest. The dividends received are credited to the respective accounts, without any deduction being made for the management of the bank; and the only portion so invested is the surplus belonging to any Depositor over the limit of £200 allowed to be lodged with the Commissioners. Mr. Shopland, the able Actuary of the bank, when examined by the Committee in 1858, was of opinion that these transactions had been satisfactory to the Depositors.†

---

* [Rule 10th of the Devon and Exeter Savings Bank is as follows:— When the amount standing in the name of any Depositor amounts to £200 principal and interest, no interest will be payable thereon. *But separate accounts may be opened by the Trustees and Managers in the names of such Depositors, and transfers made from time to time* of such sum or sums of money as will purchase one or more pounds in the 3 per cent. Government stock or annuities, so as to keep the amount of the original account under £200, which 3 per cent. stock will be invested in the names of not less than four Trustees, *for* the benefit of, and at the sole risk *of each respective Depositor, for whom such transfer and investments may be made.*]

† [The amount of stock held by the Exeter Bank under this clause is £21,383 belonging to 118 Depositors; and it is included in the returns made to the Commissioners as a portion of the total amount due to Depositors, viz. £1,020,119 (qu. 1479—1484).]

14.—In the instance of the *Perth* Savings Bank in Scotland, however, the investments under this clause are made with *Joint-stock Banks, and upon the 20th November 1858, the balance of such investments stood thus:—

With the Commissioners	£31,600
With the Perth Bank	74,200
With the Central Bank	74,200

As the interest paid by the Joint-stock Banks falls low, the Managers transfer the whole balances to the Commissioners, and *vice versâ*. Thus, on the 20th November 1855, the balance in the Commissioners' hands was £154,000. The rate of interest given by the bank to the Depositors averaged £3 per cent. In the opinion of Mr. Maitland, of the Edinburgh bank, Depositors in Scotland, being quite ignorant of the public funds, would not (for a long time at least) under any circumstances consent to invest in them, preferring their own local Joint-stock Banks.

The above arrangement is an advantageous one to the Perth Savings Bank, and there can be no doubt of its legality; but although the clause permits the Trustees to invest in Joint-stock Banks the money of Depositors—it must be at their individual request, and for their personal benefit alone. The clause does not allow a mass of Savings Bank money to be invested in the name and on behalf of the institution in its corporate capacity; in such a case, *if any loss should arise from the failure of the Joint-Stock Bank, the Trustees and Managers would be personally liable to make it good.*

---

* [The published rule of the Perth Bank is as follows:

"Funds of the Institution vested in the name of the Committee of Management, for behoof of the Depositors, in equal parts with the Perth Banking Company and the Central Bank of Scotland, at a favourable rate of interest, fluctuating with the ordinary rate of interest, but guaranteed to be always above it, and never to be below the Government rate of interest to Savings Bank Depositors." *In the reply to Qu.* 2825, *the certified Rule is given rather differently.*]

15.—By a slight *alteration in the words of sect. 12., the risk and profit of the transactions contemplated by it might be transferred from the individual Depositors to the Savings Bank in its corporate capacity; and the business of Investment Associations might be carried on in its widest sense, whether after the manner of Building Societies, which lend money on the security of houses or land, or in any other way. In the amended rules powers would have to be taken for investing according to the discretion and judgment of the Directors or managers, either with the Savings Bank Commissioners, (at a low rate of interest, viz., £2 . 10s. per cent.) or in the securities contemplated by the Friendly Societies Act, as described in our Treatise on that subject.

16.—A Savings Bank, availing itself of such powers, would be able to supersede Building Societies, because, while it could offer to its subscribers all the benefits of those institutions, it would be secure from any loss by the delay attendant on the investments of its funds, since, as soon as received, while waiting for other opportunities, the deposits may be bearing interest derivable from the Savings Bank Commissioners, or from some first-class Joint-stock Bank. It is probable, that the

---

* [The following is a clause that has been suggested:—" The Trustees of every society or bank established under this Act shall from time to time, with the consent of the Committee of Management of such society (or bank), or of a majority of the members of such society (or bank) present at a general or special meeting thereof, or in accordance with the rules of such society, invest the funds of such society, or any part thereof, to any amount, in the Public Funds, or with the Savings Bank Commissioners, or on Real or Leasehold Estate, or in such other security as the rule of such society may direct, not being the purchase of house or land (save and except the purchase of buildings wherein to hold the meetings or transact the business of such society), and not being the purchase of shares in any Joint-stock Company or other company, with or without charter of incorporation, and not being personal security, unless it consist of two responsible householders."]

Managers would soon find it to be to the advantage of their bank to invest with the Commissioners as little as possible, as new channels of local investment might in time be developed.

Some benefit might be derived from giving to non-Government Banks a wider scope of operation and investment than the mere placing of their deposits in good securities would imply; and much good might be done in the towns or villages where they are situate by allowing advances to be made for the assistance of local improvements or enterprises whereby the inhabitants, and more particularly the working classes, might be benefited.* Such advances could be made by an association or company,—which can by co-operation command large sums of money, and which delegates the management of its investment to one or more skilful persons,—with more profit and at a much lower cost than the private individual must incur. It is true that from the justly-supposed superior security of the public funds, and from the conveniences which they offer for transfer or sale, if necessary, they will always, in ordinary times, for permanent or lengthened investments, represent the lowest rate of interest which an investor can obtain, yet there are other channels that offer a higher rate of interest, which are accessible to those only who can command sufficiently large sums; and inasmuch as the better the apparent attraction of the investment over public securities, the greater the risk of loss attending it, considerable knowledge and practical experience are required to distinguish between the sound and the unsound. These advantages an association can afford to all its members, as a slight per centage on their payments will defray the cost of employing the whole time of one or more persons skilled in money matters; and the daily recurrence of occasions for investments enables the association to

---

* [See Appendix on Improvement of Industrial Dwellings.]

realize for division, from the rapidity and uniformity of its transactions, if its expenditure be moderate—a higher nominal rate of interest per cent. per annum, than the single member could obtain. This arises from the manner in which fresh interest is obtained by no delay occurring in investing the old interest; and upon a large average of transactions, the society's periods of repayment harmonize with its receipts.

17.—Non-Government Banks should be required to abstain from referring to, or professing in any way to be under Government protection or control, and they should not be allowed to adopt any name or title likely to mislead. The draft of their prospectuses,* rules, and other printed statements, should be submitted to the certifying Barrister, before publication, for his approval as not containing any matter contrary to law, and for amendment where necessary.

As regards †investments under £100 in those banks, Depositors might be allowed the following privileges:—

1. *Exemption from Stamp duty and Legacy duty,*
2. *Exemption from Income Tax on Interest,*
3. *Power to Representatives of deceased Depositors to receive without Administration any sum not exceeding £50, and*
4. *Generally the leading privileges of the Friendly Societies Acts.*

---

* [Rules suited for non-Government Banks can be obtained from the Friendly Societies Institute. See also the model Rules, in our Treatise on that subject, for the *Constitution and Management clauses.*]

† [To meet unexpected withdrawals from non-Government Banks the Savings Bank Commissioners should be empowered to make advances to them on deposit of securities, to the extent of two-thirds of the value, if they are of unexceptionable character.]

CHAPTER III.

EXTRACTS FROM RULES OF AMERICAN DEPOSIT BANKS.

Art 15.—Although, pending Savings Bank legislation, it would be premature to print here a model set of rules suited for the establishment of Non-Government Banks, yet it may be desirable to lay before our readers some of the leading regulations which govern the operations of such banks in the United States and elsewhere:—

1. "There shall be a President, three Vice-Presidents, a Secretary, an Attending Committee; an Auditing Committee, of two Trustees; a Funding Committee, of four Trustees; a Committee on lost books, of three Trustees; a Committee on clerkships and the Accountant's duties, of three Trustees; a Committee on loans of bond and mortgage, of five Trustees; and a property Committee, of two Trustees.

2. " One member of the Board, each in his turn, for one week, shall, in person, or by his substitute of another member of the Board, attend at the bank during the hours for receiving deposits, and paying drafts, to be denominated the Attending Committee. He shall have the general superintendence and management of the bank during the week of his service. He shall keep accurate minutes, and report thereon the hour when the business of the bank was finished and closed; shall see the daily receipts properly put into the vault; sign the checks payable to the order of the Accountant or in his absence the first book-keeper for the supply of cash for the bank, and for the payments at the bank to Depositors, and shall see the monies received during his week de-

posited in the bank selected by the Board. He shall have power to close the account, or to refuse the deposits of any person.

3. "The Funding Committee shall be charged with the duty of seeing to the stock investments of the funds of the bank, and the disposal of its stocks, under the direction of the Board.

4. "The Committee of Loans on Mortgage shall be charged with the examining of all applications for loans on bond and mortgage, and after the same are approved, they shall see to the completing of the securities, and of the proper certificates in relation thereto, and shall deliver the same to the Treasurer; they shall draw on the Treasurer in favour of the borrower, for the money loaned, which drafts shall be signed by a majority of the Committee.

5. "All loans shall be on productive unincumbered real estate in the city of New-York, worth at least 50 per cent. more than the sum to be loaned. No loan shall be made unless the Committee shall be fully satisfied as to the value of the property to be mortgaged, nor until they shall be furnished, by competent counsel to be employed by them, with his certificate that he has carefully investigated the title to the property, and that in his opinion the title is good, and the property unincumbered.

6. "If, after loans shall have been made, the Committee shall doubt the sufficiency of the security, they shall call in so much of the loan as will render the residue well secured.

7. "The Bank shall be at liberty to return all, or any part of any deposit whenever they may think proper.

8. "The Bank shall not be liable to pay any monies to Depositors except on a week's previous notice to the Accountant or attending Committee at the Bank, nor except on the third Mondays in January, April, July, and October: but monies may be voluntarily paid by the Bank daily, and without such notice, and without thereby waiving the right of the Bank to such notice and time of payment.

9. "Interest will be allowed at such rate as in the judgment of the Board of Managers the business of the Bank for the last six months will justify, to be declared before the third Mondays of January and July."—*Laws of the New York Bank for Savings.*

19.—The following *important clauses are from the Acts of Legislature, in reference to other Banks for Savings in the State of New York :—

1. "The Board of Trustees may, from time to time, regulate the interest to be allowed to Depositors, so that the interest allowed to Depositors having 500 dollars or more deposited with the said Bank, shall be at least 1 per cent. less than the interest allowed to others, and so that no interest or dividend, on account of the surplus fund, shall be allowed for monies which shall have been withdrawn from the Bank." (*From the Rules of the Seamen's Bank*).

2. "Amounts not exceeding 5000 dollars to any one individual may be loaned on unincumbered, productive, real estate, located within the county of   , and worth, exclusive of buildings thereon, at least double the amount to be secured thereby. In all cases of loans upon real estate, a sufficient bond, or other satisfactory personal security, shall be required of the borrower, and all reasonable and necessary expenses of the searches, examinations, and certificates of title, and of drawing, perfecting, and recording papers, shall be paid by such borrower. And it shall be the duty of the Trustees to invest, as soon as practicable, in the public stocks, or public securities, or in bonds and mortgages, all sums received by them beyond an available fund, not exceeding one-third of the total amount of deposits with the Institution, at the discretion of the said Trustees, which they may keep to meet the current payments of said corporation, and which may by them be kept on deposit, on interest, or otherwise, or loaned on Government, State, and bond and mortgage securities, or otherwise, as provided in this Act, at the discretion, and as the Trustees may direct. No part of the moneys so deposited shall be invested, except in the stocks, bonds, and securities mentioned in this section."—(*Act of* 18*th April* 1859, *Peekskill Savings Bank.*)

---

* [*Various other clauses relating to Non-Government Banks will be found in the notes to other Parts of this Treatise.*]

CHAPTER XVIII.

GENERAL REMARKS ON THE AUDIT AND MANAGEMENT OF PUBLIC INSTITUTIONS.

ART. 20.—The occasions are now becoming very numerous when associations have to be formed to effect that which individual enterprise cannot attain. In order to insure success it is becoming recognised that the management should approach as nearly as possible to the form of *Executive individuality*,* a fact which the prosperity of ordinary trading firms sufficiently demonstrates.

But as even such an executive is likely to be less cautious in the management of other people's money than its own, there arises the necessity of a thorough audit of the society's affairs and of surveillance over the executive body.

For one company that fails by dishonesty or from want of skill on the part of the chief official, ten come to grief from careless supervision. The best form of direction is an Executive Committee of five shareholders, for, judging by analogy, the prosperity of a public company can only be secured by the same system of concentrated personal management as is adopted in the great private commercial firms of this country.

---

* [In addition to executive individuality in the management, the objects of the association should be single and undivided.

The *Credit Mobilier* of France is a failure because it has attempted a *multitude of operations*, each requiring special knowledge and experience. Where the management is directed to a variety of purposes, its want of concentration renders it weak and inefficient.

An association of such a multiform character is also more affected by social disturbing causes, than where one object alone is kept in view.]

21.—Experience has, unhappily, shewn that all Joint-stock associations are liable, if surveillance be not exercised, to losses from frauds just as much as Savings Banks. The painful interest which had been awakened in the mind of the public by the extensive Tipperary and Royal British Bank *disasters, had not had time to subside before the disclosure of the startling frauds that had been perpetrated on the Crystal Palace and Great Northern Railway Companies. Rumour is also current of impending disclosures of defalcations in other institutions; and an opinion has become prevalent that the time is come for some legislative enactment to secure not only a better and closer audit of the *account-books* of a joint-stock company or bank, but also for enabling auditors to make inspection (where circumstances appear to require it) of the *minutes* of the Board of Directors and the *letter-book* of the Secretary.

Some years back we submitted to the Board of Trade the draft of a Bill for a system of audit and inspection corresponding to that which we have described in Chapter XV., as applicable to non-Government Savings Banks. The clauses recommended in the Bill, in order to carry it into effect, we give below.†

---

* [Frauds, of course, are not peculiar to any country. For example, in France, it was stated on the trial of the notorious Prost,—who was condemned to three years' imprisonment, £40 fine, and to restore £21,533 (sterling) to the shareholders he had swindled—that since 1857, the Managers of not fewer than forty companies *en commandite* had been prosecuted for fraud, and that the amount of shareholders' money which they had "absorbed" was not less than £1,600,000 sterling. The punishment, however, was not allowed to rest on Prost alone, and in this respect it may be remarked they *do* " do these things better in France," for the Court declared the members of Prost's *conseil de surveillance* responsible for the £21,000 ordered to be refunded to the shareholders, on the ground that it was owing to their neglect of duty that Prost was enabled to commit the frauds.]

Proposed Audit Clauses.

† [" 1. The Directors of each non-Government Bank or trading company in Great Britain and Ireland shall within three months after the passing of

22.—Under the proposed system, it is evident that if the Depositors or claimants do their duty, and appoint professional accountants of sagacity and experience, then the existence of such Inspectors and the possibility of their exercising their power at unexpected seasons would act as a check upon fraudulently-disposed officials and remove the opportunity which creates the crime.

That Government has hitherto taken no steps in the matter may be attributed to the unwillingness of the Legislature to

---

Proposed Audit Clauses—(continued).

this Act, and from time to time, at intervals of three years, or, in case of a vacancy, within one month thereof, summon the customers or depositors, or the persons not being shareholders, who may be creditors of the said bank or public company, to meet together at the offices of the bank or company, in order to appoint or reappoint two or more Inspecting Auditors of the said bank or company ; and the said Directors shall, immediately after such appointment, transmit the signature, name, and address of each of the Inspecting Auditors to the Board of Trade ; and the Directors of every Joint-stock Bank or public company shall cause the annual and other statements required to be transmitted under the Acts relating to Joint-stock Banks or public companies to be certified and verified by the Inspecting Auditors so appointed by the said Depositors, or others as aforesaid, in addition to the attestation now required by the said Acts, and shall also cause a certificate from the said Inspecting Auditors, as to the result of their examination of the books, to be transmitted to the Board of Trade.

2. " The summons for the election of the Inspecting Auditors as aforesaid shall be by advertisement in two or more of the local newspapers, and by announcement affixed in a conspicuous part of the offices of the bank or company, and the Depositors shall have power to adjourn their meeting or meetings for the election of Inspecting Auditors, at intervals of not more than fifteen days, as often as may appear to them necessary for the better selection of such Inspecting Auditors. And it shall be lawful for them to delegate the selection of Inspecting Auditors to a Committee of such of the Depositors, not less than twelve in number, who shall not be acting at the time as Trustees, Directors, or Managers of the bank or company. The Inspecting Auditors to be elected may be either Depositors or Accountants (publicly acting in such capacity); provided always, that in the event of no such election being made within three months after a vacancy has occurred in the office of Inspecting Auditors, the Directors shall report the same to the Board of Trade ; which shall, with all con-

interfere with the supposed right of every one to manage his own affairs as he may think best; but whilst society is willing to recognise that right, as regards private individuals, it does not follow as a consequence that it is proper when a number associate together for the purpose of monetary transactions with the rest of the community. Experience is beginning to shew that it is easier to obtain information as to the responsibility and credit of private persons, than— under the present system of audit—as to the solvency and internal honesty of associations.

23.—*As to Directors and Auditors.*—The frauds in public companies may be mainly attributed to the fact, that the Di-

---

Proposed Audit Clauses—(continued).

venient speed, appoint Inspecting Auditors for the purposes hereinafter provided.

3. "The Auditors shall have power, without notice, to attend and inspect the account-books and all other books or documents of the bank or company they may require; and from time to time may cause the books of Depositors or customers of a bank, or claims of creditors, to be produced at the offices, for the purposes of being inspected, examined, and verified with the books of the bank or company by them.

4. "It shall be lawful for the Board of Trade, and they are hereby authorised and empowered to settle and appoint the allowances to be paid for the services, pains, and labours of such Inspecting Auditors, in manner and for the purposes aforesaid, out of the funds upon which the expenses of management of the said bank or company are chargeable by the Deed of Settlement.

5. "It shall be the duty of all officers of the bank or company to produce, for the examination of the Inspecting Auditors, all books or documents in their custody or power.

6. "Any Inspecting Auditors may examine on oath the officers and agents of the bank or company in relation to its business; and may administer such oath accordingly. If any officer or agent refuses to produce any such book or document, or to answer any question relating to the affairs of the bank or company, he shall incur a penalty not exceeding five pounds in respect of each offence.

7. "A copy of the report of the Inspecting Auditors, authenticated by the seal of the bank or company into whose affairs they may have made inspection, shall be admissible as evidence in any legal proceeding."]

rectors, in too many instances, are either so engrossed in their own affairs, or possessed of too little knowledge of the details of the company they profess to govern, to enable them to be very accurately informed of its actual financial condition.

Directors would, perhaps, answer that they rely upon the appointed Auditors;—but that would be only justifiable when those officials are professional accountants.

The generality of Auditors elected by shareholders are persons having no repute for experience in matters of finance, and their audits, in consequence, are little more than an illusion. Auditors, to be of any real value, should be in the character of Committees of Surveillance, and should not be expected to content themselves with checking the vouchers for payments, and the accuracy of the items entered in the office-books. As long as it is considered a piece of interference on the part of the Auditors if they desire to extend their investigations beyond the accounts of a company, they can give no guarantee either to the Shareholders or to the *creditors that all the transactions of the Directors and officials have found a record in the books.

Hence the present system of audit is in the highest degree pernicious, for it tends to create the idea of security where none is really given.

24.—The public mind is perplexed as to how fraud can be prevented. It is urged, that when a concern is not managed entirely by one proprietor, somebody must be trusted, and that Auditors would not be able to prevent forgery or the falsification of accounts. This objection is groundless, for fraud begins when neglect of supervision in the management commences; and the best way to prevent fraud is to introduce a system which will create a fear of detection.

---

* [*By the word " Creditors" of a Bank would be meant the Customers or Depositors.*]

It is not to be expected that Directors, who meet but once or twice a-week for an hour or two, can have any very detailed knowledge of the finance of a company; and, even if they had the leisure, it does not follow that those who manage a concern, should be the best persons to audit its accounts.

Unhappily, moreover, the culpability of the Directors is not always limited to laxity of management, but appears to have had rise in some instances, if we may judge by recent exposures, from an unworthy desire to commit and conceal dishonourable operations with the funds entrusted to their care.

* The real source of the disease is the inefficiency of the system of audit now in force. The gentlemen appointed are too often the nominees of the Directors, even where they ap-

---

* [An aggrieved bank shareholder writes on this subject—" Some few years ago, when joint-stock accounts were admitted to have been 'cooked,' and when Government audit was objected to (perhaps warrantably objected to, in so far as likely to be palmed off for a Government voucher), a printed appeal for a remedy was circulated among Directors themselves; but instead of concerting proper principles of audit, the Directors, constrained to engage public accountants for the unravelling of old complications were content with engaging such gentlemen upon their permanent staff for the avoidance of like complications in the future. Since then we have seen the attestations of eminent accountants paraded at the foot of accounts, the responsibility of which, in the popular sense, they repudiate. In sooth, their own appointment having become another bit of directorial patronage, and their multifarious engagements preventing due personal tests of returns, accepted by their own subordinates from the official subordinates, such returns are carried to account agreeably to 'established precedents,' or to 'official prescription;' whereas, what is wanted is some independent and uniform system of charge and discharge, always commensurable by common standards, and intelligible to the uninitiated as well as to those behind the scenes.

"What then is required is, not to supersede routine, but to apply sagacity and experience at unappointed times, and in unexpected places, for the testing of the actual routine is sufficient for everchanging circumstances. *While simple-minded, hard-working Auditors have been pottering over huge folios which engross and divert their energies, corporate property has been fraudulently wasted notwithstanding, and that, too, by means of the very accounts which Auditors have verified.*"]

pear to be elected by the shareholders, and owe their election, not so much to their skill in investigating accounts, as to their being friends of the managing officials. Not unfrequently do they take their first lesson in auditing books at the company which they are appointed to investigate.

Nor, indeed, is it sufficient for an Auditor to be merely an honourable man, for it requires special experience to know where the hands of the "cook" may be traced in a series of accounts.

25.—We repeat, therefore, that, however excellent associations may be in principle, their success cannot be secured, when they are only nominally managed by a Board, however respectable, unless the Directors be sufficiently limited in number to secure unity of mind and regularity of system, so that the objects of the society may be carried out in its most minute details. A large, and, what is generally termed, an imposing, first-class, Board of Directors is frequently careless in the discharge of its duties. From the want of regularity in the attendance of its members, there arises a want of unity in their deliberations. Knowing little or nothing of the real working of the institution, and deceived by a certain audacity of manner and jaunty bearing on the part of their chief subordinate officer, directors not unfrequently leave the administration of its affairs too much in his hands.

Hence there arise, from his impropriety of conduct or want of capacity, a variety of circumstances, which, fostered by supineness on the part of the directors, have brought many a scheme, excellent in the abstract, to bankruptcy, and inflicted great injury on the community.

26.—To provide, then, a sufficient bar to dishonesty, or curative to lack of principle, a Committee of two professional Inspectors should be appointed, whose duty it should be to exercise a surveillance over the Executive Committee, without interfering in the acts of management, except to report what is being done to the constituents of the society or shareholders. The Inspectors should not both be simply accountants: one at least should be required to possess some legal, as well as professional knowledge, of the matters pertaining to the particular class of business they are called upon to supervise. They should be required to test the accuracy of the reports from time to time submitted by the Managers; and to watch that all their measures taken are in strict accordance with the Deed of Settlement, and the objects and principles of the society. These Inspectors should be men of fair position in life, and be adequately paid. Their tenure of office should be limited, and fresh Inspectors should be appointed—under a Rotation system—every two or three years. They should, more particularly, *not be permitted to send their clerks to do the work* which they have undertaken, and for which they have been personally selected.

Thus would they have the strongest incentive to the faithful discharge of their duties, since, by any neglect, they would not only lose the particular appointment they hold in one society, but render themselves ineligible to like offices in other institutions.

27.—If it be objected, that in some recent notorious failures the management was intrusted to men of supposed superior position in life, we answer, that in those very instances the public were deceived by an apparently repectable Board of Directors placed over the Company's officials, who, while they were not ashamed to draw large remuneration out of its funds, were yet too indolent to exercise a necessary and wholesome supervision over its affairs. This would not have occurred had there been Inspectors attached to the association, instead of a large body of directors, who had no such special experience as would enable them to detect the irregularities that were occurring.

28.—From the observations in this and the preceding Chapter, the reader will be able to form his own opinion of the benefit that would be conferred on the industrial portion of the community by the establishment of independent or non-Government Savings Banks. It will doubtless, however, be admitted that, unless stringent regulations be provided for the appointment by the Depositors of *professional Visiting Inspectors* to watch on their behalf over the operations of the bank, we may witness a repetition of the miseries occasioned by recent failures. The effect of such failures, when extending largely in a country district, can scarcely be conceived by any who have not been actually present at the scene. The inhabitants of centres of population, which have as yet been exempt from similar disasters, know little of the shock but by the distant explosion; whilst those on the spot see anxiety and distress on every countenance, all industrial confidence suspended, and, what is more painful still, numerous unfortunate Depositors—of advanced age—reduced again to the labour for which they are no longer fitted, and against which, by years of early industry, they had striven to make a provision. These sad contingencies—which honesty and prudence in the management may avert—it would be the province of the Inspectors to prevent, as far as may lie in their power, by a watchful discharge of their duties.

PART VII.

LEGISLATION ON SAVINGS BANKS SINCE THE YEAR 1859.

CHAPTER XIX.

LEGISLATION OF THE YEAR 1860,

AND POSITION OF THE SAVINGS BANK QUESTION AT THE END OF THE SESSION.

Section 1.—The nature of Mr. Gladstone's first Bill of 1860, and of the opposition thereto.

ART. 1.—Early in the Session of the year 1860 a measure was introduced by Mr. Gladstone, entitled "*A Bill to make provision for the Investment and Security of the monies received by the Commissioners for the reduction of the National Debt from Savings Banks and Friendly Societies,*" having for main objects:*—to obtain a legislative recognition of the deficiency of

---

* [It consisted of 17 clauses, but the principal provisions were:—

1st. To cancel 29 millions of the present Savings Banks stocks, and to create a new stock, to be called "The State Deposit Account, No. 1," charged on the Consolidated Fund, and to consist of about three-fourths of the gross amount, viz. 31 millions out of about 41 millions. The new stock to bear interest at 3 per cent.

2d. *To invest three-fifths of the remainder, viz. 6 millions, in Guaranteed East India Stock and other Parliamentary Securities.*

3d. To give a Parliamentary recognition, under certain restrictions, to changes in the securities held for Savings Banks.

4½ millions now existing in the amount of Savings Bank securities (see Art. 19, Part III.); to define the powers of Chancellors of the Exchequer in respect to future purchases and sales for the purposes of the State; and to authorize the National Debt Commissioners, if possible, to invest, for the sake of higher interest, a portion of the Savings Banks funds in various 'Parliamentary securities,' such as we have recommended in Art. 22, Part IV.

2.—On moving the second reading of the Bill, on the 5th March 1860, Mr. Gladstone, in a long speech full of sound information on the subject, remarked that the normal operation of the present Savings Bank system was (as we have explained in Art. 11, Part III.), that the Commissioners were buyers of stock when the market was high, and sellers when the market was low.

"This (he believed) was the main cause of the difference which existed between the assets and liabilities. .... The mode in which they proposed to manage the finances in future was, as the Hon. Member for the Tower Hamlets (Mr. Ayrton) said, by opening a great book, in which would be written the sums themselves, with a provision for the rectification of the account from year to year. Instead of holding that vast amount of stock, with its varied and fluctuating value, they would cancel a great part of it,

---

4th. To withhold interest on all Savings Bank deposits, the interest of which shall not have been claimed within ten years; to write off from the ledgers all such accounts; and to include the amount of these with the amount of the "Separate Surplus Fund" of Savings Banks; *in other words, to transfer from the banks to the Government the interest on all unclaimed deposits, merely reserving to the Depositors, or their representatives, the right to recover them with interest, if at any time the claim should be substantiated.*

5th. To thus withhold interest on about 2 millions of Savings Bank stock; —(this being erroneously presumed to be the aggregate amount of the unclaimed accounts and separate surplus funds.—See, however, Art. 43, Part I.)]

and in lieu of it enter in a book (which would contain the "State deposit account, No. 1"), the capital sum. From time to time, when the accounts were nearly balanced, that capital sum would be so regulated as to represent, as nearly as possible, the total amount of the real obligations of the State to the Savings Banks and Friendly Societies, instead of their being unaware of what was the actual amount of their engagements . . . . The third clause of the Bill was framed on the principle of maintaining the annual charge somewhere about what it was now; and when construed in connection with a subsequent clause, it provided that a limited portion of the stock should be held as dead-stock, not liable to bear interest. The principle on which this would be done was exactly analogous to that on which they now regulated by law the unclaimed dividends on the National Debt."

3.—Respecting the grand object of the new Bill, viz. to give * larger powers of investment, Mr. Gladstone observed that—
"There were certain guaranteed stocks with respect to which the

---

* [The Bill also gave power to the Commissioners to advance money for the purposes of the Exchequer Loan Fund. Mr. Gladstone said "he did not intend, in submitting that provision, to ask the House, at that moment, to give effect to any practical proposal on the subject. The power would remain dormant till the House had the opportunity of considering whether it was really desirable we should go on advancing money out of the Exchequer to the Exchequer Loan Fund Commissioners for the purpose of enabling them to lend it to various parties in the country, or whether it would not be better to transfer that function altogether to the Commissioners for the Reduction of the National Debt. He did not mean to throw any disparagement on the Exchequer Loan Fund Commission, which had proved a very useful institution, and had worked exceedingly well. *But it was certainly a question to be considered, whether a State, heavily indebted as we were, and holders of means of that kind continually falling in, ought not to use a portion of those means to carry on useful works*, in preference to advancing money for that purpose from a fund which had to be raised by taxation. . . . A Bill would have to be brought in to provide for such advances, for the receipt of the money by the Exchequer Loan Fund, and for its management."—(See Art. 23, Part IV.)]

ultimate liability of Parliament was just as full and entire as with respect to the stocks of this country. There were stocks, for example, like the Proprietary stock of the East India Company, with regard to which a certain amount of guarantee had been provided by the Legislature. The Bill proposed, therefore, that the power of investment now possessed by the Commissioners should be so far enlarged as to include that description of security. The effect of that would be, that they would in no respect go beyond stocks with reference to which Parliament had made a special provision to secure them; and at the same time they would be enabled, as to a certain portion of their assets, to get a better interest, and manage their funds more profitably for the country than heretofore. They would not, however, go beyond a certain amount, especially in a given time. He would take the Canada guaranteed loan of $1\frac{1}{2}$ million for the sake of illustration, although a considerable portion of that was now provided for. It was not at all desirable, where a third party was the debtor, and the Parliament of England only backed him with a State guarantee, that the Commissioners for the Reduction of the National Debt should acquire such a proportion of that stock as to become themselves the principal creditors. Parliament would then be placed in a false position. The Bill, therefore, proposed to limit the proportion of any stock of that character which the Commissioners might hold, as well as to limit absolutely the amount they might in any of these cases invest. The Bill also contained other powers, enabling the Commissioners to make exchanges of securities under certain circumstances; but these could be better explained in Committee. Suffice it now to say, that one of the objects of that exchange was to give the Commissioners the power of from time to time buying up certain stocks, of which the quantity was so very small in the market that they did not form a convenient medium of investment."

4.—The "State Deposit" portion of this Bill was promulgated some years ago in the public journals, and described by us in an early* publication on Savings Banks, in which we pointed out, that " by the present system of inscribing the whole of Savings Bank funds in the books of the Bank of England, no portion of it could be dealt with without incurring all the expenses of transfer; the Bank of England being paid for it as part of the National Debt, at the rate of £300 per million, for the trouble and risk of transfers, the payment of the dividends, &c., when with regard to more than three-fourths of it no transfer is ever made." The advocates of a 'State Deposit Account' at that time contended, that "if three-fourths of the amount of Savings Bank securities were converted into a debt inscribed in the public exchequer under simple regulations, nearly all the† above expense of management would be saved, and the dividends could be paid half-yearly from the public revenue, as they are now by the Bank as part of the

---

* [See the *Economist* newspaper, 1853, and the Remarks on the Savings Bank Question, in Division III. of our 'Treatise on Associations for Provident Investment,' page 111, 7th Edition, 1853.]

† ["There is still another way in which the possession of these Savings Bank funds is made to entail a loss, which in this case falls immediately on the Consolidated Fund. The Bank of England receives a commission of £300 a-year on every million of the National Debt in return for the trouble of paying dividends and regulating transfers. Something like £12,000 a-year is therefore paid to the Bank for the management of a portion of the Debt, which, being in the hands of the State itself, might just as well be cancelled at once. The absurdity of this arrangement becomes palpable enough if it is translated into an exact parallel in private life. A man with a large amount of obligations afloat may be supposed to employ an agent on commission to settle accounts every half year with his creditors. If such a debtor, by setting up a banking business, came into possession of large funds for investment, it might be reasonable enough for him to pay off some portion of his debt; but in order to parallel the conduct of the Government, he must be supposed to buy in his own bonds, and instead of tearing them up, to present them every half year to his own agent to receive dividends out of his own money, and to pay a handsome per centage for this idle transfer of cash from himself to himself."—(*Saturday Review*, March 1860).]

National Debt"—such an amount of stock being left in the hands of the Commissioners of the National Debt, as would enable them to work the account, and to meet all demands likely from time to time to be made upon them by the banks.

To give effect to this plan, it was proposed by the disciples of the Right Hon. J. Wilson that an account should be raised in the books of the Exchequer, to be called the "State Deposit Account, No. 1," to an amount equal to three-fourths of the whole liabilities of the National Debt Commissioners in respect to these deposits, which should in no way be operated upon by the Chancellor of the Exchequer, or in any other way, except for depositors' purposes; and that all the public stock representing these deposits should be cancelled, and the funded debt of the country redeemed in proportion; "the practical effect of which would be *to convert a funded debt, inscribed in the books of the Bank of England, managed at a cost of many thousands a year, into an unfunded debt, inscribed in the books of the Exchequer, and managed without any cost to the public.* A sum equal to the remaining one-fourth to continue in the hands of the Commissioners of the National Debt, as being the largest amount that it would be probable would ever be required, under any circumstances, to conduct the accounts, and to make the payments required by the banks. The interest upon the State Deposit Account to be paid to the Commissioners half-yearly, as the dividends are at present, but at different periods, which, with new deposits received, would be invested from time to time, and dealt with by cancelling so much of the funded debt, and adding to the State Deposit Account, so that it should be *always three-fourths of the whole account.*"

---

* See p. 112, Seventh Edition, before quoted (1853).

5.—This Bill of 1860 encountered prompt opposition, not only from some of the leading members of the House of Commons, but also from a very large number of Savings Banks; and petitions from all parts were presented against it. The active cause of the objection made to it by the banks was the introduction of the clause which deprived them of the profit arising from *unclaimed deposits,* by which they have a small * fund that forms a *de facto* provision against losses, &c. It was contended by the banks, therefore, that unless the whole liability for Savings Bank money, from the moment it is received, be adopted by the State, it is hardly fair that* they should be deprived of this particular fund.

As far as the Banks were concerned, it appears probable that no great opposition would have arisen, had this particular clause not been pressed, for the rest of the Bill did not affect their position in the least; but related to matters rather of public policy for the consideration of the House of Commons, than to details in which the banks were individually interested, especially as the Chancellor of the Exchequer stated that he did not propose to reduce the present rate of interest (£3. 5s.) allowed to the banks, although this is one of the measures which we have shewn, in Art. 25, Part IV., will be found necessary to make these institutions self-supporting.

6.— The opposition in the House of Commons arose mainly from a supposed disregard by Mr. Gladstone of the labours of the Committee of 1858, and of the suggestions they had put forward.

The members of that Committee, and those who thought

---

* [Distinct from the *Separate Surplus Fund.* See Art. 30 Part I.]|

* [See note, page xlv. for a regulation of the Stockholm Bank, and page xlix., relative to the agitation in New York on this very question].

with them, said they objected to the Bill because it [b] "unsettled a great deal, and settled nothing. It introduced several novel principles."

[c] "Under it a power greater than he already possessed was placed in the hands of the Finance Minister, who, as an *ex officio* Commissioner, was entrusted with the power of selling and purchasing stock to the extent of several millions. It was competent to the House to confer this power on the Chancellor of the Exchequer, but it ought to be done directly *eo nomine.*"

They asserted that the financial objects to be accomplished were simple: that the course taken by Mr. Gladstone to realize them was unnecessarily complicated: that [d] "to cancel a portion of the National Debt was a most dangerous operation, and, in some respects, inconsistent with national faith; that, in the present instance, it was useless to begin a new system of National Debt. The only reason that might be alleged was to save the money paid to the Bank of England; but if the Chancellor of the Exchequer had made proper representations to the Directors of the Bank, they would no doubt have surrendered the payment for the national benefit, without the necessity of this complex legislation. In fact, by this complicated proceeding, a new fund was created."

[e] "Such a mode of dealing with public money was quite unknown in this country. The proper way of treating the deposits would be to lay them out upon good security, taking care that too large an amount of interest was not paid, and that the money was always forthcoming."

7.—In fact, the weightiest objections to the State Deposit Account were that it was not in the form of known securities, and

---

[b] [Speech of Mr. Thomson Hankey, M.P., 22d June 1860.]
[c] [Sir Henry Willoughby, M.P., in the same debate.]
[d] [Speech of Mr. A. S. Ayrton, M.P.]   [e] [Mr. Hankey, M.P.]

also that it would contain an annual deficiency, which would not simultaneously appear in the *Cash account* of the nation. It was further asserted that:—

ᶠ" If, instead of trifling with the character of the National Debt, some £3,000,000 of new debt had been created, in the shape of Consols, the deficiency which had been created by forty years of mismanagement, and which successive Chancellors of the Exchequer had shrunk from disclosing, would have been satisfactorily adjusted. The proposal with regard to the interest,* moreover, would have the effect of diminishing the fund which existed as a guarantee against mismanagement or malversation in certain banks. If, instead of creating a new book-debt, as it had been called, the original deficiency had been made good in Consols, the interest would have been made good in the same way. But the Chancellor of the Exchequer had destroyed his Consols; and if any claim were made by the Savings Banks he would be confined to the Exchequer Bill market, instead of having the advantage of the Consols market, where the field was larger and the money more easily got. Any one acquainted with financial transactions must admit that a more inexpedient proceeding could not have been suggested."

ᵍ" It was a great question whether the Legislature should lay hold of this property of the Savings Banks, cancel the existing securities, and, by a sort of conjuring process, create fresh securities. No doubt the faith of the country would be pledged to repay the money of the Savings Banks, but the Trustees and Managers of Savings Banks, and the Depositors in them, had already a right to their money by Statute, provided they

---

ᶠ [Speech of Mr. A. S. Ayrton, M.P., 22d June 1860.]

* *On unclaimed deposits*, see page 301, note.

ᵍ [Sir Henry Willoughby, M.P.]

acted according to law. Therefore the Bill did not improve their situation in that respect."

[h] "They would rather keep the security they had than accept that offered by the Bill. Nobody disputed the liability of the Government for the money it received from the Savings Banks; and therefore the effect of the arrangements under the Bill would be to diminish the security while retaining the old management. The mode recommended by the Committee of 1858 was to adhere to the present security and alter the management."

[i] "No Committee could be more determined to investigate the question in every way; and though they had not examined Chancellors of the Exchequer, they did examine an officer whom they thought more competent to give an unbiassed opinion than even financial ministers."

[j] *"The great principle to be adopted in legislating with regard to Savings Banks was, that the property of Depositors in them should be considered to be a Trust, and a trust alone, and should not be used by the Chancellor of the Exchequer to give a factitious value to Government securities."*

[k] "These funds ought to be regarded as a Trust, and the Chancellor of the Exchequer ought not to be allowed to use them for the purpose of buying Exchequer Bills at a discount, and thus giving them a fictitious appearance of value. The Court of Chancery continually held respectable men liable for Trust money, which they had employed in the purchase of shares in companies to which they belonged in order to raise their value in the market; and it was the imperative duty of the House to provide that that should not be done by the

---

[h] [Speech of the Right Hon. Sotheron Estcourt, M.P., same debate.]
[i] [Speech of Mr. Turner, M.P.]   [k] [Mr. Malins, M.P.]
[j] [Colonel Sykes, M.P.]

Government, which a court of justice would not permit on the part of an individual."

[l] "The real question was, whether the Government, in employing the money belonging to Depositors, considered the interests of the Depositors or the advantage of the country. The right hon. gentleman said that the control over those monies must be vested in the individual at the head of the Finance Department, and instanced the Board of Control. But those systems were not analogous. The Board of Control in former times had the government of a great empire, distinct from this country, and were responsible for it; but the Chancellor of the Exchequer was responsible to the country for the finances, and he had placed under his control the deposits of individuals which had not in their origin any connection with the finances of this country, except that they implied an obligation on the part of the country to repay them. Now, was that control at all times wise, judicious, or safe? No doubt it might be so under the direction of the right hon. gentleman, but there would always remain a doubt whether some national operation which the Minister wished to carry might not be injurious to the Depositors, although beneficial to the country?"

[m] "It was not desirable the right hon. gentleman should be in the position of one who 'rigged' the market; for when the Chancellor of the Exchequer—the price of Exchequer Bills being depressed—went into the market and bought, a rise was created, but not on the sound principle of supply and demand."

8.—It was further urged as an objection to the Bill, that it had reference mainly to Investments; and that under these

---

[l] [Mr. T. Baring, M.P.]   [m] [Mr. Thomson Hankey, M.P.]

circumstances there was little chance "that other questions connected with Savings Banks, more immediately and vitally affecting them, would be settled within any reasonable time, and that many of the Savings Banks throughout the country were opposed to the Bill."

These representations so far influenced the House that it decided, by a considerable majority, when in *Committee on the 13th July, to reject the 1st clause of the Bill, although they had previously, on the 22d June, affirmed the principle of the same clause by a majority of 27.

---

* [It may be mentioned incidentally that no allusion was made by Mr. Gladstone, during the Session, to the Post Office Savings Bank Plan, which has also met with considerable opposition from the Savings Banks. Their objections have been stated at length in Part V. An experienced Savings Bank Manager has written to us recently as follows:—

"Nearly all the Post-masters in this part of the country are small shop-keepers; many of them uneducated men, unacquainted with any regular system of keeping books and accounts.

"*These parties have their private business to attend to, often to the neglect of the Post Office duties,* and certainly they are not competent to keep a set of Savings Bank books, receive monies from Depositors, and make the necessary Government returns, in addition to other business. I THINK THE PROPOSITION MOST ABSURD. Neither are these persons in a position to gain the confidence of the public.

"Many of the Depositors of this district lodge their money in Savings Banks, on account of the respectability of the Trustees and Managers, in whom they have perfect confidence, being men of the highest position in the community, both clergymen and laymen, one of whom is always in attendance when the bank is open for business."]

Section 2.—The Act of 1860, 23 & 24 *Vict. c.* 137, *" To make further provision with respect to monies received from Savings Banks and Friendly Societies."*

ART. 9.—The Bill referred to in the preceding Section having been withdrawn, another, consisting of the general investment clause only, was introduced, a few days after, and passed the Commons without opposition. It met with some resistance, however, in the House of Lords, where it was negatived on a preliminary division, although the Duke of Argyll moved a resolution declaring the passing of the Bill to be a matter of urgency; and stated that " its object was to diminish the annual loss of upwards of £100,000, which resulted to the nation from the difference of the interest which was received under the present investment of the funds, and that which was credited to the Trustees of the Savings Banks."

Shortly after the Bill was again brought forward, and became law on the 28th August 1860, in the following form :—

" Whereas, by the Acts now in force relating to Savings Banks and Friendly Societies, various provisions are enacted for regulating the mode of investing the monies received and to be received by the Commissioners for the Reduction of the National Debt from Savings Banks and Friendly Societies. And whereas it is expedient to make further provision for the investing of such monies: Be it therefore enacted by the Queen's most Excellent Majesty, by and with the advice and consent of the Lords Spiritual and Temporal, and Commons, in this present Parliament assembled, and by the authority of the same, as follows: that is to say,

" I. The powers now vested in the Commissioners for the Reduction of the National Debt in respect of all monies remitted to them on account of Savings Banks and Friendly Societies shall extend to Parliamentary securities, of whatsoever kind, created or issued under the authority of any Act or Acts of Parliament, for the interest on which provision is made by Parliament, and to any stock or debentures or other securities expressly guaranteed by authority of Parliament.

"II. The Commissioners for the Reduction of the National Debt shall, at the end of every year, report to the Commissioners of Her Majesty's Treasury, setting forth in detail the whole of the several transactions which shall have taken place during the course of the year in the investment of all monies coming into their hands for Savings Banks and Friendly Societies, and of all variations, if any, which may have taken place during such year in the securities held by the said Commissioners for those institutions, and copies of such reports shall be laid before both Houses of Parliament not later than the fifteenth day of February, if Parliament shall be then sitting, and if not then sitting, then within ten days after the next re-assembling of Parliament."

10.—The Act thus carries into effect, at the end of ten years, the recommendations we made in 1850 (see Art. 22 of Part IV.). They would probably, long ere this, have received legislative sanction, had it not been for the steady opposition of one or two leading members of the House of Lords, the justice of whose objections we cannot admit, however much we may regard the fact of their being advanced by men of eminent position.

Indeed so recently as during the debate of 1860 a distinguished authority remarked that, "whether in regard to Savings Banks, private banks, or the Bank of England, immediate convertibility was the principle which ought to be adhered to. A diminution of convertibility for the sake of a better interest was a danger which no Trustee ought to incur." On account of this, he added that he considered it would be unwise to place any portion of

Savings Bank assets in other than Government Stock and Exchequer Bills.

In objecting to the investments which are included in the term "Parliamentary securities" (see Art 22. Part IV)—on the ground that they are not so readily convertible as the public funds—he was partly right, and partly wrong. Convertibility requires two concurrent circumstances:—first, that the securities should be sufficiently extensive to have a *recognised place in the market*, so as to be familiarly known and be constantly before the mind of buyers;—the second requirement is capability of *realization* without loss, or with as little as possible; and it is well known that in this respect convertibility is lessened by placing too much of the investments on one particular security.

At present Savings Banks deposits are invested in those Government securities (Stocks and Exchequer Bills) which have the first element of convertibility; but by the circumstance of the whole amount being placed in those two kinds, the investment lacks the second element, for any attempt to get a large portion of it (such as, for example, ten millions) out of the Funds would produce an unprecedented sudden fall in the market, and a consequent heavy loss.

To make, therefore, Savings Bank investments safe (that is, convertible with comparative facility) it is essential that they should be so distributed, that whatever sum from time to time

---

* [In the Act 9 Geo. IV. c. 92, is a section (s. 56) from which it would appear to have been contemplated that, as a rule, the Commissioners should borrow in time of pressure arising from the preponderance of withdrawals over deposits, instead of selling stock. The highest rate of interest demanded during recent panics by the Bank of England has been £10 per cent. per annum, or at the rate of 16s. 8d. a month. Now, the preponderance of withdrawals over deposits rarely lasts many months; so that, if the Commissioners could make arrangements to meet

be required, may be obtained by selling a portion of several securities, and not by forcing the sale of one. (*See Art. 28, Part III., and Arts.* 8 *and* 11, *Part IV.*)

---

the call upon them by a temporary loan, less loss would be incurred than under the present practice of going into the market and effecting large sales of stock, which, occurring at a time when the funds are low, add to the downward tendency of the price and aggravate the deficiency.

Independently of the fact, that, for such a loan, the Commissioners could offer the best security possible, they would not usually require an advance until the panic or time of pressure in the money market had passed its crisis; for it is a remarkable fact, that the preponderance of withdrawals over deposits follows a panic, and is not concurrent: in other words, the actual necessity for withdrawal from the Savings Banks by the industrious classes does not arise until some five or six weeks after their employers have felt the pressure (see Art. 13. Part III). The cause of this is easily conceived.

Even if the rate of interest at which the Commissioners could borrow, say for three months, were so high as that of the Bank of England in 1857, viz. ten per cent., they would only have to pay £2.10s. for every £100 they borrowed. Now, if the rate of interest made for the same time were at three per cent., that would give them 15s., and the actual loss would be only £1.15s., so that, if the average price of their purchases had been something like that of late years, viz. 94¼, they would practically be obtaining money at a price of stock corresponding to 92½, whereas the average price realizable for stock during panic times was as low as 87 (see also Art. 11. Part IV).

Supposing then, for example, that £1,000,000 were to be called for by excess of withdrawals, the loss in the one case would be £17,500, in the other, £72,500.

Should the necessity for borrowing continue after the three months, then the rate charged for the loan (as the panic would be over) would be considerably less.

Although the amount of loss attending sales of stock for past withdrawals by Depositors has already amounted to three-quarters of a million (see Art. 16. Part III.), yet—(in times of difficulty not severe enough to be termed a 'crisis')—the actual fluctuation in Savings Banks deposits in the hands of the National Debt Commissioners is, as compared with the aggregate amount of balances, very small indeed. Under good management, even in times of ordinary panic, such as have occurred during the last fifty years, sales need rarely take place.]

Section 3.—*Position of the Savings Bank question at the end of the Session of* 1860.

ART. 11.—The withdrawal of the first Bill of 1860 leaves the question of Savings Bank re-organization still unsettled, but the discussions in both Houses have been of the highest service. They have afforded Mr. Gladstone an opportunity of pointing out the financial misconceptions that prevail on the subject; and the speeches of the friends and opponents of his measure have separated the question by a broad line of demarcation into two distinct views. It has become evident, that if Savings Banks are not to be *Independent Banks of Deposit*, such as are referred to in Part VI.—that is to say, if they are to continue in any way connected with the State—the first point to be settled (before any attempt at general re-organization) is whether the Government shall occupy with respect to their Funds the position—(1) of * *Trustees* (as advocated by Sir H. Willoughby, and the opponents to the Bill)—or (2) of *Bankers* (as contended by Mr. Gladstone, Mr. James Wilson, and other distinguished economists.)

I.—*As to the "Trustee" View.*

12.—The proposition that the State should in future treat the monies deposited in its care as a mere "Trust Fund" is accompanied by the recommendation that the whole control of

---

* ["The funds to which the measure related were not public funds; they belonged to the Savings Banks, and were only held in *Trust* by the Chancellor of the Exchequer and the Commissioners for the reduction of the National Debt." (Lord Redesdale, 20th August 1860.)]

that fund, and the supervision (by inspectors) of the Savings Banks themselves, should be delegated to a paid Government Commission (see Art. 21, Part IV.). The adoption of this idea of the duty of the State would render it necessary, that the Commission should arrange their investments and operations so that the nation should hereafter incur no pecuniary liability, and so that the Government might say, " We will manage your funds in the character of agents to the best of our ability; but we will undertake no risk of loss upon the investments which we make, and will pay you only the rate of interest actually realized from such investments." In pursuance of such a contract, the Commissioners, on investing the sums committed to their care, would credit the Banks with the securities which their deposits represented, together with all the interest realized from the same, and no more. The Commissioners would act purely as agents, as a solicitor acts for a private person who employs him to make investments, and the cost of Management would have to be defrayed out of the produce of the investments.

13.—In other words, it follows as a consequence of the "Trust Fund" proposition:—

1. That whatever security the Commission might promise to the Depositors, they would have to provide out of their own funds: thus, for example, if the Depositors be guaranteed against the frauds described in Part II., the guarantee must be attained by some system of mutual assurance such as is furnished by Guarantee Societies.

2. The investments of the Commission must produce interest sufficient (as explained p. 178), not merely to pay the interest allowed by the Banks, but to cover

the losses arising from Sales for withdrawals, delays in investment, &c.

3. An annual balance of profit and loss would have to be struck, and the depositors would have to be told at the beginning of each year what the rate of interest would be for the next twelve months; thus exposing them to fluctuation and uncertainty; a sure discouragement to provident habits.

4. If, from any cause, a *new deficiency* were to arise, that deficiency would have to be provided for out of the gross funds of the *Depositors, and be charged *pro rata* among those having deposits at the time.

It could not be made in any way a prospective or contingent liability on the State,—for if the connection of the latter with Savings Banks be simply that of a Trustee, there would be no propriety or justice in taxing the whole nation to pay a deficiency attending the investments of the savings of one section of the community. When we consider the contingencies of loss that affect all operations of investment, the advantage to the Depositors of such a condition seems doubtful.

14.—Mr. Gladstone pointed out very clearly the many grave objections to the proposition that the Legislature should leave the Depositors to all the risks attending the investment of their money as Trust-money. He observed:—

---

* [" A Trustee must act with integrity, and use a reasonable discretion, *and having done so, the persons interested in the trust are liable for any loss*. But will the House legislate on that principle for the Depositors of Savings Banks? If so, you must reconstitute the fund entirely, and begin *de novo*." (Mr. Gladstone, 22d June 1860.)]

> "I contend that the proposition is unreasonable. The property in question is subject to fluctuations of value. It would be a bad view to hold this out to the Depositors in Savings Banks—'Instead of a regular and fixed amount of interest you are to take the chance of the Funds going up or down, and four or five gentlemen are to be appointed as Commissioners, who are to do the best they can for you.' These gentlemen must sell when the funds are low and buy when they are high. The difference between the rate of interest paid and received, and the necessity of selling out at a time when the funds are low, have been the main causes of the loss on this money. Now would it be for the benefit of the Depositors to place them under all the fluctuations that result from the system proposed by the hon. member for Evesham (Sir H. Willoughby)?"

15.—An important consideration is immediately suggested by this "Trustee Fund" proposition, viz. that if it be adopted by the Legislature, no portion of the *present deficiency* (of $4\frac{1}{2}$ millions) can be allowed to remain in the Savings Bank account, because no Commission would, under the circumstances above detailed, be able safely to incur the responsibility of endeavouring to make headway against it. This point was noticed and enforced by Mr. Gladstone in the debate. He said:—

> "The principle upon which all past legislation has been founded is that this money is not the property either of the Depositors or of the Trustees, but the property of the Commissioners for the reduction of the National Debt. If you declare it to be the property of the Depositors, you must hand over to them the whole amount you have received. You have certain liabilities toward the Trustees of Savings Banks on behalf of the Depositors. There are certain assets to meet those liabilities, and the assets are of less value than the amount of those liabilities. It will be *a breach of*

faith which I feel confident this House will not entertain, if, when you have the fact established beyond doubt that the assets of the Commissioners are not equal to their liability, you hand the money over to a Commission as Trustees, without enabling them to discharge every shilling of liability.* *Such a course cannot be contemplated for a moment.*"

II.—*As to the " Banker" View.*

ART. 16.—The supporters of the "Banker" view of the Savings Bank question contend that the Government (if they are to have any future connection with Savings Banks) are compelled by the practical † necessity of the case to select the posi-

---

* [In Part III. we have shewn that all but £315,801 of the present deficiency has arisen from the past operations of the National Debt Office ' for Savings Bank purposes alone.']

† [Mr Gladstone remarked (June 22, 1860)—"It is clearly impossible we can manage them as Trustees. The time for that is past. If a trust was to be constituted, it should have been constituted when the Savings Banks were first taken in hand; but Parliament adopted a totally different system, and I think it did so wisely." ... Again, "The fact is, this doctrine of a Trust is a vast legal change in the tenure of a vast amount of property. At present the absolute proprietary right of the Commissioners is balanced by the obligation to pay back the Trustees the whole sum invested, with interest at 3¼ per cent. The basis of the present law is, that the Commissioners are in the position of Bankers. The Savings Bank money is their property, but they hold it subject to the repayment of the principal and a fixed rate of interest. The proposal of the Committee (of 1858) would be the breaking up of that system, and I declined to enter upon a task that I knew would be hopeless, of attempting to persuade this House to undo all the policy and retrace all the steps it had taken for the last 40 or 50 years, even if that change had not been accompanied with the necessity of handing over to the Commissioners, on account of the deficiency, a large sum of the public money." (*See also similar remarks of Mr. Gladstone in* 1859. Note to *Art.* 28, *Part* III.)]

tion of Bankers, and not that of Trustees. They urge, with Mr. Gladstone, that—if the State guarantees to the Depositors 'a definite rate of interest on their funds,' 'complete security for their principal,' 'power of withdrawal, whenever required, at par,' and 'freedom from any contingency of mismanagement,'—it must necessarily, in consideration of this guarantee, claim the right to do with the money received exactly what every banker is acknowledged to be entitled to do, viz. to invest it in the best way for his own security, consistently with his liabilities.

17.—In favour of this view, it is stated that by its adoption the necessity for an immediate recouping of the present deficiency of $4\frac{1}{2}$ millions (which, as we have shewn above, is an essential feature of the "Trustee Fund" idea) would be avoided. All that it requires is the formal recognition by the State of its liability for the whole amount due to the Banks, and the authority of the Legislature for the payment out of the Consolidated Fund of the annual deficiency in the investments. Its advocates propose that this liability should be acknowledged, that the present rate of interest ($3\frac{1}{4}$ per cent.) should be continued to the banks, and that any excess of interest above this, which the Savings Banks investments may hereafter produce, should be carried to the credit of the State.

18.—On this ground, Mr. Gladstone's plan of a 'State Deposit Account' is supported by many. They consider that * such an account would be of great use, as—apart from

---

* [One account (among others) should be kept in the national Ledger and called the '*Savings Bank-Deficiency Account.*' This, each year, should be made up, and any profit made in the year, over and above the charges for expenses and interest, &c., should be carried to the credit of this account, and against it should be charged any loss on the purchases and sales of stock, &c.]

the annual inspection of the deficiency it would afford—any future profit made by the investments could be carried towards recouping the present deficiency; whereas, if the new Commissioners are to treat the deposits as a Trust Fund, they would, in order to protect the Depositors from the risks of their own management, require all the margin (*if any) of future profit to form a guarantee fund against future losses.

---

* [See Art. 7, Part, IV., where we have stated our opinion that not only it is very improbable that it will be possible to invest, in the future, so as to enable a profit to be made beyond the present rate of interest allowed to the banks, but that it is unlikely (even if the deficiency were made good by a grant) that the present rate of interest can be continued.

As an illustration of the fall in the rate of interest of late years, £100 producing only £2.10s. per cent. a-year, represents 40 years' purchase. This value in good situations has, of late years, in *practice* been realized on landed property, although valuers, from custom of the last generation, continue to adopt 30 to 33 years in their estimates. With this rise in the value of land, a corresponding decrease in the interest on personal estate is steadily growing, (See Note to Art. 22, Part IV.).

Mr. Ayrton has proposed to recoupe the present deficiency by the creation of so much Savings Banks Stock as will pay the £3.5s. per cent. interest on the total amount of deposits for which the nation is now liable; but this will be only a palliative, not a remedy, for, with that rate, a fresh deficiency on the money now in hand will arise when it comes to be withdrawn by future sales, unless the average price so realized be at or above 92¾.

As regards *New Deposits*, deficiencies will also arise, if the average of the purchases they necessitate be above 92¾, and the average of future sales be below 92¾. This we have shewn to have been always the case in the past, and to be probable in future, (See Note to Art. 15, Part III.).

In fact, if the 'Trustee' view be adopted, neither can the present rate of interest be continued, nor those submitted by us in Part IV. be substituted; and as long as no more than an average of 3¼ per cent. interest be made on the investments, the rates allowed to the Banks for Depositors on the first £100 of a deposit would have (even without setting aside any thing for a guarantee fund) to be reduced to £2.18s. 4d., and for the surplus over £100, to £2.10s, or 6d. in the £ per annum. Or, placing the matter in another form, interest at the rate of ½d. in the £ per month,

19.—*Of future operations with Savings Bank Funds for State purposes.*—The adoption of the 'Banker' view of course

---

with a bonus of *one sixth* at the end of every six months, on the plan set forth at page 193.

In the debate of the 5th March 1860, Mr. Gladstone stated that "those who had the financial management of the fund considered that it was mainly owing to the nature of the terms, on which the monies were received, that their assets, in point of fact, were not equal to their liabilities." He added, however, "It followed, that when the funds were high and the rate of interest generally low, there was great disposition to invest in Savings Banks, because then the fixed rate of interest offered to Depositors something better than they were likely to obtain elsewhere; but when the funds were low the case was exactly opposite." This idea, that withdrawals only take place when the funds are low, and payments in when they are high, is not in accordance with facts. Such operations are always taking place; so much so, that, on the average, about £11 out of every £13 paid in to the Banks by one section of the Depositors, is withdrawn during the same year by them or another. (*See Note*, p. 183).

That in reality withdrawals are constantly necessary, and for proportionately larger sums than are paid in, may be seen from recent returns (Art. 44, Part II.); for while over 1½ millions of operations were made in twelve months for the deposit of money in the Savings Banks of the kingdom, more than half as many (812,488) withdrawals also occurred in the same time.

The £2 excess is all that is paid over to the National Debt Commissioners, and is what is generally laid out in the purchase of Stocks in times of plenty and high prices, and sold out when the converse takes place, *i. e.* when the withdrawals preponderate over the deposits. As we have remarked (note, p. 125), the supposition that the industrious classes have ever withdrawn with the view of speculating on a rise of the funds is a fanciful absurdity. All our experience—whether specially in reference to Savings Banks, or as an adviser for many years, in connection with "The Friendly Societies Institute," to Industrial Associations of all kinds—leads us to the conviction, that none of the Depositors would run the risk of a fall in price for the highest possible interest. For example, it is known that no Building Society could attract any members, even if it gave the finest rate of interest, where there was any chance of losing any portion of the capital on withdrawals. And even in France, so often referred to as a precedent, the poor, who seek to secure a moderate

supposes that the funds of the Savings Banks are, in that case, to be available for national purposes in the future; the State in return for the great liability it accepts to the banks, using

---

livelihood for their old age from "*rentes*"—which they are enabled to do by the fact that as little as ten francs *rentes* a year can be purchased—make their purchases as a *permanent*, and not as a temporary investment. (*See also Art. 17, Part IV.*)

The following extracts from a letter received by us (17th August, 1860) from Mr. Thomas Jeremiah, President of the largest Savings Bank in the United States (the Bowery Bank for Savings, New York) give strong confirmation to the views set forth in Part IV. The last paragraph has a valuable bearing upon the point we have so often adverted to, viz. :—that the industrious classes look more to security than to profit from Savings Banks, (see Art. 16, Part IV.) Mr Jeremiah remarks: " The importance of this subject cannot be too highly estimated in its relations to the social and moral elevation of the labouring classes. . . . .
"Your attention has been very properly drawn to the propriety of requiring notice from Depositors previous to payment: or more strictly speaking, to the right on the part of the Savings Banks to make such requisition. It is usually at periods of financial excitement that demands for payment are largely made, and it is precisely at such periods that the welfare of the Depositor himself requires that such payments should be temporarily withheld. This was abundantly demonstrated during the panic of 1857 in the City of New York. Large sums of money were drawn from Savings Banks, and considerable losses were sustained by the holders in consequence of such withdrawals. . . . .
. . . " The remedy, finally, was to refuse immediate payment except in peculiar cases, and to pay only one-tenth or one-fifth of the amount demanded, which remedy was found to be entirely efficacious, and in less than one week many of the Depositors returned with the same money they had drawn out. . . . . . . " With regard to the important subject of investing the funds of Savings Banks, it is certainly true that safe modes of investment are very limited, and may be summed up into Government and real estate securities. . . . .
" With us—where the right to invest in legal securities exists in the Board of Trustees—General, State, and City Government Stocks, form a large part of our securities, after which bond and mortgage securities only are taken. . . . . " If similar powers should be conferred upon the Managers of Savings Banks with you, I have no doubt that investments would still be made in Government [Parliamentary] securities, as being the most reliable. And even if the effect should be to cause Government securities to sell higher in the market, still the

the deposits in financial operations for the general benefit. In our chapter on past Exchequer operations (Part III.), we have shewn that the funds in question have been, on repeated occasions, wisely applied; as, for instance, when the Government took out of the market the *Bills which it had itself issued, at a time when this could be effected at a profit, and the future negotiability of such securities would otherwise have suffered by their depreciation.   This operation, *on the*

---

primary object will have been secured : the safe keeping of the earnings of the industrious poor. In any event, whether investments are made by fiscal agents appointed by Government, on behalf of Savings Banks, or by the Banks themselves through their officers, regulations such as you have adverted to must be adopted, or the value of the securities, which are the basis of Savings Banks investments, must be subject to unfavourable transitions. . . . . "You have noticed (note, p. 178) that at a very early period in the history of Savings Banks with us, laws were passed authorizing the accumulation of a [Guarantee] Fund [out of the interest] equal to 10 per cent. on deposits. This is an important provision, and one that no Depositor should object to. Indeed, I have never heard an objection to it, but, on the contrary, it has been regarded as a provision vital to the system, and a sort of balance wheel to correct irregularities, and prevent reactions unfavourable to public confidence. If, as is generally conceded, the safety of the deposits in Savings Banks is the most important consideration, and payment of interest is only secondary, then the part of wisdom undoubtedly is to secure the first condition, or to reject entirely that plea of 'benevolence,' which would ask that such institutions be at all established. . . . . "The whole subject is one in which the best minds and hearts may be profitably engaged."

Similar confirmation has also more recently been given to us by M. David, Regent of the National Bank of Denmark, and Director of the Statistical Department of State at Copenhagen, as the result of the experience of the Danish banks.]

* ["Their lordships ought to recollect that the Chancellor of the Exchequer was not a great stock-jobber, acting for his own individual advantage, but the financial agent of the country at large. In that capacity, as long as he kept within proper bounds, he was not only entitled, but it was his duty, to obtain for the public any fair advantage which his position and knowledge might place within his reach. Was he to be prevented, for example, from using any portion of the money of the

'*Banker*' *view*, was as legitimate as prudent, and those who complain of it as an interference with the Money-market have no real cause of grievance whatever. It is plain that the interests of the holders of Exchequer Bills were not damaged thereby, as the value of their property was materially improved by such operations.

The only parties that could have found fault were strangers, desirous of making investments in Exchequer Bills, who considered themselves injured by the consequent rise in price; but no one could seriously say that a debtor is not at liberty to take up his own bonds when they are in the market at a price advantageous to him.

20.—The complaint in respect to the *Funding* of Exchequer Bills (which followed the purchases) we have shown (Part III.) to be equally unfounded; because these conversions have always been calculated at the price of the particular quarter in which the Exchequer Bills were purchased.

Their results, indeed, furnish* a remarkable illustration of the law of average. As if by way of prospectively discomfiting any opponents of the operations, the average of the Fundings has proved to have been at about $91\frac{3}{4}$ price of stock, which is

---

Savings Banks for the purpose of paying Exchequer Bills? If so, the interest payable upon those Bills for a period of twelve months would be so much money thrown away, to the disadvantage and loss of the public."—*Earl Granville*, August 20, 1860.]

* [How it happens that so many persons follow the fashion of laying all the blame of the present deficiency on the various Chancellors' operations, it is difficult to conceive, except on the supposition of Archbishop Whately, that many a man, who maintains opinions which he has been told are true, and believes that good and sufficient reasons are assigned for them, is apt to conclude at once that he is convinced by those reasons, and tries to lead others to the same result; whereas the truth will often be that he has taken upon trust both the premises and the conclusion, as well as the connection between them; that he is repeating what he has heard, without performing any process of reasoning

12*s.* 6*d.* below that which we have explained to be the "price of safety" in Savings Bank operations, and also below the average price of the funds for twenty-five years:—that is to say, even if the Fundings had taken place, on the average, at $92\frac{3}{8}$, it would have been *un*-attended with a loss, because the rate of interest obtained by the Stock corresponding would have been the rate given, viz. £3. 5*s.* per cent., but as the average was $91\frac{3}{4}$, a positive *profit* to the Savings Bank income was made by the funding (see Art. 35, Part III.)

Independently of this gain in Interest for the Savings Banks the State has made for itself a profit of a similar kind, for while an apparent increase in the *nominal amount* of the National Debt was created by transferring *unfunded* into *funded* debt, an immense diminution in the aggregate debt as an *annual charge* was effected. (See Art. 40, 43, Part III., and the Appendix on the National Debt.)

These operations having extended over many years, some diminution in the particular money operated with has naturally arisen, on account of the loss of interest in temporary periods of non-investment, and the difference between the rates realized by the change of securities, &c.; but the total diminution in the value of Savings Bank Stock was only £315,801

---

in his own mind, or having made a personal examination of the points at issue.

It does not seem to have been reflected that, if Stock were sold by the Government to enable it to take up Exchequer Bills, and these Exchequer Bills were afterwards funded at the original price of the quarter in which they had been bought and the Stock sold, then the same amount of Stock would be created as was sold. No deficiency could arise in the Savings Bank fund except a trifling loss in interest, if the rate for Exchequer Bills happened to be lower than that on Stock, and this was not always the case during the operations censured.

This restoration of Stock for Stock sold is not an uncommon thing in assurance practice, where on a large advance being made for a term of years, and Stock sold for that purpose, a like amount has to be restored by the borrower in clearing off his mortgage.]

(Art. 25, Part III.), or *less than 2d. in the £* on the £41,000,000 deposited with the National Debt Commissioners.

21.—The effect of the censured changes of investment has, in fact, been admirable as far as the nation is concerned, and they were perfectly justifiable if the hypothesis of Mr Gladstone (Art. 15 of this Part) be admitted, viz : that the State is the Banker, not the Trustee, of the monies deposited in the custody of the Government. Much financial foresight was shown by the Chancellors of the Exchequer, who availed themselves of the powers they had to execute those changes.

They have been much commended by an eminent financier, Lord Monteagle, who stated, in his evidence before the Parliamentary Committee of 1858 (See Art. 39, Part III.) that in the past those funds have, indeed, been used for purposes of great importance. He observed, that at times when it has been thought right to lighten the burdens on property, by* reducing the interest on the public debt, Savings Bank funds have afforded the means of doing so by enabling the proper provision to be made for that purpose;—and that had it not been for the possession of these funds, Mr. Goulburn would not have been able in 1844 to effect that great operation which saved the country £1,300,000 a year, nor Lord Althorp that

---

* [Lord Monteagle again repeated this opinion on August 20, 1860, and remarked—" The course which had been taken by his lamented friend, the late Lord (Althorp) Spencer in dealing with the Savings Bank deposits seemed to him to be that which it was right to take. That noble lord perceived that those funds afforded him an opportunity of effecting certain economical improvements, and he had applied them to that purpose with great advantage."

Earl Granville, August 20, 1860, referring to the case of Lord Althorp, who made use of the money of the Savings Banks for the purpose of reducing the Four per Cents., also said, " It was done before the consent of Parliament was asked. Subsequently, Lord Althorp applied to Parliament, not for its assent to what he had done, but for authority to pay off the dissentient stockholders."]

in 1834, which was attended with so much advantage to the State. Mr. Gladstone also remarked with truth, that during the Crimean war these funds enabled the Chancellor to borrow with advantage and with a saving to the country, in order to bear the expenses of the war; and "that if he had then been compelled to borrow in Stock—the demands for the war being uncertain—he would have had to borrow a larger sum than was wanted, and would not only have withdrawn from the demands of commerce money that was necessary, but have entailed upon the country considerable expense."

22.—We trust, then, that in coming to a decision on this ' vexed question'—which obstructs Savings Bank reorganization by standing in the very threshold, and diverting attention from more important points—the Legislature will admit that no Government should undertake any State liability on account of the deposits of one section of the community unless it be allowed to avail itself of the advantage that may attend their possession. To this advantage no limit can be foreseen, once the principle is fully recognised.

To guard against the only objectionable part of the past operations of the Chancellors (See Art. 30, Part III), it is merely necessary that the Savings Bank Fund account in the National Ledger should be always kept strictly posted up, and that all withdrawals of Savings Bank Funds for State purposes should be set forth in an Annual Report to Parliament; so that any deficiency caused by such withdrawal may be provided for, if necessary, by a special vote, and that all Funding of Exchequer Bills required from time to time may, in future, be authorized by Parliament.

It may be observed that the recent Act (1860) enlarges rather than curtails the powers of the Minister in respect to such operations for investment and change of securities.

www.ingramcontent.com/pod-product-compliance
Lightning Source LLC
Chambersburg PA
CBHW022333230426
43664CB00040B/422